Housing the Elderly

Courtesy of Brooks Trubee
Princeton Community Housing, Princeton, New Jersey

Housing the Elderly

edited by
Judith Ann Hancock

© Copyright 1987, Rutgers—The State University of New Jersey
All rights reserved.

Published in the United States of America
by the Center for Urban Policy Research
Building 4051—Kilmer Campus
New Brunswick, New Jersey 08903

Library of Congress Cataloging-in-Publication Data
Main entry under title:

Housing the elderly.

  Bibliography: p. 287
  Includes Index.
  1. Aged—United States-Dwellings—Addresses, essays,
lectures. I. Hancock, Judith Ann.
HD7287.92.U54H69   1986   363.5′9   85-24626
ISBN 0-88285-114-4

CONTENTS

List of Exhibits vii
Introduction xiii

I. The Elderly in American Society

1. Housing the Elderly
   Anne Woodward 3
2. The Elderly in America: Their Economic Resources, Income Status, and Costs 15
   Robert H. Binstock
3. Sunbelt Update: Older Americans Head South
   Jeanne C. Biggar, Cynthia B. Flynn, Charles F. Longino, Jr., and Robert F. Wiseman 31

II. Housing Options for the Elderly

4. For Older People—Not Segregation But Integration
   Lewis Mumford 39
5. In Defense of Age-Segregated Housing
   Stephen M. Golant 49
6. Alternative Housing Modes
   J. Kevin Eckert and Mary Ittman Murrey 57
7. The Surveillance Zone as Meaningful Space for the Aged
   Graham D. Rowles 81
8. Increasing Housing Opportunities for the Elderly
   Carole R. Shifman 95

III. Housing and Personal Income: Home Equity Conversions and the Capital Gains Tax Exclusion

9. Home Equity Conversions
   Vincent J. Trichilo 121
10. Home Equity Conversions
    Michael Hoeflich 129
11. Consumer Safeguards for Financial Instruments Unlocking Home Equity for the Aged
    Maurice D. Weinrobe 135
12. Home Equity Financing of Long-Term Care for the Elderly
    Bruce Jacobs and William Weissert 151
13. Excluding Gain on the Sale of a Residence: When Should the Election be Made?
    Rolf Auster 177

IV. The Elderly as a Political Force

14. The Elderly as a Political Force
    Douglas Dobson 187
15. Setting the Elderly Housing Agenda
    Jon Pynoos 209

V. Current Programs and Emerging Issues

16. Housing Options for the Elderly
    Linda Daily 227
17. Housing Policy for Older Americans in the 1980s: An Overview
    Jerold S. Nachison and Morton H. Leeds 245
18. Future Housing Assistance Policy for the Elderly
    Raymond J. Struyk 255

Appendix:

A. Major Programs of the U.S. Department of Housing and Urban Development (HUD) to Assist the Elderly and Federal Outlays Benefiting the Elderly: FY 1981-FY 1983 ... 267
B. Pending Congressional Legislation: June 1985 273

Bibliography 287
Index 305

LIST OF EXHIBITS

I.1	Size and Proportion of Future U.S. Elderly Population	xv
I.2	Age Structure of the Elderly Population: 1977 to 2030	xvi
I.3	Living Arrangements of Persons 65 Years and Over: 1980 to 2000	xvi
I.4	Households and Families with Heads 65 Years and Over: 1980 to 2000	xvii
I.5	Need and Demand for Elderly Housing: 1980 to 2000	xvii
I.6	Number of Housing Units Needed by the Elderly: 1980 to 2000	xviii
I.7	Distribution of the Male and Female Populations 65 Years Old and Over by Living Arrangements: 1981	xix
I.8	Needed Additions to the Elderly Housing Supply: 1980 to 2000	xx
I.9	Housing Alternatives and Housing Levels	xxi
I.10	Income and Expenditures of Household Budget of Persons 65 Years and Older	xxiii
I.11	Year Housing Structure Built of Householders 65 Years and Older	xxv
I.12	Age 65 years and Older in Top Ten States: 1980	xxvii
I.13	Cities with Largest Numbers and Highest Percentage of Persons 65 Years and Older	xxviii
2.1	Distribution of Money Income Among Aged Households: 1979	22
2.2	Median Money Income for Population 65 Years and Older: 1978, by Sex, Race, and Marital Status	23

2.3	Poverty and Near-Poverty Rates Among Persons 65 Years and Older: 1979	24
2.4	Aged Couples with Incomes Below Bureau of Labor Statistics Budgets for Retired Couples: 1979	24
3.1	Migration to the Sunbelt: 1975–1980	34
3.2	Migration Streams	35
7.1	Audrey's Surveillance Zone	83
7.2	Surveillance Zone Characteristics	85
7.3	"Setting Up": Bertha's Surveillance Zone	87
7.4	Developmental Significance of the Surveillance Zone	90
8.1	Minimum Lot Area per Dwelling Unit, New Rochelle, New York and New Haven, Connecticut	100
8.2	Minimum Area per Room, New Rochelle, New York: 1969	101
8.3	What Local Governments Can Do to Encourage Infill Development	112
11.1	Effect of Annuity Purchases on RAM Monthly Payments	141
11.2	Effect of Using a Rising Property Value to Rollover a RAM at End of Initial Term	142
12.1	Relationship between Poverty Status and Net Home Equity	154
12.2	Size of Potential Yearly RAM Annuity by Poverty Status	156
12.3	Size of Potential RAM Annuity by Family Structure and Low-Income Status	156
12.4	Comparison between Estimated Risk and Actual Dependency in Personal Care	158
12.5	Comparison between Estimated Risk and Actual Rates of Institutionalization	159
12.6	Risk of Dependency in Personal Care by Family Structure	160
12.7	Risk of Institutionalization by Family Structure	160
12.8	Potential Annual RAM Annuity by Family Structure and Risk of Dependency in Personal Care	162
12.9	Percentage of Elderly Homeowners Who Could Purchase $3,580 (Plus Annual Increases for Inflation) Worth of Home Care Each Year by Family Structure and Risk of Dependence	163
12.10	Percentage of Single Elderly Homeowners Who Could Purchase Home Care Each Year Using Only the RAM Payment by Mortality Distribution, Income, and Risk	165

12.11	Percentage of Elderly Homeowners Who Could Purchase Home Care Each Year Using One-Half of Discretionary Income in Addition to RAM Payment by Mortality Distribution, Family Structure, and Risk	166
12.12	Potential Annual RAM Annuity Available for Catastrophic Nursing Home Cost Insurance by Family Structure and Risk of Institutionalization	168
12.13	Percentage of Elderly Homeowners Who Could Purchase Catastrophic Nursing Home Cost Insurance Using Only the RAM Payment by Family Structure, Risk, and Income	169
12.14	Percentage of Elderly Homeowners Who Could Purchase Catastrophic Nursing Home Cost Insurance Using Only One-Quarter of Discretionary Income in Addition to the RAM Payment by Family Structure, Risk, and Income	170
12.15	Percentage of Elderly Homeowners Who Could Pay the Premium for a Prototype Long-Term Care Insurance Policy Using One-Quarter of Discretionary Income in Addition to the RAM Payment by Family Structure, Risk, and Income	171
14.1	Distribution of Group Identifications of Persons Age 60 or Over: 1976	198
14.2	Selected Background Characteristics of Persons Age 60 and Older by Identification with Older Persons: 1976	199
14.3	Partisan Affiliation and Ideology of Persons Age 60 and Older by Identification with Older Persons: 1976	201
14.4	Political Involvement of Respondents Age 60 and Older by Identification with Older Persons: 1976	201
14.5	Support for an Expanding State Role in the Provision of Benefits to the Elderly and Perception of Elderly Status and Political Involvement among State Legislators: 1979	204
14.6	Importance of Aging Issues and Perceptions of Elderly Status and Political Involvement among State Legislators: 1979	205
16.1	U.S. Population Age 65 and Older: 1900 to 2030	228

17.1	The Continuum of Living..	249
18.1	Estimated Participation in the Open-Enrollment HousingVoucher Program	260

Acknowledgment

My deepest appreciation goes to those who gave me their support and time so generously and cheerfully, and a very special thank you to George Sternlieb, Bob Burchell, Gloria Ehrlich, Patrick Beaton, Ed Duensing, Pam Peterson, and Janet Mitchell.

Introduction

American society is facing some very tough decisions concerning housing for the elderly—decisions that will be both financially and socially costly to all Americans if they are delayed too long.

The problem is really very straightforward. Given the current trends and present programs, the demand for elderly housing will far outstrip the supply within the next 15 years. There simply will not be enough roofs to cover the heads of the older Americans. In addition to the supply problem, the housing that is available will be expensive and often not appropriate to the special needs of the elderly. And the solution to this problem? If only it were as easy to resolve as it is to define. This, however, is not the case, for the solutions to the elderly housing crunch are complex and tangled in the political maze of American social and economic policies.

The elderly merit special attention for two reasons. First, the proportion of elderly in American society will increase substantially in the next few decades, going from about 11 percent at present to approximately 18 percent within the next 50 years. Consequently, the elderly will need an increased share of available housing. Second, the elderly, because of the aging process, face significant changes—in income, health, household size, and attitudes toward life—all factors which bear on housing. Generally, they spend more time in their living quarters than when they were working; their living environment is a major influence on their activities and attitudes about life in general. Thus, the time factor coupled with the inevitable changes the elderly must cope with make it essential that they have appropriate, affordable housing. As Sandra Newman points out, the relationship between life events or changes and residential moves draws a fundamental distinction between elderly and nonelderly households. Life transitions at younger ages, which upset the balance between housing needs and housing consumption, lead to moves to different dwellings. The elderly, in contrast, rarely move, causing questions about how their at least equally dramatic life transitions and, therefore, changes in housing needs are dealt with.[1]

Thus, housing demand—the numbers alone—is a significant problem. However, the situation becomes more complex when the demand is coupled with concerns about housing availability, appropriateness, and affordability.

This book examines the problem of housing older Americans, first looking at the demographics and demand for housing and then the available housing supply, or alternatives. Personal income in the form of home equity conversions and the capital gains tax exclusion is discussed in the third section of the book. The abilities of the elderly to help themselves by influencing public policy and getting the housing assistance they need is discussed in the fourth section and is followed by an analysis of current federal programs and emerging trends. Appendices contain information about the major programs of the U.S. Department of Housing and Urban Development (HUD), federal outlays for programs benefiting the elderly, and congressional legislation pending as of June 1985.

Three common threads run through the chapters: 1) older Americans should be encouraged to live independently for as long as possible; 2) they must have a wide range of housing options; and 3) there must be closer coordination between elderly housing and the services these people need.

Housing Demand

Ideally, all elderly households should have "a decent home and suitable living environment." This goal was first officially enunciated in the Housing Act of 1949, and it was most recently reaffirmed in 1981 by the White House Conference on Aging. But what are the implications of meeting this goal?

In 1980 the elderly population, those 65 years or older, constituted 11 percent of the total U.S. population. By the year 2030, the projection is for the percentage to jump to 18.3 percent. This means that in 1980 there were 25.5 million elderly; there will be more than 55 million by 2030. Also, by the year 2030, the elderly will comprise 33 percent of the total population 25 years or older. In 1980 the elderly accounted for only 25 percent; this 8-percentage-point increase in 50 years will certainly have profound effects on all aspects of housing and living arrangements. Moreover, there will be a shift within the age structure of the older population itself. A significant growth will occur in the frail elderly, those 75 years old and older, between the 1980s and the year

Introduction

2010 especially; this sector, which comprised 37.7 percent of the elderly population in 1977, will increase to 44.2 percent by the year 2010. A slight decrease will occur after that however, and the projection is for this group to drop to 42.1 percent of the total elderly population by 2030 (see Exhibits I.1 and I.2). Even with the drop, a 5-percentage-point increase in 30 years is substantial.[2]

But households are a better indicator of housing demand than total population. In 1980, 93 percent (16.1 million) of the 25.5 million elderly lived in a household; most of the remaining 7 percent were institutionalized. By the year 2000, when the projections are for an elderly population of about 33 million, 96 percent (23 million) will live in households. In addition to this increase in the number of households, there will be a significant increase in nonfamily households, from 30 percent in 1980 to 39 percent in the year 2000 (see Exhibits I.3 through I.6). These shifts are not simply an age shift in the total population. As Benjamin Handler said in his 1982 quantitative analysis of housing for the elderly,

> Over the last quarter century, the elderly population, their households, and families have all increased faster than the total U.S. population. They have thus required an increasingly larger share of the housing stock. . . . The most drastic increase has occurred in both the number and proportion of nonfamily, particularly single person, households.[3]

EXHIBIT I.1
Size and Proportion of Future U.S. Elderly Population
(Number in population bar refers to the percent of the total population.)

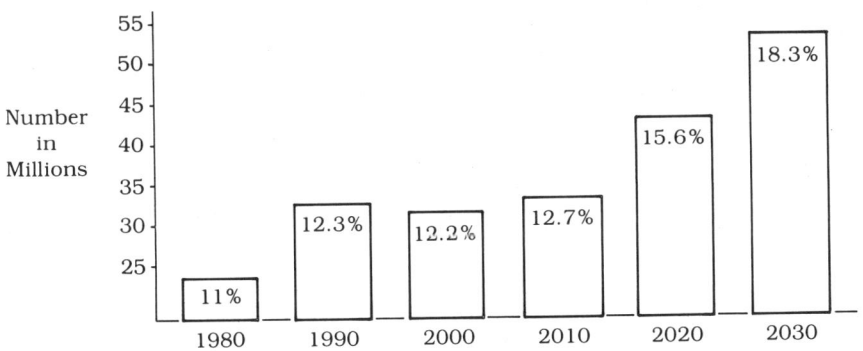

Projected Number of Elderly People

1980 = 25.5 Million	2010 = 34.8 Million
1990 = 29.8 Million	2020 = 45.1 Million
2000 = 31.8 Million	2030 = 55.0 Million

Source: Census Bureau Series II projections in "Every Ninth American," July 1982; and Katherine P. Warner, "Demographics and Housing," in Urban Land Institute, *Housing for a Maturing Population* (Washington, D.C.: Urban Land Institute, 1983), p. 3.

EXHIBIT I.2
Age Structure of the Elderly Population: 1977 to 2030

	65 to 74 Years Old			75 Years Old and Older		
	Population Size (1,000s)	% of Total Population	% of Elderly Population	Population Size (1,000s)	% of Total Population	% of Elderly Population
1977	14.6	6.7	62.2	8.9	4.1	37.7
2010	19.8	7.2	56.7	15.4	5.5	44.2
2030	31.9	10.6	57.9	23.2	7.7	42.1

Source: Current Population Reports, P-25, No. 704 (1977), Tables 8 and 11, Series II Projections in "Every Ninth American," July 1982; and Katherine P. Warner, "Demographics and Housing," in Urban Land Institute, *Housing for a Maturing Population* (Washington, D.C.: Urban Land Institute, 1983), p. 5.

The elderly population, then, has been increasing in both absolute numbers and percentage terms. And the prediction is for this trend to continue. Thus, in order to provide "a decent home and suitable living environment" for all elderly households, given the increase in elderly households from 16 million in 1980 to 23 million in the year 2000, the elderly will need 7 million more units in 2000 than they had in 1980, and this assumes that all households were

EXHIBIT I.3
Living Arrangements of Persons 65 and Over: 1980 to 2000
(in millions and percent)

	Actual				Projected	
	1980		1990		2000	
	Mil.	%	Mil.	%	Mil.	%
Total Elderly	25.5	100.0	29.8	100.0	34.2	100.0
Not in Households*	1.8	7.1	1.6	5.4	1.4	4.0
In Households	23.7	92.9	28.2	94.6	32.8	96.0
Family	(16.1)	(63.0)	(17.8)	(59.8)	(19.6)	(57.3)
Nonfamily†	(7.6)	(29.9)	(10.4)	(34.8)	(13.2)	(38.7)

* Mostly in institutions.
† Consists of a person maintaining a household while living alone or with nonrelatives.
Source: Benjamin Handler. *Housing Needs of the Elderly: A Quantitative Analysis.* Ann Arbor, Michigan: National Policy Center on Housing and Living Arrangements for Older Americans, University of Michigan, 1982, p. 7. Handler's sources for 1980 were the U.S. Bureau of the Census, Current Population Reports. *Popular Characteristics,* Series–P20, Nos. 365 and 366.

EXHIBIT I.4
Households and Families with Heads 65 Years and Over: 1980 to 2000*
(in millions)

	1980	1990	2000
Total Households	16.1	19.9	23.0
Nonfamily Households	7.3†	9.9	12.0
Family Households	8.8	10.0	11.0
Husband-Wife	(7.2)‡	(8.6)	(9.8)
No Spouse Present	(1.5)	(1.4)	(1.2)

* This is not the same as households *with* elderly members as in Exhibit I.1.

† Of these nonfamily households, 7.1 million consist of single people, and 0.22 million consist of two or more nonrelatives.

‡ Of these family households, 6.1 million consist only of husbands and wives while 1.1 million consist of husbands, wives, and others.

Source: Benjamin Handler. *Housing Needs of the Elderly: A Quantitative Analysis.* Ann Arbor, Michigan: National Policy Center on Housing and Living Arrangements for Older Americans, University of Michigan, 1982, p. 7. Handler's sources for 1980 were the U.S. Bureau of the Census, Current Population Reports. *Popular Characteristics.* Series-P20, Nos. 365 and 366

EXHIBIT I.5
Need and Demand for Elderly Housing: 1980 to 2000
(in millions)

	1980	1990	2000
Need*	18.4	22.2	25.8
Effective Demand (Households and Families with Heads 65 and over, see Exhibit 1.4)	16.1	19.9	23.0
Unsatisfied Need	2.3†	2.3	2.8

* Equals Effective Demand (households already occupying units) plus the Unsatisfied Need (those living in housing units owned or rented by others who would live independently if appropriate affordable units were available).

† In 1980, 2.3 million people lived in housing units owned or rented by others. Of these, 0.15 million were couples not living in their own households, 1.9 million were singles primarily living with relatives, and 0.3 million were singles living in nonfamily households.

Source: Benjamin Handler. *Housing Needs of the Elderly: A Quantitative Analysis.* Ann Arbor, Michigan: National Policy Center on Housing and Living Arrangements for Older Americans, University of Michigan, 1982, p. 29. Handler's sources for 1980 were the U.S. Bureau of the Census, Current Population Reports. *Popular Characteristics.* Series-P20, Nos. 365 and 366

EXHIBIT I.6
Number of Housing Units Needed by the Elderly: 1980 to 2000
(in millions)

	1980	1990	2000
Total Needed*	18.4	22.2	25.8
For Married Couples	7.2	8.6	9.8
For Family Heads (No Spouse Present)	1.5	1.4	1.2
For Other Elderly Living in Families†	2.0	1.8	1.5
For Heads of Nonfamily	7.4	9.9	12.0
For Elderly in Nonfamily Households‡	0.3	0.5	1.3

*From Exhibit I.3.

† A small proportion of these are married. The 1980 data show 0.15 married couples, at least one partner of which was age 65 or over, not living in their own households. If it is assumed that the ratio of such married couples to the number of "other elderly living in families" remains constant, the comparable figures for 1990 and 2000 are 0.13 million and 0.11 million, respectively. These numbers should then be subtracted from the "other elderly living in families" category and added to the "married couples" classifications.

‡ The difference between the number of persons in nonfamily households and the number of nonfamily households (see Exhibits I.1 and I.2).

Source: Benjamin Handler. *Housing Needs of the Elderly: A Quantitative Analysis.* Ann Arbor, Michigan: National Policy Center on Housing and Living Arrangements for Older Americans, University of Michigan, 1982, p. 28. Handler's sources for 1980 were the U.S. Bureau of the Census, Current Population Reports. *Popular Characteristics.* Series-P20, Nos. 365 and 366

decently housed in 1980, that the living patterns remain the same, and that the existing stock is maintained.

Housing Supply

Availability

Will the existing stock plus the present trends in rehabilitation and new construction be sufficient to provide a roof over the heads of the elderly? Even ignoring the issues of housing appropriateness and affordability for the moment, the answer is a resounding "No"! There will not be enough units available to come even close to fulfilling the elderly demand.

As can be seen from Exhibit I.7, at present more than 70 percent of the elderly live alone or live in a household with their spouse: about 20 percent of the men live alone and over 60 percent live with a spouse; approximately 40 per-

EXHIBIT I.7
**Distribution of the Male and Female Populations
65 Years Old and Over by Living Arrangements: 1981**

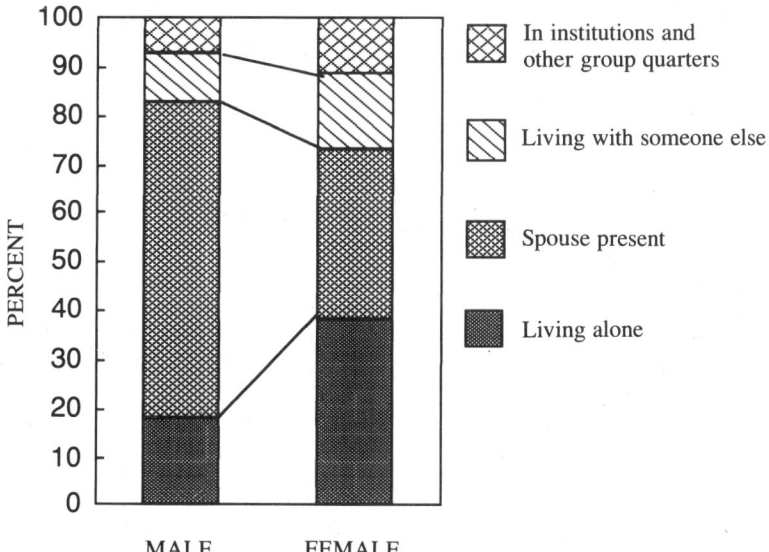

Source: Bureau of the Census, Demographic and Socioeconomic Aspects of Aging in the United States, Special Studies Series P-23, No. 138, p. 87; and United States Conference of Mayors, *Assessing Elderly Housing: A Planning Guide for Mayors and Local Officials* (Washington, D.C.: United States Conference of Mayors, 1985), p. 36.

cent of the women 65 years or older live alone and over 30 percent live with a spouse. Also, a 1984 study of the federal Section 202 program, which to date has been the most visible supplier of housing for the older population, points out that

1. women comprise 75 percent of the tenants of these projects;
2. average incomes of those living in this housing are near the current poverty level;
3. projects have low turnover rates; and,
4. waiting lists are very long—the average wait is more than a year and nearly one in four people must wait five years or more.[4]

Handler, one of the few people who has published quantitative data on this issue, believes that if the goal is indeed to have the elderly live as independently as possible for as long as possible, the demand will be for as many as 9.6 million additional units by the year 2000. The expected increase between

1980 and 2000 is for 6.8 million units. Thus there will be an "unfulfilled need" of 2.8 million units (see Exhibit I.8).[5] The cost for building these additional units is difficult to predict. But it will be costly. What kind of housing will the elderly have who are part of this "unfulfilled need?"

Appropriateness

While independent living is a desirable goal as compared to institutionalization, the elderly do have some unique needs; and in order to implement a continuum-of-living arrangement, a service component must be integrated with their housing needs. A recent HUD study of congregate housing concluded that "support services for frail elderly or handicapped persons in government-assisted housing delays the need for a move to nursing homes." Moreover, the study found that "the cost of a support services program in assisted housing (meals, housekeeping, personal care, transportation) was only about one-third the cost of care in nursing homes."[6]

Older Americans have a spectrum of personalities, and, as they age, their physical and mental abilities differ as do their needs. Thus, they require a variety of housing options with different levels of service (see Exhibit I.9). In order to better match this spectrum of personalities, abilities, and needs, the range of housing formats has increased. The American Association of Retired People recently published a pamphlet listing housing alternatives for the eld-

EXHIBIT I.8
Needed Additions to the Elderly Housing Supply: 1980 to 2000
(in millions of housing units)

	1980	1990	2000
Need*	2.3	6.0	9.6
− Expected Need	—	3.7	6.8
= Deficit	2.3	2.3	2.8
+ Replacements†	0.4	0.5	0.6
= Needed Additions	2.7	2.8	3.4
Rehabilitations‡	0.9	1.1	1.3

* Increase in elderly households plus goal of independent living.
† One-third of substandard units, i.e., those estimated to have more than one major deficiency.
‡ Two-thirds of substandard units, i.e., those estimated to have only one major deficiency.
Source: Benjamin Handler. *Housing Needs of the Elderly: A Quantitative Analysis.* Ann Arbor, Michigan: National Policy Center on Housing and Living Arrangements for Older Americans, University of Michigan, 1982, p. 33.

EXHIBIT I.9
Housing Alternatives and Housing Levels

Type of Housing Alternative	Level of Housing		
	Independent	Semi-Independent	Dependent
Single Family Dwelling	X		
Regular Apartment Rental	X		
Condominium	X		
Cooperative*	X		
Home Equity Conversion**	X		
Home Maintenance and Repair	X	X	
Shared Housing	X	X	
Accessory Apartment	X	X	X
ECHO Housing	X	X	X
Life Care Community	X	X	X
Congregate Housing		X	
Personal Care Boarding Home			X

Legend:
* Has potential as semi-independent level if congregate dining is offered within the structure.
** Has potential as both semi-independent and dependent levels if converted equity is used to cover costs of in-come care services.

Independent
Living arrangements appropriate for individuals/couples capable of handling their own housekeeping, cooking and personal care. Included in this category are such dwellings as: single family homes, apartments, condominiums, cooperatives, etc.

Semi-independent
Living arrangements which provide assistance for those who are not totally self-sufficient but capable of tending to their own personal care such as bathing and grooming. Included in this category are such dwellings as: congregate housing, ECHO housing, life care communities.

Dependent
Living arrangements which provide 24-hour personal/custodial care for more severely impaired individuals who do not need daily nursing or medical care. Included in this category are such facilities as foster homes, personal care boarding homes.

Source: A Manual of Housing Alternatives for the Elderly, Volume III, Need and Demand Projections, September, 1984, pgs. 151, 152, 155; and United States Conference of Mayors, *Assessing Elderly Housing: A Planning Guide for Mayors and Local Officials* (Washington, D.C.: United States Conference of Mayors, 1985), p. 41.

erly and giving some information about each type of housing. The formats in this pamphlet include:

- homes and apartments;
- condominiums and cooperatives;
- retirement communities;
- accessory apartments;

- echo housing (elder cottages or granny flats);
- shared housing;
- boarding homes (rooming houses);
- congregate housing;
- domiciliary care homes;
- elderly public housing projects;
- foster care homes;
- homes for the aged;
- life-care complexes; and
- mobile homes and manufactured housing.[7]

As barriers are removed, such as zoning ordinances prohibiting echo housing or accessory apartments, the quantity of each option will increase. But probably not enough. As Regnier and Byerts point out,

> The next decade will undoubtedly present even greater challenges than the last decade to the planner, developer, builder, and sponsor of new or rehabilitated housing for the elderly. The housing industry and financial institutions are facing a crisis of immense proportions. In addition, older people who own their own homes and those who rent apartments face increasing individual, familial, and financial problems as they cope with their need for shelter. . . . Even in the "good old days" of direct loans and interest subsidies, the construction target of 120,000 units per year for 10 years set by the 1971 White House Conference on Aging was never met—not even for 1 year.[8]

Affordability

Can older Americans afford the available housing? Probably not. When most people retire, their incomes are cut from one-third to one-half. Social security and pensions are their major sources of income. In the early 1980s, 25 percent of the elderly were primarily dependent on social security. Earnings, in-kind income programs (such as Medicare and Medicaid), assets, intrafamily transfers, special tax exclusions, and private pension plans accounted for the other sources of income. Housing and food were the major expenditure items in the household budget of people 65 years and older, with housing taking up 34 percent of the budget and food 21 percent (see Exhibit I.10).[9]

How well off are the elderly really? One analyst, William Lazer, recently maintained that "the spending power of the mature market may be one of the best-kept secrets left in the age of demographic scrutiny." He argues that the present generation of elderly retired with relatively poorer pensions and medical benefits than those who will retire in the coming decades. Also, he states that older people who now live alone have lower incomes than married people,

Introduction

EXHIBIT I.10
Income and Expenditures of Household Budget of Persons 65 Years and Older

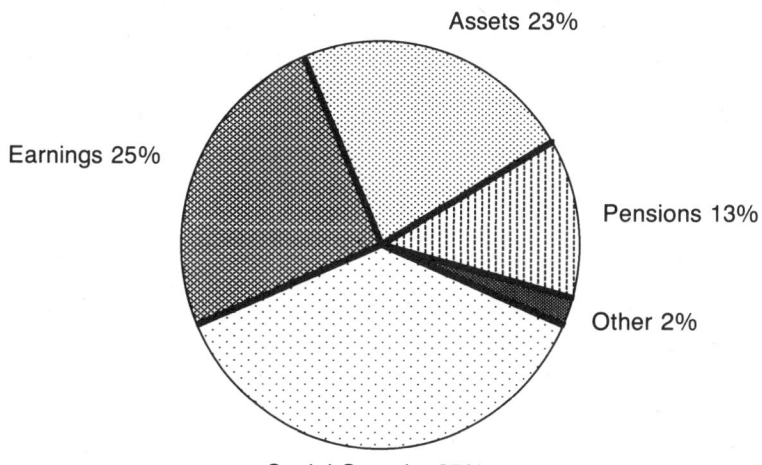

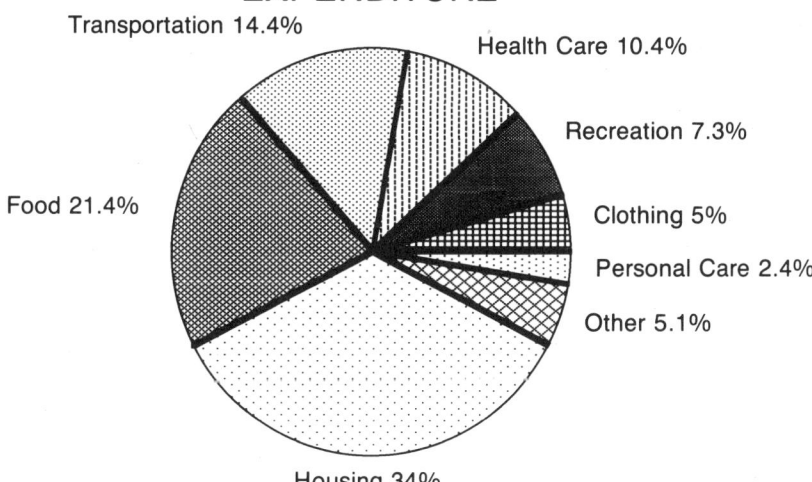

Source: Adapted from U.S. Bureau of Census, Current Population Survey, March, 1982; U.S. Department of Labor, Bureau of Labor Statistics, as reported in *Demographic and Socioeconomic Aspects of Aging in the United States,* Bureau of Census Special Report Series. P. 23, No. 138, p. 124; and United States Conference of Mayors, *Assessing Elderly Housing: A Planning Guide for Mayors and Local Officials* (Washington, D.C.: United States Conference of Mayors, 1985), p. 4.

and they feel more insecure. This insecurity affects how they spend their money, for he maintains that even though they can "afford a more luxurious lifestyle, they are less likely to indulge themselves. . . . [However] they are willing to spend on their children and grandchildren." Lazer predicts this situation will change. In the future, a larger share of income will be from sources other than social security. Moreover, he points out that by 1995 approximately 12 percent of the older Americans will have college degrees and more than 25 percent will have had some college education. As a result, this segment of the population "will seek a more graceful and elegant lifestyle, and their increasing incomes and rising levels of education will bring their consumption patterns more into line with those of younger consumers."[10]

But will the situation be different? Robert Binstock, a noted economist of the elderly population, points out that "some older people are extremely wealthy, others are economically comfortable, and still others are poor. An older black woman is more than four times likely than a white male to have an income below the poverty line."[11] In addition, he claims that "wherever the poverty line is drawn precisely, millions of older persons are clustered just above it, and their condition is not substantially different from those aging who are under it."[12] And, as for the housing of older Americans, one analyst states that "in 1979 approximately 2.3 million elderly paid excessive housing costs (over 30 percent of income for housing) and 1 million older persons still lived in physically inadequate housing. Countless others reside in neighborhoods that could be categorized as inadequate or unsafe."[13]

Katherine Warner's study of older Americans has determined that, at present, the "typical" elderly person is a woman living as a part of a married couple. This woman is a homeowner with a paid-off mortgage and lives in a 40-year-old house valued at $40,000. Her major problems are rising taxes, increasing utility costs, and difficulties getting home maintenance assistance. She worries about the future and the uncertainty of relocation.[14]

Ownership of a home can indeed be a double-edged sword. For most of the more than 70 percent elderly homeowners with a paid-off mortgage, their house is their only asset. However, many of these homes, often built more than 40 years ago, are too large for the occupants and too costly to repair and maintain (see Exhibit I.11). Energy costs and property taxes, especially, have worsened the elderly economic situation. Moreover, this asset is not spendable, and often the older Americans find themselves with no cash. Relocation is not necessarily the answer since suitable housing is often not available. The best answer appears to be programs that convert home equity into income or maintenance and repair services, such as reverse annuity mortgages (RAM), deferred payments plans (where property taxes are deferred until the house is sold or until the death of the owner), and sales plans (where the house is sold, but the elderly can stay there for as long as they desire).

Introduction

EXHIBIT I.11
Year Housing Structure Built of Householders 65 Years and Older

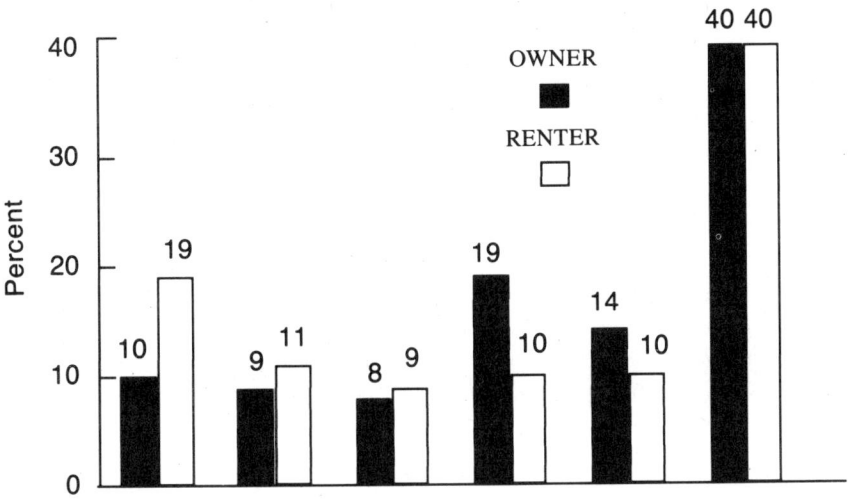

Source: U.S. Senate Special Committee on Aging in conjunction with the American Association of Retired Persons, *Aging America: Trends and Projections,* 1984, p. 91; U.S. Bureau of the Census, *America in Transition: An Aging Society,* September 1983. U.S. Bureau of the Census, Annual Housing Survey, 1980 unpublished; and United States Conference of Mayors, *Assessing Elderly Housing: A Planning Guide for Mayors and Local Officials* (Washington, D.C.: United States Conference of Mayors, 1985), p. 4.

The rental market is not in much better shape. Elderly renters constitute about one-third of the elderly households, and of these, approximately two-thirds are single people. Single elderly women renters are especially hard hit, and 56 percent of this group spend between 35 and 40 percent of their income on housing.[15] Government rent-subsidy programs have focused on the elderly poor, either through financing construction costs or by providing low-interest loans for elderly housing (Section 202 program) or by direct rent subsidies (Section 8 program). In 1982 about 50 percent of the 1.2 million public housing units were occupied by the elderly. Most new public housing constructed in the past decade has been for the elderly because of community resistance to low-income housing for families.[16] Rent vouchers and rent control may be partial answers, but questions need to be answered about how to target help to the most people who need it while minimizing the costs and disadvantages of such programs. Thus, as Warner concluded in her study,

> To deal with these trends, housing designs and public programs and policies must be shaped to work more effectively with them. . . . no maturing person is ever "typical." Older people differ as markedly from each other as do members of younger population groups. . . . Therefore, no single type of housing alternative can adequately satisfy either the needs of this group or be responsive to the resource capabilities and constraints of society.[17]

The Politics of Housing the Elderly

The elderly, then, are faced with a housing situation characterized by not enough units; and those that are available often will be inappropriate to their needs or too expensive for their pocketbooks. Can sufficient pressure be exerted at the local, state, and federal levels to relieve this situation? The answer is mixed. In some communities and in some states the older Americans probably can make some headway. In Florida, for example, where the elderly population is substantial, certainly they have a chance (see Exhibits I.12 and I.13). In states where other interests predominate, the elderly will be less effective. As Douglas Dobson points out, the elderly are not homogeneous.

> Their attitudes and political orientations are about as diverse as the population at large. Such diversity serves to inhibit a realization of the political potential of the elderly, for success in the halls of Congress and the state legislature depend, at least partially, on uniformity of articulated policy preferences.[18]

There have been successes to date, for older Americans have indeed been a prime beneficiary of federal programs. Jon Pynoos states that, "Whether due to the advocacy efforts of elderly housing interest groups or simply to the desirability of the elderly as program participants, there is little doubt that the elderly have won more than their share of federally funded housing assistance programs."[19] Public housing programs, especially, Sections 8, 202, and 236 have assisted more than 1 million households; the elderly comprised about 40 percent of all assisted households in the early 1980s, even though they represented a small proportion of the eligible population.[20]

In recent years, however, there has been a shift away from production-oriented programs to a reliance on using the existing stock. In addition, the elderly, because of the current economic situation, are now in more direct competition with other groups than they were in the past. Moreover, housing is not a high priority item for either the Reagan administration or many elderly advocacy groups who have income security and health care at the top of their agendas. Consequently, the elderly will have a tougher time making changes, and the outlook currently seems questionable for instituting a coherent housing policy. But a rich variety of initiatives are at least in the discussion stage.

EXHIBIT I.12
Age 65 Years and Older in Top Ten States: 1980

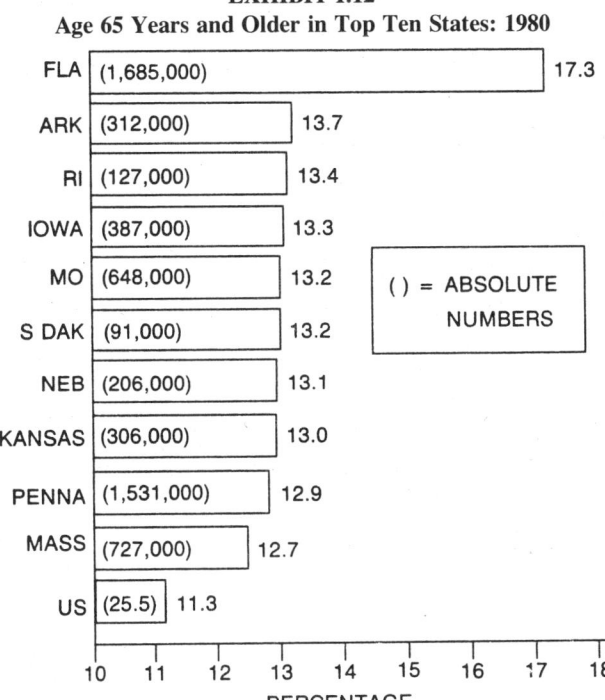

Source: U.S. Census of Population, 1980; and United States Conference of Mayors, *Assessing Elderly Housing: A Planning Guide for Mayors and Local Officials* (Washington, D.C.: United States Conference of Mayors, 1985), p. 2.

Overview of Selected Articles

The articles in this book document the situation described in the previous paragraphs, first by looking at the role of the elderly in American society and then at their needs, as well as the housing designs and financial options presently available or projected. The elderly as a political force is considered next. How much can they, and do they, influence public policies? This discussion is followed by an analysis of current programs and emerging trends. The articles, with one exception, have been published since 1980, and they represent the most up-to-date thinking about housing the elderly. The exception, the Lewis Mumford article arguing for integrating the elderly into the community rather than segregating them from the social mainstream, was first published in 1956. It is still the most ably written, comprehensive article on this topic.

EXHIBIT I.13
Cities with Largest Numbers and Highest Percentage of Persons 65 Years of Age and Older

City	Elderly Population	%	City	Elderly Population	%
New York, NY	954,671	13.5	Sun City, AZ	29,973	74.1
Chicago, IL	342,578	11.4	Miami Beach, FL	49,882	51.8
Los Angeles, CA	314,486	10.6	Hallandale, FL	18,185	49.8
Philadelphia, PA	238,037	14.1	Hemet, CA	10,854	48.3
Detroit, MI	140,790	11.7	Tamarac City, FL	13,131	44.7
San Francisco, CA	104,253	15.4	Deerfield Beach, FL	16,186	41.3
Baltimore, MD	100,707	12.8	Boynton Beach, FL	12,860	36.1
St. Louis, MO	79,742	17.6	Dunedin, FL	10,842	35.9
Milwaukee, WI	79,526	12.5	Seal Beach, CA	9,117	35.1
Seattle, WA	76,052	15.4	Delray Beach, FL	10,263	29.9
Cleveland, OH	74,596	13.0	Pompano Beach, FL	15,680	29.8
Washington, DC	74,046	11.6	Largo, FL	17,339	29.4
Indianapolis, IN	72,184	10.3	North Miami Beach, FL	9,576	26.2
Boston, MA	71,500	12.5	Clearwater, FL	22,322	26.1
Pittsburgh, PA	67,830	16.0	Sarasota, FL	12,754	26.1
Memphis, TN	67,221	10.4	Sunrise, FL	10,277	25.9
New Orleans, LA	65,229	11.7	St. Petersburg, FL	61,760	25.8
Denver, CO	62,037	12.6	Hollywood, FL	30,452	25.1
St. Petersburg, FL	61,670	25.8	Boca Raton, FL	11,732	23.7
Miami, FL	58,967	17.0	Atlantic City, NJ	9,446	23.5

Source: U.S. Bureau of Census, *1980 Census of Population and Housing, Summary Characteristics for Government Units and Standard Metropolitan Statistical Areas,* PHC 80-3; and United States Conference of Mayors, *Assessing Elderly Housing: A Planning Guide for Mayors and Local Officials* (Washington, D.C.: United States Conference of Mayors, 1985), p. 3.

The Role of the Elderly in American Society

This section focuses on the history of housing the elderly and the demographics of older Americans. The first article, by Anne Woodward, traces the changes in elderly living arrangements as the United States shifted from an agrarian society with large extended families living together to today's postindustrial society characteristics of the independent—and often isolated—housing of the elderly. She looks at federal housing policies, beginning with the National Housing Act of 1937, describes how these policies affected housing

Introduction xxix

for older Americans, and then examines design elements and housing options required by the elderly. Woodward emphasizes the need for architects and homebuilders to design and construct housing for this age group which provides both privacy and companionship, and she points to the various public service programs, housing options, technologies, and incentives that currently promote this aim. She concludes that

> we have to be willing to risk experiments. Short-term planning does us in, in the end. The persistence of homebuilding in which energy conservation is given short shrift points out the problem of building for immediate profit, not future utility. Unless we overcome the resistance to change on the part of builders and trade unions, and the addiction of architects to design for the sake of design (and not for the sake of people), by the turn of the century we could become a nation of trailers, nursing homes, and 'efficiency' apartments, with a huge inventory of obsolete, unlivable houses.[21]

How needy are older Americans? Are they really poor? Robert Binstock, in the second article, examines the economic situation of the elderly and concludes that their plight is indeed serious. With a 1979 median income of $11,316 for householders 65 years or older (unrelated single elderly people had a median income of $4,653), compared to the median of $21,201 for householders younger than 65, he argues that

> Despite contemporary portrayals of the elderly as relatively well off, millions of older persons are poor as measured by any of several absolute standards that are widely recognized. The same will hold true for millions among the future cohorts of the aged unless private and public policy conditions change substantially.[22]

Binstock maintains that Congress has an obligation to improve the standard of living for the elderly and concludes that "the challenges of maintaining or improving the economic status of the elderly in the years ahead are primarily political, not economic."[23]

The Jeanne Biggar et al. article rounds out this first section by updating information about migration of the elderly to the Sunbelt. While pointing out that most people "age-in-place," she and her colleagues argue that the 5 percent of those age 60 years or older who do relocate are, in many instances, sufficient to have a profound impact upon their new locations. Most of the elderly crossing state lines have settled in the Sunbelt states of Florida, California, Arizona, and Texas; an analysis of the data of the 1970s indicates there have been exceptionally large volume increases in Arizona (102 percent) and

Texas (94 percent) as compared to California (33 percent). This trend, coupled with the out-migration that California is experiencing, portends even greater numbers of elderly in the Southwestern states. North and South Carolina, Georgia, Mississippi, Alabama, and New Mexico have also begun to experience large increases in their elderly populations.

These authors believe the elderly will play an increasingly important role in the Sunbelt states, as well as states like New Jersey, Pennsylvania, Washington, Illinois, and Ohio—all of which rank in the top ten states receiving the largest numbers of migrants age 60 and older. The elderly will bring a more conservative view to social and political issues in these states and will substantially increase the demand for housing, retail goods, and adult recreational facilities. Also, they will force the expansion of local utilities, transportation networks, and health and municipal services. According to Biggar et al., the elderly are, and will continue to be, a potent force for change in many states.

Housing Options for the Elderly

What kind of housing does the elderly want? Do they want to live only with other elderly people or do they want to be integrated into a community along with other age groups? What unique needs do they have, and what are their options? The authors in this section address these questions, and the topics range from the issue of the segregation or integration of the elderly in communities to the variety of available housing options to zoning ordinances that expand or contract those options. But all the authors agree that older Americans must have a variety of housing alternatives to meet their needs, and that there must be more cooperation and collaboration between housing designers and the service providers of the elderly.

Lewis Mumford's article has been included because he so ably presents the arguments for integrating the elderly into the community rather than segregating them from society. He damned the trends that isolated the elderly and pushed them off to one side as the youth culture became dominant after World War II. Although this article is written in the mid-1950s—at the time the federal government seriously began to target policies for public housing for the elderly—his arguments are timeless. Mumford strongly recommends restoring the normal age distribution to communities; the elderly should not be isolated and left by themselves outside the mainstream. Moreover, he believes older Americans should not live in scattered single rooms or apartments in the community. Where possible, they should be grouped in small units of from six to twelve apartments for purposes of companionship and easier nursing care; in large cities there should be mixed age groups in highrises. Housing for the elderly must be located so there is easy access to services such as churches, libraries, and shopping. Mumford attacks zoning restrictions which encourage

Introduction xxxi

age segregation; the old and the young must be integrated so they can help each other. Through age integration and an efficient system of home health care, he argues, institutionalization, which is much more costly to society, will be deferred.

Stephen Golant, in an article written in 1985, favors age-segregated housing and aims his defense at some of the very arguments Mumford put forth 30 years earlier. Golant claims approximately 2 million (6 percent of the elderly population) reside in housing planned or organized for them and maintains there will be a "substantial" consumer market for this type of housing in the future. He argues that the criticisms leveled at age-segregated housing are not valid and discusses the advantages of this option. For Golant, older Americans living in age-segregated housing

1. share a common history so they have a greater potential for congenial personal relationships;
2. have the option of reducing involvement with the current youth-oriented culture, thereby creating their own subculture;
3. can deal with death better because they can talk to each other and can "accept with greater equanimity the inevitability of their own death";
4. can have greater physical security;
5. speak with a more potent political voice because they can vote as a bloc more effectively;
6. have better access to social services, both because of greater ease for delivery of public programs and because neighbors of their own age who understand and sympathize with their needs will be of more help than those in multigenerational communities;
7. can form cooperatives, such as special transportation programs, and because of the volume of the population, these activities can result in greater efficiencies and economies; and,
8. have predictable living environments, a factor extremely important to the well-being of the elderly because change is one of the biggest worries of this age group.

Golant concludes that age-segregated housing is not for everyone; but, he stresses, it is important that it be an option.

J. Kevin Eckert and Mary I. Murrey discuss the range of options available to the elderly, including communes and cooperatives, housesharing, mobile homes, hotels, rooming houses, and a variety of congregate housing alternatives and foster care homes. They point out that while a wide variety does exist, the elderly seem not to take advantage of the options for several reasons: for example, a very small number of elderly appear interested in intergenerational communes and cooperatives while the demand for congregate housing (housing with a minimum service package, unusually including a common dining room, some kind of medical services, and housekeeping services) outdistances the available supply. Moreover, the authors believe that considerably more needs to be known about the desirability of, and psychological effects on, the elderly of these alternatives. Housing choices are made on the basis of many forces—economic, political, psychological, and cultural. Yet, research providing insights into the interactions and complexities of these factors is lacking. Eckert and Murrey argue that there has long been a problem of aligning policies about national goals with housing needs, especially the housing needs of the disadvantaged. Research focusing directly on the links between the needs and problems of older Americans and the larger social, economic, political, and psychological forces can help realign national policies with the housing needs of the elderly.

Eckert and Murrey are concerned with the types of structures available and how these answer the needs and problems of the elderly. Graham Rowles, however, focuses on the "surveillance zone," which he defines as the "space within the visual field of a residence." This is an important area because it often is the primary way for the elderly to participate in the world outside their door. He argues that this surveillance zone can be "a source of meaning" and "a crucial link between the old person and the contemporary world." The need for this type of space, Rowles maintains, has implications for siting decisions, housing design, content and landscaping of adjacent space, and the psychological and emotional well being of older Americans. More attention must be paid to this issue he feels.

Carole Shifman maintains that changes in zoning ordinances can increase the housing options of the elderly. In her paper she looks at how age-specific zoning can be used to help the elderly live independently for a longer time, thus reducing the need for institutionalization. For example, ordinances can encourage construction of a range of housing options, or they can exclude options by restricting individuals in a single-family dwelling to related people only, thereby eliminating many shared housing alternatives. As incomes shrink and health problems increase with age, a wider variety of housing options is preferable to institutionalization, and zoning can help make these alternatives possible. Most opposition to age-specific zoning, Shifman declares, is because of beliefs that it lowers property values and that the needs of the elderly are really no different than the rest of the population. She thinks that with care the problems the opposition points to can be minimized.

It was not until 1974 that the legality of age-specific zoning was clarified. Since then, zoning ordinances have generally fallen into one of three categories: (1) ordinances that create a district for elderly or retirement housing; (2) ordinances that establish housing standards; and (3) ordinances that author-

Introduction   xxxiii

ize and regulate the addition of accessory apartments. As of 1983, for example, California was the only state using state-enabling legislation to permit echo housing—small temporary units located on the same lot as permanent homes. Zoning ordinances that especially encourage housing for the elderly include:

1. Cluster zoning, which allows units to be located in close groups yet preserves open space. The density on the lot is the same; cluster zoning affects the arrangement of the density.
2. Incentive zoning, where development is categorized and special standards are designated for all developments within a particular category. Bonuses may be awarded when this zoning is used, usually in the form of density increases, parking allowances, etc.

Zoning which facilitates infill development (encouraging construction on vacant land that may be unsuitable for commercial or industrial purposes) and adaptive reuse (using a building for other than its original purpose) can also provide housing alternatives for the elderly. Warehouses, schools, and commercial buildings that have been renovated and are now used as housing are examples of adaptive reuse.

Shifman concludes that

> General interest in relaxing rigid zoning classifications and changes in zoning provisions can encourage housing for the elderly by allowing cluster zoning, accessory and echo apartments, infill development, adaptive reuse, and an incentive zoning system. An appropriate combination of ordinances directed at housing elderly people can help to accommodate the diverse needs of a growing elderly population by providing a variety of housing alternatives.[24]

Housing and Personal Income: Home Equity Conversions
and the Capital Gains Tax Exclusion

The diminished income that elderly people receive after the retire can make it difficult for these people to retain and/or maintain their homes, especially in times of high inflation and increasing taxes. Since between 70 and 80 percent of the older Americans own their homes, quite often their house represents their major asset. Consequently, programs such as home equity conversion plans have been put in place by some states and lending agencies. These plans enable the elderly homeowners to convert their equity into income. In some cases this is done by an outright sale of the property; in other cases it occurs by cashing in some equity for an annuity. In some instances, homeowners must move (e.g. split-equity financing) while with other plans, they can remain in the house either as the owner (with a reverse annuity mortgage) or with a life lease (sale/leaseback plan). The benefits of these various programs can be substantial, but there are problems as the authors of the next four articles point out.

Vincent Trichilo outlines various types of home equity conversions available to all homeowners—reverse annuity mortgages, sale/leaseback agreements, split-equity programs, deferred payment loans, lines of credit, junior liens, and first mortgages—and briefly discusses the advantages and disadvantages of each. He points out that the programs of most interest to older homeowners (reverse annuity mortgages, sale/leaseback agreements, and split-equity financing) are rarely used; many elderly homeowners do not want to jeopardize their home equity—often their only asset—and the perceived costs and risks are too great (inflation eroding the dollar value of the money realized, lending institutions defaulting on contracts, not receiving full market value for the home, etc.). Moreover, these programs can be very complicated and confusing, and substantial financial counseling is often needed. Lenders, too, have problems with these programs because the property may depreciate, or the cost of designing, marketing, and administering the plans may not be justified unless the demand is considerably more than is the case at present.

In view of the costs and risks to homeowners, as well as the problems lenders face, Trichilo recommends creating private, non-profit organizations to educate and counsel elderly homeowners. Also, since these organizations would be non-profit agencies, they could offer loans at below-market rates and thereby increase the acceptability of the program.

Michael Hoeflich supplements Trichilo's discussion by focusing primarily on the tax implications of two home equity conversion plans—sale/leaseback agreements and split-equity financing. The advantages and disadvantages of intra-family sale/leaseback programs (between parents and children or between siblings, for example) and those involving unrelated third parties are pointed up. With this type of plan, the homeowner sells the house outright and then leases it back, usually for life. Advantages are that the elderly can remain in the house for their lifetime, and the sale may be "more acceptable" to the elderly people and their heirs than other types of home equity conversions. Disadvantages are primarily tied to income tax laws related to "fair rentals" to family members and to the capital gains tax exclusion. However, if done properly, these complications can be accommodated.

Benefits of split-equity financing appear to be many. In this plan, the owner sells the house outright, relocates, and purchases a fee ownership interest (less than 100 percent) in the new housing; thus, the elderly person is both an owner and a renter, for a lease is arranged for "fair rental" of that portion of the new housing that is not owned by the elderly person. Consequently, the older homeowner has increased cash flow because a portion of the money from

Introduction xxxv

the house sale can be invested, and the person can exclude the capital gains tax. Moreover, some portion of the property taxes and maintenance costs are shifted, and the elderly have housing more appropriate to their present needs rather than a house that generally was purchased when their living arrangements were different and they had more income. The major disadvantage with the split-equity plan is that elderly homeowners must relocate, whereas in the sale/leaseback arrangements, they can remain in their house.

Because home equity conversions can be complicated and confusing to many consumers, Maurice Weinrobe focuses on the need for consumer safeguards. He argues that regardless of the type of plan selected, there must be considerable counseling and full disclosure of such information as payment schedule, tax status and tax effects, term or duration of payments, equity position of the homeowner, prepayment penalties, rights of lenders to escalate payments of loan balances, etc. Weinrobe identifies some problem areas and suggests some safeguards. Reverse annuity mortgages and sale/leaseback arrangements, in particular, must be strengthened so they are more viable to both the lender and the consumer.

Home equity conversions can also finance long-term care. As Bruce Jacobs and William Weissert point out, costs for long-term care have mushroomed, and heavy burdens are being placed upon federal and state welfare programs; and, in some instances, because of this situation, the state is putting a lien on property in order to recover some of the costs. Most people cannot pay the large cost for long-term care from out-of-pocket expense money; consequently, if family, friends, or the government does not take over the cost, many elderly do without needed care. These authors analyze the potential of home equity to help pay these costs. They look especially at the extent to which proceeds from home equity conversions plans can pay for home care, catastrophic nursing home cost insurance, and insurance covering long-term care either in a nursing home or at home. In addition, they raise some public policy issues and outline an agenda for future research.

According to Jacobs and Weissert, there are several advantages to using home equity conversion plans to finance long-term care: (2) the elderly will be able to stay in their own homes for a longer period of time rather than being moved to a nursing home; (2) families and friends will be relieved of providing assistance; and, (3) some people will have access to care they need but do not presently have because there is no money. Moreover, elderly individuals who use a home equity conversion plan to finance long-term care would have greater choice in their health-care decisions. While recognizing that home equity conversions cannot totally replace public subsidy, these authors make the point that the elderly should give careful consideration to these alternatives, especially because of the magnitude of the costs involved in long-term care.

In addition to the various home equity conversion plans, homeowners 55 years and older have the advantage of the one-time capital gains tax exclusion, provided certain criteria are met. First enacted in 1964 and amended several times since, Sections 121 and 1034 of the Internal Revenue Code permit a person to sell a house and have a capital gain of up to $125,000 excluded from income taxes. Rolf Auster, in his article concerning this tax exclusion, points out the factors involved in getting maximum benefit from this break. He maintains this is a complex law and cautions homeowners to get financial advice so they are aware of all the ramifications of their actions and can get full benefit from the exclusion.

The Elderly as a Political Force

A wide variety of options are described in Parts II and III, but really how powerful are the elderly in making certain these options will indeed be available? Can they determine their own fate by developing and implementing policies to fit their unique needs? These two articles focus on the political arena and look at the ability of this age group to determine public policies.

Douglas Dobson is not sure of the actual power of the elderly. He admits they have the potential to play a significant role in American politics, but he is uncertain as to whether this potential will be realized. Generally political involvement increases with age, but he points out that there can be a downturn in interest and activity. In his estimation, income level and educational attainment are better factors for determining political mobilization than age consciousness. He thinks that maybe the elderly victories to date are based more on legislators' perceptions of the needs of the elderly than on the elderly as a force which shapes policies. Dobson says there is "little support for the notion that they are a distinctive, unified political force."[25] He concludes that

> the elderly of the early twenty-first century will be more highly educated, in better health, and perhaps more politically experienced than contemporary older Americans. As the present cohort is replaced by the politically active 1960s generation, it is certainly possible to visualize scenarios in which age could be a major source of cleavage in the American political system.[26]

Jon Pynoos, too, analyzes the influence of the elderly, but he looks specifically at their impact on housing policy. He argues that the elderly have not and cannot generate enough support for a national housing policy for several reasons: (1) the housing area is dominated by stronger, better organized groups such as the realtors and developers; (2) housing is only one of many interests of the elderly advocacy groups and does not have as high a priority as income security and health; and (3) the parameters for federal housing support are not within the influence of most housing advocacy groups.

Introduction

Thus, Pynoos argues, recent efforts by the elderly at the federal level have centered on keeping what they already have by shifting resources or modifying existing programs rather than by trying to significantly increase the funds or push for extensive new construction.

The primary reason the elderly have proportionately received so much more than other groups in the past is due as much to the lobbying efforts of other interest groups as to those of the elderly themselves. In the case of the Section 202 program, for example, the most successful federal elderly housing program, Pynoos says, "it is important to note that the size of the program itself has made it a smaller target for groups that oppose federally supported housing production programs."[27] Thus, it was not targeted for as much criticism and did not receive as much attention from critics as some larger programs.

In the public housing program area, the elderly influence is even more muted than in the Section 202 program. According to Pynoos, the only reason they have benefited to the large extent they have is because they are seen as "more socially desirable" than other low-income groups. Pynoos also calls attention to the fact that while the elderly did benefit more than other groups from federal housing programs, actually "only 3 percent of the elderly benefited from these programs, and ... the needs of several million elderly for housing that is affordable, safe, accessible, and suitable in terms of neighborhood amenities and services have gone unaddressed."[28] Yes, Pynoos admits, organizations for the elderly have been effective in getting issues on the agenda, especially on the agendas of the congressional committees on aging. But, he says, these committees have no power to propose legislation or appropriate funds.

As for the future agenda, "unless housing becomes a more universal as well as consumer issue, it will be difficult to generate the kind of political support needed to affect a major change in policy, such as in the case of social security."[29] But for this strategy to succeed, other interest groups will have to join the elderly. According to Pynoos, the "likely outcome" is that limited attention will be paid to this issue at the federal level. The focus will shift to state and local levels, in particular to programs concerned with new housing, shared housing, home equity conversions, and home repair and maintenance. Elderly advocacy groups will still pay attention to the federal level, especially to Section 202 housing and supportive housing for the frail elderly, but Pynoos believes these efforts, even if successful, "would continue their recent history of limited, piecemeal approaches to specific housing problems rather than attempts to overhaul the system."[30]

Current Programs and Emerging Issues

What programs presently exist for helping the elderly with their housing problems, and what current policy trends are aimed at resolving the problem of too much demand and too little supply? The authors in this section all agree that there have been, and will continue to be, major policy shifts in the decade of the 1980s. However, they examine these shifts and their implications from different perspectives.

Linda Daily looks at public policies from the point of view of how they affect a desire of the elderly to live independently as long as possible. She first looks at the institutionalized elderly by pointing out that in 1980 about 5 percent (1.3 million) of the elderly lived in nursing homes. The number is expected to double by the year 2000 so that nursing homes will then care for about 3 million elderly. In 1965 nursing home care cost $2.1 billion; it grew to $24.5 billion in 1981; and it is projected to be $75 billion in 1990. Moreover, Daily argues, congressional studies have shown that 20 to 40 percent of the nursing home residents could live in the community if adequate support services were available. But the present health care system provides greater support for institutionalization; the federal government spends only $1.00 on home health care for every $10 spent on nursing home care. The costs do not stop with care, however. With the current trend and policies, nursing homes project a need for between 300,000 and 400,000 new beds in the next decade. The government would be expected to help alleviate some of the construction costs.

Given these costs and the desirability of having the elderly live independently for as long as possible, Daily then examines the noninstitutional options for keeping older Americans in their own homes. She points to home equity conversion plans and the possibility of deferring property taxes until the home is sold or death occurs. In-home and community-based services would be of most help: adult day care, homemaker assistance, home health care, nursing care, medical equipment rental, meal delivery, and home maintenance programs need to be available. Some of these programs are provided from state or federal funds, and, Daily says, many states are trying to improve the coordination of available services as well as improve senior citizens' knowledge of them. Innovative shared housing arrangements, such as echo housing and accessory apartments, are increasing, but barriers exist to providing this type of housing in the form of zoning laws, public welfare subsidies, and federal rent subsidies. Boarding homes (rest homes, foster homes) are also being scrutinized more than in the past, and greater attempts are being made to regulate them. Since many receive significant funds from social security, Medicare, and Medicaid, and abuses gained newspaper notoriety, in 1976 Congress required states to license and regulate these facilities. Plans are also underway for the U.S. Department of Health and Human Services to play a greater role in protecting the residents of these homes.

As for federal housing policies under the Reagan administration, Daily points to the Section 8 and Section 202 programs, and the help they have given the elderly in the past. But, a redirection in federal housing policy is occurring under the Reagan administration. The private market and local initiative are viewed as the major sources in meeting needs. According to a report by the President's Commission on Housing, affordability—not supply—is the greatest housing problem faced by low-income people. Opposition to federal housing programs stems in part from their long-term financial commitments. For example, the Section 8 existing housing programs involve 15-year contracts for assistance payments.[31]

In place of the programs of the past, a housing voucher system is proposed. But critics maintain that supply is indeed a problem, and the voucher system is not an incentive for new construction—it is an incentive for raising rents. Section 202 will probably survive, but it is not enough.

Daily is particularly concerned about elderly care and housing and states that "the ideal is to keep people living independently by providing a sequence or continuum of housing arrangements and support services that meet the aging individual's needs for progressively greater care."[32] In order to meet this ideal, however, there are many long-term public policy challenges that must be faced. Program funding for all the needed services will be significant and will certainly pressure an already strained economy. Coordination of government, business, community, and volunteer services must be fostered, but politics will play a major role in determining the degree of support services and housing options available, and the response of local governments will depend upon the political power of the elderly.

Jerold Nachison and Morton Leeds agree that there will indeed be federal policy changes in the elderly housing area in the decade of the 1980s. In addition to describing the current state of the art, these authors outline trends and issues they believe will be of most importance during this decade.

Older Americans have had public housing assistance since the Housing Act of 1937, and especially since the late 1950s when construction programs primarily benefiting the moderate income elderly were initiated. Assistance in the past has come in many forms: mortgage support for nursing homes, guaranteed loans for the construction of housing for the elderly, extensive rental assistance, and, for non-profit sponsors of elderly housing, direct loans at below-market interest rates. Many of these programs, however, are now in flux or have been discontinued. If they exist at all, they have suffered cutbacks because of pressures and problems from other areas of the economy, primarily from inflation and high interest rates. These pressures have already brought about changes. For example, there is an emphasis on the use of existing stock rather than new construction; subsidies are available to local housing agencies for operating expenses; there have been cutbacks in the service sector; and, more older Americans are overhoused (living in houses with more space than they need), with large amounts of equity and little cash flow—and there is no housing available for them even if they do want to move.

These problems must be dealt with, in addition to new trends and issues that are emerging. These new trends include:

1. a major growth in the number of frail elderly. There is a need for a "continuum of living" environment which covers the time span from independent living to nursing home and hospital care.
2. a need for supplemental income because of housing deterioration and inflation. Over 70 percent of the older Americans own their own homes, homes which are largely paid for. But maintenance costs and property taxes eat away their incomes. New sources of income are now being examined in an effort to ease the strain, such as shared housing (either through renting rooms or forming cooperatives), reverse mortgages, and an emphasis on families providing more direct support.
3. consideration of more approaches to financing housing for the elderly. These include:
   a. a shift away from the elderly living in large homes to subsidized and unsubsidized apartments;
   b. a shift away from mortgage insurance for private construction loans augmented by direct loans to owners or federal underwriting of local bonds to rent-supplement and rental-assistance programs based on the "fair-market rent" concept.
   c. housing vouchers, but there is debate as to whether this approach stimulates new construction;
   d. a revision of present construction programs by simplifying mortgage insurance and rental-assistance programs, consolidating existing statutes into a block grant for state and local governments, and stressing rehabilitation rather than new construction; and,
   e. "cashing out" all welfare and related programs and giving a single payment to recipients that covers multiple needs.

These issues, then, according to Nachison and Leeds, represent the current thinking about federal housing policies for the elderly. The authors conclude that given the issues and the situation, "housing for the elderly will certainly be a major discussion topic for the decade."[33]

Raymond Struyk looks at future housing assistance for the elderly and agrees with many other authors that policies should be designed to provide a choice in living arrangements, to improve the housing quality, and to reduce the expenditures of those receiving assistance. Moreover, he argues, housing assistance should be available on an entitlement basis for at least some segment of the population. Using these assumptions as a basis, he then discusses the recent initiatives by the Reagan administration, the future of government housing policies and programs for the elderly, and the needed interventions.

Introduction

Struyk believes that Reagan administration policies have: (1) halted the growth in the number of households receiving assistance; (2) targeted assistance to poorer households; (3) reduced benefits; and (4) emphasized the use of existing stock rather than promoting new construction. Also, a housing voucher plan has been proposed but not accepted by Congress.

But what is really needed? Ideally, an entitlement program is best. Struyk favors it for several reasons. It would

1. end existing inequities;
2. remove impediments to housing adjustments which may exist because of fear of relocation and loss of assistance;
3. reduce the fear of poor, elderly homeowners of having to pay uncontrollable rents if they leave their homes;
4. be merged with the social welfare system to help limit inequities in the overall system; and,
5. be viewed as a vital part of the continuum-of-care program that must be developed.

A voucher system would help if (1) it were similar to the Section 8 existing program, (2) income eligibility could be set at 50 percent of the local area median income, (3) participants could contribute 30 percent of their adjusted incomes for housing, and (4) both homeowners and renters could participate. Struyk thinks approximately 5.3 million households would participate and that the cost would be $11.6 billion at the beginning of the program in addition to the present $5.1 billion. As for financing the proposed voucher system, he suggests

1. replacing $1.3 billion budgeted for weatherization and heating assistance by a voucher;
2. repealing forgiveness of the capital gains tax for those over 55 years of age; and,
3. containing mortgage interest deductions from the federal income tax.

Since it is unlikely that this type of program would be enacted, he concentrates his attention on two issues—construction of new rental units for the poor elderly, and a reasonable means of assisting needy homeowners.

In the past, the construction of elderly housing by non-profit sponsors under the Section 202 program was an indication of the government's concern for housing the elderly. But this is changing. The 202 program has been seriously cut back, and now there is an emphasis on leasing units rather than building new ones. Struyk maintains that in the future, the construction of new projects for the elderly beyond these low levels will occur only if newly-built projects have a well-defined role in the long-term care system. In short, they will probably have to be congregate housing facilities (i.e., housing offering a number of services in addition to shelter) that can be demonstrated to be cost-effective alternatives to intermediate care facilities *and* to providing support services to the elderly in the dwelling units they would otherwise be inhabiting.[34]

As for homeowners, Struyk says there is a choice in how best to assist the elderly—housing vouchers or the provision of in-kind maintenance services. The vouchers provide cash grants to income-eligible homeowners with dwellings which meet minimum physical standards and could be used for any purpose, including housing. With an in-kind maintenance program, services are provided directly to a homeowner by an agency. As to which of these strategies to select, Struyk maintains there is "no clear winner." But he thinks that "if national policy were being made today . . . vouchers would seem to be the better choice."[35]

Struyk agrees with Nachison and Leeds. The topic of housing the elderly will be debated fiercely, and significant changes will occur. But any housing policy that is developed in the 1980s must (1) be largely self-supporting; (2) be cost effective (have a proven track record); and (3) move housing assistance toward greater integration with the welfare and long-term care systems. The trend will probably be toward a reliance on housing vouchers for renters and possibly homeowners, but the major barrier will be financing. The goal, however, must be greater equity of similar households and greater use of federal assistance to expand the housing options of older Americans.

Summary

The problem of housing older Americans in the next few decades is indeed complex. The elderly are not a homogeneous group; they represent varied needs and interests. The answers, too, must be varied; no single answer will suffice. Experiments are now under way in numerous communities, especially with programs involving congregate housing and intergenerational housing with nonrelatives. The elderly themselves are becoming more aware of their options, and some legislation has already been put in place, such as the enabling legislation in California which permits echo housing. Other states and communities will soon follow with this and similar plans that will open alternatives to more people.

New proposals to help the elderly and their families are coming forth as evidenced by proposed congressional legislation (see Appendix B). Links between home and health care are receiving particular attention, for bills have been introduced

1. to create a home care clearinghouse in order to provide the elderly with a single place for obtaining information about federal home care programs (H.R. 167 and S. 752);
2. to improve home care services offered by the Veterans Administration for elderly veterans (H.R. 505 and S. 1007); and,
3. to expand the home care services available under the Social Security Act (H.R. 1192).

Nor have the families of the elderly been forgotten. Congress is studying bills that would

1. give a refundable tax credit for taxpayers who maintain households which include disabled elderly (H.R. 406);
2. give income tax credit for maintaining a household for dependents who are 65 years or older (H.R. 1192); and,
3. allow a credit against income taxes for expenses incurred in the care of some elderly family members (H.R. 644 and S. 779).

Elderly homeowners, too, might look for some relief in the future, for Congress is considering a demonstration program of insurance for home equity conversion mortgages for elderly homeowners (H.R. 2292). Moreover, there appears to be a strong move to oppose cuts in the Section 202 housing assistance program for the elderly and handicapped.

More needs to be done, however. But given a firm understanding of the problem and a serious commitment to seeking answers, older Americans can look forward to an increase in housing options that will allow them to remain as independent as possible.

Notes

1. Sandra J. Newman, "The Availability of Adequate Housing for Older People: Issue Areas for Advocates," *Journal of Housing for the Elderly*, Vol. 2, No. 3 (Fall 1984), 4.
2. Katherine Warner, "Demographics and Housing," in Urban Land Institute, *Housing for a Maturing Population* (Washington, D.C.: Urban Land Institute, 1983), p. 3.
3. National Policy Center on Housing and Living Arrangements for Older Americans, *Housing Needs of the Elderly: A Quantitative Analysis* (Ann Arbor, Michigan: National Policy Center on Housing and Living Arrangements for Older Americans, 1982), p. 11.
4. United States Senate, Special Committee on Aging, *Section 202 Housing for the Elderly and Handicapped: A National Survey* (Washington, D.C.: U.S. Government Printing Office, 1984), p. 3.
5. National Policy Center on Housing and Living Arrangements, p. 32.
6. National Association of Housing and Redevelopment Officials, *Monitor*, Vol. 7, No. 12 (June 30, 1985), p. 9.
7. American Association of Retired Persons, *Housing Options for Older Americans* (Washington, D.C.: American Association of Retired Persons, 1984).

8. Victor Regnier and Thomas O. Byerts, "Applying Research to the Plan and Design of Housing for the Elderly," in Urban Land Institute, *Housing for a Maturing Population* (Washington, D.C.: Urban Land Institute, 1983), p. 18.
9. United States Conference of Mayors. *Assessing Elderly Housing. A Planning Guide for Mayors and Local Officials* (Washington, D.C.: United States Conference of Mayors, 1985), p. 4.
10. William Lazer, "Inside the Mature Market," *American Demographics,* Vol. 7, No. 3 (March 1985), 48.
11. Robert H. Binstock, "The Elderly in America: Their Economic Resources, Income Status, and Costs," Chapter 2 in *Aging and Public Policy: The Politics of Growing Old in America,* ed. by William P. Browne and Laura Katz Olson (Westport, Connecticut: Greenwood Press, 1983), p. 29.
12. Ibid., p. 30.
13. Jon Pynoos, "Setting the Elderly Housing Agenda," *Policy Studies Journal,* Vol. 13, No. 1 (September 1984), 177.
14. Warner, p. 11.
15. Warner, p. 14-15.
16. Linda Daily, "Housing Options for the Elderly," *Editorial Research Reports,* Vol. 2, No. 5 (August 6, 1982), 584.
17. Warner, p. 23.
18. Douglas Dobson, "The Elderly as a Political Force," Chapter 6 in *Aging and Public Policy: The Politics of Growing Old in America,* ed. by William P. Browne and Laura Katz Olson (Westport, Connecticut: Greenwood Press, 1983), p. 141.
19. Pynoos, p. 177.
20. Ibid., p. 175.
21. Anne Woodward, "Housing the Elderly," *Society,* Vol. 19, No. 2 (January/February 1982), 57.
22. Binstock, p. 31.
23. Ibid., p. 32.
24. Carole R. Shifman, *Increasing Housing Opportunities for the Elderly,* American Planning Association, Planning Advisory Report 381 (Chicago, Illinois: American Planning Association, December 1983), p. 15.
25. Dobson, p. 140.
26. Ibid., p. 141.
27. Pynoos, p. 176.
28. Ibid., p. 177.
29. Ibid., p. 183.
30. Ibid., p. 184.
31. Daily, p. 584.
32. Ibid., p. 585.
33. Jerold S. Nachison and Morton H. Leeds, "Housing Policy for Older Americans in the 1980s: An Overview," *Journal of Housing for the Elderly,* Vol. 1, No. 1 (Spring/Summer 1983), p. 13.
34. Raymond J. Struyk, "Future Housing Assistance Policy for the Elderly," *The Gerontologist,* Vol. 25, No. 1 (February 1985), 44.
35. Ibid., 45.

I

The Elderly in American Society

1

Housing the Elderly

Anne Woodward

"Where will I live when I'm old?" Millions of graying Americans, alarmed at the fate of their parents, are starting to ask that question. With more than 400,000 men and women in the United States now entering the over-65 age group each year—most of them headed for at least another decade of life—jobs, recreation, and home and health-care services for the elderly are getting considerable attention. Government and the private sector willing, these can be rapidly instituted.

Bricks and mortar, however, are here to stay—and we must now mold the built environment to the more than 12 percent of the population who will, by the year 2000, by elderly (over 65). Given the current conservative climate, where do we start? By prodding architects out of their preoccupation with other design problems. By enlisting planners and private organizations to fight obsolete zoning regulations. And above all, by convincing homebuilders after short-term gains that people of all generations seek living options unavailable in our present inflexible housing.

The three-bedroom detached house in the suburbs, for instance, remains the typical dwelling in the United States, representing two-thirds of all our housing. More than 750 thousand three-bedroom houses were built in 1980, compared to only 75-80 thousand townhouses and condominiums. Whom does this ideal three-bedroom detached house—often some distance from shopping—really

---

Published by permission of Transaction, Inc. from SOCIETY, Vol. 19, No. 2, copyright © 1982 by Transaction, Inc.

serve? It serves the nuclear family with two or three growing children, and one or two cars; not the one in every nine Americans now over age 65, and even less the family of three or four generations who may need, or wish, to live in closer proximity.

Recently, there has been considerable debate about whether the extended family, in the good old days, was ever as close as we have been led to believe. Certainly multigenerational living was easier to achieve in an agrarian society, and it apparently worked for many people. Also, our multiple migrations—from the western movement to population shifts into and out of cities—must have pulled families apart.

In any case, it is clear that, from the 1930s on, many factors combined to isolate the elderly. That decade saw the beginning of zoning and private covenants prohibiting two-family dwellings on one lot, the proliferation of small houses—newly affordable under FHA—and a widespread ignorance of, or indifference to, the housing needs of the elderly. As Winston Churchill put it, "We shape our buildings, and then our buildings shape us." By 1950, the youth-cult and experiments in single-generational living, in communes of the 1960s, contributed to a growing apartheid, as youths warned "don't trust anyone over 30." From 1960 to 1970, while the number of persons 65 and over increased by more than 20 percent, the number of multigenerational households decreased by 10 percent. By 1978 a mere 9 percent of all older Americans lived with adult children, although 42 percent reported they "depended" on their children for other support. Figures from the 1980 census are still being analyzed. But it seems likely that in addition to younger persons who have never married or are divorced, the elderly make up a good proportion of the single-person households that now constitute nearly a quarter of all U.S. households.

In addition to solitary living, two other living arrangements for the elderly now substitute for multigenerational households: the institutionalization or "warehousing" of infirm older persons in nursing homes and homes for the aged, and, for the more affluent elderly still in relatively good health, the privately developed retirement community. Well-intended government policy may have contributed to the isolation of the impoverished elderly with legislation authorizing funding of public housing for the low-income aged in 1956. That year, reflecting on the trend, Lewis Mumford was moved to declare that "probably at no period and in no culture have the old been so completely rejected as in our own country, during the last generation."

The question has been raised: Is the rejection a two-way street? Do the elderly really want to remain with the rest of society? In Mumford's day, even cities were still relatively free from violent crime. Now, faced with purse snatching on the street and violent invasions of their homes, older persons sometimes seek out the comparative safety of a home for the aged or a specially guarded retirement community as a haven from abuse and perhaps also from other hostile elements of daily life: traffic congestion and noise, haste and rudeness in public places and on public vehicles, the clamor of young children at play. It should come as no surprise, then, that some studies have shown that, contrary to expectation, many elderly persons find high-rise apartment living quieter and safer than living in a house.

For some of the relatively affluent elderly, withdrawal now means a flight to a privately developed retirement community—most often in the sunbelt—or to an apartment or apartment-hotel that provides its own restaurant and shopping facilities on a small to spectacular scale. Middle-income groups may rely on homes for the aged provided by the Veterans Administration, labor unions, churches and synagogues, or other beneficent organizations with which they are associated. But many of these homes have long waiting lists.

Despite the public protest, homes for the aged not sponsored by charitable organizations are frequently mere rooming houses in old buildings that are basically firetraps and, despite licensing and occupancy regulations, seem difficult for authorities to monitor. Against living in these poorly staffed and managed homes, many low- and middle-income elderly prefer to take their chances on their own. Nursing homes, the last resort, are generally regarded as housing only for the most infirm cases. Ironically, the Government Accounting Office (GAO) has established that between 15 percent and 40 percent of the elderly now living in nursing homes could live in a normal community if special homemaker and health-care services, and transportation, were available to them.

Challenging the Experts

There is a drastic need for experts in several disciplines to look at home and community design and ways they might function for the elderly. Safety, convenience, and ease of home maintenance are obvious, worthy objectives. But the real challenge may lie in how to achieve an ideal balance between privacy and human contact, since these depend to some extent on individual preferences. Most elderly persons seek some companionship with their peers to indulge in shared memories and common concerns over health and families. But they also desire the comforting awareness of life's continuity that comes with the mix of generations. It is clear we will need many options.

Fortunately, some forward-thinking planners are beginning to realize that services to the elderly who live independently—such as Meals on Wheels, and health and homemaker services—should be taken into consideration in locating building sites and planning traffic patterns. Other planners have suggested housing options which aim at preserving in individual communities the approximate proportion of older persons in the population as a whole. Mumford articulated this goal a quarter-century ago, but it was never pursued in any meaningful way, except in some planned new communities. Several new towns in Europe and Australia did successfully incorporate imaginative design for the elderly into development plans. And in Reston, Virginia, as in some of Britain's new towns, special housing for the elderly is located on the perimeter of shopping centers, with access to nearby shops and medical clinics. The early collapse of the new-town movement in the United States in the 1970s, however, slowed any innovation here, and we are largely faced with working within existing land-use patterns.

Frank Spink of the Urban Land Institute suggests interesting but costly uses of property in city suburbs, which are gaining in elderly households while central cities are losing. The first involves adding to or converting unused space in elementary schools as service centers for the elderly. Schools could become day-care centers, or, filling an even greater need, temporary convalescent homes, utilizing existing cafeteria and nursing services to assist those unable for short periods to manage for themselves at home. Spink also recommends construction of in-fill housing—small, one-bedroom units specially designed for the elderly—on the land between existing, larger homes. This would mean higher density in low-density areas, but it would permit the elderly to own or rent homes in familiar neighborhoods, with about the right degree of isolation and privacy. Ideally, these suburban in-fill units would be situated reasonably close to suburban shopping areas or the school centers. To accomplish the transition, services now commonplace in urban areas would have to be made available farther out: delivery of or transportation to shopping, food, and medical services, as well as access to recreational opportunities. How can we achieve such radical redesign of our suburbs? Tax incentives would be vital. And other guarantees, probably similar to those instituted to permit the preservation and rehabilitation of our cities, would also have to be created.

Architects design upon demand. With 25 million Americans already over 65, it is somewhat shocking to learn that only around seventy members of the American Institute of Architects (AIA) specialize in housing for the elderly, and that no one, apparently, is clamoring for multigenerational schemes. Fortunately, the executive director of the AIA, David Meeker, a former Assistant Director for Community Development of Housing and Urban Development, is alert to the possibilities. He acknowledges that "under present economic and social pressures, the extended family may reassemble as an economic unit" and exert pressure on architects to think about houses to accommodate several generations.

And what of the home builders? Obviously, they are looking for profit and build for the market as they perceive it. And as a nation, we have only very recently begun to recognize and accept new family living patterns and the dramatic increase in the number of elderly. These developments give rise to new market demand. Who will do the innovating? Only 10 percent of all homebuilders construct more than a hundred housing units a year. These larger firms are usually in a better financial position to take risks than the smaller, average homebuilder, who completes less than fifteen units a year. Yet the smaller firms have been more adventurous in seeking new markets. After young "homesteaders" started rehabilitating older city houses in the 1970s, smaller firms pioneered in the construction of townhouses in urban, then suburban, areas. Perhaps these homebuilders will not develop innovative designs for tomorrow's aged.

What is the incentive? First, home-buyers, mindful that a small cost-saving today could necessitate an enormous investment in changes tomorrow, should make their voices heard. They should demand that houses now being built will suit their needs in twenty or so years. This may prompt a little more social concern. However, other efforts will be needed if we are really to progress beyond the omnipresent inflexible house and the bigger and bigger home for the aged. Government may have to stir homebuilders with better carrots and sticks. As Meeker admits, "both in coordination and process, our present instruments are increasingly less important and relevant to today's housing." Some new possibilities? HUD could cooperate in the development of new housing types and financing mechanisms. FHA and the Veterans Administration regulations could stipulate a limit on loans for home building unless the product would be suitable for the new population mix. Then, with tax incentives and other logical guarantees, private enterprise should respond. Among the alternatives architects and builders might consider are: double-houses, multigenerational group-living arrangements, congregate housing of suitable size and design, and basic houses or other new structures with flexible design features.

Creative Alternatives

Seventy-one percent of all persons over 65 own their own home. Is there any way those who wish could stay there until they are too feeble to care for themselves? Their empty nests—the aging, oversized homes in cities and older suburbs—are often unsafe, too big, and awkward to care for. The average lifespan of a house is estimated to be fifty years; and half of the elderly still live in housing built before World War II. The high cost of modernization, plus increased taxes, make maintenance difficult. Present tax deductions for improvements or partially subsidized repairs are apparently inadequate. HUD admits that the present FMHA Section 504 Home Repair Loan Program, available to the elderly of low income, is rarely used because of the loan repayment schedules. If better financing could be arranged, and zoning changed to make possible remodeling to a "double," some, but not all, of the problems might be resolved. A reliable tenant in a rental unit could provide extra security, supplemental income, and even transportation in emergencies.

The "double" is also a good bet for the family worried about an aging parent or wanting parents nearby, but not underfoot. In these cases, provision of not only health and homemaker services, but some relief from the constant strain of care taking is essential. To preserve privacy and pursuit of special interests, an addition to the family home, or conversion of space to a completely separate "grandparents unit," is most desirable. But in most cities—Los Angeles and Houston among the exceptions—zoning regulations prohibit such conversion.

How can houses be remodeled so that there is living space for an elderly person or couple? Often there are basements in city townhouses that can be converted to living quarters suitable for renting to students or young professionals. But families hardly wish to put their aged parents in damp or dark basements. Duplex houses—living quarters that mirror-image each other side by side—are scarce but useful. One-floor "double" brick houses with three bedrooms each, dubbed "executive bungalows," have been successful with middle-income families in Dallas; they are near stores and recreation. Stacked apartments, one over another in an older home, like the "triple deckers" of Massachusetts, could be fine, except for the stairs. However, in ground-level townhouses, conversion of the lower level into an apartment for the elderly works out well, with use of the top two floors for a younger family—provided care is taken through use of thick carpets, carpet pads, and other sound-abatement devices to ensure that noise from above is not transmitted to the apartment below. Inner conversions of space are more likely and offer interesting, if costly, design challenges. But most "doubles" will have to be created out of existing housing. With land at a premium, remodeling, not new building, is the wave of the future, for at least a couple of decades.

The tax deductions for interest paid on home mortgages, and also for remodeling and repairs to rental units, are helpful but need simplifying. What is missing is any special deduction for remodeling to modernize or maintain a full-time "granny flat." (A bill to allow a credit for household expenses to any taxpayer who maintains a household with a dependent 65 years old or over was proposed in the 96th Congress—but languished in committee. This, too, might be resurrected.)

The concept of several generations sharing living space is not limited to members of the same family. A Presbyterian minister, the Reverend Dennis Day-Lower, developed in the Back Bay area of Boston a model, non profit "shared living project," in which fifteen unrelated persons, aged 20 to 80, have lived together since July, 1979. Day-Lower started with Title III seed money from the Administration on Aging and obtained additional funds from private sources to convert a former rooming house for primarily low-income residents (in accordance with HUD guidelines). Residents pay from $150 to $250 for private rooms, some with baths, in the Victorian row house with one large kitchen, common all-purpose living-dining space, one kitchenette on each floor, and a roof-top garden. The essential privacy is maintained. And none of the elderly residents are so disabled that they cannot contribute physically, socially, or mentally to management of the project. The apparent success of the Boston project has encouraged Day-Lower to establish "Inter-generational Housing Services" in Philadelphia to advise on the other extended "family" living arrangements. Privately supported by churches and individuals, the center expects to engage in direct consulting and technical assistance on similar shared-living projects, develop educational material for interested persons, act as a resource to local groups on the removal of legal barriers to shared-living projects, and establish a nationwide network for information exchange. Day-Lower cites at least fifty shared houses now around the country—some rented, some individually or jointly owned.

There have also been experiments accommodating a few rental units for the elderly in condominiums. In essence, the individual owners of condo units carry the older residents, who pay a flat monthly rent according to income and receive regular condo services—maintenance, utilities, etc.—free of additional charge. There are several advantages to this situation. Elderly residents receive protection and pleasant surroundings at minimum cost. And while the cost to residents who "carry" them is minimal when divided among many unit owners, the benefits of having a few elderly persons readily available for temporary child care or home management may be important.

Group living for the elderly should not be ruled out. It has worked in Scandinavian countries, and many gerontologists, including Marie McGuire Thompson of the International Center for Social Gerontology, affirm its usefulness. The Urban Institute estimates that a million Americans require this living arrangement, but this is somewhat debatable. It is necessary now because so few alternatives and home services are available. Group living is a practical solution when independent living, living with a family, or living with an extended "family" of different age groups is undesirable or impossible for physical, emotional, or financial reasons. As long as the building housing an elderly group is not too large, and as long as it is located in a community where the elderly are not completely isolated from other age groups, shops, medical centers, and neighborhood activities, this is not necessarily a bad solution. Unfortunately, new buildings for the elderly appear to be being built farther and farther out into the countryside, where land is cheap. And new or renovated buildings in the center city—and even in some new communities like Reston, Virginia—get bigger and bigger, also for maximum financial return.

There is some agreement that, socially, the ideal group housing for elderly occupants contains six to twelve units to a building. The ideal building is located in a mixed-age community, in pleasant surroundings, but close to amenities; the ideal design takes into consideration regional preferences and the ethnic or other cultural differences of the occupants. In other words, the best group living facilitates not only the necessary services to the elderly, but also friendship informtion. Peers, in such situations, add to or substitute for the emotional and other support of the family. In most such congregate housing in the United States, the minimum age limit is 62. In Europe, it is often 55—which may make for a better mix.

The idea of a house as a changing process rather than a fixed object has intrigued architects for some years. The concept was strongly advocated at a Stanford Research Institute Conference in 1967, and since then a number of attempts have been made to design and build both an adaptable conventional house and a more radical "core" house to which self-contained units, requiring only furniture, could be added or subtracted according to the needs of the occupants. The "typical" housing consumer, like the "typical" American family, is becoming more and more diverse. The press has recently pointed out the many young persons now returning to their parents' households—for economic reasons—and the benefits and friction this may generate. Thus, the time seems particularly ripe for developments to accommodate changing family roles, provided home builders and the construction trades overcome their resistance to innovation.

For the most part, builders have been frightened away from experiments as a result of an unfortunate experience with the "basic house" in 1970-71. In an effort to keep down costs, builders constructed a dwelling without amenities like fireplaces or dishwashers or larger rooms. The idea never caught on; although the buying public had been asking for more affordable homes, few purchased this stripped-down model. At the January 1981 annual meeting of the National Association of Home Builders, however, the concept resurfaced as one way to make houses affordable despite high interest rates. And the American Institute of Architects tends to agree. A few initial experiments in "core" housing to which other units could be hooked were also less successful. Olin Corporation attempted some "flexible" modular units in the new town of Jonathan, Minnesota, in 1971—dwellings with a basic service core of kitchen, two bathrooms, and an all-purpose area to which bedroom modules could be added on one side, and a living-dining room on the other. (There was even talk of having rentable units that could be added for a special need at a special, specified time.) The cost of moving the additional modules into place, however, proved prohibitive—at about the same cost as moving a trailer. Grumman Modular Buildings experimented with modules made with structural steel stacking frames with both fixed and movable walls and partitions, but never went into mass production. The idea undoubtedly has merit, but the ideal formula has yet to be found. And once it is found it will take a carefully thought-out public relations campaign to lure people away from their desire for the single-family detached unit built on conventional lines, the dreamhouse useful for only limited family years. Perhaps people can become educated to become less fixture-oriented—seeking only houses with rooms rigidly dictating specific functions such as dining rooms, bedrooms, etc.—and become more space-oriented.

Little has been said to date about the usefulness of flexible housing as a solution to the needs of the elderly. But it may be significant that in Japan, where families traditionally take care of aging parents, houses are made more flexible through the use of moveable screens which can open up space or close off rooms for privacy. Architects and interior designers, who in recent years have removed doors to create an illusion of greater space, might well consider installing screens, "pocket" doors, or large, hinged doors that fold back to multiply room use (and, as a side-benefit for the elderly, make the passage of a wheelchair practical). Some experiments with design of a conventional adaptable house that could accommodate the handicapped or elderly, however, are now taking place. Under contract with HUD, the National Association of Home Builders Research Foundation has recently completed two houses (one in Las Vegas and the other in Loveland, Colorado) and four apartment units (two in Bethesda, Maryland, and two in southern Florida) to show that new design standards, making the house adaptable for handicapped (or elderly) persons, would not necessarily be prohibitive in cost. Adaptations in the houses and apartments were, for the most part, available on the standard market. They included such small changes as levers rather than door knobs as handles; wider doors—36 rather than 32 inches wide—and light switches and plugs at waist level; and stronger bathroom walls to accommodate bars and rails that might be added later. The largest cost was for items not now available, such as kitchen countertops that could adjust to different heights. The countertops had to be custom-made but, should they come into mass-production, would not be excessive in cost. HUD is currently evaluating this "adaptable" housing for new American National Standards Institute (ANSI) buildings standards, but from the cost aspect only. HUD reports no interest in seeing how the living arrangement work out with occupancy, despite the fact that handicapped persons have now occupied the first-completed homes for several months.

Long-Term Planning

Persons over 75 currently make up the fastest growing age group in the United States, but only about 46 percent of this group are able to function without help (as opposed to 71 percent of persons age 65 to 74, according to the Government Accounting Office). Despite all medical effort to prevent or alleviate loss of sensory acuity, for example, people still have to expect this physical deterioration to begin at around age 70. And even with the trend toward better general health for the aged, handicaps due to a particular illness become noticeable at this time of life. As a result, architectural and interior design features—special treatments of light, color, and texture as well as physical space—become increasingly important.

The elderly, moreover, require safety features to guard them not only from crime, but also from accidents. Accidents in the home cost the nation $2.5 billion annually, and the elderly are particularly vulnerable. These facts have not been ignored. The Department of Commerce has issued safety guidelines for those who want to construct homes that have the potential to be relatively accident-free. Accommodations for the handicapped, which have won wide attention, are now commonly used in reputable homes for the aged and nursing homes. This is encouraging. But it is only a beginning. If older persons are really to maintain their independence for as long as possible—alone, in a family setting, or with a surrogate family—builders must give some thought to incorporating special design as accepted practice in standard homes (and, where suitable, shops and medical clinics.

Some design elements deserve special review:

- *Special alarm systems.* In Britain an alarm system alerts neighbors that the older person is having difficulty at home: the older person's residence contains switches in each room which turn on a bright blue light outside the front door, in plain view of neighbors and passersby, as a signal for help. Other alarm systems, including an alarm bell that also opens the front door, are being experimented with here. Such house systems would complement Med-Alert, the device worn on the body which can signal a receiving station that help is needed.
- *Aid to physical movement.* Awning and crank-operated casement windows (except for the arthritic) should replace double-hung windows, which are awkward and often stick. Non-slip floors, with no raised thresholds, and levers rather than door knobs would be helpful. Handrails should be installed where appropriate, and at the proper angle. (Marie McGuire Thompson reports that too many handrails are now being used in homes for the aged.)
- *Sensory aids.* Changes in textures and contrasting colors for walls and floors, risers and treads on stairs, etc., would reinforce perceptions of depth and location. A proper balance of lighting—not too bright, not too dim—would eliminate glare and sharp contrasts.

Predictions for the future are mostly perilous. The Institute for the Future, for example, conducted a study in 1971 of "Some Prospects for Residential Housing by 1985." One way-off-base prediction: "A gradual lowering of the prime interest rate of 7 to 7.5 percent by 1980, followed by a rise to 8 percent by 1985 is expected." Experts, moreover, disagree. At about the same time that the Institute's report was also predicting that "building codes will undergo extensive revision emphasizing standardization mechanisms which permit a greater degree of innovation and use of mass-production techniques," architect Peter Blake was telling a Washington, D.C., audience—not half in jest—that "building costs and unemployment may be so high in the future that we will have to go back to construction with handmade bricks."

New technologies, we now expect, may offer resources in the future that will improve life for the elderly no matter where they live. Advanced and computerized communications systems seem the most obvious and promising development, since they could reduce the feeling of isolation and permit better medical and other monitoring. Developments in health fields also make us inclined to predict longer, healthier lives, with decline and death following quickly at the end.

So we have to consider several possible scenarios. And we have to be willing to risk experiments. Short-term planning does us in, in the end. The persistence of homebuilding in which energy conservation is given short shrift points out the problem of building for immediate profit, not future utility. Unless we overcome the resistance to change on the part of builders and trade unions, and the addiction of architects to design for the sake of design (and not for the sake of people), by the turn of the century we could become a nation of trailers, nursing homes, and "efficiency" apartments, with a huge inventory of obsolete, unlivable houses.

Herein lie the economic and aesthetic incentives to constructing an attractive environment that does not exclude the elderly. It deserves attention. But the emotional gain may be even greater. If in our building and planning we grasp this opportunity to show loving care for the elderly and a desire to incorporate them into our lives, the guarantee of our own future may be the biggest payoff of all.

Suggested Readings

Brown, David. "Housing for the Elderly: Federal Subsidy Policy and Its Effect on Age-Group Isolation." *University of Detroit Journal of Urban Law,* 57:2 (Winter 1980).

Folsom, James C. "Architectural Uses of Space and Texture to Prevent Disorientation in the Elderly." Paper presented at conference on *Improving the Quality of Life of the Elderly through Environmental Design.* New York Academy of Medicine/AIA New York City Chapter. October 1980.

Kasschau, Patricia L. *Aging and Social Policy.* New York: Praeger Publishers, 1978.

Pastalan, Leon A. "Housing for the Elderly." Paper presented at the 1981 Michigan *White House Conference on Aging.*

2

The Elderly in America: Their Economic Resources, Income Status, and Costs

Robert H. Binstock

An axiom of public rhetoric in America, from the Townsend Movement of the 1930s until the late 1970s, was that most older persons are poor. By the end of the 1970s, however, this axiom had been rather suddenly discarded. Beginning in 1978, the American public was flooded with media stories and social policy analyses that portrayed the elderly as having been "lifted out of poverty" by government programs, private pensions, savings, and employment opportunities. Typical of such portrayals was a 1980 cover story in *U.S. News and World Report*, which proclaimed:

> Stereotypes die hard, but few are as stubborn as America's outmoded images of older people: The impoverished widow, the decrepit man banished to a nursing home.
>
> Those situations still exist, but they have become rare... Retirees are not too badly off.[1]

At the same time that the stereotype of poverty among the elderly was being transformed, journalists, scholars, and public officials began to recognize the

---

From *Aging and Public Policy: The Politics of Growing Old in America,* edited by William P. Browne and Laura Katz Olson, Westport, Connecticut: Greenwood Press, 1983, pp. 19–33. Reprinted by permission of Greenwood Press.

economic implications of an aging population. Attention was directed to the "graying of the budget," that is, the demographic age changes and public program benefit structures that have led to a situation in which the federal government currently expends more on aging than on national defense.[2] Moreover, on the basis of reliable predictions of increases in the number of older Americans and assumed continuity in present program benefit structures, projections were made that the 25 percent of the federal budget that was expended on the aging in 1981[3] would reach 40 percent early in the next century[4] and 63 percent by the year 2025.[5] On the basis of such projections, some journalists began to suggest that American society could not afford to maintain collective public efforts to sustain the economic burden of an aging population.[6]

Taken together, the new stereotype of the economic status of the aging and the recognition of the budgetary implications of population aging began to suggest that older Americans are living off the fat of the land and pose a threat to the American economy. The business-oriented *Forbes* magazine expressed the notion in an exceptionally hyperbolic fashion in a 1980 feature entitled "The Old Folks": "The myth is that they're sunk in poverty. The reality is that they're living well. The trouble is there are too many of them—God bless 'em."[7]

Concern for the present and future costs of an aging population was also heightened in the late 1970s by projected short-term and long-term deficits in the Social Security trust funds. Despite substantial increases in Social Security taxes enacted in 1977,[8] the transition of the American economy to slow growth and high rates of unemployment and inflation indicated that the pay-as-you-go funding of Social Security, with taxes from today's workers paying for benefits of today's retirees, would not be viable in 1982. Long-term problems with the funding of Social Security in the twenty-first century were identified in relation to the changing demographic age structure of the American population. The ratio of Social Security beneficiaries to taxable workers is projected to rise sharply when the post-World War II baby boom begins to reach retirement age after the year 2010.[9]

Public proclamations of concerns about the solvency of the trust funds have apparently undermined another long-standing axiom of American politics: widespread public faith in the mythology of the Social Security program. Most Americans have long believed that Social Security benefits are like insurance annuities that they have paid for with premiums deducted from their paychecks through Federal Insurance Contribution Act (FICA) withholdings. They have paid their payroll taxes while trusting that something on the order of a contract exists that binds the U.S. government to pay them retirement benefits in accordance with their earlier payroll tax deductions. But in the context of growing official proclamations about the capacity of the Social Security system to meet future benefit commitments, public trust has been undermined. A 1979 nationwide survey indicated that more than four employees in five have less than full confidence that Social Security will be able to pay the benefits "owed them" when they retire.[10]

After several decades of relative immunity from political problems,[11] income-maintenance policies affecting the aging have suddenly become a major social policy issue on the agenda of American politics. Little attention was paid to aging policies in the three 1976 Carter–Ford presidential campaign debates,[12] but in the 1980 televised debate between Carter and Reagan, a major issue was their respective views on the future of financing for the Social Security program. In the first year of his administration, President Reagan put forth major proposals for policy changes substantially affecting benefits available to current and future generations of older Americans through federal income-maintenance programs.

In light of this swiftly changing scenario, the purpose of this chapter is to provide a context in which contemporary discussions of income-maintenance policies toward the aging can be interpreted. To be sure, many broad and specific issues bear upon the politics and policies of the economics of aging. Not the least of them are the value assumptions concerning the division of collective and individual responsibility for income adequacy in old age. But, given the scope of a single chapter, the most essential issues would seem to be those that bear upon current assertions that the aging are relatively well off and that American society may soon not be able to afford programs that sustain the economic security of the elderly.

Accordingly, three central topics will be addressed in a brief, overview fashion. First, What are the economic resources available to the elderly in America? Second, What is the income status of older persons? And third, Can American society continue to bear the economic costs of maintaining an adequate income status for its older citizens?

Economic Resources of the Elderly

In order to consider the income status of the elderly as well as the cost implications of maintaining or enhancing their status, it is useful to review briefly the different kinds of economic resources available to older persons in America.[13] These resources include earnings from participation in the labor force; a wide variety of public and private programs that pay cash and in-kind benefits; special tax exemptions for the aged; intrafamily transfers; and assets accumulated by older persons.

Earnings

About 8 percent of persons sixty-five years of age and older are active in the work force. Their earnings constitute about 23 percent of the aggregate money income received by older Americans.

The distribution of earnings as an income source for older persons has narrowed steadily over the past three decades. In 1951, for example, over half of the couples sixty-five and older in the United States received income from earnings; by 1976 this percentage had declined to 40 percent. For single men the decline in this period was from 34 to 21 percent. Although the proportion of single older women receiving earnings rose from 13 percent in 1971 to 23 percent in 1962, by 1976 it had declined to 14 percent.

Social Security

The largest of the economic resources available to older Americans is the national Social Security program. Old Age Survivors Insurance (OASI) benefits paid under the Social Security program constitute 38 percent of the aggregate money income of the older population.

Participation in the Social Security system is compulsory for employed Americans except for those in certain excluded groups, such as employees of the federal government. The program, established in 1935, is funded through a flat-rate payroll tax contributed in equal amounts by employees and employers (in 1982, 6.7 percent from each on wages and salaries up to $32,400 annually). The system is financed by a pay-as-you-go basis, with a limited reserve.

Workers become eligible for OASI benefits by choosing among several retirement-age options available to them. They can receive the full benefits to which they are entitled, starting at age sixty-five if their earnings are below a specified ceiling used to determine their retirement status. They can opt for earlier retirement at age sixty-two, but receive reduced benefits throughout their remaining years. Or they can delay retirement beyond sixty-five, adding to the amount of benefits to which they are entitled (and receive benefits at age seventy-two, and beginning in 1983 at age seventy, regardless of the amount of additional income they receive from earnings).

The amount of benefits paid is calculated through formulas based upon the worker's history of participation in the system. In January 1982, the monthly benefit for an individual with maximum covered earnings and retired at sixty-five was $679.30; a worker with an average earnings history received $535.40; a worker with an earnings history equivalent to the nationally established minimum wage received $355.30 in retirement. The total amount of OASI benefits paid out in fiscal year 1981 was estimated at $97.1 billion.

Public Employee Retirement Systems

A variety of government employee pension plans make up 6 percent of the aggregate money income of older persons. These include retirement systems for civilian and military personnel of the federal government as well as employees of states, municipalities, counties, school districts, and other special district governments.

The federal civilian employee retirement system was first established in 1920. Today, it encompasses sixty-eight retirement systems for federal personnel, covering virtually all employees of the national government. In fiscal 1981, retirement benefits to federal civilian employees totaled an estimated $16.7 billion. The military retirement system currently awards benefits of 50 percent of pay after twenty years of service. In fiscal 1981, total military retirement expenditures were $13 million.

More than six thousand public employee pension plans are administered by the state and local governments of the United States, covering 85 percent of their workers. Although such plans began in the nineteenth century, their major growth took place in the 1940s and 1950s. By 1978, the total benefit outlays of these systems were estimated to be $10 billion. State and local government workers can also elect to be participants in the national Social Security system; currently, about 70 percent of state and local employees are covered by Social Security in addition to their own plans.

Private Pension Plans

About one-half of the private work force is covered by private pension plans, but they constitute only 7 percent of the aggregate income of the elderly. Coverage is primarily limited to large, unionized manufacturing firms. In 1981, total retirement benefits paid through private plans was estimated to exceed twenty billion dollars. About 21 percent of the retired population sixty-five and over is receiving income from private pensions. The national government regulates certain aspects of private pension plans through provisions of the Employee Retirement Income Security Act of 1974, which affects vesting (for job changers), funding, and management of pension funds.

Means-Tested Cash Assistance

A national cash-assistance program, Supplemental Security Income (SSI), pays benefits to older persons whose other sources of income do not bring them up to a designated income level established by the federal government. SSI is funded from general tax revenues. Eligibility and benefit amounts are determined through income and assets tests. State governments are encouraged (and in some cases required) to add their own benefits to the federal benefits. In fiscal 1981, the national government paid out an estimated $2.6 billion in SSI benefits.

In-Kind Income Programs

In-kind income consists of goods or services available to the aged without expenditure, or at least at a rate below the market value of the service. The federal government's Medicare and Medicaid health insurance programs are important examples. Another is subsidized housing. Still another is the nation's food stamp program, through which more than one million persons age sixty and over receive coupons that can be used to purchase food in retail stores. The value of coupons received depends on both the income of recipients and the number of persons in a family, and eligibility for the program is means tested.

In fiscal 1981 the federal government expended an estimated $45 billion in in-kind benefits to the aged. Medicare accounted for $35.8 billion; Medicaid expenditures were estimated at about $6.0 billion; public housing subsidies comprised about $2.3 billion.

While in-kind benefits do not contribute to the money income of the aged, they clearly are an important economic resource for older Americans. Measuring the value of these benefits, however, poses some difficult conceptual issues. For instance, the value that recipients themselves place on some in-kind services and goods (such as medical care or housing) may well be substantially less than the market price. Consequently, as will be made evident below, assessments of the income status of the aged can vary considerably in accordance with different interpretations of the impact of in-kind benefits.

Special Tax Exclusions

Substantial benefits are provided to the elderly through a variety of national, state, and local tax provisions. One important tax exemption for older persons is the nontaxation of Social Security benefits. Another is property tax reductions, which are granted in all states for elderly persons. The most common type of reduction is a "circuit breaker," through which tax relief is tied to need as defined by taxpayers' income levels in relation to their property tax liabilities. Another common method of property tax relief is the "homestead exemption." Under this mechanism, before the tax rate is applied, a state excludes a portion of the assessed value of a single-family home from total assessed value. A few states allow deferral of property taxes until an elderly owner dies or sells his or her residence, and a few freeze the tax rate in force when the aged person reaches a certain age, usually sixty-three or sixty-five.

Intrafamily Transfers

Another resource to be considered is intrafamily transfers of money, goods, and services to the aged. But very little is known about the magnitude and nature of transfers among family members (for example, from children to parents or vice versa). In the most recent study, economist Marilyn Moon found that intrafamily transfers altered the well-being of about 28 percent of aged families.[14] However, relatively large transfers flow both ways—with slightly more aged families receiving assistance than assisting younger children.

Assets

Many of the aged own assets that provide housing, serve as a financial reserve for special or emergency needs, contribute directly to income through interest, dividends, and rents, and generally enhance the freedom with which they spend their available income. Assets provide about 19 percent of the aggregrate money income of the aged.

Most assets can be sold and thereby converted to money that can be used to buy goods and services. But one should distinguish between liquid assets and nonliquid assets. Nonliquid assets usually require more time to convert. If an aged family has significant nonliquid assets, such as housing, as long as they are determined to keep that housing and not sell the property that asset is not convertible into income to be used for day-to-day living. In effect, the asset is "locked in."

In fact, a high proportion of older people own a home or have an equity in it. About 80 percent of elderly couples and 57 percent of one-person elderly households live in an owned home. The amount of mortgage debt on those homes is usually very low; in fact, about four-fifths of elderly homeowners own their homes free of any mortgage.

Until recently in the United States, there was no available financial mechanism that would permit people to sell the equity in their home, get back money over a period of time, and still be able to live in the house. Since January 1, 1979, however, the Federal Home Loan Bank Board has allowed federally chartered savings and loan associations to offer reverse annuity mortgages. Under this type of mortgage, a homeowner may sell some equity in the house, receiving in return a fixed monthly sum based on a percentage of the current market value of the house.

Income Status

Given these various economic resources, how well off are the elderly? Two principal approaches for addressing this issue are, first, to examine the distribution of income among the aged and, second, to apply various measures of income adequacy.

Income Distribution

The aged, as a group, have cash incomes significantly lower than the incomes of the younger population. In 1979, the 8.8 million householders sixty-five and older had a median income of $11,316, compared with a median income of $21,201 for families with householders younger than sixty-five; unrelated individuals sixty-five and older had a median income of $4,653, compared with a median income of $9,706 for younger unrelated individuals.

Exhibit 2.1 shows that the majority of aged households in 1979 had cash incomes of less than $10,000 a year; only slightly over 13 percent of aged units had incomes higher than $20,000. A breakdown of income distribution by race, sex, and marital status, as depicted in Exhibit 2.2, shows that incomes tend to be lower among older women, members of minority groups, and single persons.

Cash Income Adequacy

Among a variety of measures that can be employed to assess the adequacy of incomes received by the aged, three absolute standards are used by the federal government for official pruposes: the national poverty index, the "near-poor" index, and the hypothetical budgets for an urban elderly couple that are constructed by the U.S. Bureau of Labor Statistics (BLS).

The poverty index is based on a formula that considers the cost of food needed for a temporary subsistence diet (as determined by the Department of Agriculture) and the proportion of family income that is typically spent on food. Different indexes are developed to take into account factors such as family size, number of children in the family, age and sex of the family head, and farm and nonfarm residence. The thresholds are updated annually according to changes in the

EXHIBIT 2.1
Distribution of Money Income Among Aged Households: 1979

Income	Total Households (thousands)	Percent of All Households
Under $5,000	4,985	31.0
$5,000–$9,999	4,961	31.0
$10,000–$14,999	2,708	17.0
$15,000–$19,999	1,360	8.0
$20,000–$24,999	758	5.0
$25,000–$29,999	503	3.0
$30,000–$34,999	276	2.0
$35,000–$39,999	175	1.0
$40,000–$49,999	214	1.0
$50,000–$74,999	151	1.0
$75,000 and over	61	0.3
Total	16,152	100.0*

*Percentages do not add to 100 because of rounding.
Source: U.S., Bureau of the Census, *Current Population Reports,* Series P-60, "Money Income and Poverty Status of Families and Persons in United States, 1979." Advance Report (Washington, D.C.: Government Printing Office, 1980).

EXHIBIT 2.2
**Median Money Income for Population 65 Years and Older:
1978, by Sex, Race, and Marital Status**

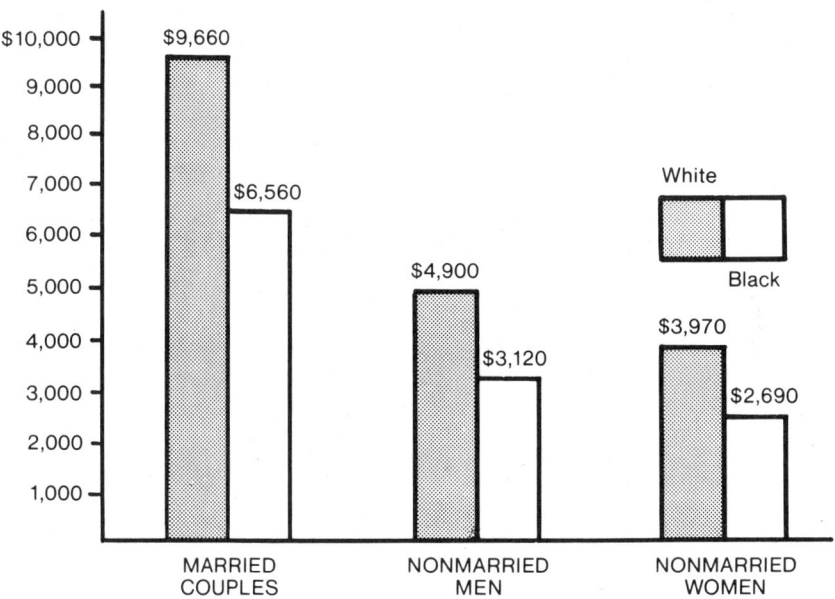

Source: Unpublished data from the U.S. Social Security Administration.

Consumer Price Index. In 1981, the poverty line was $5,470 for an aged couple and $4,350 for an aged individual.

The poverty rate among the elderly population declined from 35 percent to 14 percent between 1959 and 1978 but rose noticeably in 1979 to 15.1 percent. In the same year the poverty rate for the entire population was 11.6 percent. (See Exhibit 2.3.)

The near-poverty measure was developed to reflect a more adequate nutritional standard. It equals 125 percent of the poverty threshold for a given population. As is shown in Exhibit 2.3, near-poverty rates for the aged population are also high, indicating that substantial numbers of the elderly live on incomes only slightly above the official poverty level. Older women and minorities experience significantly higher rates of poverty.

The U.S. Bureau of Labor Statistics constructs three budgets for urban retired couples based on the prices of items on a hypothetical shopping list of goods and services. Prices are updated by changes in the Consumer Price Index for those

EXHIBIT 2.3
Poverty and Near-Poverty Rates* Among Persons 65 Years and Older: 1979

Group	Numbers (in thousands)	Percent in Poverty	Percent Poor and Near-Poor
Total	23,743	15.1	24.7
Male	9,783	11.0	18.5
Female	13,960	17.9	29.0
White	21,446	13.2	22.4
Male	8,803	9.5	16.3
Female	12,643	15.8	26.6
Black	2,020	35.5	49.2
Male	847	26.9	40.4
Female	1,173	41.7	55.5
Spanish origin	562	26.1	38.4
Male	259	22.8	—+
Female	303	29.0	—

* In 1979, the national poverty line was $4,364 for an aged couple and $3,472 for an aged individual; the near-poor lines were $5,455 and $4,340, respectively.
+ Dash indicates figures not available.
Source: Unpublished U.S. Bureau of the Census data for 1979.

goods and services. In 1979, there were approximately 6.1 million husband and wife couples with heads sixty-five and older whose incomes could be compared with the lower, intermediate, and higher standards of living described by the BLS budgets. One-third of these couples could not meet the intermediate budget level, as indicated by Exhibit 2.4.

EXHIBIT 2.4
Aged Couples with Incomes Below Bureau of Labor Statistics Budgets for Retired Couples: 1979

BLS Hypothetical Budgets	Budget Levels	Number of Couples (in millions)	Percent of Couples with Incomes Below Standard
Higher budget	$12,669	3.8	62
Intermediate budget	8,562	2.2	36
Lower Budget	6,023	1.1	18

Source: U.S., Congress, Senate Special Committee on Aging, *Developments in Aging,* 1980, part 1 (Washington, D.C.: Government Printing Office, 1981), xviii.

Impact of In-Kind Benefits

As the foregoing discussion should make clear, interpretations of the rate of poverty among the aged can vary considerably, depending upon the absolute standards of income adequacy that are applied. Similarly, even if one holds standards of income adequacy constant, the rate of poverty will change if one adds to the cash income distribution among the aged the impact of other economic resources such as tax exclusions, intrafamily transfers, home equity, and in-kind benefits.

Among the studies that have attempted to assess the impact of these resources on the income adequacy of the elderly, perhaps the most widely cited has been a Congressional Budget Office (CBO) estimate that in 1977 the inclusion of in-kind benefits would reduce the rate of poverty among the elderly from 14 to 6 percent.[15] Indeed, this particular study has been widely quoted to support the journalistic assertions that the elderly are now relatively well off.

The CBO study and similar analyses of in-kind benefits are technically correct but somewhat misleading. For example, let us consider the fact that Medicare and Medicaid in-kind transfers comprise the bulk of nonmoney benefits included in this analysis, which calculates their value as if they were health insurance premium subsidies. The insurance value of these two programs accounted for 98 percent of all in-kind benefits attributed to older persons in 1978.[16] When the value of these two programs is examined in the context of an actual budget, the misleading aspects of the picture conveyed by the CBO analysis become apparent.

According to the budgetary components of the official poverty indexes, an elderly couple that had made it up to the poverty line in the year that the CBO conducted its analysis would have had $50 per month per person for clothing, transportation, utilities, furniture, taxes, personal and property insurance, and medical and dental care. The average expenditures for medical and dental care are clearly assumed to be minimal. Yet, in the same year, out-of-pocket medical and dental expenses alone averaged more than $50 a month for each elderly person.[17] Thus, even with extensive Medicare and Medicaid benefits, many couples that had made it up to the poverty line, or even exceeded it, would have had little or nothing left for clothing, transportation, utilities, and all other items after paying their out-of-pocket health-care expenses. In short, receiving in-kind benefits from the government may change the category in which one is officially classified by government economists, but it does not necessarily lift one out of poverty in a functional sense.

How Well Off Are the Elderly?

Obviously, the income status of older Americans is most accurately understood in terms of disaggregated descriptions. Some older persons are extremely wealthy, others are economically comfortable, and still others are poor. An older black woman is more than four times likely than a white male to have an income below the poverty line. Whether society has a responsibility to better the economic status of those who are below the poverty line, the near-poor line, and/or the BLS budget standards is, of course, an issue that can only be resolved through the political process.

It can be stated, however, that the assumptions used to construct the poverty index (by which 15.1 percent of the elderly are classified as poor) do not accurately reflect the income needs of an older person.[18] A consequence of these inaccurate assumptions is that the poverty line imposes an exceedingly harsh measure of economic security. Consider the budget of an aged couple that had reached the poverty line in 1980 and therefore was not classified as poor. According to official assumptions, the couple would have had, for instance, $16 per person for food each week. Not suprisingly, many analysts and official reports have suggested that higher standards than the poverty line should be used for measuring the economic security of older persons. Indeed, the original creator of the poverty indexes, Molly Orshansky, recently estimated that 36 percent of the aged "have too little income of their own to live by themselves."[19]

It is clear that wherever the poverty line is drawn precisely, millions of older persons are clustered just above it, and their condition is not substantially different from those aging who are under it. As Borzilleri has pointed out, an extra $25 a week could remove about three million elderly out of poverty as officially defined.[20] This would make the official record look different but would hardly have a major impact on the living standards of the recipients.

Costs

Scholars, journalists, and public officials have raised serious questions about the economic capacity of American society to maintain the burden of an aging population. Because this issue has emerged relatively recently, few scholarly analyses have addressed it directly. Nonetheless, two recent leading studies make it possible to draw some useful, though tentative, conclusions.

As indicated at the outset of this chapter, dramatic estimates have been made that 40 percent of the federal budget will be spent on the aged early in the next century, and 63 percent by the year 2025. These numbers do not rest on assumptions that policies will be changed to improve the income status of current and future cohorts of the elderly poor. Rather, they reflect assumptions of continuity in current policies, predictions of increased numbers of older persons, and estimates concerning such matters as the rate of increase in health-care costs, trends in inflation, rates of real economic growth, and other macroeconomic factors.

Numbers that express the percentage of federal expenditures devoted to a single function such as "benefits to the aged" or "defense" may be important political symbols. But they do not necessarily represent unsustainable economic burdens. The central question to be answered in this discussion is, Can the American economy afford to continue, well into the next century, the current policies through which it provides benefits to the elderly? Evidently it can, according to a recent study that has addressed this issue.

An analysis published in 1981 by economists Robert L. Clark and John Menefee has shown that maintenance of current benefits per older person in real terms (1978 dollars) through the year 2025 would require a smaller proportion of the gross national product (GNP) in the years ahead than it does at present, if the consumer price index is used as the measure of inflation for benefit levels.[21] They point out that the percent of GNP required to finance federal benefits for the aged in 1978 was 5 percent. Maintenance of benefits per person in real 1978 dollars, according to their analysis, would require 3.8 percent of GNP in the year 2000, 3.3 percent in 2010, and 3.8 percent in 2025.

To date, most of the public discussion of the economic implications of an aging population has been confined to policy issues concerned with maintaining the viability of existing governmental mechanisms that provide income benefits to the elderly through specific, established formulas. An additional issue, of course, is whether the American economy can sustain the costs of improved income adequacy for the elderly through any mix of economic resources that might be available to older persons.

Despite contemporary portrayals of the elderly as relatively well off, millions of older persons are poor as measured by any of several absolute standards that are widely recognized. The same will hold true for millions among the future cohorts of the aged unless private and public policy conditions change substantially.

If one considers the substantial array of economic resources available to the elderly briefly sketched earlier in this chapter, it should be apparent that a variety of public and private strategies could be pursued to enhance the income status of the aging. Expansion of opportunities for older persons to earn income through employment might be achieved through government and private sector strategies to eliminate age-based job discrimination, retrain and reeducate older workers, and restructure jobs to permit more flexible working arrangements. Government could create additional incentives to promote increased personal savings. Appealing strategies for unlocking home equity and other nonliquid assets can be developed. Public policy and/or collective bargaining could promote the expansion and inflation-indexing of private pensions and health insurance benefits. Successful policies to promote general economic productivity and growth could provide large bases of employment and taxation for sustaining public income transfers to the elderly through cash and in-kind benefits.

This plethora of possible strategies, however, obfuscates the issue of whether the American economy can sustain the costs of an improved level of income adequacy for the aged. A complex chain of assumptions must be fulfilled for each strategy to result in increased income for older persons, and the relationship among such strategies and their requisite assumptions is intricate. Moreover, most of these strategies cannot substantially solve the income problems of those subgroups within the aging population who are frequently without significant employment histories—the frail elderly, older women, and minorities.

One of the more useful approaches for considering the capacity of the American economy to provide income adequacy for the elderly was undertaken by the Technical Committee for the 1981 White House Conference on Aging (WHCOA), which addressed the "Implications for the Economy" of population aging. In the context of an overall study of "Economic Policy in an Aging Society," it examined the probable aggregate economic effects of an expanded public income transfer program that would be used as a direct measure for addressing income-adequacy problems of the elderly through the year 2005. While the WHCOA Committee recognized that other policy alternatives might have some impact on improving income adequacy for the aging, it explicitly observed that "only an income transfer program directly targeted on the poorest elderly can have a significant impact."[22]

In analyzing the economic impact of increased transfers that would guarantee adequate income for all older persons over the next twenty-five years, the committee chose a relatively high absolute standard of adequacy, an income consistent with the BLS Intermediate Budget for Retired Couples. In addition, it posited that such transfers would only be made to those below the BLS standard and would be financed by the increased taxes rather than by a redistribution of tax revenues.

The WHCOA committee's analysis led to the finding that such a program of increased income transfer and taxation "would not have a significant effect on the overall economy."[23] To be sure, such a program would add to federal expenditures; the analysis indicated that $19 billion would be required to fund the program in 1981, but the amount needed would decline to $12 billion (in current dollars) by 2005. Nonetheless, this technical committee found that an intermediate and ongoing direct guarantee of the adequate income to all older persons for the next twenty-five years would have no harmful effects on the American economy.

No definitive judgments can be made on the basis of either this WHCOA committee report or the analysis conducted by Clark and Menefee. They are among the first in what will undoubtedly be a spate of serious technical studies examining the implications of an aging population for the American economy. But they do provide early indications that the challenges of maintaining or improving the economic status of the elderly in the years ahead are primarily political, not economic.

Notes

1. *U.S. News and World Report*, September 1, 1980, p. 500.
2. See, for example, Robert B. Hudson, "The 'Graying' of the Federal Budget and Its Consequences for Old-Age Policy," *Gerontologist* 18, pt. 1 (October 1978):428–40.
3. U.S., Office of Management and Budget, *The Budget of the United States Government: Fiscal year 1981* (Washington, D.C.: Government Printing Office, 1980).
4. Joseph A. Califano, Jr., "U.S. Policy for the Aging—A Commitment to Ourselves," *National Journal* 10 (1978):1576.
5. U.S. Congress, Senate, Special Committee on Aging, *Emerging Options for Work and Retirement Policy* (Washington, D.C.: Government Printing Office, 1980):24.
6. See, for example, Robert J. Samuelson, "Aging America—Who Will Shoulder the Growing Burden?" *National Journal* 10 (1978):1712–17.
7. *Forbes*, February 18, 1980, p. 51.
8. Public Law 95-216
9. See U.S., President's Commission on Pension Policy, *Coming of Age: Toward a National Retirement Income Policy* (Washington, D.C.: Government Printing Office, 1981), pp. 21–26.
10. Louis Harris and Associates, Inc., *Study of American Attitudes Toward Pensions and Retirement*, commissioned by Johnson and Higgins (New York, February 1979).
11. See Martha Derthick, *Policymaking for Social Security* (Washington, D.C.: The Brookings Institution, 1979).
12. Yosef Riemer and Robert H. Binstock, "Campaigning for 'the Senior Vote': A Case Study of Carter's 1976 Campaign," *Gerontologist* 18 (December 1978):517–24.
13. The data presented in the following discussion of economic resources are combined from the following sources: President's Commission on Pension Policy, *Coming of Age: Toward a National Retirement Policy* and *Appendix* (Washington, D.C.: Government Printing Office, 1981); U.S., Office of Management and Budget, *The Budget of the United States Government: Fiscal Year 1981* (Washington, D.C.: Government Printing Office, 1981); and unpublished data from the U.S. Social Security Administration.
14. Marilyn Moon, *The Measurement of Economic Welfare: Its Application to the Aged Poor* (New York: Academic Press, 1977).
15. U.S., Congressional Budget Office, *Poverty Status of Families Under Alternative Definitions of Income*, Background Paper No. 17, rev. (Washington, D.C.: Government Printing Office, June 1977).
16. Thomas C. Borzilleri, "In-Kind Benefit Programs and Retirement Adequacy," *National Journal* 12 (1980):1821–25.
17. U.S., Congress, Senate, Special Committee on Aging, *Developments in Aging: 1978*, part 1 (Washington, D.C.: Government Printing Office, 1979), p. 42.
18. See U.S., Congress, House, Select Committee on Aging, *Poverty Among America's Aged, Hearing*, 95 Cong., 2nd sess., August 9, 1978; and U.S., President's Commission on Pension Policy, *An Interim Report* (Washington, D.C.: Government Printing Office, 1980).
19. U.S., Congress, House, Select Committee on Aging, *Poverty*, p. 203.
20. Borzilleri, "In-Kind Benefit Programs."
21. Robert L. Clark and John Menefee, "Federal Expenditures for the Elderly: Past and Future," *Gerontologist* 21 (1978):132–37.
22. U.S., White House Conference on Aging, Technical Committee on an Age-Integrated Society—Implications for the Economy, *Economic Policy in an Aging Society* (Washington, D.C.: White House Conference on Aging, 1981), p. 29.
23. Ibid., p. 2.

3

Sunbelt Update: Older Americans Head South

*Jeanne C. Biggar, Cynthia B. Flynn,
Charles F. Longino, Jr., and Robert F. Wiseman*

Florida is still the number one state in attracting older migrants, but the popularity of North Carolina has soared. Arizona may overtake California as the number two state in attracting older movers, and Texas may become the third most popular Sunbelt destination for older migrants by 1990.

Among the ten states receiving the largest number of migrants aged 60 and older, five are Sunbelt states.[1] The top four are Florida, California, Arizona, and Texas. North Carolina ranked seventh.[2] Since 1960 the number of Americans aged 60 and older who move to the Sunbelt has nearly doubled, from 469,000 in the five years from 1955 to 1960, to 925,000 between 1975 and 1980. Most of this rise occurred during the 1970s.

Fifty percent of all older interstate migrants between 1965 and 1970 went to the Sunbelt. From 1975 to 1980, 56 percent of them were headed for a Sunbelt state. The number of older migrants increased in every Sunbelt state during the past two decades, with growth accelerating in most of the states since 1970.

The number of older migrants moving to Arizona, North Carolina, and South Carolina more than doubled during the last decade, and in New Mexico and Texas it nearly doubled. North Carolina jumped from 27th place in 1960 in volume of older movers to 7th place in 1980 as the number of older movers to the

---

From *American Demographics*, 6, 12 (December 1984), 22–25. Reprinted with permission from *American Demographics*, © 1984, Ithaca, N.Y.

state increased by 141 percent. Commercial retirement communities in the mountain areas around Asheville and in the central Piedmont near the Research Triangle are providing new retirement options for older people.

The number of older people moving to South Carolina jumped by 122 percent in the 1970s. The state is likely to become a significant retirement destination during the 1980s.

Among other southeastern Sunbelt states, Mississippi experienced an 80-percent increase, Alabama a 77-percent increase, and Georgia a 70-percent increase in their number of older migrants. Louisiana's volume of older migrants grew the least—up only 45 percent. Despite the increases, these southeastern states are overshadowed by the other Sunbelt states. They will have to fight to maintain their share of older migrants in the 1980s.

The western Sunbelt states of Arizona, California, New Mexico, and Texas will compete among themselves during the 1980s for the status as the second-most popular destination for older migrants (after Florida). Between 1975 and 1980, California had attracted 8.8 percent, Arizona 5.7 percent, and Texas 4.5 percent of all interstate movers aged 60 and older. Arizona's volume of older migrants, however, increased 102 percent during the 1970s, compared to California's increase of only 33 percent. Texas experienced a 94-percent increase in volume, but then Texas is a larger target on which migrants can set their sights. If these trends continue, both Arizona and Texas may surpass California in attractiveness to older migrants. New Mexico also experienced a 94-percent increase during the 1970s, indicating the successful development of retirement communities there.

Elderly Mobility

Older Americans are not the only ones moving to the Sunbelt. Forty-four percent of all migrants during the 1975 to 1980 period moved to one of the 12 Sunbelt states. California, Florida, Texas, and Virginia ranked first through fourth, respectively, as the favorite Sunbelt destinations of all interstate migrants. Proportionately, however, the flow of older people to the Sunbelt exceeded the general flow of migrants in three states—Florida, Arizona and New Mexico.

People of retirement age are less mobile than younger people. While nearly 10 percent of all Americans—20 million people—changed their state of residence between 1975 and 1980, less than 5 percent of people aged 60 and older did. Of the 36 million people in the older age group, 1.7 million of them changed residence between 1975 and 1980. Of the 20 million Americans who moved, only 8 percent were aged 60 or older.

In Florida, 24 percent of migrants to the state between 1975 and 1980 were aged 60 and older. In Arizona 16 percent of migrants were older Americans. Slightly over 8 percent of New Mexico's in-migrants were aged 60 and older. In the other Sunbelt states, however, older migrants were just joining the crowd, since they comprised less than the 8-percent national share of migrants aged 60 and older.

Where They Come From

Although all of the Sunbelt states received large numbers of older migrants between 1975 and 1980, only Arizona, California, Florida, North Carolina, and Texas drew above average numbers of older movers from non-Sunbelt states.

As the leading destination state, Florida attracted large numbers of older migrants from Connecticut, Indiana, Massachusetts, Michigan, New Jersey, New York, Ohio, and Pennsylvania.

Number-two ranked California received significant numbers of older movers from eight states—Arizona, Colorado, Hawaii, Illinois, Nevada, Oregon, Texas, and Washington. A decade ago, Missouri movers were more likely to head for California, but now they move to Texas. Minnesota movers also used to favor California, but now Arizona attracts more of them. (See Exhibit 3.1.)

Since the 1960s, the majority of older movers from midwestern and northwestern states chose California. But by the late 1970s, third-place Arizona was drawing significant numbers of older people from the non-Sunbelt states of Illinois, Michigan, Washington, Minnesota, Iowa, and Wisconsin. Minnesota, Iowa, and Wisconsin are newcomers to this list of states sending migrants to Arizona. The western states of Colorado and California have also contributed significantly to Arizona's in-migrants.

Between 1975 and 1980, Texas attracted new streams of older migrants from Kansas and Missouri, while continuing to receive in-migrants from Arkansas and Oklahoma outside the Sunbelt, and from California, Arizona, New Mexico, and Louisiana in the Sunbelt.

In the past, most of the older migrants in the East went as far south as they could go—to Florida. But by 1980, North Carolina had emerged as the second most popular destination for older movers in the eastern Sunbelt. North Carolina drew older in-migrants from South Carolina and Virginia, as it had during the 1960s, but new streams of migrants came into the state from Florida, Maryland, and New Jersey during the 1975 to 1980 period. There is no evidence, however, that older migrants are choosing North Carolina instead of Florida, even though both states drew migrants from New Jersey. Since Florida's in-migration continued at record highs during the last decade, it is more likely that North Carolina is attracting a different group of movers.

Sunbelt to Sunbelt

During the last two decades virtually every Sunbelt state has exchanged older migrants with neighboring states. Only Florida failed to gain many migrants from its neighbors, although elderly Floridians have moved to Alabama and Georgia,

EXHIBIT 3.1
Migration to the Sunbelt: 1975–1980

Sunbelt State	In-Migrants of All Ages (Aged 5+)	Older In-migrants (Aged 60+)	Share of National Interstate Migration				Older Migrants as a Percent of All Migrants
			Aged 5+	(Rank)	Aged 60+	(Rank)	
Alabama	320,000	20,000	1.6%	(25)	1.2%	(27)	6.3%
Arizona	598,000	94,000	2.9	(8)	5.7	(3)	15.7
California	1,877,000	145,000	9.2	(1)	8.8	(2)	7.7
Florida	1,801,000	429,000	8.9	(2)	25.9	(1)	23.8
Georgia	582,000	26,000	2.9	(9)	1.6	(14)	4.5
Louisiana	325,000	13,000	1.6	(24)	0.8	(35)	4.0
Mississippi	213,000	15,000	1.0	(33)	0.9	(31)	6.9
New Mexico	207,000	17,000	1.0	(34)	1.0	(30)	8.3
North Carolina	538,000	38,000	2.6	(14)	2.3	(7)	7.0
South Carolina	332,000	20,000	1.6	(23)	1.2	(25)	6.1
Texas	1,436,000	75,000	7.1	(3)	4.5	(4)	5.2
Virginia	695,000	34,000	3.4	(4)	2.1	(11)	4.9
Total Sunbelt in-migrants	8,924,000	926,000	43.8		56.0		10.4
Total other interstate migrants	11,434,000	728,000	56.2		44.0		6.4
Total interstate migrants	20,358,000	1,654,000	100.0		100.0		8.1

Note: Fifty-six percent of older interstate migrants moved from Frostbelt to Sunbelt between 1975 and 1980, compared to less than half of all interstate migrants. Florida received 26 percent of all older migrants.

EXHIBIT 3.2
Migration Streams. Major interstate streams of older migrants from the frostbelt to the sunbelt states: 1975–80

From 1975 to 1980, the 20 largest Frostbelt to Sunbelt migration streams of older migrants went to Florida, California, Arizona, Texas, and North Carolina.

and more recently to North Carolina. People living in the states bordering Florida may not want to move to a climate even warmer and more humid than the one in which they already live. On the other hand, elderly Floridians may be moving north in search of lower living costs, less crowded communities, or the change of seasons.

In the late 1970s, more older Sunbelt residents went to Texas than to any other Sunbelt state. Substantial numbers of older migrants to Texas came not only from neighboring Louisiana and New Mexico, but also from Arizona and California. Between 1965 and 1970, Texas returned migrants only to New Mexico, but by 1980 older Texans were moving out to Louisiana and California as well. Nevertheless, Texas gains more from other Sunbelt states than it loses.

There is no significant flow of migrants between Arizona and New Mexico. This is unusual considering that most neighboring Sunbelt states exchange migrants even when they have similar climates, and considering that Arizona has been growing in popularity among older movers from other areas.

Out of the Sunbelt

Not all older movers head for the Sunbelt. Some leave the South for the North. Florida and California have been sending significant numbers of older people to states outside the Sunbelt. Older people leaving Florida between 1975 and 1980 headed for Michigan, Pennsylvania, New York, and Ohio. Some of these people had moved South in the 1950s and 1960s and have been returning to their former states of residence, perhaps at the onset of physical or financial problems, or at the death of their spouses.

California sent large streams of older people to Oklahoma, Utah, Washington, Arkansas, Colorado, Idaho, and Missouri. The out-migration streams from California may be composed of long-term California residents who are moving away to retirement homes elsewhere—in the Ozarks of northern Arkansas or southern Missouri, for example.

Another explanation for California's out-migration streams is long-term return migration. During the first half of this century, California drew fortune-seeking migrants from the East. People who moved to California in their early adulthood are now older and free from job ties and may be returning to their home states to retire.

Conservative Politics

There is no question that the older movers of the 1980s will benefit the communities where they settle by increasing the demand for housing, retail goods, and adult recreational facilities. At the same time, while few will work or depend on welfare, they will force the expansion of local utilities, transportation networks, and health and protective services.

The new older residents will bring with them the more conservative attitudes typical of the older generation. In the future, local bond issues for school construction in Sunbelt communities may gain fewer votes than legislation creating new adult recreation programs. If Florida is an example of the political change in store for the Sunbelt states, increased conservatism can be expected: Recently Florida voters supported a proposition to cut the state budget by $2.4 million. While local Sunbelt governments will enjoy the economic growth brought by the influx of relatively affluent older consumers, they will be challenged to expand governmental services in a political climate that is becoming resistant to expansion of the public sector.

Notes

1. In this article the Sunbelt refers to 12 states—Alabama, Arizona, California, Florida, Georgia, Louisiana, Mississippi, New Mexico, North Carolina, South Carolina, Texas, and Virginia.
2. The other five are New Jersey (5), Pennsylvania (6), Washington (8), Illinois (9), and Ohio (10).

II

Housing Options for the Elderly

4

For Older People—
Not Segregation But Integration

Lewis Mumford

Probably at no period and in no culture have the old ever been so completely rejected as in our own country during the last generation. As their numbers have increased, their position has worsened. The breakup of the three-generation family coincided here with the curtailment of living space in the individual household; and from this physical constriction has come social destitution as well. Unwanted in the cramped small home, even when they are loved, and too often unloved because they are unwanted, the aged find their lives progressively meaningless and empty, while their days ironically lengthen. The years that have been added to their portion have come, unfortunately, at the wrong end of their lives.

Now the problem of housing the aged is only one part of the larger problem of restoring old people to a position of dignity and use, giving them opportunities to form new social ties to replace those that family dispersal and death have broken, and giving them functions and duties that draw on their precious life experience and put it to new uses. "Old age hath yet his honor and his toil," as Tennyson's Ulysses put it. The first step toward framing a sound program is, I believe, to examine the human situation as a whole, not to center attention solely upon the

---

From *Architectural Record,* May 1956. Reprinted by permission of *Architectural Record* and L. Mumford. All rights reserved.

problems of destitution, chronic diseases, and hospital care. We shall not, perhaps, be able to care for the aged, on the scale their needs and our national wealth demand, until we are ready to put into the rebuilding of human communities something like the zeal, the energy, the skill, the dedication we give to the monomaniac production of motor cars and super-highways.

As things are now, the process of aging seems to go through three stages. The first, which begins around the age of forty-five, but may not be final for another twenty years, brings liberation from biological reproduction and increasing detachment from the active nurture of children within the family. For the sake of their own growth and independence, young people start at the earliest possible moment to live by themselves. Poverty or a housing shortage may prolong the two-generation family or even restore, in shaky desperation, the three-generation family. But in general early marriages and early childbearing hasten the hiving off of the next generation.

Sometime during this period of transition, those who have maintained a household big enough for a large family find their quarters empty but burdensome: for they are too expensive for their incomes and even too large to keep clean, except at an extravagant cost in menial service. In cities, this leads either to a remaking of the single family house, if owned, into multiple dwellings, or to removal to a small apartment. This shrinkage of space is often accompanied by other losses, such as the breaking of neighborhood ties, the abandonment of a garden and a workshop; and that in turn brings about a further contraction of opportunities and interests. Mark the result: well before senescence has set in, even people in the upper income groups, in robust health, may find the orbit of their lives uncomfortably narrowing, in a way not adequately compensated by increased local mobility in the motorcar and increased opportunities for general travel.

The second stage in senescence is that of economic retirement: withdrawal at the age of sixty-five, often enforced by benign pension provisions, from the active working life. Unfortunately our wide practice of automatic retirement often brings on a severe psychological crisis: but even if we showed greater flexibility in imposing retirement, still at some moment, early or late, this blow would fall. In addition to removing a worker from the main sphere of his life-interest and competence, it often halves his income or—as the recent Twentieth Century Fund report shows—cuts it down to a starvation level. At the same time, for those who have invested their energies too exclusively in their work, retirement tends to make their whole life seem meaningless. If at this moment, the community sharpens the crisis by weakening other social connections, too, it may psychosomatically aggravate the physical disabilities that begin to dog this period.

The final stage, that of physiological deterioration, is more variable than the cessation of reproduction or work. Whether the old are happy or bitter, active or

Courtesy of Brooks Trubee
Princeton Community Housing, Princeton, New Jersey

frustrated, depends partly upon how long the period of health and vigor is in relation to that covered by the lapse of biological functions that leads to death. But also it depends partly upon how well the community's efforts are directed toward preventing minor impairments from turning, through lack of prompt and adequate care, into major disasters. In any event, senescence proper brings about a gradual slowing down of the vital processes, the deterioration of bodily functions, eyesight, hearing, locomotion, fine coordinations, memory. With this goes a loss of self-help and with that, self-confidence. In the end this loss may necessitate institutional care, in a nursing home or a hospital. Since the cost of such institutional care, if prolonged over any considerable period, taxes heavily even the upper 10 percent of our income groups, every effort must be made, not merely to lengthen the period of active health, but to restore, through neighborly cooperation and friendly oversight, the kind of voluntary care that the three-generational family once made possible.

If we carry our analysis far enough, we shall find, I think, that the three phases of old age—liberation from reproduction, economic retirement, and physiological breakdown—demand a common solution. We shall also find that no present institution, certainly no simple architectural scheme, and no mere extensions of existing services, will supply that solution.

The main point I would make is that the transition from middle-aged maturity to old age is a long process; and if we meet it imaginatively at the earliest period possible, instead of waiting till the last desperate moment, we can make the transition without a jar, and in some degree turn a crisis, full of cruel decisions and bitter acceptances, into a positive and fruitful phase of life. Even more, by extending active life on the upgrade, we can perhaps shorten the period, now so burdensome, when it is on the downgrade. By contrast, the worst possible attitude toward old age is to regard the aged as a segregated group, who are to be removed, at a fixed point in their life course, from the presence of their families, their neighbors, and their friends, from their familiar quarters and their familiar neighborhoods, from their normal interests and responsibilities, to live in desolate idleness, relieved only by the presence of others in a similar plight. Let us ask rather by what means we can restore to the aged the love and respect that they once enjoyed in the three-generation family at its best.

Unfortunately for any such aim, specialization, mechanization, institutionalization, in a word, segregation, are the order of the present day: a meaningless, effortless, parasitic, push-button existence is now put forward as the beautiful promise of an advanced technology, indeed, the ultimate goal of our whole civilization. If those terms were actually final ones, I, for one, should hardly be concerned with the fate of the aged for it should be plain that a whole society that can conjure up no better goals is already moving swiftly toward early euthanasia, or at least toward mass suicide. If we wish something better for ourselves, we must be prepared to put forward a program, at every phase of life, that challenges many of the dominant habits and customs of our society and moves boldly in a contrary direction.

At some point in conceiving a good habitat for the aged, we must of course come to an architectural solution; but we must not for a moment imagine that the architect himself, even when backed by ample financial resources, can provide the answers that are needed, or that beauty and order and convenience alone are sufficient. One of the most generous quarters for the aged I have seen is the old Fuggerei in Augsburg, built in the sixteenth century, composed of one-story row dwellings, giving privacy to each old couple, with a handsome fountain and a chapel. But this "city for the aged and poor" is set apart from the rest of the town; though it has beauty and order, it lacks animation; at best it is only a handsome ghetto. The objection against this solution was indignantly put to me by an old man in another comely quadrangle for the aged near Manchester: a modern building set in ample grounds looking inward on a spacious grassy close; also with a little chapel where the dead rested before burial. At first glance, the peace and beauty of this spot seemed "ideal"—but the inmates knew better. They now had, alas! only one occupation: remaining alive. When the bell tolled, it tolled not only for the departed: it ominously summoned those who were left. "All we do here," said my bitter informant, "is to wait for each other to die. And each

For Older People 43

Courtesy of Brooks Trubee
Princeton Community Housing, Princeton, New Jersey

time we ask ourselves: 'Who will be next?' What we want is a touch of life. I wish we were near the shops and the bus station where we could see things."

To normalize old age, we must restore the old to the community. In order to make clear what this means, let me assume that we have a free hand and can plan a whole neighborhood community, as one does in an urban re-development area in the United States or a New Town in Britain. If we establish the right relationships under such ideal conditions, we shall have a clearer view of what to aim for in situations where only a piecemeal solution is possible. We cannot have even a good half-loaf unless we know what ingredients should go into a whole loaf.

The first thing to be determined is the number of aged people to be accommodated in a neighborhood unit; and the answer to this, I submit, is that the normal age distribution in the community as a whole should be maintained. This means that there should be from five to eight people over sixty-five in every 100 people; so that in a neighborhood unit of, say, 600 people, there would be between thirty and forty old people. Any large-scale organization of habitations for the aged, which upset this proportion, should be avoided. And this brings us to the second requirement. For both companionship and easier nursing care, the aged should not be scattered in single rooms or apartments through the whole community; but neither should they be thrown together in one large barracks labelled by the architecture, if not the signboard, Old Peoples' Home. They should rather be grouped in small units of from six to perhaps a dozen apartments. The old monastic rule, that one needs a dozen members to form a community, has had long enough trial to give one confidence in it as a rough measure: when there are less than a dozen, a single cantankerous individual may have a disruptive effect. When there are too many together, they bring on institutional regulations. As an old Navy man once pertinently remarked: there is freedom on a destroyer but not on a battleship.

But once a reasonable degree of closeness is established between small groups of the aged, there is much to be gained by giving them apartments on the lower floors of two- or three-story houses whose upper floors will be occupied by childless people in other age groups: there is likewise reason for providing a covered way or arcade, to make visiting back and forth easier in inclement weather, and to serve as a sheltered place for chatting and sunning at other times. This mixing of age groups within a housing unit primarily designed for the accommodation of the aged would make it possible for those past sixty-five, who found stairs difficult, or who wanted to be more accessible, to adapt themselves to their infirmities with with no greater hiatus than moving downstairs.

Now it happens that the number of people over sixty-five in a community are roughly the equivalent of the number of children under six or seven; and in meeting the needs of both extremes pretty much the same conditions hold. Young children need special protection and bodily care; they must be guarded from wheeled vehicles; their difficulties in locomotion and coordination when under three make it desirable to avoid unnecessary obstacles and long flights of stairs. Even psychologically, there are parallels between the self-absorption of the young child and the tendency to withdrawal and inner concentration that mark the last phase of senescence. In a well-designed neighborhood unit, the aged should be able to go to any part of it, including the shopping area, the library, the church, the community center, without crossing a traffic artery; indeed, without if possible climbing a step. Someday, when our motorcar production is designed to fill varied human needs, rather than the requirements of the assembly line, we will produce electrically-powered rolling chairs for the aged, which can go safely anywhere a pedestrian can go. That will lessen one of the serious handicaps of old age, if medical remedies for arthritis and feeble limbs remain ineffective. But until then, the ambit of the five-year-old child and the seventy-five-year old senescent is their normal walking distance. Once these conditions are fulfilled in a neighborhood unit, a larger life would begin to open before the aged.

Now we are ready to rebuild, in our ideal scheme, the other facilities and activities and services that were once performed, more or less effectively, by the three-generation family. And just as the young proceed with their growth through multiplying their contact with the environment and enlarging their encounters with people other than their families, so the aged may slow down the processes of deterioration, overcoming their loneliness and their sense of not being wanted, by finding within their neighborhood a fresh field for their activities.

But before such an environment can be created, we must challenge the whole theory of segregation upon which so many American communities, not least those that call themselves "progressive," have been zoned; zoned so that one-family houses and apartment houses, or row houses and free-standing houses, cannot be built side-by-side; zoned so strictly for residence that in many suburban communities one cannot buy a loaf of bread or a tin of tobacco without going a mile or two by car or bus to the shops. The pernicious effect of this kind of zoning was first adequately characterized by the Committee on Community Planning of the American Institute of Architects as far back as 1924, and time has abundantly proved all their contentions. Under our zoning ordinances, it is impossible to give either the young or the old the kind of occupational and environmental variety that both a superblock and neighborhood unit should have.

In a mixed community, however, many opportunities for service, both voluntary and paid, would open to the aged. Gardening is an occupation that can be carried on at odd hours, and that can be adapted to the strength and staying power of the old: when a community is well planned, with sufficient amount of parked and gardened open space, it makes greater demands for collective care than it can now often afford. Certainly old people with a turn for gardening should have a little garden plot of their own, too, to look after. Similarly, other opportunities for handicraft should be met by the provision of workshop facilities; making toys, repairing mechanical fixtures, binding books, painting furniture would not merely provide older people with new forms of work: it would, even more importantly, give them the human contacts that a more restricted life fails to offer. Such little shops would have a further educational value for the younger members of the community: indeed, they might be incorporated, with a separate entrance from outside, in a modern school, with great advantage to both the old and the young, who now too often miss the precious experience of intercourse with their grandparents' generation. I know a small town where the carpenter's shop, situated in the old residential area, is the place where school children come to get little repair jobs done; and their contact with the carpenter himself is an affectionate and rewarding one. Such a program would be far more efficacious, psychologically speaking, than putting the aged to work on some monotonous specialized task, producing in quantity for the market, under factory conditions.

In addition there are other services that the aged can perform only in a mixed community, beginning with their most obvious service as baby-sitters. This again, at a dollar an hour, has become a prohibitive luxury even in middle-class communities; and the hazards of leaving the young to the sometimes irresponsible care, if not criminal levity, of inexperienced adolescents only underline the desirability of enlisting the old in the same fashion as they would have been used in the three-generation family. In addition, there are many experienced old women, proud of their skill at baking a cake, or even cooking a whole dinner, who would think better of themselves and their life if they might cook and bake occasionally for pay. By having such opportunities, old age pensions and annuities might be made to go a little farther, with greater happiness for both the server and the served. To cause the aged to spend all their time glued to a television set is to damn them prematurely to a second childhood. Though these passive amusements have their place in the life of the aged, especially for the crippled and bedridden, there is little reason for reducing their lives as a whole to such a soporific routine. What the aged need is activities: not just hobbies, but the normal participation in the activities of a mixed community.

No single institution, however amply financed and humanely planned, could provide anything like the range of interests that a mixed neighborhood community would do, once age ceases to be regarded as a disease best treated in an isolation ward. Still there usually comes a time in everyone's life sooner or later when he requires specialized nursing and medical care. The skillful organization of such care is the duty of the community as a whole; but some fatal inertia has kept our hospital services in an antiquated centralized patter, and has prevented the creation of small nursing homes, close at hand for family and neighborly visitors, who could, if the hospital were conveniently at hand, take over no small part of the otherwise prohibitively expensive nursing service.

Even before active hospitalization there is need for a public organization of visiting nurses and visiting houseworkers, such as are now provided for on a national scale in England and likewise in certain individual American cities. Here again, by drawing upon all the resources of the community, a much more favorable situation can be created than the most elaborately equipped central institution can provide. I look forward to a day when a small nursing home, for illness and for maternity cases, will be part of the normal requirement of a neighborhood; perhaps as a direct adjunct to a medical clinic and a visiting nurse service. Only when these normal functions of the family are drawn back into the circle of the neighborhood community is there any prospect of our catching up with our needs without raising to a prohibitive height the present cost of institutional care.

Now we can put together these requirements for the aged. They should, first of all, be part of a normal mixed community, whether they become members of it at twenty-five or at seventy-five. Their quarters should be undistinguishable outwardly from those of other age groups; but they should be sited, as far as possible, where there is a constant play of diverting activity, near a shopping center or a school, so that their chance of being visited, casually and effortlessly, will be increased. Frequent visits, though short, are more refreshing than formal visits, tediously prolonged, that leave desolate intervals of loneliness between them. Many people would find their own family life replenished if the grandparents, though not under their feet, were near at hand; and above all, the young would be the gainers from this; for there are special bonds of sympathy between them and their grandparents' generation, through its very detachment, which often makes them far more ready to heed their advice than that of their own parents. Who

For Older People

can say how much delinquency and brutalized mischief in our American towns may not be due to the very absence of a warm, loving, reciprocal intercourse between the three generations?

Through their nearness to each other, in small units, personal contacts within their own group may easily pass beyond the pleasantries of daily intercourse, the hospitalities of a cup of coffee in the afternoon or a friendly game of cards or checkers or chess at night; it would also involve visiting each other when ill and performing little services for each other. Everything that makes the aged more independent, yet more confident of the fact that their presence is welcome, increases their capacity to love and be loved: and it is only, in the end, by providing an environment in which the gifts of love may be more easily interchanged, that old age can be kept from shrinking and drying till what is left of life is only a dismal waste. But to say this is also to say that there is no easy shortcut to improved care of the aged: to do well by them, we must give a new direction to the life of the whole community. If we fail here, we shall, in prolonging life, only prolong the possibilities of alienation, futility, and misery.

5

In Defense of Age-Segregated Housing

Stephen M. Golant

The image conveyed is often one of old people huddled helplessly behind closed doors, deprived of communication with the outside world, with virtually no friends or neighbors beyond their immediate residence. The elderly are portrayed as outcasts, existing in a stifling atmosphere without stimulation from the young and productive members of society. Such is the spectre raised by senior citizen housing and retirement communities—or geriatric ghettoes, to use the harsh term applied by their critics.

It is conservatively estimated that almost 2 million elderly persons aged 60 and older, about 6 percent of the U.S. elderly population, permanently reside in housing and communities that have been deliberately planned or organized for their occupancy. These statistics do not include the elderly in institutions (e.g., nursing homes) or the many millions of elderly who occupy unplanned age-segregated apartments and neighborhoods. The latter population concentrations have resulted primarily from the residential inertia of people who have chosen not to move upon retirement—they literally have aged-in-place.

A reliable projection of the future number of elderly in planned age-segregated housing units is unavailable. What is certain, however, is the presence of a substantial consumer market for these accommodations. Moreover, because of the large projected growth of the elderly population in this country, the demand for these living arrangements will steadily increase. By the year 2020 approximately 71 million people will be 60 and older, some 24 percent of the total U.S. population.

Although occupied by a substantial number of the U.S. elderly, age-segregated or retirement housing is a concept that is often roundly criticized. Yet the elderly people who live in these settings persistently report high levels of satisfaction with their residences. This article attempts to explain this paradox and in so doing offers a defense of this often maligned, yet very significant housing alternative for senior citizens.

The Critics Are Biased

While having in common an age-segregated social situation, planned senior housing and retirement communities consist of an extremely diverse array of residential accommodations. Lumped in this category are retirement villages, mobile home parks, federally subsidized low-rent apartments, retirement hotels, non-profit sponsored low-rent apartments for the elderly, garden and highrise apartments, condominium complexes, and life-care facilities (or congregate housing).

Not surprisingly, the features and facilities found in these different types of housing vary dramatically. Some offer 24-hour medical supervision and nursing care, others only the telephone number of an on-call physician; some provide on-site meals and counseling (information and referral) services, others only access to home-delivered meal programs; some have completely equipped, well-supervised leisure-oriented facilities, others contain only a make-shift card room off the building's main lobby; some have architectural designs sensitive to the needs of old people, while others are merely hastily converted conventional housing.

Generalizations about the occupants of these age-segregated residences are also not easily made. The healthy and the sick, the young-old (age 60-74) and the old-old (aged 75 and older), the active and the inactive, the poor and the wealthy, the middle-class and the skid-row bum, blacks and whites—can all be found in these accommodations.

Although states such as Arizona, Florida, and California are correctly identified as having the majority of these age-segregated accommodations, they can be found in almost all regions of the United States and are located throughout cities, suburbs, and rural areas.

Despite this housing and population diversity, there is a single-minded stridency in the criticisms leveled against age-segregated housing. It is argued that a society tolerating and encouraging such housing is cold-hearted, unsympathetic, and inhumane, is blind to the needs of its aged citizenry, and discriminates against a population group because of its age. Critics contend that these segregated living arrangements isolate the old from the rest of society, prevent old people from sharing their wisdom and experiences with the young, lead to old people's having a restricted set of friendships and neighbors and contribute to low morale and feelings of uselessness and rejection in some elderly persons.

However, when these charges are carefully scrutinized, it becomes apparent that they are inspired by personal emotions and ideologies rather than by careful factual analysis. They are inconsistent with the findings and reports of most social and behavioral scientists, social workers, and counselors studying and serving elderly populations, and with the overwhelming number of anecdotal experiences reported by elderly persons themselves.

The critic's most fundamental contention is unfounded, namely that old people who occupy age-segregated housing become physically and socially isolated from the rest of society. In fact, the large majority of these elderly have strong links to the "outside world." They often belong to clubs and organizations whose members include young and old alike: they eat and shop in establishments patronized by all age groups; they visit with kin, friends, and neighbors—of all ages—on a regular basis; they communicate daily by mail and phone with persons who are considerable distances away; and their spheres of activity often extend beyond their immediate residences.

Of course, there are old people in age-segregated settings with chronic illness and severe physical and mental impairments who are unable to leave their dwellings. However, only a relatively small percentage of the elderly in retirement housing persistently suffer from these restrictions. Occasionally, they may be temporarily "place-bound" and have mobility problems because of poor weather, short-term illnesses, unavailable transportation, and so on; but they suffer from no greater constraints in their activities than elderly occupants of conventional housing.

Advantages of Senior Housing

The most effective reply to critics of age-segregated or retirement housing is to emphasize the many positive functions and attributes of these accommodations. They result in more supportive and protective environments than those found in places occupied by people of all ages.

A major social and psychological attraction of retirement housing is the elderly occupants themselves. They are obviously more capable than younger people of understanding and sympathizing with the problems faced by people as they become old. They have shared such potentially stressful experiences as coping with loneliness when grown children leave home, dealing with the excess time generated by leaving one's job, adjusting to the continual presence of one's spouse, being able to perform fewer physical activities than in youth, and so on. Because they were born and raised at similar times, old people are also more apt to share a common history. They have lived through similar events—the disruptions of

World War II, the economic stresses of the Great Depression, and the fascinating but frightening products of technological change. Because they have very similar life concerns and backgrounds, members of an older peer group are more likely than younger persons to serve successfully as friends, neighbors, and acquaintances. Thus, the age-segregated setting offers an older person a large potential number of congenial personal relationships.

Living in an age-segregated setting also gives elderly people the option of reducing their involvement with a society that seems overly preoccupied with the desirability of youth, the rewards of employment, and the joys of child-raising—a society that offers pitifully few clear guidelines as to how individuals are expected to conduct their lives when they retire. Old people in age-segregated settings can literally create their own subcultures, surrounding themselves with other elderly people who value their worth, understand their contributions, similarly interpret the meanings of their lives and environment, and offer satisfying role models.

One potentially stressful aspect of old age, in particular, can be dealt with effectively in age-segregated housing. Evidence suggests that old people living together are better able to deal with the prospect of their own deaths. Because they can "talk out" their fears of dying with other concerned older people and constructively confront the relatively frequent deaths of others, they are often able to accept with greater equanimity the inevitability of their own death.

Age-segregated residential settings perform another function of special significance to elderly people. Surveys and polls eliciting older people's assessments of their major housing and environmental concerns repeatedly emphasize their fear of being attacked and robbed either inside their homes or in their neighborhoods. Well-guarded and fenced-in retirement villages and condominium complexes and all-night doormen and desk clerks in retirement hotels and high-rise apartments all produce a level of protection against intruders that is often unavailable in housing and communities occupied by all age groups. In some residential settings, older people have organized themselves to carry out "watchman roles" or have served as "buddies" for their peers when they take walks and short trips to the store. Additionally, the visibility of population concentrations of the elderly has given police forces a rationale for patrolling these areas more frequently.

The occupancy of residences and environs relatively secure from the threat of crime can reduce both the victimization rates of elderly people and their well-founded fears of confronting the criminal element. However, a caveat is in order: When these "organized" defenses are absent, the concentration of elderly people in one place may increase the dangers of attack by criminals who are attracted by the presence of a large number of especially vulnerable victims.

Old people who occupy retirement housing not only are better able to protect themselves; they may more effectively exercise their rights and voice their opinions. A greater potential exists for a "single-minded" electorate to influence the outcomes of local voting referendums. The residential concentration of elderly people becomes a political base from which to influence local issues and a source of support for national, state, and city organizations that are representing the interests of elderly people. A notable illustration is Adult Action, an organization representing adult communities in the state of Arizona, which through its lobbying efforts, succeeded in having a bill passed designed to exclude families with children in certain residential areas of Arizona.

On balance, one must be careful not to ascribe too much political influence to these residential concentrations of older people. Although the older population displays a higher voter turnout than any other age group, current evidence does not indicate that elderly persons vote uniformly on particular social issues. However, the impact of living in an age-segregated neighborhood or community on older people's voting behavior has yet to be investigated carefully.

The residential segregation of elderly people may serve a more fundamental function—sustaining human life. Although the majority of old people can satisfy their own needs, there comes a time when physical or mental impairments—either of a temporary or permanent nature—seriously jeopardize this ability. In most cases, friends, relatives or sympathetic neighbors assist in these critical times, but older people without these supports will often have to rely on the organized social welfare system. However, unless elderly persons in need take the initiative for obtaining help, their detection by social workers and professional agency staff is difficult. This is especially true for elderly persons who lead socially isolated lives.

In contrast, elderly occupants of age-segregated housing who require assistance are more likely to come to the attention of nearby elderly residents or of a concerned building manager.

Since many residents in retirement housing are involved in activities in their dwellings, there are more opportunities for noticing an elderly neighbor in need of help. The resident can either assist the person or notify the appropriate professional agency. Even without neighborhood assistance, elderly persons in retirement housing are more likely to have their needs evaluated or monitored by representatives of church, civic, or government-sponsored organizations and agencies.

Another positive consequence of age-segregated housing arises because old people have similar retirement-oriented life styles and social and medical problems, and so require similar goods and services. This consumer demand produces certain economies of scale whereby goods and services can be delivered more effectively and efficiently at lower average costs.

Examples of activities that result in efficiencies and economies include: the formation of grocery cooperatives; the availability of special transportation vans to take the elderly to preferred destinations; the delivery of hot meals (meals on wheels); the hiring of managerial and janitorial personnel trained to understand and address the needs and problems of old people; the dissemination of information about services and programs relevant to senior citizens; and the development of architectural design features (e.g., bathroom grab bars) to help older people cope better with age-related declines in their sensory and motor skills.

Planned retirement villages and large apartment or condominium complexes designed for the elderly possess a less obvious feature: they are relatively unchanging, predictable living environments. This is in contrast to age-integrated neighborhoods and communities that can undergo unexpected and undesirable changes in their population, dwelling, and land use attributes. On the one hand, once thriving middle-class or working-class areas may become the home of poorer, welfare populations and be occupied by stores and shops that denigrate the residential character of the place (such as taverns and adult book stores). On the other hand, neighborhoods occupied by poorer populations may become gentrified. The housing stock is renovated and revitalized and thereby becomes attractive to wealthier, professional residents. This inevitably results in the displacement of many current residents who cannot afford to pay high rents or to buy condominiums. Either the threat or reality of such scenarios produces considerable stress and anxiety for elderly residents whose life styles often center around their immediate surroundings.

In contrast, such fears and unsettling consequences are avoided by the elderly resident in the planned retirement setting, where land uses, population makeup, and activities are carefully controlled. Whereas elderly persons in conventional housing have little guarantee that their neighborhood will retain its attractive features, the elderly occupants of retirement housing are assured that their dwellings and environs will remain unchanged in the foreseeable future. For elderly persons, this certainty and predictability are important virtues in a society perceived as rapidly changing and sometimes intolerant of its elderly citizenry.

Opponents Fear Old Age

It was pointed out that the elderly persons who occupy age-segregated housing and communities represent a broad cross-section of the American population. However, certain groups of elderly persons are more likely than others to find these residential accommodations attractive. The gerontologist, Dr. Irving Rosow, has contructed a population typology that appears especially appropriate to predict the age-segregated preferences of elderly people. Rosow distinguished three groups of elderly persons who differed according to their beliefs about themselves and others as old people (their age-identification patterns). Two of these groups are predicted to be disposed favorably to age-segregated living arrangements.

The first group of elderly strongly identifies with their age peers. They perceive many important similarities between themselves and other elderly people.

They understand and respect the needs, capabilities, and activities of other elderly persons; they share with them the joys and fears of late life; and they similarly see themselves as "outsiders" in a youth-oriented society. Thus, they feel especially comfortable when associating with people of their own age.

The second population group displays "deviance" patterns of age-identification. These elderly persons look to younger persons as standards or examples by which to judge and compare their behavior and appearance. They hold more positive self-images when they perceive fewer age differences between themselves and other people; they do not want to be reminded constantly of their oldness. For these elderly people, the probability is greater that by associating with younger people they will become painfully aware of their unproductive lifestyles, traditional values, and frail bodies. On the other hand, older persons who confine their contacts—and thus their comparisons—to older people can more easily sustain an image of themselves as youthful and active.

While the above two groups of elderly will more favorably evaluate the prospects of living in age-segregated housing—albeit for different reasons—this is not true of the third group. Its elderly members display "dissociation" patterns of age-identification. They will vigorously deny their oldness—and all its varied concrete and symbolic manifestations. They attempt to dissociate themselves from other elderly people. They are apt to consider any recognition of their being old as tantamount to admitting they are unattractive and unwanted members of society. Both in their behavior and their appearance, these persons take great pains to exempt themselves from membership in anything that smacks of a senior citizen group. They look with suspicion on the use of age as an indicator of anything—"you after all are only as old as you feel and act." These persons would be predicted to take a dim view of living in a residential complex containing predominantly old people. They would avoid at all cost any visible association with a group with which they do not wish to be identified.

Although there is no research on the question, it is conceivable that the most vocal critics of age-segregated living arrangements display dissocation patterns of age-identification. Because they personally view old age as a very dismal, unattractive stage of life, they find it incomprehensible that older persons would voluntarily choose to live exclusively with other elderly people. Thus, these critics—whether they are old or young themselves—consider segregated housing to be an extremely repugnant concept. These accommodations can be rationalized only as repositories of elderly persons who have very limited housing choices. They blame the existence of retirement housing on a youth-oriented society that turns its back on its elderly citizenry and seeks to abandon them in isolated ghettos. Because these very same people venerate youth, they can be quite tolerant of, even enthusiastic about, the benefits of "young singles" or "young married" highrise apartments or condominium buildings. The paradox that these are also age-segregated residential situations—but of the young—never occurs to them.

Conclusions

Stripped of its emotional content, most criticism of age-segregated or retirement housing is without foundation. There is nothing intrinsically evil, malicious, or immoral about advocating that large numbers of older people live near each other. Neither geographic nor social isolation is a necessary result. It is easy to demonstrate the many positive social, economic, and psychological consequences of planned residential concentrations of the elderly. For many senior citizens, the attributes of these accommodations will improve the quality of their retirement years. Of course, there are elderly people who have personally valid reasons for disliking and rejecting this housing alternative. These accommodations will not satisfy the residential preferences of all, or even the majority of elderly persons. Nor should they. But it is important for retirement housing to remain as a housing option for people when they are old.

6

Alternative Housing Modes

J. Kevin Eckert and Mary Ittman Murrey

Alternatives Within the Community Residence Category

Communes and Cooperatives

Several articles in recent years have discussed cooperative and communal style living for the elderly (Lawton, 1981a; McConnell and Usher, 1979; Streib and Streib, 1975). It is apparent that the number of elderly who are involved in or who might be interested in this particular alternative arrangement is extremely small. As Lawton noted, there are no firm estimates of the number of people of any age who live in true communcal style. Such utopian communities seemed to have reached their peak in the 1960s and early 1970s. They corresponded with other social movements of that era and were centered particularly in the values of the young adult cohorts of that time. Pooling of financial resources, sharing household tasks, providing mutual support, and experimentation with supposedly untried ways of life were all characteristics of original communal arrangements. Cooperative and communal arrangements exist today in which older adults do live, but they are hard to document and little if any research has been done in such contexts. One example is provided by Maggie Kuhn, the founder of the Gray Panthers, who has converted her own home and another one nearby into a cooperative. In Lawton's words,

---

From *Elderly People and the Environment,* eds. Irwin Altman and Joachim F. Wohlwill, Vol. 7 in *Human Behavior and Environment,* New York: Plenum Publishing, 1984, pp. 103–128. Reprinted by permission of Plenum Publishing Corporation and K. Eckert.

"Life there is totally independent, always stimulating, and embodies every ideal of affective and instrumental exchange among people of all ages. But there are few Maggie Kuhns" (Lawton, 1981a). This statement is especially apropos since it points to a key factor in the success of such arrangements—the need for a strong charismatic leader and persons who share unique personal qualities. This particular housing arrangement puts a premium on individual characteristics and values and relies heavily on individual preference as a factor in choice.

While many gerontological planners and policymakers may herald the ideal of communal and cooperative living as a good idea for older people, it does not seem to be a particularly attractive alternative to present cohorts of older adults. For example, a three-year demonstration project in Kansas City was unable to open a communal house because older people could not be found who were willing to share space and household responsibilities. A total of more than 3,000 older persons were contacted about the program, yet only 100 were interested enough to request additional information, and almost none were willing actually to move into the home. Lawton (1981a) cited another expensive project on retirement cooperatives funded by the Administration on Aging (October 1978). He noted that the product of this project amounted to a grandiose plan for a national network of living, social, and employment cooperatives with little data to support the feasibility of the idea.

Comments of Streib and Streib (1975) on the improbability of widespread development of truly communal living for the elderly are well taken and reflect factors operating at several levels of our ecological framework. Their prediction is based on three factors: (a) the structural constraints of contemporary society which result in a fear on the part of most community residents of unconventional or "unnatural" family types; (b) the conditions and attitudes of the elderly themselves relevant to maintaining freedom, autonomy, and privacy; and (c) the relatively negative attitudes of the young communards toward including older people in their communities.

We need to know a great deal more about the feasibility and internal organization of communes and cooperatives. Better information on the prevalence of this arrangement would be most helpful with special attention directed toward regional and local differences in values and attitudes. For example, one might predict that such arrangements could flourish in some cosmopolitan areas of the United States. Future research should also address changes in attitudes toward communalism among adjacent cohorts of the elderly.

House-Sharing

Housesharing can take two forms: either renting a room to another person or converting a portion of a home into an apartment. The most typical form is to rent a room without remodeling. In such cases kitchen privileges are allowed as well as use of other living spaces. Housesharing is different from other rooming home arrangements in that it has emerged as a planned activity conducted by social agencies with the expressed purpose of convening owners and tenants. McConnell (1979) states that sharing a home develops from at least three factors operating at the individual level and related to enablement: financial status, companionship, and health. In a study done in Los Angeles county, McConnell reported that homeowners rated "help in emergency" and "companionship" as the most important advantages of housesharing. Gillan (1976) notes that in college towns it has been typical for older persons, mostly women, to take in a college student as a roomer. In the past matching of tenant to homeowner was done informally. More recently, intermediaries have been developed to interview and screen both owners and applicants, matching them against criteria voiced as important by both sets of clients. These arrangements may entail a simple verbal rental agreement or an elaborate communal contract in which all expenses, chores, and facilities are shared equally (McConnell, 1979).

McConnell and Usher (1979) provide data on several home-sharing programs in operation in the United States. Project Share, based in the Family Service Association of Nassau County, New York, is the largest project of its kind. This OAA Title III-funded project deals with both short- and longer-term finances. Recent data on this project show that as of March 1982, 1,083 owners and tenants had been served, 541 of whom were together as of that time (Inz, personal communication, 1982). As noted by Lawton (1981a), home-sharing meets short-term as well as longer-term residency needs and problems. The number of turnovers points to the need for short-term residencies to meet transitory housing problems like eviction or late occupancy. McConnell (1979) provides information on other house-sharing programs in San Jose, California (Project Match), and in San Francisco (Project Share). Further information can be obtained on sharing housing from the Shared Housing Resource Center located in the Gray Panthers headquarters in Philadelphia.

The potential for house-sharing seems great. Inz (personal communication, 1982) reports that since Project Share was initiated over 1,000 requests for information have been made. Approximately 70% of persons 65 and over are home owners and 97% of them live in "uncrowded" units (Wallin, 1972). However, this vast potential for housesharing must be weighed against the attractiveness of this arrangement to the present cohort of elderly. As noted by Lawton and Bader (1970), the importance of privacy increases with age. At the level of individual preference, the loss of privacy brought on by house-sharing may be its greatest liability. In the future, however, factors operating at the macrosocial level, such as the possibility of reduced funds for home maintenance programs and other assistance, may turn more elderly to housesharing as a last resort.

Reliable information concerning this alternative is increasing with the development of the Shared Housing Resource Center in Philadelphia. At this point research is needed on macrosocial forces which might foster or inhibit the future growth of this alternative. As well, a further exploration of cohort differences in individual values such as privacy and independence must be undertaken. While we espouse these values at the macrosocial or cultural level, successive numbers of elderly may show increased variability in the personal importance they attach to these values.

Mobile Homes

The mobile home is a rapidly growing alternative to home ownership. In this chapter, *mobile home* refers to a freestanding and stationary housing form usually anchored to a plot of land. These units provide completely furnished housing in one package; and newer mobile homes have concealed wiring, sockets in each room, insulation, and modern plumbing. They are compact and function much like an efficiency apartment and allow for independent living (Elrod, 1979). Rausch and Hoover (1980) provide very important data on the structural characteristics of mobile homes and the elderly who reside in them. A considerable portion of the 65-year-old and over population live in mobile homes. In 1975, 17% of the population occupying mobile homes were elderly; as of 1976, 4.9% of all people over 65 lived in mobile homes. A key factor for the increase in mobile home occupancy appears to be the opportunity they afford for home ownership, still a highly valued role in our society (Meeuwig, 1970). The vast majority of elderly living in mobile homes own their units (92%), with 61% of them having paid cash for them (Rausch, 1979). Modern mobile homes can be purchased with FHA loans either by contacting the lender directly or by going through a mobile home dealer approved by the lender (Elrod, 1979). Initial lower cost, however, may be offset by site rentals, higher financing charges, and higher depreciation (Weitzman, 1976).

Approximately half of all mobile homes are located on individual plots of land in small groups, while the remaining half are in groups of six or more and are referred to as mobile home parks (Rausch and Hoover, 1980). Monthly lot rentals in these parks can range from $50 and upward. As a rule, utilities are extra, as are clubhouse and recreational fees in the newer parks (Elrod, 1979). Residents of units located in the larger groups have greater access to utility and service systems (Rausch and Hoover, 1980), which might be a function of the larger groups' being located closer to public utility, water, and sewer systems. However, because of their peripheral or rural locations, mobile homes generally have poorer access to municipal services than other housing types.

The durability and quality of construction of mobile homes is an important variable in assessing this type of housing. Newer and more expensive units built after 1965 are not necessarily of higher quality than older units. Hazardous heating and electrical system breakdowns occur in greater proportion in these units and present serious hazards to all age groups. Rausch and Hoover (1980) point to the need for more uniform codes to regulate the manufacture of mobile homes.

Distance from resources coupled with other utility problems suggests that everyday environmental demands are greater for mobile home dwellers (Lawton, 1981a).

Mobile home communities have been shown to possess unique social environments, and several studies exist which address the microlevel dimensions, the individual and social characteristics, of these environments for older persons in particular (Fry, 1977; Hoyt, 1954; Johnson, 1971). Both Johnson and Fry estimate that age-graded mobile home parks have mushroomed around urban centers primarily in states with warm climates. Fry has conducted the most recent field studies of two small age-graded mobile home communities which differed in terms of degree of risk related to land tenure and the role of the developer. In the first community, Casa Del Oro, the role of the developer was marked by default; whereas the developer for the second community, Equus Estates, continued to be a patron and sponsor. The two communities also differed in terms of three other features: (a) more white-collar workers lived in the former and more blue-collar workers in the latter; (b) Casa Del Oro was located 10 miles outside Tucson, Arizona, whereas Equus Estates was within city limits; and (c) Casa Del Oro residents owned their lots, whereas those in Equus Estates rented theirs.

In both communities the basic social unit was a household marked by the absence of children. The households were integrated into the community through informal cliques and organized programs centered in a recreation hall. Cliques formed on the basis of residential proximity, mutual interest activities, and geographic origin. However, the social life at Casa Del Oro was more intense and complex than at Equus Estates. Fry attributes this intensity and complexity to the greater responsibility on the part of Casa Del Oro residents to protect, manage, and maintain their investment. At Equus Estates one's investment was limited to monthly rent plus utilities and the cost of moving the mobile home if things did not work out. In general, the commitment to community life was not as great. Fry's study points to the interaction between sociality (an aspect of the microsystem) and modes of ownership (a feature of the exosystem) in small-scale, age-graded communities. She suggests that the degree and quality of interaction among community residents will be in part determined by the type of investment (renting or owning) they have made in the setting. The greater the investment, the greater the degree of interaction and organization. Despite the need to examine how functional these communities would be as their residents' physical capabilities decline, it is apparent that the attractiveness of this alternative as a source of moderately priced housing is likely to increase in the future.

Condominiums and Cooperative Apartments

Condominiums differ from cooperatives. Cooperative apartments typically are organized on a corporate basis. A corporation is formed which buys the land and building; then a mortgage is taken out on the property and shares are sold to tenants (Kratovil, 1974), who purchase long-term leases from the corporation and pay rent to the corporation for the right to possession. The rent covers a pro-rata share of amounts needed to cover the mortgage debt, taxes, and operating expenses (Elrod, 1979). In the case of a condominium, on the other hand, the purchaser buys and receives a deed to his apartment unit or townhouse and an individual nonpartitionable interest in the common areas (Kratovil, 1974).The buyer obtains a mortgage in a manner similar to that involved in buying a house. FHA financing is available for condominium purchase. Units are taxed separately and an association enforces rules and regulations.

Both condominium and cooperatives can offer advantages to the elderly with the financial resources to purchase them. They combine features of rental living, such as freedom from exterior home maintenance and yardwork, with the benefits of homeownership tax benefits and equity (Elrod, 1979). The closeness of neighbors can meet needs for social interaction and safety.

On the negative side, condominiums and cooperatives are not cheap. When the monthly maintenance fees and mortgage payments for condominiums and lease rental fees for cooperatives are taken into consideration, they cost as much as, and in some cases more than, conventional housing and yield less space. Inflation causes these expenses, especially maintenance fees, to rise steadily. For persons on fixed incomes such increases could rise to a point at which the condominium or cooperative is no longer affordable (Elrod, 1979). In addition, condominium and cooperative owners are much more dependent upon one another for preservation of their interests than are renters or homeowners (Henry & Wittie, 1978). As Fry (1977) discovered for mobile home park residents who owned their land, increased risk and interdependence can stimulate the formation of social groups and interaction—a positive feature for some people.

Conversion of rental apartments to either condominiums or cooperatives can have a dramatic negative impact on the elderly. They often live in buildings which are prime targets for conversion, and they are the least able to cope with it, both economically and psychologically. Conversion takes valuable rental units off the market in urban areas with depressed construction of new replacement units (Wood, 1977). Furthermore, it displaces people who can afford a monthly apartment rent but do not have the capital necessary to purchase a condominium or cooperative. Elrod (1979) notes that the cost for a condominium unit may be 150 times the monthly rent for an apartment, and maintenance costs and taxes may cause 35% higher monthly payments for a rental unit converted to a condominium unit. The United States Department of Housing and Urban Development (1975) predicts, however, that pressure for condominium conversion will probably continue.

One critical area needing further research is the human cost of converting apartments to either condominiums or cooperatives. For example, to what extent are the elderly being displaced through conversions, where do they go if displaced, and what are the human costs in terms of deteriorated morale, health status, and overall quality of life?

For the elderly who have the initial capital to purchase a condominium or cooperative, we need to know the impact of rising inflation rates on their quality of life. How do people without income growth potential cope and adjust to rapidly increasing living costs?

Hotels and Rooming Houses

Of the 6.8 million elderly who live in urban areas, approximately 397,000 live on a relatively permanent basis in accommodations which are referred to in the literature as "single-room occupancy" (SRO). This type of housing includes three kinds of living units: (a) partial single-room units (no access or shared access to kitchen facilities and/or bath); (b) single-room units (renter-occupied one-room housing units); (c) renter-occupied housing units in a residential hotel, rooming house, or a permanent unit in a transient hotel (Haley, Pearson, & Hull, 1981).

The populations found in these units are not homogeneous but represent the gamut in terms of age, income, social connectedness, sex distribution, and so on. For example, some case studies of SRO units have tended to support the stereotype that persons living in these environments are loners (Stephens, 1976) outside the mainstream of society, who are "socially terminal" (Siegal, 1977) or marked by maladaptation (Shapiro, 1966, 1971). Some other case studies have pointed to the heterogeneity of the SRO population in terms of housing quality and type, personal biography, age, health, modes of adjustment, and so on (Eckert, 1979, 1980; Erickson and Eckert, 1977; Sokolovsky and Cohen, 1978). At present, data are lacking to construct a comprehensive profile of elderly hotel and rooming-house dwellers and their housing. We know that, as the SRO category is defined formally, it could include small boarding residences where a single bedroom is rented by the week or month as well as converted houses and apartment buildings in urban areas where rental payments cover a room but where residents must eat meals in local restaurants and cafeterias (Goode et al., 1980). Central to the SRO category are the hotels, which can vary dramatically in size, condition, rent, and social climate.

As noted by Goode et al. (1980), much of the research concerning the elderly residents of hotels and rooming houses has been narrowly focused on specific subgroups, most often differentiated by characteristics of the accommodation. Albrecht (1969) and Teski (1979) focused on retirement hotels; Kowall (1970, 1973, 1976), Sokolovsky and Cohen (1978), Eckert (1979, 1980, 1982), Erickson and Eckert (1977), Stephens (1976), and Ehrlich (1976) have concerned themselves with small and large inner-city SRO-type hotels; some others have concentrated on skid-row or tenement accommodations (Ehrlich, 1976; Erickson and Eckert, 1977; Siegal, 1977; Shapiro, 1971); at least one researcher,

Zorbaugh (1929), focused on the unique social situation afforded by rooming houses, a situation that was more common in the early years of this century (Hareven, 1976).

As we noted above, research on some types of SRO housing and subpopulations has been quite prolific over the past decade. Several common conclusions about SRO accommodations, living arrangements, and social life run through this body of research. Numerous researchers have noted that hotels and rooming-house environments provide formal and informal supports for their older residents (Albrecht, 1969; Eckert, 1979, 1980; Ehrlich, 1976; Erickson and Eckert, 1977; Kowall, 1976; Shapiro, 1971; Sokolovsky and Cohen, 1978; Stephens, 1976). These supports are provided in a way that allows for reciprocal social exchanges which tend to maintain one's sense of autonomy, control and self-respect (Eckert, 1979; Kowall, 1976; Shapiro, 1971). Many SRO accommodations are located in or near urban commercial zones which provide convenient and important services (restaurants, shops, transportation) to meet their older residents' needs (Eckert, 1979, 1980, 1982; Erickson and Eckert, 1977; Goode et al., 1980).

When one decides to live in a hotel or rooming house, one receives more than just a room. Basic housekeeping services are usually included in the rent along with furniture, linens, and heat. Desk clerks, resident managers, maids or owners act as security personnel, watching out for the residents themselves as well as controlling the presence of outsiders. In times of emergency these persons sometimes provide direct support to or a liaison function for residents. Living close to other older persons of similar background or circumstances can create a climate in which mutually supportive and beneficial social relationships emerge (Eckert, 1979; Sokolovsky and Cohen, 1978). As summarized by Goode et al. (1980), this nontraditional housing has to varying degrees many of the features considered important in planned housing for the elderly. More important, it exists, and it appears to meet the housing needs of some older people.

Case studies and studies based on census data indicate that older people who live in SRO accommodations are different from those living elsewhere (Ehrlich, 1976; Erickson and Eckert, 1977; Stephens, 1976; Tissue, 1971). Lawton (1981a) reports that residents in hotels and rooming houses are characteristically male; 3.4% have never married, 3.0% are widowers, and 6.0% are divorced or separated. An overall profile of the elderly who live in hotels and rooming houses reveal that, in comparison to older people living elsewhere in the community, they are more likely to be never married or widowed, living alone, over 75, and living in poverty (Goode et al., 1980). These findings suggest that a significant proportion of this population is probably not only frail but at risk both physically and socially (Erickson and Eckert, 1977, 1979; Goode et al., 1980).

Life course trajectories that lead to living in SRO accommodations vary, but it appears that a relatively large proportion of older persons chose this housing during an earlier stage in life. The choice was determined partly by the existence of few other low-cost housing alternatives and partly by a style of life and personal conditions that made housekeeping responsibilities difficult to assume (Eckert, 1980; Kowall, 1976). With functional health reasonably intact, such environments provide a niche for some individuals, at a lower cost, than other environments could. Some others are in SRO accommodations because there is no available alternative, for example, the very old who moved into a hotel because they had outlived all relatives and friends and had no other place to turn or those who have been discharged from an extended-care mental hospital or prison. For these individuals multiple problems and marginal social adjustment may make life miserable.

Public and private development efforts pose a serious threat to SRO establishments and the people who live in them. Public misunderstanding and disdain for this housing, housing policies indifferent to the needs of SRO residents, urban renewal, gentrification, and historical preservation have led to a depletion of valuable SRO housing stock and alterations in key neighborhood services so critical to supporting this residential way of life (Eckert, 1979; Ehrlich, 1976; Kowall, 1970, 1973; Levy, 1968). Hotels and rooming houses must be viewed as an integral part of their larger neighborhoods and local communities. Without the infrastructure of services available in these environments, the needs of older residents will not be satisfied.

At present, research is under way to assess the effects of forced relocation and environmental change on the elderly living in SRO hotels in a West Coast city (Eckert, 1982). This study is the first to consider the consequences of relocation and urban change on the elderly hotel resident. It employs a quasi-experimental research design comparing measures of mental and physical health status, social networks and supports, and psychological adjustments before and after moving for an experimental and comparison group of older persons. Those in the comparison group were randomly selected from hotels similar in characteristics and contiguous to those being destroyed.

In general, the group experiencing relocation showed little negative change in measures of health and well-being before and after moving. However, a subpopulation of people who rated their health as poor appeared vulnerable to relocation stress. These persons were at risk in terms of selected physical health measures prior to relocation and continued to be at risk after being relocated. This finding points to the importance of disaggregating elderly persons in terms of their health status. Those in poor health are at risk; they must be identified and assisted through special services (Eckert, 1982). Data from this research further point to the importance of the infrastructure of supports both within the hotel and the local neighborhood for older urban residents.

At the macrosocial level, federal housing policy is the major stumbling block to improving the housing conditions of the single poor (Levy, 1968; Fielding, 1972; Kowall, 1973). As Kowall (1976) so cogently notes, HUD regulations requiring self-contained units—that is, private use of complete bathroom and kitchen facilities—in existing housing preclude SRO tenants and management from housing assistance programs necessary to arrest the deteriorating buildings.

At the national level, the impact of urban change, be it renewal and development or deterioration and decay, on the elderly is not known. Research in various cities and localities throughout the United States indicates that there is a problem. Large-scale national research, although unlikely to gain funding at present, is nonetheless called for.

Alternatives Within the Congregate Housing Category

Another broad category of residential type in which alternatives can be identified is known as *congregate housing*. Although the term has no satisfactorily accurate definition, *congregate* will be used here to refer to housing that offers a minimum service package that includes on-site meals served in a common dining room, plus one or more services such as on-site medical or nursing service, personal care, or housekeeping (Lawton, 1976). The precise number of available congregate units is not known, but what is known indicates that they are in short supply and are in great demand. Lawton (1981a) offers the estimate that their numbers do not exceed 30,000 to 40,000 units including both assisted and nonassisted housing. This housing attracts both those who are fully independent and those with some limitations in physical capability.

The typical resident in congregate housing is white, female and single or widowed. Unlike SRO hotels and rooming houses, this housing has far more women than men. In a study done by Urban Systems Research and Engineering, Inc. (1976), it was found that 75% of the residents were 75 years of age or older and 7% were black. Residents in congregate housing said that they had moved from their own houses or apartments to congregate quarters as a security against the uncertainties of old age.

The elements of congregate housing such as on-site meals plus services can be seen in recently developing smaller-scale alternatives. Brody (1979) has distinguished the congregate category (which she refers to collectively as group homes) into two levels: small congregate group homes and high-support group homes. Two emerging alternatives will be discussed which fit this category: Share-a-Home and community housing.

Share-a-Home

The Share-a-Home concept can be categorized under what Brody calls small congregate homes. These arrangements provide some mix of hired help to shop and cook; maintenance and housekeeping; and social service consultation. All appear to be under the auspices of some organization. The original Share-a-Home idea was started in 1969 by James Gillies when a group of 20 elderly persons jointly leased a 27-room house and facilities. Since that time the concept has grown, and at least ten additional "families" live in a variety of housing, ranging from a former Catholic convent to a spacious mansion. In 1972 Gillies established a nonprofit tax-exempt organization to assist in the formation of new families and to coordinate their ongoing operation. The organization performs "a kind of surrogate parent role for the ten families now in operation" (Streib, 1978).

In Gillies's words,

> Any senior adult may live in Share-a-Home. The only requirement is that members be ambulatory and able to manage their own personal care. There are no initiation fees—no founders fees—no contracts. Members pay only their fair share of expenses monthly, excluding personal items like clothing and medical expenses (Gilles, 1979).

From a sociological perspective, the Share-a-Home model represents a new kind of social group in American society which blends in one location both familial and bureaucratic functions (Streib, 1978). Although it is not a traditional family, it has some of the affective and support characteristics of families and has been considered a family on some legal grounds (Sussman, 1976). It also has some of the characteristics typical of bureaucratic organizations, such as a board of directors and formal rules of operation. As "amalgam" groups, Share-a-Home families try to deal with both the uniform and nonuniform tasks and needs of some older Americans (Streib, 1978).

With programs in operation throughout the country, the Share-a-Home model is receiving considerable attention as an alternative mode of living for the elderly. For an ever-growing number of elderly men and women who do not wish to live alone, it is a way of life which allows people to retain self-respect and a degree of autonomy in an atmosphere of caring without institutional restraints (Gillies, 1979).

The concept of Share-a-Home presents several interesting research questions. First, if such groups to demonstrate qualities of families, how do they cope and adjust to the loss and replacement of members over time? Second, what are the personal characteristics of people who opt for Share-a-Home, and what are the characteristics which are seen as desirable in others? Third, what problems arise as members of a Share-a-Home decline in capability and greater support services are required?

Community Housing

Another form of alternative housing which fits into the broad congregate category is what Brody (1978) refers to as intermediate or community housing.

Similar to the Share-a-Home model, community housing utilizes existing housing stock with the provision of backup services to maintain an individual's independence and autonomy. The original community housing model was developed and sponsored by the Philadelphia Geriatric Center (PGC) to provide innovative options for older persons. As described by Brody (1979), it consisted of nine one-family, semidetached homes located in a residential neighborhood adjacent to the PGC campus. Purchase and conversion of each house to contain three private efficiency apartments and a shared living room was accomplished with the aid of mortgages insured through the Section 236 Rehabilitation Program of the Federal Housing Administration. Rent supplements to eligible persons allowed the apartments to be rented at reduced rates.

Basic rental fees include institutional assistance with janitorial and building maintenance; cleaning of the common areas; a "hot line" phone connected to the PGC switchboard for medical or other emergencies; access to the Center's group recreational, religious, and social activities, and social services at application and moving phases (Brody, 1978). Residents are expected to do their own shopping, cooking, and housekeeping. However, home-delivered frozen main meals and light housekeeping could be purchased from PGC. Medical care is not provided, and tenants retain their own personal physicians (Brody, Kleban, and Lebowitz, 1975).

Brody (1978) found that a major motivation for older people who moved into this housing was fear, isolation, and loneliness because of the high crime rate in

Courtesy of Brooks Trubee
Princeton Community Housing, Princeton, New Jersey

the neighborhoods in which they lived. Deteriorated housing stock and depletion of family and friends living nearby was another related stimulant.

Despite the deliberate design of the environment for independence, the tenants who moved in were less healthy than a comparison group who did not move; their social needs were reflected in that the housing appealed almost exclusively to those who lived alone (Lawton, 1981a). The overall evaluation of the housing has been positive (Brody, 1978).

This kind of housing holds promise if existing agencies can be encouraged to expand their programs to handle small residences (Lebowitz, 1978). Relying on existing housing stock, community housing offers familiarity, independence, security, social opportunities, and the group support of the sponsoring organization (Lawton, 1981a).

A factor at the level of the exosystem limiting the development of the above-mentioned alternatives is restrictive zoning ordinances in many communities against the occupation by unrelated persons of a single-family residence. Although neighborhood residents may not object to a group of unrelated elderly living together, they may fear that any unconventional arrangement of people might set a precedent for other unrelated groups which they would see as undesirable. However, Elrod (1979) reports that several states have permitted unrelated persons to occupy a single-family residence notwithstanding an ordinance prohibiting such occupancy.

Courtesy of Brooks Trubee
Princeton Community Housing, Princeton, New Jersey

Alternatives Within the Domiciliary and Personal Care Residential Category

The National Center of Health Statistics defines domiciliary and personal care residence as follows: a residence is considered domiciliary care if it offers one or two of eight named personal care services (e.g., help with eating, bathing, toileting, grooming); it is personal care if three or more of these services are offered (National Center for Health Statistics, 1976). Domiciliary and personal care can be seen as a hybrid residential type which offers personal care services but not medical/nursing services (Lawton, 1981a). Estimates are that 500,000 to 1,500,000 elderly, disabled, and mentally ill citizens live in over 300,000 domiciliary residences nationally (Report of the House Select Committee on Aging, 1979). The vast majority of these facilities are private, for-profit enterprises. The primary source of payment is Supplemental Security Income (SSI), although other sources include Social Security, veterans' benefits, and federal funds under alcohol and drug abuse programs (Report of the House Select Committee on Aging, 1979).

A particularly thorny issue regarding any discussion of this residential type revolves around nomenclature. Domiciliary facilities are known in different locations by different names, such as foster homes, board and care homes, and sheltered care homes (U.S. General Accounting Office, 1979a). Many states recognize several categories of adult care homes, applying a variety of standards to the different categories. An "adult foster home" in one state is referred to as an "adult congregate living facility" in another state. Furthermore, social service agencies differ in criteria, with some defining a boarding home as any facility which houses four or more SSI recipients not related by blood or marriage (National Citizens' Coalition for Nursing Home Reform [NCCNHR], 1981). At the level of residential type, Lawton (1981a) provides some help by stating that domiciliary facilities differ from congregate housing in that they are more institutional, containing shared bedrooms and few options for independent function. Congregate housing usually has a private dwelling-unit with either private or public cooking and dining facilities. Congregate housing is more often under nonprofit sponsorship and houses more residents.

Although there are certain characteristics at the level of the individual which may be ascribed to boarding home residents in general—they are often elderly, poor (SSI recipients), mentally impaired, and without close family ties—there are wide variations. Some are elderly and sick; others are younger, retarded, deinstitutionalized patients. Some have criminal records (NCCNHR Report, 1981). The most vulnerable are the sick elderly who have been deinstitutionalized from state hospitals (NCCNHR Report, 1981).

Although there are some reputable and well-run boarding homes, a considerable number appear to provide poor care clearly contrary to the mental and physical health of their residents. Poor sanitation, inadequate provision for medical care, unavailable social services, housing and safety code violations, and inadequate diet are some of the problems contributing to a marginal quality of life for boarding home residents (NCCNHR Report, undated).

Some states have required licensing of boarding homes, but the standards are minimal and enforcement almost nonexistent. Enactment of the Keyes amendment to the Social Security Act (1976) requires states to establish, maintain, and insure enforcement of standards covering such matters as admission policies, safety, sanitation, and protection of civil rights. However, there are several major obstacles to enforcement: no provision for financial assistance to implement enforcement or inspection of homes; and a misdirected penalty of reduced SSI payments to recipients who reside in a facility that does not meet state standards. Standing alone as the only penalty, this provision punishes the victim rather than the operator.

Foster Care Homes

Within the domiciliary and personal care category, the concept of *foster home* deserves special attention. As with other variations in this category, definition is a problem. For example, what is considered a foster home varies among and within states. Variation in definition within a state can depend upon the supervisory or regulatory body of government. In New York state, for instance, there are several types of foster care programs sponsored by the Department of Mental Hygiene, Department of Social Welfare, or Veterans' Administration (Sherman and Newman, 1977). Definitions of the characteristics of a foster home, as well as of the personal characteristics of residents, differ substantially between these sponsoring departments (Newman and Sherman, 1979).

Lawton (1981a) provides two general defining criteria of foster homes: (a) a single-family household, with (b) no more than four nonrelatives living in a household as paying residents. Another central criterion which several authors specify as highly desirable (Sherman and Newman, 1977; Silverstone, 1978) is the creation of an atmosphere in which patients or residents are treated as family members and participate in normal family activities. The concept of a family-like primary group is a key factor differentiating foster care from "mere boarding homes" (Sherman and Newman, 1977). A decent foster family living arrangement should offer an adult in need of care—over and above basic essentials—relatively permanent primary group relations wherein his or her individualized, affectional, and unpredictable needs are met. In such a context the resident is expected to reciprocate by trying to meet these needs for other primary group members. The foster family potentially offers closer links to the community of which the foster family is a part and independence from the conforming tendencies of institutional populations (Silverstone, 1978).

Variation in type and quality of foster homes is great, and caution must be exercised in assuming that security, social, and privacy needs are actually met. Lawton (1981a) notes that it cannot be assumed simply because they are part of the community and small in scale that foster homes offer a style of life that is any richer than that offered by some institutions.

In terms of community attitudes toward foster homes, their small size contributes to the likelihood of their going unnoticed and therefore being reasonably well accepted. Sherman and Newman (1977) warn against saturating any community with too many family care homes to protect against visibility and consequent hostility. The potential for foster care homes and other domiciliary care facilities will most likely remain high, based on (a) the number of old people with chronic health problems and (b) the rise in the number of people who live alone.

Several research efforts are currently underway which should significantly add to our understanding of domiciliary care nationally. For example, the Hebrew Rehabilitation Center for the Aged (HRCA) is presently completing a study which will determine the availability and cost of domiciliary care (i.e., board and care) and the services that are provided to older persons in supportive residential settings. The research objectives of this study address issues at all four levels of our ecological housing model. The stated objectives of the study include the following:

- To determine the supply of different types of domiciliary care for the elderly.
- To determine the costs of each type of domiciliary care for the elderly.
- To assess the impact of federal and state policies on the supply of supportive residential settings, including funding sources and regulations, licensing requirements, and limits on entry of service providers.
- To determine how elderly persons enter these facilities.
- To identify types of services provided to elderly residents of such facilities.
- To identify the extent and types of linkage between these facilities and other community providers.
- To assess the appropriateness, adequacy, and quality of domiciliary care services, based on the needs of elderly residents, provided by such facilities.
- To identify the characteristics and levels of impairment of elderly persons who are best suited to be served in each type of facility.

Another grant has been awarded to the Denver Research Institute to review board and care homes and the various systems that have been developed for managing services to the elderly residents in homes that require some level of protective services. The central objectives of this study are to review state standards and regulations for board and care homes, with special attention given to the enforcement and effectiveness of the Keyes amendment. The study will also provide recommendations for enforcement mechanisms at the state and national levels.

Specific Phenomena at the Macrolevel

Although it is important to talk about specific types of housing arrangements, one must not isolate them from larger societal forces which are constantly changing their existence, form and user population. Several factors operating at the macro- or societal level of our ecological model affect the development of new housing modes for the elderly. Gentrification, a crisis in available rental units, erosion of the income of the elderly through inflation, and proposed cutbacks in federal housing programs and human services all impact alternative housing for the elderly.

The upgrading of the class composition and housing stock within a neighborhood is called *gentrification*. Between the middle and late 1970s, this phenomenon was evident when a movement of upper middle class and wealthy into certain inner city areas occurred. A 1975 survey estimated that privately initiated renovation efforts were under way in 70% of the American cities with populations over 250,000 (Myers, 1978). The reason for the shift is complex but includes such factors as fewer numbers of couples with children requiring schools and suburban environments, increased appreciation of the cultural attractions in the city, proximity to work, and the relative housing bargain available as compared to the suburbs. The new residents occupy either renovated housing structures or newly built condominiums or apartments built especially for the higher-priced market. The surrounding environment also may undergo dramatic change as new shops, restaurants and other businesses that cater to the new market move in. With development usually comes displacement of the working-class or poorer residents, who cannot afford to buy their converted apartments or to pay increased rents and property taxes for their housing, be it apartment, rented hotel room, or private home. It has been demonstrated that gentrification is more likely to occur in tracts that house more elderly. A general out-migration occuring simultaneously with gentrification of older households from the inner city, increasing as one moves closer to the center, indicates that the elderly are being displaced by the shift (Henig, 1981).

For the elderly who own their own homes, gentrification usually means increased property taxes as well as increased maintenance costs. These added costs are often too much to bear for people on fixed incomes, who are forced to move or in some cases to take in boarders, thus stimulating indirectly the development of the house-sharing alternatives. In addition there have been reports of realtors pressuring older people to sell at prices lower than market value, taking advantage of their lack of knowledge of the current market (Myers, 1978).

Renters of apartments or hotel rooms are especially hard hit by gentrification. The renovation of older apartment structures or hotels for occupation by upper-income tenants or other uses raises rents far beyond what they have previously been. Some apartments become converted into condominiums while some hotels are destroyed or converted into office space. In the case of condominium conversion, current renters usually have first option on buying their apartments, but costs of $30,000 and more are prohibitive to older persons on fixed incomes. In 1977, 30% of all elderly households were renters. Of this group 40% had incomes below $5,000; another 32.6% had incomes between $4,500 and $10,000; and only 8% had incomes above $20,000. Forty-two percent of all elderly renters live in apartments which rent for at least $150. These are the rental units which tend to be converted. A majority of elderly are already paying over 25% of their incomes to live in units renting for from $150 to $250 (Select Committee on Aging, 1981a, p. 48). Thus the conversion of apartments into condominums potentially affects a large number of elderly who cannot afford further rent increases. The owner-occupants of converted buildings clearly tend to be young professionals. Nearly two-thirds are individuals who hold a professional or managerial position; about one-half are 35 or younger, whereas only one-fifth are over 55 and only 9% are over 65 (Select Committee on Aging, 1980a). What happens to the older displaced tenants? Although federally funded high-rises have been built for a small number of them, these are not adequate to house the vast majority. For those people who are not lucky enough to be housed in new or public housing, a move into a poor and more dangerous neighborhood may be their only choice (Myers, 1978). A large national study found that one-half of all former residents of converted buildings had some difficulty in finding housing, with elderly, nonwhite and lower-income former tenants reporting more difficulty (in Select Committee on Aging, 1980a, p. 99).

The reasons for the unfortunate fates of large numbers of the elderly who are displaced are better understood when placed in the context of the current rental crisis. The nation's lowest recorded rental housing vacancy rate and shortages of affordable rental units have resulted in this crisis. The primary causes are the low level of moderately priced, new private construction and the losses of existing stock to conversions to condominiums and abandonments (U.S. General Accounting Office, 1979b). A call by the current administration for the replacement of subsidized housing construction by the government, the traditional means of assistance, by a system of vouchers or certificates to be used on the open market will only add to this crisis by failing to stimulate the building of new low-cost housing. In addition, without mandated changes in the existing housing stock and market (i.e., rent control, stricter landlord-tenant laws), the poor have little choice but to remain or to move to poor-quality housing.

Although slightly more than 70% of older persons own their own homes, the structures tend to be older, in poorer condition, and of lower value than the rest of owner-occupied housing (Carp, 1978; Baer, 1976). In addition, elderly homeowners tend to be poor, with a vast majority having incomes under $4,000 (Select Committee on Aging, 1980a, p. 48), although they tend to pay a proportionately higher amount of their income in property taxes (Baer, 1976). There is need to provide mortgage, insurance, and maintenance supports to enable older people to remain in their homes and enjoy a comfortable quality of life. If the elderly can stay in their own homes, the likelihood of house-sharing will remain a viable housing alternative.

Recent trends to reduce the federal government's financial and administrative involvement in housing and human service programs will have both a direct and indirect impact on the development of alternative housing for the elderly. For example, expanded rent subsidy programs under Section 8 requiring the elderly to pay only 25% of their income for rent could have provided much needed assistance to persons living in SRO units. However, proposed budget cuts may reduce by 33% the number of presently subsidized units. Section 236, which provided rent supplements for persons living in the community housing alternative, could be similarly affected.

The quality of housing available for the share-a-home alternative may be affected through reduced funding for the Community Development Block Grants (CDBG) and consolidation of Section 312 loans, Weatherization and Urban Development Action Grant Programs. Section 312 provided loans for repairs when CDBG grant funds did not cover complete costs. Without additional funding, the only source for low-interest, home-repair loans will be eliminated.

The development of less desirable housing alternatives for the elderly could be influenced through decreases in medical payments. Expanding needs, tightening eligibility, and lowered reimbursement could stimulate the development of low-quality board and care homes—in effect, a "bootleg" nursing-home industry.

The development of innovative housing alternatives for the elderly demands a commitment of policymakers at the local, state, and federal levels of government. The possible elimination of very promising alternative housing, such as the congregate housing demonstration program, signals a distressing future trend.

In summary, the negative factors include the lower quality of the elderly's housing and the reduction of funds for home maintenance, housing subsidies, and government-sponsored housing. The call of a replacement of construction with vouchers will force elderly to find their own housing on an open private market which is unresponsive to the needs of the poor. There is no solution offered for people at risk of being displaced by the processes of gentrification, relocation for private redevelopment and renewal, and condominium conversion. Property taxes may be rising, often in response to gentrification. Increases in fuel costs because of gas and oil deregulation, as well as cuts in energy assistance and weatherization, will force many older people to make choices among decent housing, adequate nutrition, or keeping warm.

Future Research and Conclusion

Alternative housing for the elderly encompasses a broad range of residential types and specific housing arrangements. To date, research exploring alternative housing has been diverse in method and objective. Research in the future would benefit from clearer specification of research problems, theoretical and conceptual frameworks, and attempts at anchoring these in an ecological framework. There is a need for research on alternative housing which explores the interaction between levels in our ecological model. Although such research is complex, of a large scale, and expensive, it is nonetheless necessary. Research of this type will begin to consolidate and order the bits and pieces of data we now possess and assist in theory building. Although it is sometimes easier to conduct research on individuals within their immediate environmental context, factors operating at the level of the local neighborhood and larger society should not be ignored.

The making of choices among possible alternative housing arrangements is a result of complex multilevel factors ranging from political and economic forces (macrolevel) to psychological and cultural characteristics (microlevel) of the individual. However, the larger social, political, and economic forces and processes within a particular changing society are the primary determinants in explaining and accounting for the existence and range of housing alternatives and in the variation in choice between groups of elderly, as well as the changes in these housing options over time.

An insightful review of housing literature (Eribes, 1979) reveals that the most common and persistent problem is the "inability of public policy in aligning national goals with the needs of shelter of the especially disadvantaged." This inability of public policy to meet the housing needs of the disadvantaged is not altogether surprising since housing is a private industry with an inherent interest in making profit. Although the federal government has attempted to provide subsidized housing, only a small portion of the needy were served; and now even these meager attempts are threatened. The power of political and economic forces can be demonstrated in the complete and unhesitating elimination of congregate housing in the face of years of research demonstrating its benefits. To address the housing needs and problems of the elderly, then, we must directly face and change these forces, which are the source of the major problems.

References

Albrecht, R. "Retirement Homes in Florida." *University of Florida Institute of Gerontology Series.* 1969, *18*, 71-82.

Altman, I., and Lett, E.E. "The Ecology of Interpersonal Relationships: A Classification System and Conceptual Model." In J. E. McGrath (ed.), *Social and Psychological Factors in Stress.* New York: Holt, Rinehart & Winston, 1970, pp. 177-201.

Baer, W.C. "Federal Housing Programs for the Elderly." In M. P. Lawton, R. J. Newcomer, and T. O. Byerts (eds.), *Community Planning for an Aging Society: Designing Services and Facilities.* Stroudsburg, Pa.: Dowden, Hutchinson & Ross, 1976, pp. 81-98.

Barker, R.G., and Barker, L.S. "The Psychological Ecology of Old People in Midwest, Kansas, and Yoredale, Yorkshire." *Journal of Gerontology,* 1961, *16,* 144-149.

Bell, W. "Urban Neighborhoods and Individual Behavior." In M. Sherif & C.W. Sherif (eds.), *Problems of Youth: Transition to Adulthood in a Changing World.* Chicago: Aldine, 1967, pp. 235-264.

Berry, B.J.L. (ed.), *City Classification Handbook.* New York: Wiley, 1972.

Brody, E.M. "Community Housing for the Elderly: The Program, the People, the Decision-making Process, and the Research." *The Gerontologist,* 1978, *18,* 121-129.

Brody, E.M. "Service-Supported Independent Living in an Urban Setting: The Philadelphia Geriatric Center's Community Housing for the Elderly." In T.O. Byerts, S.C. Howell, and S.A. Pastalan (eds.), *Environmental Context of Aging.* New York: Garland STPM Press, 1979.

Brody, E.M., Kleban, M.H., and Liebowitz, B. "Intermediate Housing for the Elderly: Satisfaction of Those Who Moved in and Those Who Did Not." *The Gerontologist,* 1975, *15,* 350-356.

Carp, F.M. "Housing Organization and Designs for the Elderly." Prepared for the *AAS Intergovernmental Research and Development Project Workshop on Health and Human Resources: The Elderly.* Warrenton, Va.: Airlie House, December 12-14, 1978.

Chapman, N.J., and Beaudet-Walters, M. *Predictors of Environmental Well-Being for Older Adults.* Paper presented at the Annual Meeting of the Gerontological Society, Dallas, November 1978.

Cowgill, D.O. "Residential Segregation by Age in American Metropolitan Areas." *Journal of Gerontology,* 1978, *33,* 446-453.

Eckert, J.K. "Urban Renewal and Redevelopment: High Risk for the Marginally Subsistent Elderly." *The Gerontologist,* 1979, *19,* 496-502.

Eckert, J.K. *The Unseen Elderly: A Study of Marginally Subsistent Hotel Dwellers.* San Diego: Campanile Press, 1980.

Eckert, J.K. "Dislocation and Relocation of the Urban Elderly: Social Networks as Mediators of Relocation Stress." *Human Organization,* 1982, 42(1), 39-45.

Ehrlich, P.A. "Study of the 'Invisible Elderly': Characteristics and Needs of the St. Louis Downtown SRO Elderly." In *The Invisible Elderly.* Washington, D.C.: The National Council on the Aging, 1976, pp. 7-14.

Elrod, L.H. "Housing Alternatives for the Elderly." *Journal of Family Law,* 1979, *18,* 723-759.

Eribes, R. "The Housing Puzzle: Do the Pieces Fit?" *Public Administration Review,* 1979, *5,* 445-499.

Erickson, R.J., & Eckert, J.K. "The Elderly Poor in Downtown San Diego Hotels." *The Gerontologist,* 1977, *17,* 440-446.

Fielding, B. "Low-Income, Single-Person Housing: What's Happening as a Result of the 'Congregate Housing' Provisions of the 1970 Act?" *Journal of Housing,* 1972, *29,* 133-136.

Fry, C.L. "The Community as a Commodity: The Age Graded Case." *Human Organization,* 1977, *36,* 115-123.

Gillan, R.B. "Zoning for the Elderly." In M.P. Lawton, R.J. Newcomer, and T.O. Byerts (eds.), *Community Planning for an Aging Society: Designing Services and Facilities.* Stroudsburg, Pa.: Dowden, Hutchinson & Ross, 1976, pp. 99-105.

Gillies, J.W. "Share-a-Home—A New Lease on Life." *Generations,* 1979, 3(3), 26.

Goode, C., Lawton, M.P., and Hoover, S.L. *Elderly Hotel and Rooming House Dwellers: The Population and Its Housing.* Philadelphia: Philadelphia Geriatric Center, 1980.

Haley, B.A., Pearson, M., & Hull, D.A. *Urban Elderly Presidents of Single Room Occupancy Housing (SRO's), 1976-1980.* Paper presented at the 34th Annual Meeting of the Gerontological Society of America, Toronto, Canada, November, 1981.

Hareven, T.K. "The Last Stage: Historical Adulthood and Old Age." *Daedalus,* 1976, *4, 105,* 13-27.

Henig, J. "Gentrification and Displacement of the Elderly: An Empirical Analysis." *The Gerontologist*, 1981, *21*, 67-75.
Henry, L.J., and Wittie, R.A. "Uniform Condominium Act: Key Issues." *Real Property, Probate and Trust Journal*, 1978, *13*, 437-539.
Hoyt, G.C. "The Life of the Retired in a Trailer Park." *American Journal of Sociology*, 1954, *59*, 361-371.
Inz, J. "Personal Communication," April 1982.
Johnson, S.K. "Idle Haven: Community Building Among the Working-Class Retired." Berkeley: University of California Press, 1971.
Kahana, E.A. "A. Congruence Model of Person-Environment Interaction." In M.P. Lawton, P.G. Windley, and T.O. Byerts (eds.), *Aging and the Environment: Directions and Perspectives*. New York: Garland STPM Press, 1980, pp. 97-121.
Kendig, H. "Neighborhood Conditions of the Aged and Local Government." *Gerontologist*, 196, *16*, 148-156.
Kowall, C. "New Housing for Furnished Room Inhabitants." Mineograph. New York: Office of Special Purpose Housing, Housing and Development Administration, 1970.
Kowall, C. *SRO Housing—A National Need* (Mimeograph). New York: Office of Special Purpose Housing and Development Administration, 1973.
Kowall, C. *The Federal Housing Program and Its Response to the Needs of the SRO Elderly Residents*. A position paper for the 2nd Conference on the Invisible Elderly. St. Louis: St. Louis University, Institute of Applied Gerontology, 1976.
Kratovil, R. "Condominiums and Co-Ops." *Real Estate Law*, 1974, *3*, 381.
Lawton, M.P. "The Relative Impact of Congregate and Traditional Housing on Elderly Tenants." *The Gerontologist*, 1976, *16*, 237-242.
Lawton, M.P. *Environment and Aging*. Monterey, Calif.: Brooks/Cole Publishing Company, 1980. (a)
Lawton, M.P. "Housing the Elderly: Residential Quality and Residential Satisfaction." *Research on Aging*, 1980, *2*, 309-328. (b)
Lawton, M.P. "Alternative Housing." *Journal of Gerontological Social Work*, 1981, *3*, 61-80. (a).
Lawton, M.P. "An Ecological View of Living Arrangements." *The Gerontologist*, 1981, *21*, 59-66. (b)
Lawton, M.P., and Bader, J. "Wish for Privacy by Young and Old." *Journal of Gerontology*, 1970, *25*, 48-54.
Lawton, M.P., and Hoover, S.L. *Housing and Neighborhood: Objective and Subjective Quality*, Philadelphia: Philadelphia Geriatric Center, 1979.
Lawton, M.P., and Nahemow, L. "Ecology and the Aging Process." In C. Eisdorfer and M.P. Lawton (eds.), *Psychology of Adult Development and Aging*. Washington, D.C.: American Psychological Association, 1973, pp. 619-674.
Lawton, M.P., and Yaffe, S. *Victimization of the Elderly and Fear of Crime*. Philadelphia: Philadelphia Geriatric Center, 1979.
Lebowitz, B. "Age and Fearfulness: Personal and Situational Factors." *Journal of Gerontology*, 1975, *30*, 696-700.
Lebowitz, B. "Implications of Community Housing for Policy and Planning." *The Gerontologist*, 1978, *18*, 138-143.
Lee, T. "Urban Neighborhood as Socio-Spatial Schema." In H.M. Proshansky, W.H. Ittelson, and L.G. Rivlin (eds.), *Environmental Psychology*. New York: Holt, Rinehart & Winston, 1970, pp. 349-370.
Levy, H. "Needed: A New Kind of Single Room Occupancy Housing." *Journal of Housing*, 1968, *25*, 572-580.
McAuley, W.J. "Age, Desired Characteristics of the Residential Environment, and Likelihood of Residential Mobility." Paper presented at the Annual Meeting of the Western Gerontological Society, Denver, March 1977.
McConnell, S.R. "House Sharing: An Alternative Living Arrangement for the Elderly." *Generations*, 1979, *3*(3), 24-25.
McConnell, S.R., and Usher, C.E. *Intergenerational House-Sharing*. Los Angeles: University of Southern California, Andrus Gerontology Center, 1979.

Meeuwig, M.J. "Housing and Activities of the Elderly." *Journal of Home Economics,* 1970, *62,* 592–597.
Moos, R.H., and Lemke, S. "Multiphasic Environmental Assessment Procedure: Preliminary Manual." Palo Alto, Calif.: *Social Ecology Laboratory,* Stanford University School of Medicine, 1979.
Moos, R.H., Gauvin, M., Lemke, S., Max, W., and Mehren, B. *The Development of a Sheltered Care Environment Scale: A Preliminary Report.* Paper presented at the Annual Meeting of the Gerontological Society, San Francisco, November 1977.
Murray, H.A. *Explorations in Personality.* New York: Oxford University Press, 1938.
Myers, P. *Neighborhood Conservation and the Elderly.* Washington, D.C.: The Conservation Foundation, 1978.
National Center for Health Statistics. "In Patient Health Facilities." *Vital and Health Statistics, 1976, 14*(16). Rockville, Md.: U.S. Department of Health, Education, and Welfare, 1976.
National Citizens Coalition for Nursing Home Reform. *Boarding Home Issues: A Resource Sheet.* Washington, D.C., May 1981.
National Citizens Coalition for Nursing Home Reform. *Boarding Home Abuse: An Outgrowth of the Deinstitutionalization Process.* Washington, D.C., undated.
Newcomer, R.J. "An Evaluation of Neighborhood Service Convenience for Elderly Housing Project Residents." In P. Suefeld and J.A. Russell (eds.), *The Behavioral Basis of Design* (Vol. 1). Stroudsburg, Pa.: Dowden, Hutchinson and Ross, 1976, pp. 301–307.
Newman, E.S., and Sherman, S.R. "Community Integration of the Elderly in Foster Care Family Care." *Journal of Gerontological Social Work,* 1979, *1,* 175–186.
Peterson, J.A., Hamovitch, M., and Larson, A.E. *Housing Needs and Satisfactions of the Elderly.* Los Angeles: Ethel Percy Andrus Gerontology Center, University of Southern California, 1973.
Rausch, K.J. "Mobile Home Movement." *Generations,* 1979, *3*(3), 34.
Rausch, K.J., and Hoover, S.L. *Mobile Home Elderly: Structural Characteristics of Their Dwellings.* Philadelphia: Philadelphia Geriatric Center, 1980.
Regnier, V.A. "Neighborhoods as Service Systems." In M.P. Lawton, R.J. Newcomer, and T.O. Byerts (eds.), *Planning for an Aging Society.* Stroudsburg, Pa.: Dowden, Hutchinson and Ross, 1976, pp. 240–257.
Regnier, V.A., Eribes, R.A., and Hansen, W. *Cognitive Mapping as a Concept for Establishing Neighborhood Service Deliverly Locations for Older People.* Paper presented at Eighth Annual Association for Computing Machinery Symposium, New York City, 1973.
Rosenberg, G.S. *The Worker Grows Old.* San Francisco: Jossey-Bass, 1970.
Rosow, I. *Social Integration of the Aged.* New York: Free Press, 1967.
Select Committee on Aging, U.S. House of Representatives. *Fires in Boarding Homes: The Tip of the Iceberg.* Washington, D.C.: U.S. Government Printing Office, April 25, 1979.
Select Committee on Aging, U.S. House of Representatives. *Condominium Conversions.* Comm. Pub. No. 96–246. Washington, D.C.: U.S. Government Printing Office, August 29, 1980. (a)
Select Committing on Aging, U.S. House of Representatives. *Income Status of the Rural Elderly.* Comm. Pub. No. 96–253. Washington, D.C.: U.S. Government Printing Office, August 29, 1980. (b)
Select Committing on Aging, U.S. House of Representatives. *Analysis of the Impact of the Proposed Fiscal Year 1982 Budget Cuts on the Elderly.* Comm. Pub. No. 97–273. Washington, D.C.: U.S. Government Printing Office, April 6, 1981. (a).
Select Committing on Aging, U.S. House of Representatives. *Impact of Fiscal Year 1982 Budget Cuts on the Elderly.* Comm. Pub. No. 97–284. Washington, D.C.: U.S. Government Printing Office, April 6, 1981. (b).
Shapiro, J. "Single Room Occupancy: Community of the Alone." *Social Work,* 1966, *11*(4), 24–33.
Shapiro, J. *Communities of the Alone: Working with Single Room Occupants in the City.* New York: Association Press, 1971.
Sherman, S.R., and Newman, E.S. "Foster-Family Care for the Elderly in New York State. *The Gerontologist,* 1977, *17,* 513–519.

Siegal, H. *Outposts of the Forgotten, New York City's Welfare Hotels and Single Room Occupancy Tenements.* Edison, N.J.: Transaction Books, 1977.

Silverstone, B. "The Social, Physical, and Legal Implications for Adult Foster Care: A Contrast with Other Models." In N.K. Haygood and R.E. Dunkle (eds.), *Perspectives on Adult Foster Care.* Cleveland, Ohio: Human Services Design Laboratory, Case Western Reserve University, 1978, pp. 29-37.

Sjoberg, G. "Community." In J. Gould and W.L. Kolls (eds.), *Dictionary of the Social Sciences.* New York: Free Press, 1964.

Sokolovsky, J., and Cohen, C. "The Cultural Meaning of Personal Networks for the Inner-City Elderly. *Urban Antropology,* 1978, *7,* 323-342.

Stephens, J. *Loners, Losers, and Lovers.* Seattle: University of Washington Press, 1976.

Streib, G.F. "An Alternative Family Form for Older Persons: Need and Social Context. *The Family Coordinator,* 1978, *27,* 413-420.

Streib, G.F., and Streib, R.B. "Communes and the Aging." *American Behavioral Scientist,* 1975, *19,* 176-189.

Struyk, R. "The Housing Situation of the Elderly Americans." *The Gerontologist,* 1977, *17,* 130-139.

Sussman, M.B. "The Family Life of Older People. In R.H. Binstock and E. Shanas (eds.), *Handbook of Aging and the Social Sciences.* New York: Van Nostrand, 1976, pp. 218-243.

Teski, M. *Living Together: An Ethnography of a Retirement Hotel.* Washington, D.C.: University Press of America, 1979.

Tissue, T. "Old Age, Poverty, and the Central City." *International Journal of Aging and Human Development,* 1971, *2,* 235-248.

U.S. Department of Housing and Urban Development. *Condominium/Cooperative Study 1-7.* Washington, D.C., July 1975.

U.S. Department of Housing and Urban Development. *How Well Are We Housed? 5. Rural.* Washington, D.C.: Office of Policy Development and Research, 1976.

U.S. Department of Housing and Urban Development. *Report to Congress: Rental Housing: A National Problem That Needs Immediate Attention.* Washington, D.C.: November 8, 1979. (a)

U.S. Department of Housing and Urban Development. *Report to Congress Identifying Boarding Homes Housing the Needy Aged, Blind, and Disabled: A Major Step Toward Resolving a National Problem.* November 19, 1979. (b)

Urban Systems Research and Engineering. *Evaluation of the Effectiveness of Congregate Housing for the Elderly.* Washington, D.C.: U.S. Department of Housing and Urban Development, 1976.

Wallin, P.L. "Home Ownership Problems of the Elderly." *Clearinghouse Review,* August-September 1972, *6,* 227-232.

Weitzman, J. "Mobile Homes: High Cost Housing in Low Income Market." *Journal of Economic Issues,* 1976, 576-597.

Wood, E.F. "Condominium Conversion and the Elderly." In J.A. Weiss, *Law of the Elderly.* New York: Practicing Law Institute, 1977, 323-336.

Zorbaugh, H.W. *The Gold Coast and the Slum: A Sociological Study of Chicago's Near North Side.* Chicago: University of Chicago Press, 1929.

7

The Surveillance Zone as Meaningful Space for the Aged

Graham D. Rowles

> Yeah, everybody who comes in here says, "My goodness, you can see all over town. You really have it nice here." . . . I don't know what I'd done if it hadn't been for this window you know . . . I think if everybody had something like this, they wouldn't feel so closed in.
> —Peggy, 71 years old

> The outside space is more important than the inside space, I think.
> —Lucinda, 64 years old

In recent years there has been much concern with exploring the meaning of "home" as a distinctive realm of space (Bachelard, 1969; Bollnow, 1967; Buttimer, 1980; Eliade, 1959; Loyd, 1975; Porteous, 1976; Rakoff, 1977). It has been argued that home may come to assume considerable emotional significance for old people (Gelwicks, 1970; Holcomb, 1980). However, concern with the meaning of home has tended to blind us to the importance of other spaces.

Immediately outside each dwelling is an area that can be viewed from the windows. This space within the visual field of a residence may be formally defined as the *surveillance zone*.[1] This zone mediates between the sacred space of home and the more remote community environment beyond the visual field. For many

---

From *The Gerontologist*, 21, 3 (June 1981), pp. 304-11. Reprinted by permission of *The Gerontologist*.

The research reported in this article was supported by a grant from the NIA (AG 00862).

old people, particularly the housebound who may spend much time at the window, the surveillance zone represents a primary focus of participation in the world beyond the threshold.

Several studies have suggested the significance of the surveillance zone as the area in which the activities of young children can be monitored by their parents (Fanning, 1967; Hart, 1979; Jacobs, 1961; Jephcott, 1971; Michelson, 1969). However, little in-depth study of the structure, use, and meaning of this space for old people has been undertaken, even though in a 1974 national study of housing for the elderly, 46.8% of the sample interviewed responded positively to the question, "Do you spend much time sitting by a window to watch people or views outside?" (Howell, 1976). In this study the surveillance zone is explored as an arena for "watching" and "being watched," in which visual reciprocity facilitates the emergence and maintenance of practical and social support from neighbors, and as a space which often comes to provide an important source of ongoing environmental participation and a sense of identity for the old person. These observations are viewed as themes within a developmental perspective on the role of the surveillance zone in the old person/environment transaction. Finally, some implications for the location, design, and landscaping of housing for the elderly are considered.

Growing Old in an Appalachian Community

The environmental experience of old people living in Colton,[2] a dying Appalachian mountain community, has been explored over the past 3 years (Rowles, 1980a). Approximately 400 people live here. Much of the population consists of elderly persons who remain despite a deteriorating physical setting. Using an experiential methodology (Rowles, 1978b), 15 long-time residents of Colton ranging in age from 64 to 93 years have been worked with intensively. Through three summers' residence in the community and weekly visits during the remainder of the past 3 years, the author has established an interpersonal climate in which it has been possible to reveal dimensions of experience that are customarily taken for granted. In exploring the significance of surveillance zones in these old people's lives, lengthy tape-recorded conversations have been complemented by semi-structured interviews, discussions with neighbors, participant observation, the mapping of surveillance zones, and photography (including aerial photography to define spatial relationships within the area surrounding each home).

Characteristics of Surveillance Zones

It is useful to start by describing physical characteristics of surveillance zones in order to provide a measure of the arena potentially available to each old person. There is considerable variation among the participants in the maximum visual range of surveillance (Exhibit 7.1). For some, like 89-year-old Bertha, the surveillance zone, as a result of home location and topography, provides visual access across the entire valley. At the other extreme, for Jennifer Rose, 70 years old, living on a wooded stretch of highway outside Colton, the available visual field is limited to a few yards and incorporates no inhabited buildings. Most par-

EXHIBIT 7.1
Audrey's Surveillance Zone

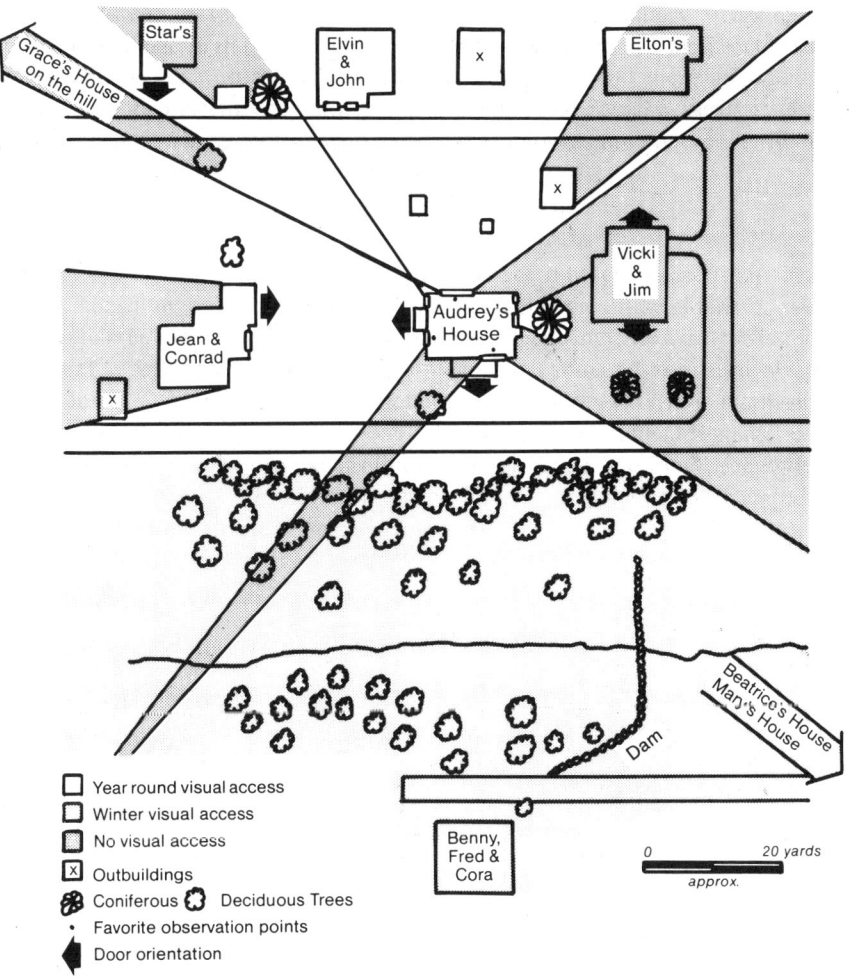

ticipants fall between these extremes. Their visual field embraces several adjacent houses.

Surveillance potential involves more than proximity. Consideration of the area surrounding 81-year-old Audrey's home reveals important directional variation (Exhibit 7.1). Audrey is surrounded by residences. She has a clear view of Jean's and Conrad's house and the home of Elvin and John (two men in their fifties) who share a home to the rear of her house. However, visual access to her closest neighbor's home (Vicki's and Jim's) is limited by the position of an evergreen tree and by the nonalignment of windows between the two homes. These barriers, reinforced by incompatible door orientation, have a significant impact on her relationship with this neighbor:

> She doesn't watch me like the others do, because she can't see from her window.... She said, "I'm sorry. I don't think I do enough for you like the other neighbors do."... She said, "I look over at night, but you know the way my windows are arranged, from the living room I can't see at all."... I said, "Why Vicki, you really are not my next door neighbor either because there is no door opening from your house towards me." When they come out, the go out on the other side, they never come over on this side.

The seasons also affect the visual range of surveillance. In the summer when the leaves are on the trees Audrey cannot see across the valley to the home of Benny, the youth for whom she babysat when he was a child and with whom she maintains a strong relationship as a surrogate "grandmother."

One effect of such surveillance zone characteristics is that each participant has tended to develop a pattern of surveillance favoring particular directions and using only those windows providing a good visual panorama (Exhibit 7.2). Audrey uses windows in the front, in the back, and to one side of her house. Other participants make frequent use of a single window. In sum, each individual's home provides a distinctive potential for visual participation in the space outside. How exactly is the surveillance zone transformed from an opportunity into a resource?

Use of the Surveillance Zone

Much time is spent *watching*. Many of the participants profess to wandering from window to window during the day as they monitor events outside. In addition to the change of vista this affords, it also reduces the chances of being perceived as "nosy." As Lucinda notes:

> They always told me it was bad manners to stare out the window at somebody. If I'd look out the window, I'd kind of do it from behind the curtain.

EXHIBIT 7.2
Surveillance Zone Characteristics

Participant	Maximum Visual Range (Yards)	Number of Windows Used	Orientation of Windows Used		
			Front	Back	Sides
Jennifer Rose	50	1	X		
Audrey	200	4	X	X	1
Nell	200	2	X		
Rebecca	200	2	X	X	
Beatrice†	400	3	X		2
Walter†	400‡	2	X		1
Nakoma	400	3	X		2
Lucinda(1)*	800	1	X		
Lucinda(2)	400	2	X	X	
Asel	800‡	3	X	X	1
Mary	800	4	X	X	1
Bill	800	2	X		1
JoNell	1200	—	No evidence		
Bertha	1200	1	X		
Peggy	1200	2	X		1
Dan	1600	3	X		2

* Lucinda relocated during the course of the research.
† Married couple.
‡ Reduced by poor vision.

Some watching has a practical purpose. Bertha watches for the newspaper carrier; Audrey looks for the mailman; 93-year-old Asel oversees a garden that is the center of his life. In the summer, he will stand at his kitchen sink and watch for stray dogs or other predators which might disrupt the order of his immaculate rows of vegetables. Monitoring the activities of children is a favorite pastime. This may on occasion take a more active form as the old person, acting as surrogate parent, intervenes to arbitrate disputes or impose sanctions on unruly behavior.

Sometimes watching can lead to actions transcending the "nosiness" of which old people are often accused. Nell, 84 years old, recounts an incident related to monitoring activities outside the house at the foot of the hillside where she lives:

> One evening they came home from work, and Karen (their child) got out of this side of the car, and I thought, it looked like she didn't shut the door. . . . I didn't

pay much attention to it, I was busy crocheting in the living room and had my television on. About 9:00 p.m., I came out here and it looked like there was a light on in the car. They had gone to bed. I could tell, their lights were all out. So, I called down, I said, "Peter, this is your nosy neighbor, Nell, on the hill. Looks to me like there is a light on in your car." He said, "Oh my goodness." He said if I hadn't called him, the battery would have gone clear down. He said, "Well, I'm glad we've got nosy neighbors like that."

Many old people engage in a process of "setting up" for watching. They select windows providing the best vantage and then arrange their furniture and provide themselves with supports to facilitate monitoring space outside. Generally, windows are selected to provide for viewing active rather than passive scenes. Supports for observation range from prudent placement of a chair to more elaborate and frequently unconscious forms of "setting up." Audrey, whose balance is sometimes a little unsteady, likes to stand leaning against the back of a chair placed by her front window. Peggy has her telephone, her C.B. transmitter, notepads and pencils, her latest sewing project, and the television remote control all within easy arm's reach. Perhaps the best example of this process is provided by the way in which, aided by her family, Bertha set herself up during an illness when she was confined to her bed (Exhibit 7.3). The entire room was rearranged so that she had access to all her needs within arm's length of her bed. A key component of this "setting up" was placement of the bed to facilitate watching events outside. She could see who came to the door, keep an eye on her neighbors, and watch the trains.

During the summer, the process of surveillance is made easier by the ability to sit outside and to watch and be watched from the porch (Lozier and Althouse, 1975). As Audrey notes:

> I can see everybody that goes by. Everybody waves to me. And I don't know some of the people, but they wave too.... I guess they feel a little old lady is sitting there. They think, "Well, maybe, she's lonesome."

A second important use of the surveillance zone stems from this visual reciprocity. In addition to watching, there is the important support provided by *being watched*. Most of the Colton elderly have established close relationships with neighbors in their surveillance zone that incorporate systems of signals to monitor each other's well-being. Audrey provides a good example of such a system as she describes how she is watched by neighbors to the rear of her home.

> They watch for the curtain to be opened in the morning. He (Elvin) told me that. He said, "Do you know, you get up about eight?" I said, "Yes, I do." He said, "Well, at that time, I'm usually standing there at my kitchen window with a cup of coffee in my hand watching for your curtains to be opened."

EXHIBIT 7.3
"Setting Up": Bertha's Surveillance Zone

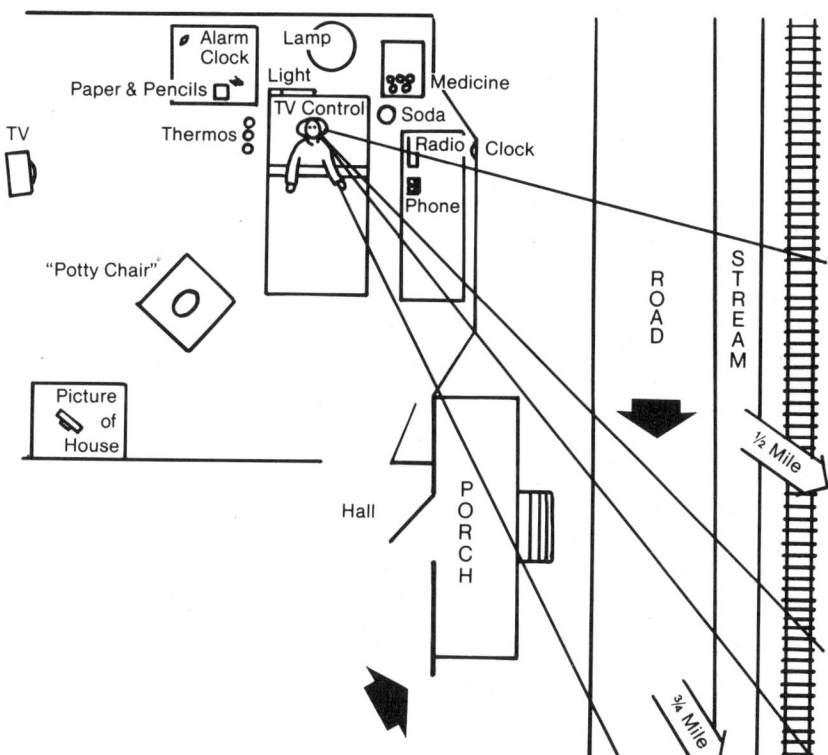

She went on to describe how Jean, another neighbor, watched for her to open the drapes in her bedroom each morning: "There's a signal. I couldn't lay in bed sick very long, because they'd find me," she concluded. A sense of security derives from such knowledge.

Continual visual contact between the old person and neighbors often facilitates the development of *practical support*. This is especially important for the many old residents of Colton who live alone. Nell provides an excellent example of such everyday support. Neighbors within her surveillance zone bring in the mail from the roadside mailbox, pick up items from the grocery store, provide assistance with interpreting tax forms, and fix leaky faucets. They also provide opportunities for getting out. Like many of her peers, Nell is transported to church by neighbors within the surveillance zone. During winter, the level of practical support is sufficient to sustain her for several months without ever leaving home.

In some cases, support is available from family members. It enables the old person to remain independent longer than might otherwise be possible. Asel's youngest daughter lives within view of his kitchen window. Each day she brings his lunch at noon. Her husband calls in before he leaves for work to bring the medicine Asel might otherwise forget to take.

Practical support from within the surveillance zone is especially important during crisis situations. When a youth broke into the rear of her house, Nell had just enough time to telephone Bill on the street below before she was assaulted. He was able to reach her home in less than a minute. This probably saved her from injuries more severe than the cracked ribs she sustained. Less spectacular emergencies may also be dealt with by neighbors within the surveillance zone. In time of illness, they will handle visitors, call the old person's family to keep them informed of their loved one's status, and if hospitalization is necessary, will often take in the mail, service the furnace, and in general act as guardians of the old person's home.

Practical support invariably is coupled with strong *social support,* sustained through frequent visits and telephone calls. Audrey talks about the visits she receives from her neighbor Elvin:

> About every Sunday afternoon, he comes down for an hour. If there is anybody here, he doesn't. If he sees a car he doesn't. But if not, on Sunday, he'll come down for an hour to see me. I enjoy him.

Indeed, over time, as a cluster of people within the old person's surveillance zone develop stronger and stronger functional and social ties, and as a sense of mutual obligation evolves, this arena gradually becomes a distinctive social space (Buttimer, 1969; Lozier and Althouse, 1975).

The Surveillance Zone as a Source of Meaning

To fully understand the significance of surveillance zones in the lives of the Colton elderly, it is necessary to view this space in the context of the old person's total life experience. When Audrey stands and gazes at the falling snow, and when Asel sits watching the workmen remove rubble from the burnt-out shell of the house next door—what are they thinking? How does this activity fit into their lives?

First, the space, and the process of surveillance it fosters, provides a crucial link between the old person and the contemporary world outside, a sense of ongoing *participation* in events. Monitoring the rhythm of life in the contemporary space provides a "field of caring." Often involvement extends to vicarious participation. As Audrey wistfully observes:

You know after you've gone to church all your life, it's hard not to be able to. I sit here and look out the window and watch them all go, and then I turn the TV on and listen. It's the next best thing. . . . Sunday, I look out more, because I'm watching people go to church. Since I can't go to church, I watch the cars go by, watch Jean and Conrad leaving, McCories, all of them . . . and then at noon, I watch them all come back.

Asel reveals the same process when he explains how he sits watching the men work on the demolition of the house next door and works out how he would tackle the job. For a time he can participate vicariously, almost turning back the clock.

Participation in outside space has an historical as well as a contemporary aspect. This may be especially important to old people immersed in reminiscence or engaged in the process of life review that studies have suggested are important facets of old age (Butler, 1963; Lewis, 1971; Lieberman and Falk, 1971; McMahon and Rhudick, 1967; Merriam, 1980). The surveillance zone may provide a mirror to the old person's life. If the person has lived in the community for many years, as is the case with most of the participants in this research, physical cues within the visual field may act as symbols of the past and provide a stimulus to reflection. Within Jennifer Rose's visual field, there is a half-constructed garage her husband started to build 30 years ago. The project was never completed. It remains as a physical legacy that stirs fond memories. Beatrice, 84 years old, when she looks out of her front room can see the broken dam that many years ago impounded many gallons of water. In the winter this provided a skating rink for the children. The pond is now filled with silt, but each time she looks at it, there is the potential to revive memories of her youth. The scene within the surveillance zone also serves to sustain memories of people who inhabited this space. I found that Nell could trace an elaborate social history of each home within her surveillance zone, replete with vivid accounts of incidents that transpired many decades ago.

Contemporary events within the surveillance zone may also trigger reminiscence and encourage a form of "gazing" behavior I have often noted as old people stare out of their windows, seemingly becoming oblivious to my presence. I asked Audrey to share her thoughts as she stared out at a recent snowfall: "I thought about my poor mother doing all that dressing on me, and putting me out there. And oh, just little things." Such "little things" may be extremely important in maintaining a sense of identity.

Developmental Significance of Surveillance Zones

In seeking to assess the significance of the surveillance zone in old people's lives, it is useful to adopt a developmental perspective and to consider this space in relation to changing activity levels over the lifespan (Exhibit 7.4). We may hypothesize that the surveillance zone assumes particular importance during two stages of life, although for different reasons. In childhood, this space is the arena in which the child is allowed to play; an arena defined by parental sanctions of surveillance which limit the wanderings of the child. Space within sight of home may thus come to assume special significance (Hart, 1979). As the child grows and is permitted to venture farther afield, this space becomes progressively less important. During adulthood, because much time is spent away from home, the surveillance zone may be of limited consequence.

As physiological capability declines in old age, the surveillance zone once again assumes increasing importance, one of a variety of transitions that occur in the old person/environment transaction as the individual becomes increasingly environmentally vulnerable. Most views of aging acknowledge reduced mobility and a gradual constriction of the old person's activity space (Montgomery, 1977; Pastalan and Carson, 1970; Windley et al., 1975). As this transition occurs, progressively more time is spent at home. However, this is something of an oversimplification. There are a variety of compensations in other dimensions of the old person's environmental experience (Rowles, 1978a, 1980b, 1981). In "an hypothesis of changing emphasis" I have suggested that vicarious involvement in environments displaced in space (the worlds of children) and/or time (places of one's past) often becomes a substitute for physical participation. As these transitions occur, there is some reorientation in the functional role of particular realms of space and in the affective meaning with which they are imbued. Home becomes a more salient space in terms of both the individual's time and emotional

EXHIBIT 7.4
Developmental Significance of the Surveillance Zone

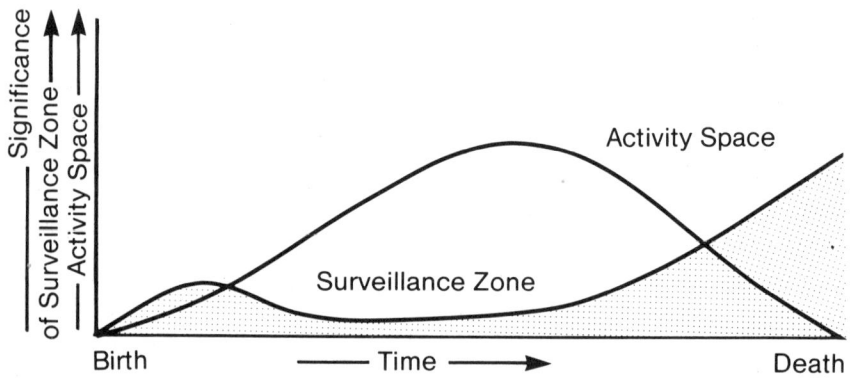

investment. More important in the context of this discussion, adjacent space, the surveillance zone, becomes a more pervasive component of the individual's lifespace as it begins to assume the array of functions I have described. For the housebound or institutionalized old person, the surveillance zone may come to represent the major arena of direct contact with the world outside (Rowles, 1979). Considering these transitions in association with other postulated developmental changes—an increased propensity for reminiscence and the process of life review (Butler, 1963; Merriam, 1980)—it becomes possible to see how the surveillance zone, in additon to its practical and social significance, can become a focus of meaning for the elderly, long-time resident of a community.

Some Implications

There is considerable variation in the characteristics, use, and meaning of the surveillance zone among the old people of Colton. This raises important research questions. Is the surveillance zone important to *all* old people? Is it experienced in the same manner, or are particular themes within surveillance zone utilization more significant to certain subgroups? Does the significance of the surveillance zone vary systematically with age or health status? What role does personality play in surveillance zone utilization? To what extent is interpersonal variation merely a function of location and the different surveillance zone potentials generated by alternative housing arrangements and designs? The Colton elderly are long-time residents of old single-family-housing stock. They have had the time to accumulate the temporal depth of meaning within their surveillance zones that makes them reservoirs of cues to reflection. Are old people without similar length of residence, of those who relocate to new housing, able to harness surveillance zones, or must they forego the identity-reinforcing function of this space? What is the role of this space in other environmental settings? In urban neighborhoods? In special housing for the elderly? In institutional settings?

Several philosophical dilemmas also emerge. One of the most interesting concerns attitudes toward old people. It is perhaps appropriate to reassess a prevalent association between the watchful elderly neighbor and images of "the busybody": such behavior may be no more than an adaptation to more limited personal circumstances. On the other hand, this acknowledgement raises the crucial problem of reconciling legitimate privacy needs with the supportive potential of surveillance. Assuming such dilemmas can be resolved, what are the implications for providing improved living situations for old people?

First, there are ramifications with regard to the *location and orientation of new housing*. Siting in settings surrounded by other homes is clearly desirable. Prudent orientation can also facilitate the creation and use of surveillance zones, although here the issue of privacy must be considered, particularly in an intergenerational context. Some young families may resent the prospect of being constantly watched, however beneficial this may be for their elderly neighbor. Location and orientation affording the potential for overlooking "active" scenes is also preferable to the provision of tranquil vistas of rustic beauty.

Advantages of location and orientation can be complemented by *housing design* (Howell, 1980). Complementary door orientation facilitates both visual and social contact. The height of window ledges and the size of windows can also foster or preclude surveillance. Bertha explains why she adamantly refused to move to Dallas to live in her daughter's modern ranch-style house:

> The windows is [sic] all up so high that you can't see out. These new houses, you know, the windows, they aren't down like this. They're up high, and all the people keeps draperies and everything all over the windows, so you can't see out. And I like to see out. If I had to stay in that house, all that time, and couldn't see out, and couldn't go no place... I'm better at home.

One strategy to overcome this problem, utilized by Peggy, was replacement of her small living room window with a picture window with a lower sill that provided a clear vista across the center of Colton. Interior design and arrangement of rooms in both new and refurbished housing could also be undertaken to more fully acknowledge the importance of surveillance zones and facilitate the process of "setting up."

Moving outside the house, greater sensitivity to the *content and landscaping of space within the surveillance zone* can enhance the environmental experience of the old person. The need for such awareness is illustrated by Beatrice as she talks about the impact of her neighbor Jeff's recent construction of a workshop on the side of his house on her relationship with his wife, Sarah:

> Ever since Jeff built all that stuff in between us, we said we might as well live ten miles apart. We don't see each other you know. We used to look out the kitchen window and wave, and point and make signs. And we could tell when they got up, and they could tell when we got up and went to bed. . . . It's different now.

How often do we unwittingly impoverish the lives of old people and increase their isolation by closing them in through construction, design modification, or merely by planting a tree?

Perhaps the most important implications are attitudinal. It is necessary to seek deeper understanding of the particular meaning of the surveillance zone to old people. To the child, space immediately beyond the threshold is a source of adventure, the scene of first explorations and, at the same time, an arena of security under mother's watchful gaze. To the old person, it may become not only a source of functional support but also a symbol of continuity and continuing participation within a world from which one is physically withdrawing. Yet we have an unfortunate propensity for homogenizing space and viewing its use in unidimensional terms. As we pass by the house where the lady is always peeking out from behind the curtain, we may feel a certain resentment at her nosiness. On her part, she may feel a twinge of guilt at her behavior. In reality, neither party understands the significance of a scenario that is far from trivial.

Notes

1. The surveillance zone, defined as space within the visual field of home, assumes increasing significance as people grow older and spend more time at home. Using insights from a 3 year participant observation study in an Appalachian community, this paper describes characteristics of the surveillance zone and explores its meaning for old people. The process of monitoring events outside, the emergence of watchful reciprocal social networks, and the potential of the surveillance zone for generating a sense of personal identity are explored. Implications for locating and designing environments for the elderly are traced.
2. Colton is a pseudonym, as are all proper names in this chapter.

References

Bachelard, G. *The Poetics of Space.* Boston: Beacon Press, 1969.
Bollnow, O. "Lived Space." In N. Lawrence and D. O'Connor, *Readings in Existential Phenomenology.* Englewood Cliffs, NJ: Prentice Hall, 1967.
Butler, R.N. "The Life Review: An Interpretation of Reminiscence in the Aged." *Psychiatry,* 1963, *26,* 65–76.
Buttimer, A. "Social Space in Interdisciplinary Perspective." *Geographical Review,* 1969, *59,* 417–426.
Buttimer, A. "Home, Reach, and the Sense of Place." In A. Buttimer and D. Seamon (eds.), *The Human Experience of Space and Place.* London: Croom Helm, 1980.
Eliade, Mircea. *The Sacred and the Profane.* New York: Harcourt, Brace and World, Inc., 1959.
Fanning, D.M. "Families in Flats." *British Medical Journal,* 1967, *18,* 382–386.
Gelwicks, L.E. "Home Range and the Use of Space by an Aging Population." In L.A. Pastalan and D.H. Carson (eds.), *Spatial Behavior of Older People.* Ann Arbor, MI: University of Michigan–Wayne State University, Institute of Gerontology, 1970.
Hart, R. *Children's Experience of Place.* Irvington, New York: Halsted Press, 1979.
Holcomb, B., and Parkoff, B. "Sex Differences in the Role of Home Place Among the Elderly." Paper presented at the annual meeting of the Association of American Geographers, Louisville, Kentucky, 1980.
Howell, S.C. "Designing for the Elderly: Windows." Design evaluation project, Department of Architecture, Massachusetts Institute of Technology, Cambridge, 1976.
Howell, S.C. *Designing for Aging.* Cambridge, MA: M.I.T. Press, 1980.
Jacobs, J. *The Death and Life of Great American Cities.* New York: Vintage Books, 1961.
Jephcott, P. *Homes in High Flats.* Edinburgh: Oliver and Boyd, 1971.
Lewis, C.N. "Reminiscing and Self-Concept in Old Age." *Journal of Gerontology,* 1971, *26,* 240–243.
Lieberman, M.A., and Falk, J.M. "The Remembered Past as a Source of Data for Research on the Life Cycle." *Human Development,* 1971, *14,* 132–141.
Lozier, J., and Althouse, R. "Retirement to the Porch in Rural Appalachia." *International Journal of Aging and Human Development,* 1975, *6,* 7–15.
McMahon, A.W., and Rhudick, P.J. "Reminiscing in the Aged: An Adaptational Response." In S. Levin and R.J. Kahana (eds.), *Psychodynamic Studies on Aging: Creativity, Reminiscence, and Dying.* New York: International Universities Press, 1967.

Merriam, S. "The Concept and Function of Reminiscence: A Review of the Research." *Gerontologist,* 1980, *20,* 604–608+.
Michelson, W. *Man and His Urban Environment: A Sociological Approach.* Reading, MA: Addison–Wesley, 1970.
Montgomery, J.E. "The Housing Patterns of Older People." In R. Kalish (ed.), *The Later Years: Social Applications of Gerontology.* Montery, CA: Brooks Cole, 1977.
Pastalan, L.A., and Carson, D.H. (eds.). *Spatial Behavior of Older People.* Ann Arbor, MI: University of Michigan–Wayne State University, Institute of Gerontology, 1970.
Porteous, J.D. "Home: The Territorial Core." *Geographical Review,* 1976, *66,* 383–390.
Rakoff, R.M. "Ideology in Everyday Life: The Meaning of the House." *Politics and Society,* 1977, *7,* 85–104.
Rowles, G.D. *Prisoners of Space? Exploring the Geographical Experience of Older People.* Boulder, CO: Westview Press, 1978(a).
Rowles, G.D. "Reflections on Experiential Fieldwork." In D. Ley and M. Samuels (eds.), *Humanistic Geography: Prospects and Problems.* Chicago: Maaroufa Press, 1978(b).
Rowles, G.D. "The Last New Home: Facilitating the Older Person's Adjustment to Institutional Space." In S. Golant (ed.), *Location and Environment of the Elderly Population.* Washington, DC: V.H. Winston and Sons, 1979.
Rowles, G.D. "Growing Old 'Inside': Aging and Attachment to Place in an Appalachian Community." In N. Datan and N. Lohmann (eds.), *Transitions of Aging.* New York: Academic Press, 1980(a).
Rowles, G.D. "Toward a Geography of Growing Old." In A. Buttimer and D. Seamon (eds.), *The Human Experience of Space and Place.* London: Croom Helm, 1980(b).
Rowles, G.D. Geographic Perspectives on Human Development." *Human Development,* 1981, *24,* 67–76.
Windley, P.G., Byerts, T.O., and Ernst, F.G. *Theory Development in Environment and Aging.* Washington, DC: Gerontological Society, 1975.

8

Increasing Housing Opportunities for the Elderly

Carole R. Shifman

The median age of the U.S. population is on the rise. In fact, people over the age of 65 are proportionately the fastest-growing group in the United States.[1] Between 1970 and 1980, this segment of our population grew from 20.1 to 25.5 million, an increase of approximately 28 percent.[2] Projections show that this group will more than double in size between 1977 and 2035.[3] As the impacts of this trend become more apparent, cities will have to consider ways to address the housing needs of this aging population.

In recent years, a variety of financial, legislative, and programmatic responses to the need for housing for the elderly have been developed. This report will focus on one of these approaches: the adoption of special zoning ordinances. Zoning is a limited approach, but, used in conjunction with other approaches, it may be useful in encouraging a range of housing alternatives to meet the needs of elderly people.

There are arguments in favor of zoning ordinances designed for elderly populations and arguments against such zoning. Nevertheless, there is a growing body of legal precedent to support the practice, and the use of zoning as a means of encouraging the provision of housing for the elderly appears to be increasing.

Reprinted with permission from *Increasing Housing Opportunities for the Elderly,* PAS Report 381, copyright 1983 by the American Planning Association.

This report considers arguments for and against age-specific zoning for the elderly, as well as the history of such zoning. The report also will explore recent regulations and trends in the use of zoning as a mechanism for addressing the housing needs of the elderly. It will highlight as well the impact of some innovative zoning mechanisms on housing developments for older people.

There is no established definition of "elderly" on which all communities agree. The term is used to refer to people of a broad range of ages, usually anywhere from 55 years old and up. Some zoning ordinances define elderly differently for various housing alternatives; others adopt one of several definitions used by federal agencies for particular programs. Some ordinances do not define elderly at all. In this report, "zoning for the elderly" will refer to ordinances geared to the needs of a population that meets the delineated criteria in a particular ordinance, program, or area.

Arguments in Favor of Zoning for the Elderly

Older people's housing needs differ from those of the general population, particularly as they advance in age. In a paper presented at the American Planning Association's National Conference in 1980, Katharine Warner, of the University of Michigan, noted that 70 percent of elderly people own their homes. Yet, in many cases, either physical limitations and/or economic constraints make it difficult for older people to repair and maintain these houses. The situation is compounded by the fact that a significant number of these households consist of single women who may have little or no experience in home maintenance. Warner cited studies indicating that many older people would welcome a more maintenance-free housing situation.

These elderly homeowners may also be "overhoused." In other words, older people often remain in the homes in which they raised their families. This creates a twofold problem: first, the home is usually larger than an elderly couple or individual needs and is able to maintain, and second, such overhousing contributes to a shortage of housing for younger families. Relocation to housing specifically designed for the needs of an elderly population or remodeling to provide accessory apartments is appropriate in many situations.

Whether older people prefer to live in relatively segregated situations, or whether they prefer to live among people of all age groups probably depends on the individual. Housing experts and gerontologists tend to agree, however, that housing for elderly people should be located near public transportation, commercial establishments, and medical and support services. General public sentiment is increasingly opposed to unnecessary institutionalization of elderly people. Instead, efforts are being made to develop housing alternatives for the elderly that will facilitate privacy and independence, while providing necessary support services. In-home (or on-site) provision of medical care, meals, housekeeping services, and recreational facilities is particularly desirable as residents become infirm or too old to care for themselves.

Zoning can be used to address these "elderly specific" needs in several ways. First, ordinances can authorize a range of housing alternatives; each alternative, from accessory apartments to high-rise developments, may be designed to address the needs of different groups of elderly people.

Second, zoning ordinances can help to make such developments economically feasible. There have been indications that without some modification of density and/or parking requirements developers will not build housing for the elderly.

Third, many zoning ordinances emphasize traditional single-family developments. Thus, they may restrict the number of unrelated individuals who share a single-family house, prohibit the installation of an additional unit in a traditional house, or prevent placement of a separate unit on a single-family lot. These restrictions preclude the development of congregate housing, accessory apartments, and echo housing, respectively, all of which are increasingly popular housing alternatives for older people. In order to address the specialized housing needs of elderly people, through these techniques and others, local zoning ordinances must be modified. It is important that these modifications be designed carefully to ensure that housing for the elderly is developed under proper standards, protecting both the elderly population and the community at large.

Arguments Against Zoning for the Elderly

Although adoption of zoning modifications for elderly residents is generally accepted, there are reasons why a city might want to avoid such zoning amendments. Among these reasons are the potential exclusionary impact of zoning for the elderly, the possibility that housing needs of elderly residents are not significantly different from the rest of the population, and the fear that elderly-specific zoning might result in lower property standards.

Conceivably, zoning for the elderly could be used as a tool to discourage young families from settling in a community. An ordinance that is very narrowly drawn may, in fact, be an attempt to avoid the high costs of additional public schools and recreational facilities that are traditionally associated with young families. Granted, it is possible that an ordinance tailored to the needs of the elderly could have an exclusionary impact; the same can be said of any zoning ordinance directed at the needs of a particular population. Certainly an ordinance can be carefully designed to avoid exclusionary impacts and yet address the needs it is intended to meet.

Some opponents of zoning for the elderly point out that the housing needs of people aged 55 and up tend to mirror those of the general population. To support this argument they cite the results of a recent study of parking space requirements in developments for the elderly in Maryland.[4] These findings contradict the generally accepted assumption that elderly people have fewer cars and drive less than the general population. Instead, the study found that car ownership and the driving habits of elderly people depend more on their health, income, and living situation than on their age alone. Using this fact, opponents argue that the housing needs of elderly people vary as much as the housing needs of nonelderly people and are met through traditional zoning mechanisms.

Elderly people are not a generic group. Their housing needs and preferences may differ with age, health, income, class, and location, to name a few variables. However, it is clear that many elderly people, particularly as they grow older, do develop specialized medical, social, and physical needs that can be met by design. Careful studies of the elderly population in a particular city can indicate exactly what their needs are. A special ordinance narrowly tailored to meet those specific needs will avoid reliance on questionable generalizations.

Finally, zoning ordinances for the elderly frequently authorize higher density, smaller units and fewer parking spaces per unit than are required for other residential developments. Opponents of elderly-specific zoning argue that, in addition to inaccurately reflecting the needs of the elderly population, these allowances might result in lower property standards. This contention is based on the fear that units developed for elderly residents will be inadequate for future use by young families or other nonelderly populations. However, recognition of the need for specialized housing for elderly citizens should not be used as a justification to authorize housing that is substandard. Ordinances that allow special standards for housing for the elderly must ensure that the requirements are adequate. If ordinances are carefully developed with minimum standards and proper documentation of the needs of elderly couples and individuals, there is no reason why the housing developed under those ordinances should not suffice for younger couples and individuals as well.

The Legality of Age-Restrictive Zoning

Prior to 1974, the legality of age-restrictive zoning[5] was unclear. This uncertainty was based partially on case law that reflected the traditional theory that a zoning ordinance may regulate the use of the land, but not the user. Since zoning for the elderly was not considered entirely legal, such early ordinances were usually quite narrow in scope.

In 1974, local authority to use age-restrictive zoning was clarified. In the *Village of Belle Terre v. Boraas,* 416 U.S.1 (1974), the Supreme Court indicated that restricting occupancy of an area to a certain group of people was permissible, as long as the restriction had a valid legislative purpose and was accomplished "reasonably." Subsequent decisions upheld the legality of age-restrictive zoning and extended local authority to do so in a fairly broad manner. Thus, zoning ordinances for the elderly drafted after 1974 tend to be more comprehensive than their earlier counterparts.

It is important to note, however, that age-restrictive zoning ordinances may not interfere with a person's constitutionally protected right to live with members of his/her extended family.[6] Most zoning ordinances designed to regulate housing for the elderly delineate certain characteristics in order to establish occupancy standards for projects. For example, the ordinance adopted in Brunswick, Ohio, in 1983, restricts occupancy in the following way.

> Occupancy is restricted to persons *60 years of age or older* with the following exceptions.
>
> A. A spouse under 60 years of age married to one over that age.
> B. Children over 18 years of age residing with at least one parent over 60 years of age.
> C. Adults under 60 years of age if their presence is required to minister to an occupant over 60 years of age.
> D. Adults of any age who are related to, or on the basis of friendship desire to live with, an occupant who is 60 years or older.
> E. Handicapped or infirm adults over age 18 whose disability requires the special amenities and services of a senior citizen complex.[7]

It is conceivable that circumstances (young, orphaned grandchildren living with elderly grandparents, for example) could create a living situation that violated the above requirements. Should a city attempt to evict an elderly occupant because of such a living arrangement, it is likely that the age-restrictive ordinance would be struck down. It is probable that a court would find that the ordinance violated the elderly individual's freedom of choice as to family living arrangements.

Ordinances drafted before the *Belle Terre* decision generally reduced parking space allocations, or allowed higher density levels in certain zones, or both, but did not go much further.

Based on an assumption that elderly people have fewer cars and visitors than younger people, reduced parking space requirements were the most frequent concessions made to developers of housing for the elderly.[8] In 1966, New Haven, Connecticut, allocated one parking space for every two units of housing for the elderly, while in 1967, Pittsburgh, Pennsylvania, reduced the allocation to one parking space for every three units.[9]

Maximum density limits were generally increased in early zoning ordinances for the elderly. This was done, first, to make developments for the elderly more economically attractive, and second, because elderly families are usually smaller than their younger counterparts.[10] Minimum lot areas per dwelling were also reduced in early zoning ordinances for developments for the elderly. (See Exhibit 8.1.)[11] Other increases in density not only include more units per acre but allow less open space overall. Furthermore, some communities, such as New Rochelle, New York, in 1969, decreased the minimum area per room allowed in housing for the elderly. (See Exhibit 8.2.)[12]

The majority of these regulations were adopted in the late 1960s and are still in effect today. In New Rochelle, for example, there have been no significant changes in the zoning provisions for the elderly since their adoption in 1969. The planning department noted that three projects for the elderly have been built under the original standards and, although there has not been any activity lately, the ordinance is still considered acceptable.[13]

Later Ordinances

More recent ordinances that focus on the needs of the elderly still allow reduced parking requirements and higher densities; however, they tend to be much more comprehensive in scope than earlier ordinances. There is more interest in authorizing a range of housing alternatives for elderly people. Another important trend reflects interest in helping elderly people stay in their homes and communities through the use of accessory apartments or, more experimentally, "echo housing." Exemplifying these general trends, zoning ordinances adopted from 1974 to the present tend to fall into one of three basic categories.

First, there are ordinances that establish a particular zoning district for elderly or retirement housing. Cities that have adopted this alternative include Zion, Illinois; Plano, Texas; and Kansas City, Kansas. Second, municipalities such as Brunswick, Ohio and Clearwater, Florida, have drafted ordinances that establish

EXHIBIT 8.1
Minimum Lot Area per Dwelling Unit:
New Rochelle, New York and New Haven, Connecticut

City and Zoning District	Elderly	Efficiency	Other
New Rochelle	700 sq. ft.		2,500 sq. ft.
Garden apartments	(after six		(after two
R3B, R4	units)		units)
New Haven			
Low-middle density	1,750	2,500	3,500
High-middle density	1,000	1,400	2,000
General-high density	1,000	1,400	2,000
Residence-office	1,000	1,400	2,000

EXHIBIT 8.2
Minimum Area per Room, New Rochelle, New York: 1969

Zoning District	Elderly	Other
Garden apartments, R-3B, R4	150 sq. ft. first room; 100 sq. ft. other rooms	400 sq. ft. first room; 200 sq. ft other rooms

standards for housing for older people in assorted residential districts. Third, some areas have chosen to authorize and regulate the addition of an "accessory" apartment to a single-family home. Greenwich and Westport, Connecticut, have done so, as have Montclair, New Jersey; Babylon, New York (Long Island); and Princeton, New Jersey. The use of echo housing—a small, temporary unit placed next to or behind a permanent home—is the most recent innovation in zoning for the elderly. So far, it has been authorized only in California, through state enabling legislation.[14]

Zoning Districts for the Elderly

In 1983, the City of Zion, Illinois, adopted an ordinance establishing an "EH" (elderly housing) district for people aged 60 and above. The district overlaps certain previously established districts in which the type of specified development is permitted by right. The ordinance requires one parking space per unit and otherwise requires that EH structures conform to the zoning requirements of the immediately surrounding zone.[15]

Courtesy of Richard Reinhold
Amish "grossdawdy" houses in Lancaster County, Pennsylvania, have accessory apartments for elderly relatives.

The ordinance adopted by Plano, Texas, in April 1982, outlines extensive standards for zoning for the elderly. It creates a "RH" (retirement housing) district in which housing for the elderly is permitted by right. The housing may be of various types and sizes, as long as the provisions of the ordinance are met. Housing for the elderly is also allowed in other districts by a Specific Use Permit. The ordinance[16] defines retirement housing and occupant eligibility as:

> A development providing dwelling units specifically designed for the needs of ambulatory elderly persons. To qualify as Retirement Housing, a minimum of 80 percent of the total units shall have a household head of 60 years of age or older. The remaining proportions may qualify by meeting one of the following conditions:
>
> A. The household head is 55 years of age or older;
> B. A unit is occupied by the surviving member(s) of a household, regardless of age, and the household head meeting the age requirements, and who was a resident at the time of his death, had died;
> C. A unit is occupied by management personnel and his/her family (the total of such dwelling units shall not exceed one per 100 dwelling units, or portion thereof, in the project).

The ordinance also authorizes special accessory uses such as barbershops, cafeterias, and libraries to provide on-site services for residents and guests. Parking requirements, lot sizes, and maximum density requirements are established as well. The following minimum safety standards are also required:

A. All doors shall be of sufficient width to accommodate wheelchairs.
B. All areas of public use shall have doors of sufficient width to accommodate wheelchairs.
C. Wherever steps are located, ramps or elevators shall be provided in addition.
D. Cooking units shall have no open flame.
E. Emergency signal facilities shall be provided in each residential unit and shall register a signal at a central location.
F. Electric outlets shall be located at least 24 inches above floor level.
G. Grab bars shall be located around all tubs and showers.
H. Toilet areas shall be adaptable for the installation of grab bars.
I. All floor surfaces shall be nonskid.
J. Central heating and air conditioning shall be individually adjustable for each residential unit.

Although the Plano ordinance is fairly new, officials feel that it has worked well. One project has been developed, and, as Jeffrey Zimmerman, Senior Planner, explained, "We can modify certain provisions as necessary, but the basic framework is set."[17] Plano is unusual because, although its population is fairly young, it has adopted a board zoning ordinance that stresses the need for noninstitutional housing alternatives for elderly people. As Zimmerman noted, "What's important is that Plano is prepared for future growth and development."

A similar ordinance, in Kansas City, Kansas, authorizes "District E-3." The ordinance, adopted in 1973, mandates that within District E-3 "no building or land shall be used and no building shall be . . . erected, converted, or structurally altered unless otherwise provided in this article, except for . . . A) elderly housing, B) nursing homes, and C) accessory buildings and uses customarily incident [to the] above uses. . . ."[18]

The ordinance also specifies landscaping and sign requirements, as well as maximum density. There has been little activity under this ordinance, and the city is in the process of revising it. Kansas City is currently considering an ordinance that would regulate different types of housing development for elderly people in all residential districts in Kansas City.[19]

Housing for the Elderly

The senior citizen housing ordinance from Brunswick, Ohio, is an example of zoning that regulates developments for the elderly in various residential districts. The purpose of Chapter 1276 is broad. It is designed:

- A. To provide appropriate sites for the development of such housing and related facilities in locations convenient to Brunswick's social and welfare facilities and convenient to shops, public transportation, and other needs of the senior citizen;
- B. To regulate the intensity of development so as to provide ample outdoor livable space, to retain a sense of personal identity, intimacy, and human scale within the development;
- C. To provide in such developments, ample-sized meeting rooms and recreational facilities for the comfort and convenience of the occupants; and
- D. To regulate the bulk, height [and] spacing of buildings, and the circulation and parking pattern within the development in order to obtain adequate light, air, privacy, and open space for passive recreation and landscaped amenities.[20]

To achieve these purposes, Brunswick restricts occupancy to people over 60 years of age, with various exceptions for spouses, children over the age of 18, and handicapped adults who may require support services similar to those for elderly residents. The ordinance also outlines main and accessory uses, planning and site criteria, and design features. Although there have been inquiries from developers, there has been no development under Brunswick's ordinance, largely attributable, city planners feel, to the recession and a lack of construction generally. Once building resumes, the ordinance is expected to encourage housing for the elderly.

The Clearwater, Florida, housing for the elderly ordinance is innovative. It stresses deinstitutionalization for many groups of people, including "well" elderly. It also emphasizes the benefits of congregate living for elderly people and provides a wide range of alternatives to meet their needs. The ordinance, adopted in 1982, authorizes and regulates congregate living facilities, residential retirement developments, and life care facilities for elderly people, as well as for dependent children and people who are developmentally disabled, mentally ill, or physically disabled. These facilities may be located in various districts.

The provisions of the ordinance dealing with elderly citizens are limited to people who are 55, 60 or older (depending on the program and area). The facilities range from homes for two or three elderly residents, to small clusters of congregate homes, to residential hotels and larger facilities. As the following excerpt indicates, particular building, parking, and density requirements vary according to type, size, and location of the development. The ordinances specifies that:

1. The permitted density shall be governed by the following minimum lot area and width requirements based on the number of residents to occupy the dwelling units:

Number of Residents	Lot Area	Lot Width
Seven (7) to Nine (9)	5,000 sq. ft.	50 ft.
Ten (10) to Fifteen (15)	8,000 sq. ft.	75 ft.
Sixteen (16) to Twenty-two (22)	12,000 sq. ft.	100 ft.

2. Off-street parking shall be provided on the basis of two (2) spaces for the first six (6) residents, plus one (1) space for each space for each additional six (6) residents or fraction thereof. In addition one (1) space shall be required per two (2) nonresident employees on the maximum working shift.[21]

Clearwater has had great success with this ordinance. Since 1982, 12 facilities (each housing 12 or more elderly residents) have been opened; additionally, two larger projects have been approved.

Accessory Apartments and Echo Housing

Some recent zoning ordinances authorize either accessory apartments[22] or echo units. Accessory apartments are independent units contained within a single-family house. In contrast, echo housing is a small, temporary housing unit, often a modified trailer or prefabricated unit, placed in the rear or side yard of a single family home. One goal of these alternatives is to allow elderly people to retain as much independence and privacy as possible while facilitating the provision of support services and medical care.[23] Some municipalities view these alternatives as a way of providing rental income for elderly homeowners. In addition, ordinances authorizing accessory apartments or echo housing may reflect a desire to keep elderly people integrated into the community and to avoid unnecessary institutionalization. Since all of these benefits can be achieved in some measure by accessory apartments and echo housing, any ordinance that authorizes either has the potential to help elderly citizens, whether specifically targeted toward them or not.

Greenwich, Connecticut, has had a housing for the elderly accessory apartment ordinance since July 1981. The explicit purpose of the ordinance is to "promote the availability and maintenance of housing to benefit elderly persons whose numbers constitute a significant and growing portion of the town's population."[24]

In the past two years, Greenwich has had 40 applications for conversions, 70 percent of which are from elderly people.[25] The ordinance essentially authorizes the installation of an apartment into any single-family home and establishes the following standards:

1. Either the primary or converted unit shall be owner-occupied, and one of the units shall be occupied by a person 62 years of age or older.
2. The floor area of the converted unit may not exceed 70 square feet.
3. A converted unit in an accessory building shall be permitted only on a lot having at least twice the minimum lot size required by the zone.
4. The accessory use as defined in Sec. 6-95(a)(4) providing for roomers or boarders shall not be permitted in either the primary unit or converted unit.[26]

Once the age restriction is complied with, Greenwich does not require that there be any family relationship between the inhabitants of the accessory and primary units.

Montclair, New Jersey, has adopted an ordinance that is similar to the Greenwich ordinance. It authorizes:

§224-6. Additional dwelling unit for parents as conditional use

A. The Planning Board may grant a conditional use so as to permit within a single dwelling unit the establishment of accommodations for one (1) additional housekeeping group, with separate kitchen and bathroom facilities, for use by the parent or parents of one (1) of the owner-occupants or tenant-occupants if, after a public hearing pur-

Courtesy of Lancaster County Office of Aging and Edward Guion
The "Elder Cottage," is an innovation of the Lancaster County, Pennsylvania, Office of the Aging. These units are removable, low in energy costs, and designed specifically to meet the needs of their elderly residents. The other three views are of this one-bedroom unit.

Courtesy of Lancaster County Office of Aging and Edward Guion

Increasing Housing Opportunities for the Elderly 107

Courtesy of Lancaster County Office of Aging and Edward Guion

Courtesy of Lancaster County Office of Aging and Edward Guion

suant to the Municipal Land Use Procedure Ordinance, the Board finds and requires that an application complies with the following:

1. The exception requested is for the purpose of accommodating not more than two (2) members of a family who are a parent or the parents of one (1) of the owner-occupants of the dwelling unit and who are of such an age or of such condition of health as to require special consideration.
2. No rent, fee, or other charge of any sort is to be made or collected by the owner-occupants or tenant-occupants of the dwelling unit from the parent or parents accommodated by the exception, and affidavits so stating shall be submitted annually by both parties at the time of application for certificate of occupancy renewal.
3. The additional housekeeping accommodations are to be established without structural alterations except those deemed necessary by the Board to provide bathroom and kitchen facilities, and the resulting arrangement must not be such as to divide the dwelling into two (2) separate dwelling units capable of independent occupancy.
4. The dwelling unit, building, and premises will comply with all other laws and ordinances in all respects if the application is granted.
5. The said owners will prepare and enter into a written agreement with the Town of Montclair, in form sufficient for recording in the Office of the Register of Essex County, which said agreement shall be subject to the approval of the Town Counsel, whereby the said owners will agree that such use of the premises shall terminate at such time as the applicant no longer owns or occupies the said premises or at such time as the parent or the parents no longer occupy te said premises, whichever shall first occur.[27]

The scope of this provision is so narrow that it has only been used three or four times in the past 10 years. The provision seems extremely impractical since homeowners are restricted from recapturing their investment upon resale. Peter Steck, Director of Planning and Community Development in Montclair, noted that "The ordinance is so restrictive, it's almost a disincentive in all but emergency situations."[28]

Babylon, New York, adopted an accessory apartment ordinance after a study indicated that over 10 percent of the houses in Babylon contained illegal accessory units.[29] Although anyone can apply for an accessory apartment permit, fees are reduced for elderly applicants. Similarly, although the ordinance does not specifically target older people, one of its goals, cited by the planning department, is to help elderly people keep their homes by providing them with an additional source of income.[30]

In order to install an accessory apartment in Babylon, certain standards must be met:

a. The two-family dwelling must be *owner-occupied.*
b. The two-family dwelling must have one on-site parking space per dwelling unit (a total of two parking spaces for each two-family dwelling); the parking spaces must be paved with asphalt, concrete, or other similar materials.
c. Each unit of the two-family dwelling must have a minimum of 500 habitable square feet. The rental unit of the two-family dwelling is to be limited to a maximum of two bedrooms.
d. The two-family special permit requires that the dwelling have only one front entrance; all other entrances will be on the side or in the rear of the dwelling. An entrance leading to a foyer with entrances leading from the foyer to the two dwelling units will be accepable.
e. The two-family dwelling must comply with all requirements for two-family dwellings as per the New York State Building Code and all the laws and housing regulations of the state of New York and the town of Babylon and be maintained in a neat and orderly manner.[31]

The Princeton, New Jersey, "flat ordinance," like the Babylon ordinance, does not expressly address elderly needs; however, it has the potential to do so. The ordinance authorizes the addition of an accessory apartment to a single-family or semi-detached home, subject to certain size and design requirements. There is no reason why such an apartment could not be added for the purpose of housing elderly tenants or a parent. Since the city does not keep records on occupancy of accessory units, it is unclear whether elderly people are using the ordinance.[32]

Echo housing is fairly new in the United States. In 1981, the state of California (and some localities) passed enabling legislation designed to encourage the use of echo housing for elderly people. The act reads:

1. Steps must be taken to encourage the creation of more residential units for persons over the age of 60.
2. There is a serious shortage of housing units for persons over the age of 60.
3. There is an important need to maintain senior citizens in independent living situations and also to encourage housing arrangements that prevent isolation of elderly persons and to reunite families. . . .

Section 65852.1
Notwithstanding Section 65906, any city, including a charter city, county, or city and county may issue a zoning variance, special use permit, or conditional use permit for a dwelling unit to be constructed, or attached to, a primary residence on a parcel zoned for a single-family residence, if the dwelling unit is intended for the sole occupancy of one adult or two adult persons who are 60 years of age

or over, and the area of floor space of the dwelling unit does not exceed 640 square feet.[33]

As yet, few local echo housing ordinances have been adopted. However, a recent report, "Echo Housing: A Review of Zoning Issues and Other Considerations," discusses probable forms such ordinances might take. To ensure that the units will actually be temporary and primarily benefit elderly people, it is likely that echo housing ordinances will involve granting a permit to specific individuals as the sole occupants of an echo unit. Occupancy of the echo unit is likely to be restricted to either elderly or handicapped residents, and ordinances will probably require that the property owners reside in either the primary or echo unit.[34] The ordinance would probably establish minimum lot sizes, maximum heights, and lot coverage, as well as access paths and parking. It is possible that such an ordinance might also limit building materials and placement.

Innovative Zoning and Housing for the Elderly

The impact of zoning and development standards on the cost of housing is currently a major issue in the field of housing and real estate development. Since a serious problem for elderly people is the rising cost of housing, recent zoning modifications that authorize smaller, higher density, so-called "affordable housing" for families can have a significant impact on housing for elderly people as well.[35]

Examples of zoning techniques that might facilitate development of good housing for the elderly at lower cost include cluster zoning and incentive zoning. There are also land-use and architectural approaches—like infill developments and adaptive re-use—that might increase the availability of affordable housing for the elderly and may require changes in zoning law. Echo housing and accessory apartments, discussed earlier, also fit into this category. Some alternatives might require only a Special Use Permit; others would require major revisions of the zoning ordinance. Nevertheless, if implemented with a sensitivity toward the design needs of an elderly population, these approaches could encourage development of more housing for elderly people.

Cluster Zoning

Cluster zoning allows structures to be situated in close groups, thus preserving more open space. The overall density of the lot is the same; it is merely concentrated in certain areas of the lot. In a recent article entitled "Zoning Responses to a Maturing Population," Lazlo Papp notes that cluster development is well suited to the needs of an elderly population in several ways. First, it maximizes security by arranging units close enough to each other to establish an informal surveillance network. If located on level ground, clustered units increase accessibility by avoiding steep grades and steps. Furthermore, since the open space is shared by all residents, maintenance can be shared as well. Finally, Papp notes that since most cluster housing is regulated through a planned unit development process, a municipality can ensure that the resulting housing is appropriately developed and constructed to address the needs of the elderly residents.

An example of cluster development for elderly people is Legion Village in Hanover, Massachusetts. Legion Village consists of 60 apartments located on a 12-acre parcel of land. The units are concentrated in three groups of 20 apartments each and are distributed on only about one-third of the lot area. The additional land is easily accessible for recreation, or it can be used for additional housing in the future.

Legion Village is designed to encourage community interaction and security, and it is located on level land to facilitate accessibility.

Infill Development

Infill development may be facilitated by designing special zoning provisions to encourage building on vacant parcels of land. Parcels that may be inappropriate for industrial or commercial development may be suitable for well-designed housing for the elderly. Since infill lots are often found in previously developed areas, they may offer proximity to commercial and recreation centers and use otherwise vacant sites on a productive manner. Exhibit 8.3 provides more information on how local governments can encourage infill development.

A example of infill development for the elderly is Sheridan Apartments, a 57-unit complex in Palo Alto, California. Built on only 37,600 square feet of land, it is located in a residential area close to restaurants, stores, parks, and public transportation. The city of Palo Alto assembled four vacant lots that were then sold to the developer. In spite of the development's high density, it is carefully designed to preserve individual privacy and to address other needs of its elderly residents.

Incentive Zoning

With incentive zoning, development is divided into broad categories and establishes certain standards for all developments in the category. Additionally, "bonuses" (usually in the form of density increases for residential developments) may be awarded to a development that meets other desirable criteria. For example, the "Land Development Guidance System for Planned Unit Developments," adopted by Fort Collins, Colorado, awards density increases to encourage construction on infill lots and the development of low-income housing.

Although the Fort Collins system does not specifically designate housing for the elderly as a potential objective for receiving a density bonus, it could easily be modified to do so. Density bonuses may be available to residential develop-

EXHIBIT 8.3
What Local Governments Can Do to Encourage Infill Development

Goals	Implementation Methods	Community Examples
Stimulate developer interest in infilling	Publicity campaigns and meetings with real estate interests; Design competitions.	Colorado Springs, Col. Omaha, Neb. State of New Jersey St. Paul, Minn. Minneapolis, Minn.
Remove obstacles created by government	Reduced delays in project review; Code revisions.	Kansas City, Mo. Livermore, Calif. Winston-Salem, N.C. Colorado Springs, Col. Seattle, Wash. Montgomery County, Md. Omaha, Neb. Modesto, Calif. Portland, Ore. Phoenix, Ariz.
Create neighborhood support for infilling	Review meetings; Special procedures; Area targeting.	Baltimore, Md. Minneapolis, Minn. Phoenix, Ariz.
Address market weakness or uncertainty	Lower risk; Advantageous financing; Demonstration projects; Maintenance and rehabilitation; Service upgrading; Interim uses.	Dallas, Tex. Minneapolis, Saint Paul, Minn. Los Angeles, Calif. Birmingham, Ala. Springfield, Ill Chicago, Ill. Bronx, N.Y. Oakland, Calif. New York, N.Y. Wilmington, Del.
Address site-specific problems	Increased land availability; Cost of land and improvements reduced; Infrastructure problems corrected.	San Diego, Calif. Portland, Ore. Polk County, Iowa San Mateo County, Calif. Duluth, Minn. Phoenix, Ariz. Omaha, Neb. Baltimore, Md. New York, N.Y.

EXHIBIT 8.3 (Continued)
What Local Governments Can Do to Encourage Infill Development

Goals	Implementation Methods	Community Examples
Increase land availability	Eminent domain; Land swapping; Vacant land taxed at higher rates; Land banking.	St. Louis, Mo. Omaha, Neb.
Combine infill incentives in effective strategies	Package tools and techniques; Use of state and federal assistance.	

Source: Real Estate Research Corporation, *Infill Development Strategies*, Washington, D.C., published jointly by the Urban Land Institute and the American Planning Association, 1982.

ments that meet certain criteria, including proximity to various services, type of housing, energy-efficient construction, and safety equipment.

Conceivably, a similar ordinance could award density bonuses (or parking allowances, setback revisions, etc.) to encourage development of housing for the elderly. Criteria might include location, amenities, design, and safety features.

Adaptive Reuse

Adaptive reuse involves renovating an older building for a use other than its original one. It may require a special use permit, a zoning variance, or other special permission. Warehouses, factories, churches, schools, and other older buildings are all finding new uses. Although buildings are frequently renovated to provide housing, reuse has also resulted in office and commercial space. Reuse may be undertaken by private companies, or a project may be developed in conjunction with local agencies and government funds.[36]

In recent years, adaptive reuse has been a popular technique for providing housing for elderly people. It has particular advantages for doing so. Buildings suitable for reuse are usually located in developed areas, offering proximity to commercial and recreational facilities; they often include distinctive architectural features that encourage a sense of pride and identity in residents; and, most important, adaptive reuse is generally less expensive than constructing new housing with similar features. Thus, reuse is attractive to developers and may result in lower costs for elderly tenants.

Adaptations of old buildings for housing for the elderly have been undertaken on both a small and large scale. For example, the Polish National Home, in Chicopee, Massachusetts, is an example of a smaller scale, adaptive reuse project. The building (constructed in 1912) and its annex (constructed in 1914) have been converted into 50 apartments for the elderly. The rehabilitation was par-

Courtesy of Nick Wheeler
The Car Barn in New Bedford, Massachusetts, is a former garage and warehouse that has been renovated and adapted for reuse as housing for the elderly.

tially financed by Neighborhood Strategy Area loans through the Department of Housing and Urban Development. Rents for the apartments ranged from $329 to $475 in 1982 and are subsidized through HUD's Section 8 Program.

The Car Barn in New Bedford, Massachusetts, includes 114 apartments for elderly residents, various community rooms and recreational facilities, and a trolley museum. The building was constructed in 1910 by the Union Street Railway Company. It was subsequently used as the municipal bus garage and a supermarket warehouse. In the 1970s, the Barn was placed on the National Register of Historic Places. The city of New Bedford accepted a proposal from the Claremont Company and the Boston Architectural Team to renovate the Car Barn.

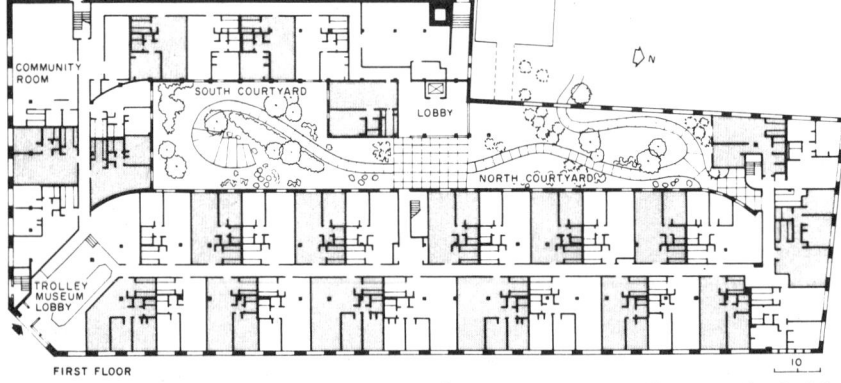

Reprinted from Architectural Record, July 1982, © 1982 by McGraw-Hill, Inc., with all rights reserved.
The site plan, above, shows how the Trolley Museum has been incorporated into the residential area.

The Car Barn is divided by two outdoor courtyards. It offers residents ample communal space, and a central location.

Summary

Although many cities continue to modify only parking and density requirements in zoning for elderly residents, it is becoming more common to adopt comprehensive housing for the elderly ordinances similar to the one enacted by Clearwater, Florida. Such ordinances provide a municipality with alternatives to address the needs of its elderly population. General interest in relaxing rigid zoning classifications and changes in zoning provisions can encourage housing for the elderly by allowing cluster zoning, accessory and echo apartments, infill development, adaptive reuse, and an incentive zoning system. An appropriate combination of ordinances directed at housing elderly people can help to accommodate the diverse needs of a growing elderly population by providing a variety of housing alternatives.

Notes

1. Warner, "Housing for a Maturing Society."
2. Myers, "Aging in Place," p. 12.
3. Warner, "Housing for a Maturing Society."
4. Smith, Thomas, *Flexible Parking Requirements,* PAS Report No. 377, American Planning Association, 1313 E. 60th St., Chicago, IL 60637, 1983.
5. For more information, see Conners, "Valid Discrimination in Zoning."
6. See *Moore v City of East Cleveland,* 431 U.S. 494 (1977). In *Moore,* an ordinance that defined "family" so narrowly as to prohibit a grandmother from living with her children in a "single-family" zone was struck down. The decision noted that freedom of choice as to family living arrangements is protected by the due process clause of the Fourteenth Amendment.
7. Zoning Ordinance, City of Brunswick, Ohio, No. 82-83.
8. Spicer, *Zoning for the Elderly.*
9. Ibid.
10. Ibid.
11. Zoning Ordinance, City of New Rochelle, R-3B, R4; Zoning Ordinance, City of New Haven, Art. III, Sec. 13, A.1.c. and Sec. 14, A.1.c; and Art. IV, Sec. 22, C.1.
12. Zoning Ordinance, City of New Rochelle, New York, Annex A, Part I, Sec. 15.1, Districts R3B, R4.
13. Phone conversation with A. DiNovo, planner, New Rochelle, New York, August 19, 1983.
14. Amendment to Sec. 65852.1 of the state of California Government Code, 1981.
15. City of Zion, Illinois, Zoning Ordinance No. 83-0-5, adopted January 18, 1983.
16. City of Plano, Texas, "Retirement Housing," Zoning Ordinance No. 82-4-9, April 12, 1982.
17. Phone conversation with Jeffrey Zimmerman, planner, City of Plano, Texas, August 19, 1983.
18. Kansas City, Kansas, Zoning Ordinance, Sec. 27.82.1(1), adopted in 1973.
19. Phone conversation with T. Shelman, planner, Kansas City, Kansas, August 11, 1983.
20. City Brunswick, Ohio, Zoning Ordinance, Chapter 1276, Sec. 1276.1, adopted June 28, 1982.
21. For a detailed discussion of accessory apartments in general, see PAS Report No. 365.
22. City of Clearwater, Florida, Zoning Ordinance, No. 2772-82, adopted August 19, 1982.
23. Frederick H. Bair, Jr., "Aging in Place," paper presented at the American Planning Association Conference, Seattle, Washington, April 1983.

24. Town of Greenwich, Connecticut, Zoning Ordinance, Sec. 6-99, adopted June 26, 1981.
25. Conversation with Diane Fox, planner, Greenwich, Connecticut, August 8, 1983.
26. Town of Greenwich, Connecticut, Zoning Ordinance, Sec. 6-99.
27. Town of Montclair, New Jersey, Zoning Ordinance, Sec. 224-6.1, amended September 29, 1980, by Ord. No. 80-44.
28. Phone conversation August 9, 1983.
29. *Report on Illegal Two-Family Dwellings in the Town of Babylon, New York*, Planning Department, City of Babylon, New York, January 1979.
30. Phone conversation with A. Forcillo, Director of Planning, Babylon, New York, August 10, 1983.
31. City of Babylon, New York, Zoning Ordinance, Sec. 6.
32. Phone conversation with P. Kneski, Town Engineer, Princeton, New Jersey, August 9, 1983.
33. State of California Government Code, Sec. 65852.1, adopted 1981.
34. Hare, P., and Hollis, L., *Echo Housing*.
35. This discussion is adapted from Lazlo Papp, "Zoning Responses to a Maturing Population," in *Housing for a Maturing Population*, Urban Land Institute, 1983.
36. For a further discussion of adaptive reuse, see also PAS Report No. 319, August 1976, "Recycling Public Buildings."

References

General Materials

"Age Restrictions in Land-Use Control." *Zoning and Planning Law Report*, Vol. 2, No. 8, June 1979.

American Society of Planning Officials (now American Planning Association), 1313 E. 60th St., Chicago, IL 60637. "Zoning for the Elderly." Richard B. Spicer. Planning Advisory Service Report No. 259. 1970.

American Planning Association, 1313 E. 60th St., Chicago, IL 60637. *Accessory Apartments: Using Surplus Space in Single-Family Houses*. Patrick H. Hare, with Susan Conner and Dwight Merriam. Planning Advisory Service Report No. 365. 1981. 25 pp.

———. Planners Press, jointly with the Urban Land Institute. *Infill Development Strategies*. Real Estate Research Corporation. 1982. 144 pp.

Bair, Frederick H., Jr. "Aging in Place"; "Retirement—Better Use of Housing and Human Values." Paper presented at the American Planning Association Conference, Seattle, Washington. 1983.

City of Fort Collins, Planning and Development Department, P.O. Box 580, Fort Collins, CO 80522. 1981. 7 pp.

Conners, Donald L. "Valid Discrimination in Zoning: The Young and the Old." American Law Institute–American Bar Association report. Available from the American Bar Association, 1155 East 60th St., Chicago, IL 60637. 1981.

Hare, Patrick H., and Hollis, Linda E. "Echo Housing: A Review of Zoning Issues and Other Considerations." American Association of Retired Persons, 1909 K St., N.W., Washington, DC 20049. 1983. 32 pp.

Myers, Phyllis, *Aging in Place: Strategies to Help the Elderly Stay in Revitalizing Neighborhoods*. The Conservation Foundation, 1717 Massachusetts Ave., N.W., Washington, DC 20036. 1982.

Rush, Richard, "The Age of the Aging," *Progressive Architecture*, August 1981, p. 59.

"Sharp Rise of Elderly Populations in 1970s Portends Future Increases." *New York Times*, May 4, 1981, p. 1.

Urban Land Institute, 1090 Vermont Ave., N.W., Washington, DC 20005. *Housing for a Maturing Population*, 1983.

Warner, Katharine, "Housing for a Maturing Society." Paper presented at American Planning Association Conference, Cincinnati, Ohio. 1980.

Ordinances

City of Babylon, New York, "Temporary Two-Family Dwelling," Local Law 9, 1979.

City of Brunswick, Ohio, "Senior Citizen Housing," Ordinance No. 83-82, adopted June 28, 1982.

City of Clearwater, Florida, "Amendment No. 1, Special Living Facilities, Housing Element of the Comprehensive Plan," Ordinance No. 2772-83, adopted August 19, 1982.

City of Kansas City, Kansas, " 'E-3' Elderly Housing District," Sec. 27-82.1, adopted 1973.

City of Montclair, New Jersey, "Additional Dwelling Unit for Parents as Conditional Use," Code Sec. 224-6.1.

City of Plano, Texas, "Retirement Housing," Ordinance No. 82-4-9, adopted April 12, 1982.

City of Zion, Illinois, "Establishment of E-H Zoning District," Ordinance No. 83-0-5, adopted January 18, 1983.

Town of Greenwich, Connecticut, "Conversion to Additional Dwelling-Elderly Housing," Sec. 6-99, adopted June 1981.

Town of Westport, Connecticut, "Conversion of Dwelling for Elderly Persons." Sec. 32-1.

Township of Princeton, New Jersey, "Flats," Sec. 10B-274 of the Princeton Township Code.

III

Housing and Personal Income: Home Equity Conversions and the Capital Gains Tax Exclusion

9

Home Equity Conversions*

Vincent J. Trichilo

The concept of Home Equity Conversion is not new within the financial markets since individuals have used the equity in their homes for many years to finance a variety of needs such as education, debts, major purchases, and for investment purposes.

The receipt of income to supplement regular income by converting equity is a relatively new idea. Demand for this type of financial restructuring is almost nonexistent in this area, and it is with this in mind that this paper is prepared.

Home equity conversion plans are designed to help house-rich and cash-poor homeowners unlock the value of their homes and connect it to working capital, or to pay for services necessary for continuance of a set life-style.

The working capital could be used for many purposes such as: paying for children's education, restructuring debts, investing in other ventures, and to create a reserve fund to draw upon when needed.

Equity conversion can also be used to pay for repairs on a structure, to maintain it for normal usage, or to modify a structure to make it energy efficient in order to save operating expense.

A report prepared by the Special Committee on Aging of the U.S. Senate states, "Approximately 12.5 million homes are owned by Americans over 65

---

* Statement prepared for United States House of Representatives, Select Committee on Aging, Subcommittee on Housing and Consumer Interests. *Home Equity Conversion. Hearing at Mattydale, New York, October 22, 1983.* Washington, D.C.: Government Printing Office, 1984, pp. 22–26.

years of age, 80 percent of these are owned free and clear. For the majority of these older homeowners, the equity they have accumulated represents their single, largest asset; their major lifetime investment." This report also states that the estimated equity totals more than $600 billion.

The study also recites that one-fourth of all low income elderly homeowners could raise their incomes above the poverty level, and two-fifths of low-income homeowners over age 75 could also do this by utilizing the equity in their property.

Historically the mechanism for conversion of equity has been the fixed rate mortgage, as either a first mortgage or a junior lien against the property. Lately, and especially within the last 3 to 4 years, other methods of financing have come to the market place: the Reverse Annuity Mortgage, the Sale/Leaseback Plan, and the Split Equity Mortgage. In addition some variation of the second mortgage is being used.

Each of these programs will be discussed in turn as to operation.

Home Equity Conversion Programs

Reverse Annuity Mortgage (RAM)

The reverse annuity mortgage is the opposite of a conventional mortgage loan. The loan is paid to the homeowner in monthly payments, the amount determined by the amount of some equity borrowed against the interest rate and the length of the loan. Therefore, the amount of interest owed rises as the amount drawn increases, until the time specified or until the home is sold.

The value of the house at the time of the mortgage agreement determines the maximum loan amount. Because of the cost to the lender and the potential risk that the home may decline in value, reverse loans are not made for the full amount for which the house might be sold. Also some lenders believe that homeowners with some continuing equity investment in the house will maintain it better. Usually, the loan amount is between 60 to 80 percent of the appraised value of the property. Some lenders are developing reverse mortgage arrangements with adjustable rates and share appreciation features.

The following example illustrates how the RAM program works: A reverse mortgage loan of $120,000, at a fixed rate of 14 percent charges, would yield a monthly income of $463. If an initial disbursement of $5,000 is made to pay off an existing mortgage or make repairs on the house, the monthly income would be $386. After 10 years, the loan must be repaid or renegotiated.

The RAM program began with a level monthly payment reverse mortgage loan with a fixed interest rate and fixed term. Now it is offering a graduated payment RAM with fixed interest rate and fixed term—monthly payments increase by 6 percent annually—and a renegotiable RAM, with payments linked to the Consumer Price Index (CPI) and a variable interest rate—the payments and interest are adjusted at 3-year intervals. The RAM program offers the option of an initial loan disbursement, which the owner could use to purchase a deferred annuity to provide income when the loan terminates. However, the annuity will not pay off the RAM loan or assure life tenure in the home.

Lenders participating in the RAM program placed a ceiling of $150,000 on the maximum loan amount, which also is limited to 80 percent of the property's appraised value. Fees and charges are limited to 1 percent of the loan amount, plus the appraisal cost ($100 to $150) and normal closing costs, including escrow and title insurance fees.

Homeowners who have obtained reverse mortgage loans have used funds for a variety of needs. One recently widowed woman used the monthly payments as income until she could restructure her finances and sell her home. Others have drawn upon home equity to meet medical expenses, or to pay for in-home or nursing home care for a spouse. Some of the older borrowers have taken out a loan in the expectation that the term would match or exceed their life expectancy, while the loan would provide them with income for a more comfortable existence in the present; in doing so, they accept the risk that they may, in fact, live longer and have to sell the home to pay the loan.

Other proposed variations of the reverse annuity mortgage would invest some or all of the home equity loan or provide an annuity which would yield a lifetime income for the homeowners. None of the reverse loan plans available now offer a guaranteed income for the remainder of the borrower's life. A long-term mortgage plan guaranteeing income to age 100 has been proposed by a New Jersey corporation called American Homestead.

Sale/Leaseback

The sale/leaseback arrangement is one of the oldest methods of equity conversion. One form, called rents viageres, has existed in France for a number of years and has been used in the United States. Some sale/leasebacks have been completed, where children purchase the home for their parents.

There are a number of ways to structure a sale/leaseback. All involve an investor who purchases the elderly seller's home and grants the seller life tenancy at a specific rental payment. For investors, a major incentive for participating in sale/leaseback is the depreciation of the property for tax purposes. Also the seller may be able to take the one-time capital gains deduction of up to $125,000 on the sale, available to homeowners over age 55.

The elderly seller may receive payment in a variety of ways: a lump sum; in equal monthly payments based upon an annuity purchased by the investor; or in monthly mortgage payments from which the monthly rent is deducted. The method used will depend upon the income needs of the elderly homeowner and the tax situation of both the seller and the investor. The sale agreement establishes a contractual relationship between the investor and the seller which clearly spells out the elderly individual's right to continued occupancy, the rent schedule, and other financial responsibilities, and assigns responsibility for the future maintenance and care of the property. If the arrangement involves monthly mortgage payments, the agreement specifies the disposition of the remainder owed, should the elderly person die before completion of payment.

Sale/leasebacks have the advantage that all of the transaction is complete at the beginning, giving the older homeowner a view of future income and expenses which must be calculated against potential inflation. The elderly seller is protected against buyer default by the mortgage and the annuity purchased at the time of sale.

The following example shows how a sale/leaseback might work: A 79-year-old widow sells her house, appraised at $80,000 to an investor for $63,200, a 21-percent discount. She receives a downpayment of $6,320 (10 percent) and a 12-year promissory note for the $56,880 balance. She receives a monthly payment of $679 from the investor, including interest at 10 percent per year, from which she pays rent of $285 back to the investor, leaving $394 as net income. The buyer purchased an annuity which will maintain the $697 monthly payment after the note is paid off.

Split Equity

The HELP program, Home Equity Living Plan, Inc., of Buffalo, N.Y., is a publicly sponsored home equity conversion program. It was the idea of a city councilman, who remembers his own mother's inability to use the equity tied up in her home to meet her living needs. The plan was capitalized by $1.3 million in community development block grant (CDBG) funds.

The HELP program is a split equity arrangement. The homeowner is guaranteed a lifetime tenancy estate to the property, while the public body becomes the owner of a remainder interest. The homeowner retains title to the house until death (in case of a couple, until both die). If the corporation fails to deliver the promised payments, it forfeits its rights to the house. In essence, the monthly payments to the owner represent a long-term installment purchase of the property.

The following example illustrates how the program works: In August 1981, HELP, Inc., signed a contract with a woman, age 66, in which the corporation agreed to rehabilitate her $16,000 house and to pay all her future expenses of major maintenance, insurance, and taxes, plus a cash annuity of $624 per year for the remainder of her life. In exchange the woman relinquished the residual equity in her house. When she dies, the corporation will take title to the house and sell it to recover its investment.

Deferred Payment Loan (DPL)

The deferred payment loan is another means by which elderly homeowners can draw upon home equity to maintain and repair their homes, thus preventing loss of the property value. These loans permit homeowners to defer payment of all principal and interest either for a specified term or until the house is sold.

For older homeowners who may wish to move to smaller living quarters or into other housing arrangements, deferred payment loans permit rehabilitation and repairs which make the house more salable or may increase its value. Other homeowners use such loans to make repairs and changes which permit them to remain in their homes comfortably and with greater self-sufficiency for the remainder of their days or until other housing is needed. Homeowners whose monthly incomes are too small to qualify for conventional loans could use deferred payment loans to create an income-producing unit in the home, which would provide greater monthly income and could be used to repay the loan at term.

In Wisconsin, a statewide program used public and private non-profit agencies to make deferred payment loans to low-income elderly homeowners in certain targeted neighborhoods requiring rehabilitation. State revenue funds were used to provide about $4.6 million in loans—668 loans averaging about $6,900—for home repairs.

Some other states, for example, New Jersey, make low-interest home improvement loans or life grants to older homeowners in designated neighborhoods, which do not have to be repaid until title is transferred. Also, in two states, California and Oregon, elderly homeowners are able to defer payment of property taxes until their home is sold or the estate settled.

Home Equity Line of Credit

A new method of recapturing your equity in property is the Line of Credit Loan System, whereby a line of credit is granted based upon a percentage of value of the property. Homeowners may draw checks against this line of credit for any purpose. Interest rate is based on an index picked by the lender and will vary as the index changes.

Junior Liens and First Mortgages

These traditional ways of financing the equity in a house are still the most used of all programs. They involve nothing more than applying for a regular loan at a lending institution. These loans are available at a fixed rate and at adjustable rates.

The major disadvantages to this type of loan is usually the cost of acquiring the loan and also in qualifying for the monthly payments incurred.

Availability

The programs mentioned above, other than the First Mortgage, Junior Mortgage, and the Line of Credit loan, are seldom, if ever, used in the New York area.

The lack of programs other than the normal loans (First Mortgage, Junior Loans, and Line of Credit) is due to: (1) lack of demand by the consumers, (2) lack of understanding by homeowners in the value of their equity, (3) lack of desire of homeowners to jeopordize their interest in property, and (4) cost and risks which is covered below.

Cost and Risks

Equity conversion involves both costs and risks for the homeowner. Depending upon the method of conversion, the costs could be in the form of interest and various fees or commissions. The owner may receive less for the property than full market sale value and not receive the benefit of appreciation in the property's value over subsequent years.

Many homeowners would consider it risky to deplete their home equity during their own lifetime. Owners also must consider the possibility that the lender or program provider might default on monthly payments and the potential erosion of the dollar value of monthly payments over years due to inflation.

For many older homeowners, debt-free ownership of their home represents a hard won lifetime accomplishment. Understandably, they may be reluctant to assume any new mortgage debt or relinquish complete ownership of their homes.

In reverse equity loans, the main risk is that the homeowner will live longer than the term of the loan and will have to sell the home to repay the loan. Also, there is some risk that the home will depreciate in value over the term of the loan. In split equity and sale/leaseback arrangements there is a danger that the investor or sponsoring public body may be unable to make the monthly payments which the elderly person depends upon for income. With annuity plans, the homeowner takes the risk that they will not live long enough to justify the higher cost of the annuity. With all fixed income payment equity plans, there is the risk that inflation will erode the spending value of the payment and the homeowner will not have enough income to meet basic needs.

Consumer Safeguards

Home equity conversion can be a complicated and confusing process. These techniques are new and it will be some time before sufficient experience is developed to provide national models and widespread knowledge of the process both among lenders and consumers.

Because of the novel character of home equity conversion, plans may contain provisions which even the most well-informed consumer would not be able to properly evaluate. Also because of the limited availability of home equity plans, the traditional market mechanisms which winnow out inferior or defective products may not operate.

Care is needed to minimize the financial risks faced by elderly homeowners and the potential for failure or fraud in home equity conversion. For many, home equity represents their only asset of any size and once it is used up, the older person may have few other financial resources. Therefore, society has an interest in making certain that the rights and interest of the elderly homeowner are protected. Homeowners considering equity conversion should seek sufficient counseling and legal advice to fully understand the potential consequences.

The major element for protection of homeowners is that of disclosure. Virtually all of the instruments and legal documents for home equity conversion—reverse mortgages, sale/leaseback, or deferred loans—will be complicated and difficult for a lay person to understand. Therefore, the elderly homeowner should be provided with information which explains the program clearly and simply and which provides a basis for comparison with alternative plans. The homeowner should be able to see the amount of income which would result under various payment schedules and interest rates.

Lender Problems

One of the major problems lenders may have with the RAM, Sale/Leaseback, Split Equity, and Deferred Payment Plans is one of public relations, for the plans may be tied to the time when an elderly homeowner may be forced to sell because he has outlived his plan, or when heirs may argue that their parents were not advised properly or lacked the business acumen to make this type of decision.

In most cases, these types of loans would have to be designed, marketed, and serviced at costs equal to regular programs. Should demand not exist, these costs might not justify having the programs available.

Another lender concern is how to control physical depreciation of property, to minimize further risk in this area.

Summary

In view of a very limited study of the program in the New York area, it appears that because of consumer disinterest and the cost factor involved to lending institutions to set up programs of limited usage, some very basic steps must be taken to make these programs available and worth-while. Also, some consideration should be given to setting up private non-profit organizations which could offer loans at below market rates, thereby increasing the acceptability of programs. Also steps should be taken to educate the elderly in the value of property equity and to direct their energy toward the steps needed to implement the programs locally.

10

Home Equity Conversions*

Michael Hoeflich

The plight of older American homeowners squeezed by stationary or decreasing incomes and increasing housing costs is one which is attracting substantial attention among housing professionals. The problem is relatively simple. Large numbers of older Americans are finding that their incomes are not sufficient to cope with the rising costs associated with home ownership, e.g., taxes, utilities, repair and, concomitantly, that their principal asset is the very house the upkeep of which is consuming too large a portion of their income. Unfortunately, a house does not produce net cash income that can be used for expenditures. Instead, it represents illiquid wealth. The purpose of the various home equity conversion devices that are currently being developed is to find a means by which the illiquid wealth represented by unencumbered and appreciated housing owned by older Americans can be utilized to generate additional current cash income without forcing the elderly to sacrifice home ownership. In this statement I would like to draw attention to two forms of home equity conversion which I believe to be promising: (1) sale-leasebacks and (2) split-equity financing.

---

*Statement prepared for United States House of Representatives, Select Committee on Aging, Subcommittee on Housing and Consumer Interests. *Home Equity Conversion. Hearing at Mattydale, New York, October 22, 1983*. Washington, D.C.: Government Printing Office, 1984, pp. 53–56.

The first, and to my mind, the simplest sale-leaseback transaction used as a home equity conversion device would be a sale-leaseback effected between elderly parents and their own child or children. In this simple scenario, elderly parents would sell a fee simple interest in their home (presumably unencumbered by any liens) to their children and then immediately execute a lease for a certain term with renewal options (or, if tax problems could be overcome,[1] a lease for a life term) at a fair market rental. The children either could pay cash for the house or finance a portion of the purchase price through a third party lender or on the installment basis through their own parents as the financing party. In the latter case the only "outsiders" needed in such a transaction would be professional advisers, i.e., lawyers and accountants to structure the transaction and provide necessary documentation.

From the tax perspective, a number of issues, even in this simple transaction, will be significant. First, of course, are issues raised by doing the transaction entirely among family members. In this regard, Code Sec. 280A(d)(3), as amended in 1981, will be crucial. This recent change in the law permits the rental of a principal residence to a family member at a "fair rental" without incurring the general restrictions on deductibility of expenses imposed by IRC Sec. 280A on such transactions. Second, since the sale would be between members of a family, it is quite important that there be some clarification (administrative or legislative) that such a sale would not prohibit use of the IRC Sec. 121 one-time capital gain exclusion by the sellers. Also, it will be necessary, if the sale takes the form of a purchase money installment contract, that the parties pay particular attention to the tax accounting rules of IRC § § 267 and 453.

Another issue from the tax aspect which would arise in connection with the proposed transaction is whether a sale with a leaseback for the life of the seller will, under current case law, cause the IRS to attack the transaction. Generally, current case-law would suggest that a lease in excess of the estimated useful life of the property sold will be counted as a negative factor in determining whether or not there has been a valid sale for tax purposes (thereby permitting the buyer to claim depreciation deductions).[2] In most cases, the homes to be sold by elderly parents will be quite old. Recent literature suggests many of these homes will be at least 30 years old at the time of sale. A lease for life to elderly parents might be attacked on the grounds that it is more likely than not that such a lease will exceed the useful life of the home. In most analogous cases to these, decided prior to the Economic Recovery Tax Act of 1981 when remaining useful lives have had to be determined in regard to older commercial buildings, remaining lives have been generally determined to have been quite short. It should be noted that this particular problem could arise even in a non-family transaction. Nevertheless, the familial nature of the transaction may complicate this issue and the question of "intent" to effectuate a true sale is even more questionable.

In spite of potential difficulties with a sale-leaseback transaction between parents and children, there are a number of very attractive possible benefits to be gained from an intra-family transaction.[3] First, of course, is the ability to circumvent the capital markets and the transaction costs which can often be quite high in tax shelter syndications. Avoidance of substantial incidental fees can lead to significantly improved yields for the children as investors. Indeed, this potentially higher yield may increase the likelihood that such transactions are upheld for tax purposes, if audited, since a true market yield, or one a bit higher, may indicate the presence of a valid business purpose, on the children's side, for the transaction. Second, and perhaps most important, a sale effected between parents and children may be far more acceptable to potential parents/sellers than a sale to unrelated third parties. A number of surveys have indicated a fear, on the part of elderly homeowners, that a sale of their home to a third party will unfairly deprive their children of a rightful inheritance. For instance, in a survey of elderly residents of Lake County, Illinois, conducted in 1982 by the Program for Housing Research and Development of the University of Illinois, nearly one-fifth of those surveyed believed that their homes were a "family asset" worthy of retention within the family.

The second type of sale-leaseback transaction, in its simplest form again, would be a sale-leaseback involving unrelated third parties. Here, clearly, questions of scale enter the picture. First, we may probably assume that the average home sold nationwide will not achieve a sale price in excess of $100,000. Furthermore, if one assumes that at least 80 percent of the sale price will be leveraged, then a single sale-leaseback of such an average home may require perhaps no more than $20,000 in equity, a sum far too small to interest any traditional real estate syndicator. Rather, it seems quite clear that to tap the traditional market it will be necessary to "pool" numbers of such sales so as to generate a large enough equity base to justify syndication. Such pooling of properties is common in public limited partnerships in real estate, as well as in mortgage-backed investment transactions, so the concept should encounter little investor resistance. The alternative to pooling and syndication would be to forego traditional syndication methods entirely and instead find "brokers" willing to act as intermediaries between potential sellers and buyers. However, the advantages of pooling and syndication ought not to be overlooked. First, of course, are economies of scale to be obtained in a syndication, such as lower incidental fees in the aggregate and, possibly, the availability of lower-cost financing. Second, use of a pooling and syndication method can also lead to diversification in the holdings, both geographical and economic. Such diversification in mortgage pool investments has met with investor approval and ought to be positively greeted in this context. The major difficulty in such a pooling arrangement, however, will be practical, i.e., how to ensure overall supervision of diverse small properties.

A major disadvantage of utilizing a pooling/syndication technique in connection with sale-leasebacks of older Americans' homes, however, is the danger that in so doing the emphasis of the parties will shift from primarily one of aiding the older American sellers to one of maximizing the profits of the investors. Such a shift in emphasis might well result in victimization of the elderly unless carefully guarded against.

The second possible home-equity technique which might prove to be of great value is split-equity financing, a technique that I am currently researching in conjunction with the staff of the Housing Research and Development Program at the University of Illinois at Champaign-Urbana. The split-equity concept differs in certain significant respects from the sale-leaseback technique described above. The most significant difference, one which affects the elderly sellers, is that while the purpose of the sale-leaseback technique is to "unlock" a portion of accumulated housing equity without having the elderly seller relocate, the split-equity technique presupposes that the elderly seller will relocate, particularly to purpose-built, smaller, and more energy-efficient housing. Second, while in the sale-leaseback scheme, the elderly seller will exchange fee ownership (i.e., full legal ownership) for a long-term lease-hold, in the split equity context the elderly seller will purchase a fee ownership interest (albeit less than 100 percent) in his new housing and will thus be both owner and renter (of that portion of the fee he does not own) rather than just a renter.

The simplest example of a split-equity arrangement would be as follows: an elderly homeowner would sell his existing house to an unrelated buyer (by normal means) and exclude up to $125,000 of the gain on sale pursuant to IRC § 121. Then, the elderly seller would determine the type of new housing unit he desires to move into. Presumably, the seller would have already contracted to purchase an interest in this new unit contingent upon sale of his existing home. Second, the elderly seller would determine what percentage of ownership he desired, e.g., 30 percent, 50 percent, 70 percent. The remaining percentage would be purchased by an investor, either a family member or an unrelated party, for instance, a pool/limited partnership arrangement. The elderly seller could then invest the remaining proceeds of the sale of his first house either in an annuity, municipal bonds, or another investment vehicle yielding current income. He would also execute a long-term lease with the investor to rent that portion of his unit owned by the investor at a fair rental.

The benefits of the split-equity arrangement are several. First, for the elderly seller, there is the benefit of acquiring new, purpose-built housing designed to suit precisely the needs of older Americans, i.e., increased energy efficiency, easy maintenance, proper size. Second, the elderly seller now has increased cash flow (some of which will be used to pay rent due to the investor/owner). Further, a portion of local real property taxes will be shifted to the investor/owner, thereby reducing maintenance costs to the elderly. Finally, the elderly seller/buyer has the advantage of retaining a true equity ownership in his new home, rather than becoming a pure renter. For the investor/owner, either related or unrelated, there are the same tax advantages as there would be in the sale-leaseback situation, e.g., depreciation. There is also an additional potential advantage for the community. While the sale-leaseback technique leads to retention by the elderly of their older homes, homes which are often too large for elderly households and too difficult for them to properly maintain, the split equity technique puts these older, larger houses onto the market, making them available to younger families who would utilize them more fully as well as more easily maintain them. Of course, to the extent the elderly household desires to stay in its current housing, in spite of underutilization, maintenance, and other problems, the split-equity technique will not meet with a warm reception. For those elderly families, however, who are willing or desirous of relocation to better, more suitable housing but want, at the same time, to increase cash income and maintain a true equity interest in their housing, the split-equity technique is promising.

Notes

1. Such a sale with a retained life interest currently is believed not to qualify for the IRC § 121 gain exclusion.
2. Cf, Financial Accounting Standards Board, Statement 13, Accounting for Leases (1976), as amended, for parallel accounting treatment.
3. Such brokering is common in certain types of tax-sheltered equipment leasing transactions.

11

Consumer Safeguards for Financial Instruments Unlocking Home Equity for the Aged

Maurice D. Weinrobe

The Nature of Consumer Safeguards

Financial instruments that will allow the elderly to tap equity from owned residences will put the beneficiaries of such plans at a distinct disadvantage vis à vis the providers of funds.[1] These plans and instruments will be introduced to potential recipients at a time of their lives when they are skeptical and accustomed to being warned about "get rich" or "do well" schemes, and in many cases to individuals who have not had primary responsibility for household financial arrangements. Beyond the matter of the personality characteristics of the potential recipients, the programs being offered in all likelihood will be confusing, at least initially.

In addition to their relatively confusing and even alien character, plans to unlock home equity may contain provisions that the average well-informed

---

From *Journal of Housing for the Elderly,* Vol. 2, No. 2 (Summer 1984), 55-71. Reprinted by permission of The Haworth Press, Inc., 28 East 22nd Street, New York, NY.

This study was undertaken on behalf of the Home Equity Conversion Project, a project financed in part by the State of Wisconsin and the Administration on Aging. The helpful comments of Ken Scholen, Don L. Ralya, Bronwyn Belling and Trudy A. Ernst are acknowledged.

consumer would not be able to evaluate. For example, most consumers can not evaluate whether they should consume food products with specific additives, or whether they should accept the services of one plumber rather than another. The problems of uncertainty and incomplete information are often made tractable in a market economy by the process of competition. Most of us do not know whether we should purchase radios with tubes or transistors, but with the help of the market our decisions largely are made for us—decidedly inferior products do not pass the market test. But for decidedly inferior products to be eliminated from consideration there must be a superior alternative (tubes were not always inefficient in radios), and another characteristic of plans to unlock home equity is that in the early years of their existences they will probably be offered by only a few providers. The discipline of the market will not be equally vigorous for all aspects of plans to tap home equity. Some financial parameters of the plans could be kept under control by the market (such as the mortgage interest rate in a reverse mortgage), while other plan features would have no similar force to ensure that the characteristic is for the best interest of financial institution and senior/homeowners (such as a prepayment penalty).

It is clear that decisions of the elderly on the disposition of their principal asset are extremely important decisions, and decisions in which the public has some interest. If a number of elderly persons made decisions that in retrospect were determined to have been unwise, society would pay part of the price for the error. This could be true for cases where houses were disposed of or retained.

The subject of consumer safeguards is a catalogue of restrictions and interferences with the market. It is a blatant statement that the market has, will or should not work. Consumer safeguards are a correction to the market, and as such one should be very careful in identifying safeguards to make sure that the market correction is in response to a market failure. Anyone can suggest, and rightly so, that lower interest rates are in the interest of the consumer. But just because a safeguard is beneficial to the consumer—even the consumer who is a senior/homeowner—is not to say that such safeguard is socially desirable.

In this paper a set of consumer safeguards for instruments to unlock home equity for the elderly will be reviewed. In all cases the attempt will be to identify a problem that exists in an unfettered market situation, and then suggest how the social situation could be improved with the introduction of a consumer safeguard. Even though home-equity release plans can be extremely diverse, there are problems common to either all instruments or broad classifications of instruments. In the second part of this paper issues relating to consumer safeguards in general are discussed. In part three reverse annuity mortgage safeguards are investigated, and in part four safeguards for sale and leaseback arrangements for elderly persons are considered.

General Consumer Safeguards[2]

Consumer safeguards can come into existence from a number of outside institutions. Virtually all financial institutions face some type of regulation, and depository institutions in particular face very specific regulation. Sometimes the regulations are national in scope, sometimes restricted to an individual state. The important thing is that while one can talk about matters that are similar to all kinds of instruments to unlock home equity, seeing a rule or regulation put into effect that will affect all instruments equally is very unlikely.[3]

The most common safeguard problem is that of disclosure. Virtually all instruments that allow the elderly to tap home equity will be difficult to understand. If senior/homeowners are to be able to make intelligent decisions, two conditions must be fulfilled: the instruments offered must be explained fully but straight-forwardly, and for situations in which more than one instrument or plan is being offered, the alternatives must be comparable.

The comparability of plans is not a simple matter.[4] There are many simple criteria on which plans can be compared (e.g., measures of rate of return on investment, net monthly payments, present value of expected payments, etc.), but a summary measure is not always appropriate. In searching for a new automobile I may be interested in the fuel efficiency of available cars, but I will not base my decision solely on that factor. For adequate comparison of plans, attention must be given to assembling and providing data on a range of key items. The following items are indicative of the kind of information that should be disclosed: the schedule of monthly payments or net monthly payments to senior/homeowner; the expected payment schedule if it is noncertain; tax status and tax effects of payments; term or duration of monthly payments; equity position of homeowners after a specific period of time (at term if appropriate); for variable interest rate plans, some measure of the effect of a specific rate change on payments and loan balance (for example the effect of a limit change in the interest rate, positive and negative, at the first rollover point); prepayment penalties; and rights of lender to escalate payments of loan balance. This list is illustrative, but it does convey the importance of not only describing a plan, but doing so in a format that allows comparison.

Instruments for equity recapture are fundamentally different from other loan or sale/leaseback decisions in their explicit orientation towards the elderly.[5] This must be taken into account in designing disclosure materials. In fact, the provider of funds or the intermediary should be obligated to do more than disclose. It should be mandatory that any individual applying for an instrument that will tap home equity be given full financial counseling with respect to that instrument.

Disclosure, counseling, and comparison should apply to virtually any home equity conversion plan being considered. Beyond these basic issues, different classes or types of instruments have very different problems. In the next two sections attention is directed to the two major classes of instruments. The discussion will still be general in that such matters as variable interest rates and non-level payments schedules will not be given special attention. Such specific aspects of the plans would merit equally specific safeguards.

Reverse Mortgages

Reverse mortgages, or reverse annuity mortgages (RAMs), involve a loan secured by a residence.[6] Some portion, or all, of the proceeds of the loan may be used to purchase any annuity. Both the loan and the annuity purchase should involve safeguards. The following are variables in a RAM: the interest rate, term to maturity, initial disbursement of cash to the borrower, and the loan-to-value ratio (LTV). It is not unusual to put limits on these, or similar, variables in an attempt to aid the consumer. If one is to urge that this be done, however, there should be a principle for the market interference.

One of the more common market restrictions is the usury ceiling. The overwhelming professional opinion is that attempts to protect people from high interest rates, and other situations that reduce consumer well-being, are rarely effective in achieving their announced intention. It is far more often the case that flows of funds are simply reoriented away from the protected use.[7] The most probable effect of an interest limitation on RAMs would be a dearth of RAMs actually written.

A second potential restriction on RAMs would be a limit on term to maturity. It is possible to ensure that senior/homeowners do not get themselves into a bind by taking out a RAM that is too long, but it is also true that extending term to maturity seriously diminishes the monthly payments on a RAM, and it is unlikely that the situation of an extreme term to maturity would arise in an unconstrained market environment. A term constraint would at best be redundant. Similarly, the effect of a large initial disbursement reducing monthly payments should keep potential borrowers from trying to pull out excessive equity at the front end of a loan. Again a constraint in the form of a safeguard is unnecessary. The final variable, the LTV, presents a slightly different situation.

A reverse mortgage has the reverse risk profile of a standard mortgage. In the earliest phase of a RAM, the property behind the loan provides unquestionable security for the loan. For a standard mortgage, the first few years are the riskiest. As a RAM approaches the term to maturity, the loan balance nears its maximum. The risk of a RAM is a result of the loan balance behavior relative to property value. The future loan value is scheduled, but the future house value is difficult to predict—it depends on individual and market circumstances. Thus the ultimate LTV is inherently risky. Because regulators of depository intermediaries are responsible for the protection of depositors, it is appropriate to place restrictions on the scheduled LTV, based on initial property value (i.e., rather than a predicted property value).[8]

The quantification of the maximum LTV should be based on experience and the actuarial risk of default. This is a difficult magnitude to estimate as it involves not only mortality, but other factors that would lead to an early termination of a RAM, and property value as well. The other factors that would lead to early termination would in part be dependent on the consumer safeguards adopted. As for property value, I have been unable to find any studies that compare the values of properties owned by elderly persons to all residential properties.

As a complement to the above, a senior who wished to get as much value as possible from a property should have the right to refinance a RAM at any time, basing a new loan on a reappraised property. Appropriate limitations on the refinancing would be that the interest rate would be changed to the rate then current, and that the maximum LTV (based on reappraised value) would still be in effect.

In addition to consumer safeguards on the loan parameters of RAM, it is also appropriate to consider potential aspects of the loan. The following items are worthy of consideration: requirements for lender conduct at the term of maturity; loan acceleration prior to term; rights of the senior/homeowner on the sale of a RAM; and prepayment and termination penalties.

The most difficult procedural RAM matter is how to treat things at the term of the loan. The issue is a very simple one. At the maturity of the loan the borrower is faced with a decision that involves the possible forced sale of a residence. There are two distinct possibilities worth considering: required annuity purchase; required lender re-scheduling of a loan. (See Weinrobe, 1983.)

The individual's problems at the term of a RAM could conceivably be taken care of by purchasing a single premium deferred annuity at RAM origination.[9] The annuity could either pick up interest only on the loan (essentially allowing the senior to remain in a house with no additional income payments) or interest plus old monthly income payments.

In a study of reverse annuity mortgages completed for the Reverse Annuity Mortgage Program of the San Francisco Development Fund, computer simulations were run using a simple RAM incorporating annuity premiums as an initial loan disbursement (Kaplan, Smith and Associates, 1981). The annuity premiums are for a "no death benefit" annuity—an annuity form with the lowest premiums available.[10]

For an $80,000 final loan balance, interest only payments at 12 percent per annum would be $1,000 per month. If a 70-year-old man wished to purchase an annuity to generate $1,000 per month at the end of ten years (the end of the presumed term for a RAM), it would cost $25,745. This amount would be an initial disbursement of funds by the lender—i.e., it would be part of the RAM. But $25,745 at 12 percent annual interest (compounded monthly) for ten years equals $84,968. Thus, the annuity purchase itself would prevent the RAM from having any payments to the senior, and in fact the flow of payments would have to be from senior to lender just to keep the maximum loan balance at $80,000. (The payments would be $17.94 per month.) If the 10 year, 12 percent RAM had been originated without an annuity, the monthly payments to the senior would have been $347.76. A variety of different annuity situations are shown in Exhibit 11.1, with their effects on monthly payment.

The annuity simulations of Exhibit 11.1 are not appealing in terms of their effect on the within term monthly payment to senior. The possibility of requiring an annuity purchase as a consumer safeguard for a reverse mortgage would seem out of the question given the relationship between annuity premiums and mortgage interest rates.

Required rescheduling of a RAM loan is a second possible safeguard for dealing with the loan termination point. In fact, the initial RAM regulations of the Federal Home Loan Bank Board (FHLLB) adopted in 1978 included a provision: "If the mortgage has a fixed term, refinancing shall be made available at market rates current at the time payment is due."[11] This language was imprecise, but might be interpreted as requiring the lender (S&L) to refinance the RAM at maturity subject to a new appraisal and the originally specified maximum loan-to-value ratio, which would mean that the amount of the monthly payment in the second place of the mortgage would be a variable. This is best seen with an example. If a RAM was originated on a $100,000 with a target loan-to-(original) value ratio of 80 percent, the ultimate loan balance would be $80,000. If the original RAM was for 10 years at 11 percent, then level monthly payments would have been $365.32. Now assume the senior/homeowner wishes to extend the RAM for an additional five years. Exhibit 11.2 indicates that within even a rather modest range of annual house inflation rates (4 to 8 percent) the possible monthly payments for the additional five years would range from $-236.11 to $489.20.

Because the additional monthly payments are so sensitive to property value, the FHLBB type regulation is by no means a guarantee that the senior will be able to continue to live in her or his house, but it does provide a backstop for some situations. In that light it is a desirable kind of consumer protection

EXHIBIT 11.1
Effect of Annuity Purchases on RAM Monthly Payments*
(RAM with ultimate loan balance of $80,000 and interest rate of 12 percent)

	Annuity Generates Monthly Income of $1000	
		Monthly RAM Income During Term of RAM
Male–70	10 year RAM	$– 17.94
	15 year RAM	38.75
Female–70	10 year RAM	– 134.15
	15 year RAM	– 13.62
Male–75	10 year RAM	121.84
	15 year RAM	103.81
Female–75	10 year RAM	42.16
	15 year RAM	74.85
	Annuity Generates Monthly Income of $600	
		Monthly RAM Income During Term of RAM
Male–70	10 year RAM	$128.34
	15 year RAM	87.30
Female–70	10 year RAM	58.61
	15 year RAM	55.89
Male–75	10 year RAM	212.21
	15 year RAM	126.34
Female–75	10 year RAM	164.41
	15 year RAM	108.97
	No annuity—Monthly Income of $0 Post RAM	
	10 year RAM	$347.76
	15 year RAM	160.16

*Monthly income derived using annuity premium as initial disbursement of RAM. These income figures are meant to be descriptive of a phenomenon, and are heavily dependent on annuity premiums used in the simulation. The annuity premiums were obtained from Occidental Life Insurance Company, and were effective 8/18/80 through 9/1/80. The premiums are for a deferred life annuity, single premium, no refund, no death benefit.

Source: Special Study on Reverse Anniuty Mortgages, Reverse Annuity Program of the San Francisco Development Fund, 1981.

clause. It does the lender no harm (as long as the new RAM can be written at "then current rates") and it offers the senior an element of protection. If there are only a few financial institutions offering RAMs, this type of safeguard is

EXHIBIT 11.2
Effect of Using a Rising Property Value to Rollover a RAM at End of Initial Term

Interest Rate: 11 percent
Initial Loan Term: 10 years

	Property Appreciation Rate**		
Initial Property Value	$100,000	$100,000	$100,000
Property Value at End of 10 Years	149,082	181,939	221,961
Monthly Payment to Senior:*			
First Ten Years	365.32	365.32	365.32
Next Five Years	−236.11	90.21	489.20
Final Loan Balance***	119,266	145,551	177,569

*For both the first ten years and second five years, monthly payments are set up so as to reach an end of term balance of 80 percent of the beginning of period house value.
** Annual rate of appreciation compounded monthly.
*** Using a disbursement of $80,000 at rollover.

all the more important as one lender's reluctance to roll over a RAM may leave the senior/homeowner with no alternative source of funds. The lender is also protected by such a safeguard as it sets out the obligation in the context of reasonable profitability. The lender should by no means be forced to extend a loan which would be unsecured.

One can go much farther in designing arrangements to protect the senior at term. This could involve pooled loan arrangements or pooled annuities, depletion insurance, or a requirement that the lender "have a built-in leasing arrangement and/or purchase agreement which would enable the borrower to continue to occupy his home even though he may have forfeited any right to title or have passed title to the [lender] . . ."[12] Each of these possible arrangements is directed at a critical issue, but until insurers indicate a willingness to enter into such arrangements at rates that will not seriously disrupt the monthly payment, or until it seems clear that lenders are willing to pool loans, it would be premature to require as part of the RAM contract that such safeguards be adopted. If the market can effectively provide such options, it should not be necessary to require them as safeguards. They will dominate loan plans without such options. If the market cannot provide such options, it is fatuous to require them.

The treatment of the maturity on a RAM is a difficult issue. If a senior is short-sighted or enters into an agreement not expecting to survive the term to maturity, but then does in fact survive, she or he could be forced out of the house. But against this, if a senior can be adequately made aware of the risks involved, does in fact benefit by taking the income flow from the capital asset over time, and then must settle the debt by sale of the property, one can reasonably ask whether any injustice has been done. Much depends on the question of how much credible information has been dispensed at the origination point. A complete and thorough counseling at origination should screen individuals so that those who choose to take out RAMs are not only aware of the possibilities, but find their personal objectives coincident with them.

A second set of procedural issues relates to acceleration of the loan balance due. The simplest case of the right of a lender to accelerate payment of the current loan balance is death of the borrower. It would seem apparent that with the death of the borrower the purpose of a RAM is exhausted and the lender should be permitted to accelerate. But the general issue is more complicated and when the focus moves from death to other possible conditions for acceleration, the desirability or propriety of acceleration becomes less clear.

Consider the following events, each of which might be considered a proper occasion for loan acceleration: the sub-letting of a portion of the residence, a move-out (temporary or permanent), and changes in the physical or mental condition of the borrower.[13] In these instances, the action implies a change in the status of the senior homeowner. The purpose of acceleration in these instances would be to recognize that the borrower no longer requires the flow of payments associated with the RAM.

In a standard mortgage agreement a lender is dependent on a financially secure borrower who can be expected to continue to pay monthly obligations. Anything that jeopardizes the standing of the borrower also jeopardizes the quality of the loan. The reverse mortgage is not dependent on the financial standing of the borrower.[14] It is appropriate for a lender to be concerned with the quality and value of the residence in question, and to take actions or reserve the right to take actions to protect against declines in property value. The interesting thing about the various events under discussion that might merit acceleration clauses is that they do not directly affect the value of the residence.

The effects of even the potential for acceleration associated with these events could be important. A clause providing that a move-out would be sufficient to trigger acceleration could only have a detrimental effect on a senior seeking to experiment with other possible living arrangements. Similarly, an acceleration clause for cases of diminished physical or mental capacity would not only be difficult and perhaps expensive to prove, but might force an elderly person from one of the only elements of stability in her or his life.

In sum, it is well to consider carefully just what the objectives are of any loan acceleration contingencies. From the point of view of the consumer, it may be that such clauses inhibit action and reduce the attractiveness of a

RAM. If they really serve no purpose to the lender, then their inclusion should be prohibited in RAM loan agreements.

A third procedural RAM issue deals with the sale of a RAM. It is possible that a lender would want to sell a RAM to an individual or institution. Obviously, the obligation of the lender to honor all commitments to the senior/homeowner is vitally important and must be safeguarded.

A fourth RAM issue is the right to prepay. One ordinarily thinks of loan termination simply as pre-payment, but in the case of a RAM loan termination is a two part or even two phase operation. The flow of disbursements to the senior/homeowner can cease (while the loan balance continues to accumulate interest), and the senior can pay off the existing loan balance prior to scheduled maturity. There is a strong case for allowing senior initiated actions of both phases without penalty.

The absence of prepayment penalties is often mandated on standard mortgages. This is presumably done because of unequal information on borrower and lender sides of a transaction and because of the likelihood that individual circumstances will arise that necessitate prepayment of a loan, and a lender should not be in a position to sit in judgment on whether a prepayment is honorable. On both grounds the case is stronger for a prohibition of prepayment penalty with a RAM. In addition, since a RAM is by design a negatively amortizing loan, it is appropriate to allow a senior/homeowner the right to order a cessation of loan disbursements.

It is therefore appropriate that RAMs include the following consumer safeguards: (1) the borrower may repay a RAM in full or part without penalty; and, (2) that the borrower may initiate the reduction of the monthly payment in part or in full, in which case the loan balance would continue to accrue interest at the originally scheduled interest rate.

This completes the discussion of consumer safeguards associated with RAMs. It is not a comprehensive discussion. There are many legal issues that arise, other issues associated with all mortgages, and issues associated with specific RAMs. If there is a theme to be recapitulated, it is that the mortgage contract must be a bit more flexible than a standard forward mortgage, in keeping with the special situation of senior/homeowners. The safeguards that have been suggested will make a RAM instrument a better instrument for *borrower and lender*. Indeed, without these safeguards it is unlikely that a RAM instrument would have any viablity in the marketplace.

Sale/Leaseback Plans

The sale/leaseback arrangement is one of the oldest working plans allowing elderly persons to liberate home equity. Guttentag (1975) describes the rentes viageres which has existed in France for quite some period of time as a simple sale/leaseback program. However, even though the concept has existed and been used for years, the amount of formal interest in this type of arrangement (apart from transactions between related parties, such as between parents and children) is small.

In theory there are many ways that a sale/leaseback arrangement could be set up. The investor (an individual, a pool, or a financial institution) could agree to purchase with a lump-sum payment, purchase with an annuity type series of payments, purchase with the senior taking back a mortgage, etc. Similarly, the arrangement could be set up so that the senior has the right to life tenancy, or the right to a more limited tenancy. The safeguards that would be appropriate to a sale/leaseback would largely be dependent on the nature of the specific agreement. The most important set of consumer safeguards would deal with the lease. Because the elderly person is putting her or himself into a situation of extreme dependency on the place of residence and the investor, it is vital that the lease be drawn up to protect against contingencies that could force the senior to leave the home. Thus, future rents should be specified or made part of a formula, and conditions for eviction should be specific. Matters such as temporary move-outs, the allowance of additional tenants, and diminished physical and mental capacity, should be addressed clearly. Without unusual protection on these kinds of items, the senior/homeowner could be in an extremely vulnerable position. Lastly, responsibility for repair and maintenance should be clearly specified.

A second set of safeguard issues relates to the terms of the sale itself. Again, these items require a specific sale/leaseback plan for a detailed discussion, but some generalities can be offered. To the extent that a substantial mortgage is involved, the term of the mortgage should be related to life expectancy. This would result in an income stream to the senior that would continue for a desirable amount of time, but also would mean that any annuity purchased as part of the transaction would be relatively inexpensive. A second sales related issue is that of the terms of the sale. It is undesirable to have suggested constraints on the price and downpayment, but it should be kept in mind that important tax considerations abound that relate to a sale/leaseback transaction. It would be extremely helpful to have sale/leasebacks proceed according to some model arrangement where all important tax considerations have been taken into account.

While all of the suggestions of the previous paragraph would probably provide for a better sale/leaseback, it is wrong to conclude that regulatory or statutory safeguards should be adopted to require them. Once again, they are sensible to all parties concerned and there is no reason to believe market failure should arise.

A third matter, and case that would be helped along by a consumer safeguard, stems from the recognition that the sale/leaseback may put the senior in a position of seller, banker, and tenant. These roles are complex and confusing. Any sales arrangement involving a loan must have suitable protection for the lender to be confident of recourse in case of default. A sale/leaseback should be designed so that the senior can have speedy recourse in the case of a cessation of payments from the investor. Because these mortgage payments will in all likelihood be the principal source of income to the senior, a lengthly delay in declaring default and instituting an action leading to foreclosure could be serious and even dangerous. Because the foreclosure process would be different from that enjoyed by financial institutions, different statutes or regulations should control the process.

The above comments on sale/leaseback arrangements are primarily related to private arrangements—i.e., between a senior or elderly couple and a private individual or firm. Sale/leaseback plans have also been proposed with public agencies or cooperatives as the purchaser. Once again, the variety of possibilities of such public programs are quite large and the appropriate consumer safeguards would differ from one to another, but there is an important common issue that bears note. Whenever a sale/leaseback agreement is entered into the seller is giving up a property right. Precisely what is being received in return is less exact. In some cases the exchange could be for a fixed amount of cash; in others for a mortgage; and in others for an annuity. It is with an annuity arrangement that the following is concerned.

An annuity is a promise to pay for an extended period—typically life or life plus a period of time. The guaranty of any annuity is a matter of contract. Reference has been made repeatedly to conditions under which a senior's rights to occupancy may be terminated. These same issues arise in the case of an exchange of annuity for a property. The senior should be protected against any connection of the annuity with house tenure But beyond specific clauses that protect the elderly homeowner/leasee, it is appropriate to be concerned with the ability of any purchaser to continue payments over the life of the elderly person. If a mortgage is written in exchange for the property, the senior can proceed with foreclosure in case of a default. If an annuity is purchased from an insurance company, then one is dealing with a regulated body. If, however, the annuity is the liability of a public or private body, it may be the case that the future payment is not fully guaranteed, and that the property right of the senior is impaired. A reserve fund or guaranty should be established in the case of any sale/leaseback arrangement that involves the exchange of a property for the promise of an annuity. This would provide protection to the senior to ensure that any promised flow of income to the senior is independent of the general state of the housing market or even the aggregate economy at some future point in time.

Conclusion

In this paper the subject of consumer safeguards for financial instruments that allow the elderly to tap home equity has been reviewed in general and in particular. It is impossible to develop a complete catalogue of consumer safeguards for such instruments, but one can hope to highlight some of the more important issues and concerns, and to suggest some types of restrictions on financial instruments that protect the borrower without leaving the lender disaffected.

It is very unlikely that the financial instruments that have been discussed here will come into existence barren of consumer safeguards. There are already some restrictions on RAMs in the regulations of the Federal Home Loan Bank Board and in state statutes and regulations, and it is probable that as the instruments gain use, other financial regulators will insist on safeguards for their use. The biggest concern should be not whether, but which, consumer safeguards. It is too easy to take the side of either lender or borrower, and with either bias the effect could be decimating. Because these instruments are quite novel there will be some hesitancy to become involved on both sides of the market. Elderly homeowners are not eager to jump into a new plan about which they or their families know little, and which may involve a question of whether they will be able to live out their lives in their own home. Similarly, lenders have not shown themselves to be overeager to begin making loans that involve a bigger forward than immediate commitment of funds. It must be remembered that consumer safeguards are constraints on the market—restrictions on one side or the other. As such, by their nature they make an instrument less attractive than it would have been to at least one side.

Care should be exercised in the development of each safeguard. Particular attention should be devoted to the general effects of any provision, in addition to any immediate effects. As long as one is aware of the variety of implications of a market restricting action or regulation, it is likely that the best interests of all concerned will be served. Put differently, a consumer safeguard that results in few or no loans to the elderly has not served the purpose for which it was intended.

Notes

1. There have been a number of recent publications on the general subject of home equity conversion for the aged. A good reference with an up-to-date bibliography is Scholen and Chen, 1980.
2. An extensive discussion of the need for consumer safeguards on residential mortgages may be found in Weinrobe, 1977.

3. This is also true of consumer safeguards on residential mortgages, and specifically on variable or adjustable rate mortgages. The evolving process of regulating consumer safety has been a kind of regulatory competition with one type of financial intermediary looking to regulators of other intermediaries as inspiration for their own regulatory body.
4. On the difficulty of comparing plans for the release of home equity, see Guttentag, 1980.
5. There is no logical necessity that reverse mortgage or residential sale/leasebacks be oriented towards the elderly, but they often are, and that is the subject of this paper. It is interesting to note that reverse mortgages in particular could be very well suited for other purposes, such as financing higher education or financing expenses during a period of reduced income. Two reasons that these instruments are oriented toward the elderly are: the remaining tenure horizon of the elderly is relatively brief; and, a great percentage of elderly persons own their homes and are house rich/income poor. See Scholen and Chen, 1980, Part I.
6. There is some confusion over the terms reverse mortgage and reverse annuity mortgage. A reverse mortgage provides a flow of income either as a result of a rising loan or a fixed loan which is used to purchase an annuity. Either of these streams of income can be described as an annuity: "a series of equal payments made at equal intervals of time." (Greene, 1977, p. 463) The difference between the two instruments is that the rising loan has a fixed maturity date and the fixed loan with purchased annuity typically continues to generate income for the life of the annuitant. It is entirely appropriate to discuss reverse mortgages with or without a purchased annuity.
7. In a word, credit is fungible. Two of many papers that focus on this matter with respect to housing market credit are Arcelus and Meltzer, 1973, and Hendershot and Villani, 1977.
8. A closely related matter is that a borrower who survives the term of a RAM will be dependent on any residual equity for her or his well-being. If no annuity has been purchased (as will often be the case due to the magnitude of annuity premiums relative to RAM interest rates) the existence of a large residual equity will be one way for a senior/homeowner to generate more future income. But one can legitimately question the social propriety of requiring that such a large equity be preserved. Indeed, the largest residual equity would result from no RAM at all. It seems more appropriate to provide full information to a RAM borrower and then allow the borrower to make the decision that suits her or his individual circumstance.
9. Other annuity programs could be discussed but the point is well covered by this suggested arrangement.
10. That is, this type of annuity has the lowest premium. The actual premium schedule used in the simulations comes from Occidental Life Insurance Company. Few insurance companies offer this particular annuity and Occidental's premiums were available. Other companies may have lower premiums.
11. Timms and Mataya, 1979, p. 36.
12. These restrictions are included in some existing RAM agreements.
13. Like so many aspects of RAMs, the responsibility of secured financial status is the reverse of a standard or forward mortgage. It is important that the provider of a RAM, the lender, be sufficiently credit worthy that the senior/homeowner can be certain that the RAM payments will continue for the contracted life of the loan.
14. The very worst situation would be for the income and security of the senior to be tied to the value of the property itself. The essence of the sale/leaseback is that the senior is giving up the uncertain future value of the property for a certain present value. If income (including the likelihood of the continuity of income) is tied to the property value, then the senior is bearing the downside risk of property value changes and selling off the upside of potential appreciation. That is highly inappropriate.

References

Arcelus, Francisco, and Meltzer, Allan H. "The Markets for Housing and Housing Services." *Journal of Money, Credit and Banking.* February 1973, Vol. 5, No. 1, pp. 78-99.

Greene, Mark R. *Risk and Insurance,* 4th edition. Cincinnati, Ohio: South-Western Publishing Co. 1977.

Guttentag, Jack M. "Creating New Financial Instruments for the Aged." *The Bulletin 1975.* New York University Center for the Study of Financial Institutions, 1975.

_____. "Criteria for Assessing Home Equity Conversion Plans," Mimeo, November 1980.

Hendershot, Patric H., and Villani, Kevin. "The Federally Sponsored Credit Agencies: Their Behavior and Impact," in Robert M. Buckley, et al. (eds). *Capital Markets and the Housing Sector: Perspectives on Financial Reform.* Ballinger Publishing Co., Cambridge, MA, 1977.

Kaplan, Smith and Associates. *Special Study on Reverse Annuity Mortgages.* Reverse Annuity Mortgage Program of the San Francisco Development Fund, 1981.

Scholen, Ken, and Chen, Yung-Ping (eds.). *Unlocking Home Equity for the Elderly.* Ballinger Publishing Co., Cambridge, MA, 1980.

Timms, Ronald H., and Mataya, James M. *The Reverse Mortgage Loan.* United States League of Savings Associations, Chicago, IL, 1979.

Weinrobe, Maurice D. "Analysis of Consumer Safeguards for AMIs," in Donald M. Kaplan (ed). *Alternative Mortgage Instrument Research Study,* Vol. III. Federal Home Loan Bank Board, Washington, D.C., 1977.

_____. "Home Equity Conversion Instruments with Fixed Term to Maturity: Alternatives to End of Term Pay-Off." *AREUEA Journal.* Vol. 11, No. 1, Spring 1983.

12

Home Equity Financing of Long-Term Care for the Elderly[1]

Bruce Jacobs and William Weissert

Financing long-term health care for the elderly has become increasingly difficult as the population ages. In the past two decades, expenditures on health and related services for the chronically ill have mushroomed. Though nominally responsible for financing long-term care (for example, that following a hospital stay for an acute illness), the Medicare program picks up less than 4 percent of all nursing home costs. Recently, some public sector support for in-home services has emerged, but the programs are quite small relative to the total scope of the problem.

Today the burdens of long-term care are borne in three principal ways. In the public sector, the Medicaid program provides the lion's share of support for nursing home care of poor patients, the vast majority of whom are elderly. As it is now structured, the program puts substantial economic pressures on state governments, which finance approximately half the public sector expenditures, and on prospective patients, who must be virtually impoverished before they qualify for aid. Both groups have taken steps to relieve these pres-

---

From U.S. Department of Health and Human Services, Health Care Financing Administration, *Long-Term Care Financing and Delivery Systems: Exploring Some Alternatives. Conference Proceedings*, ed. by Patrice Hirsch Feinstein, Marian Gornick, and Jay N. Greenberg. Washington, D.C.: U.S. Government Printing Office, 1984, pp. 82–94.

sures. State governments have attempted to limit costs by regulating the supply of nursing beds and by putting liens on on the estates of Medicaid patients. States are now authorized to put a lien on the homes of recipient patients who do not have a spouse or a disabled child living in the home and who are not expected to return to the community. There have also been recent proposals to secure some financial contribution from the children of Medicaid patients in nursing homes.

For most long-term care patients, financing of nursing home stays, initially and preponderantly, consists of out-of-pocket expenditures. The majority of older Americans will never be hit with a major nursing home bill. Only a minority of them will enter a nursing home, and most stays are reasonably short (less than four months long). However, the economic consequences of a long-term stay are usually devastating. In a kind of nursing home roulette, elderly Americans face the risk of catastrophic health costs that today accumulate at an average rate of more than $1,000 per month, with some institutions charging more than three times that rate.

Historically, the families of persons in need of long-term care have avoided major out-of-pocket expenditures by providing much of the care themselves, and this appears to remain the case today (Shanas, 1979; Weissert, 1983; Weissert and Scanlon, 1983). However, a substantial increase in the labor force participation of middle-aged women (the daughters and principle family caregivers for the dependent elderly) and the equally dramatic increase in the percentage of elderly people who do not live with other family members have combined to constrain the supply of family care.

Very few prospective elderly nursing home patients can afford extended stays using only their current income. There is also a great reluctance to utilize liquid assets that have been accumulated over a lifetime. In any event, most older Americans do not have easily spendable assets sufficient to finance very extended long-term care (Friedman and Sjogren, 1981). The combination of low probability and high cost of lengthy nursing home stays would seem to provide a natural market for an insurance instrument that pools the risk borne by elderly people. However, private insurers have been reluctant to issue policies for this purpose at prices the elderly might be expected to pay out of their current incomes.

Not surprisingly, some of the aged and their families have taken other steps in anticipation or against the risk of an expected nursing home stay. Medicaid has strict guidelines on the total liquid assets that may be held while a patient is eligible to receive financial assistance. To conform to these guidelines, some older people have transferred assets to children or other family members. Though recent federal regulations limit this behavior, hiding assets will no doubt remain a strategy chosen by some. However, it is not desirable for prospective nursing home patients to appear to be without any resources, because private-pay patients are routinely give priority in admissions to privately owned facilities.

Thus, we have a long-term care system in which large costs are imposed on unfortunate families and individual elderly persons; state governments face substantial expenditure pressures from the Medicaid program; and most of the elderly are unlikely to be able to finance, out of current income, an extended nursing home stay, catastrophic health insurance, or major in-home care. Moreover, the incentives embedded in the system often distort difficult decisions about patient placement, level of care, and private financing. No single policy intervention would eliminate all the financial strain, anxiety, and value conflicts that accompany long-term care decisions. Nor can greatly increased public sector financing of long-term care be realistically expected within the foreseeable future. There is, however, one source of private financing that could relieve some of the economic and emotional strain of long-term care. That source is the accumulated equity the elderly have in their homes.

In what follows, we analyze the potential use of home equity to help pay for long-term care. The amounts of home equity held by the elderly and the yearly incomes that can be derived from it are estimated using data from the Annual Housing Survey. The Health Interview Survey and the National Nursing Home Survey are then analyzed to estimate the risk of need for some kind of long-term care and the risk of institutionalization in particular. We then gauge the extent to which the proceeds from home equity conversion could pay for home care, catastrophic nursing home cost insurance, and long-term care insurance covering either nursing home stays or home care. Finally, we raise some of the public policy issues that emerge from our findings, and we specify an agenda for further research.

Home Equity Conversion

Home ownership is the dominant housing mode of the elderly population. Three-quarters of all elderly-headed households are owner-occupied. Nearly 16 million elderly people (that is, those over 65) live in about 12 million homes they own, and more than 80 percent of them have paid off their mortgages.[2] For a variety of reasons (including both consumption benefits and tax advantages), most Americans have invested the bulk of their savings in their homes by the time they reach the age of 65. One study found that the median proportion of total assets held as net home equity (total home value minus remaining mortgage debt) was 70 percent (for elderly homeowners). For unmarried women (mostly widowed) the analogous figure was 83 percent (Friedman and Sjogren, 1981).

The average amount each elderly homeowner has tied up in her home now exceeds $50,000, and the aggregate equity owned by the elderly is now more than $600 billion. Moreover, high levels of net home equity are not enjoyed solely by upper income elderly. About 65 percent of all elderly poor are homeowners, and many low-income elderly people have substantial assets in their homes. Exhibit 12.1 shows that 22 percent of the poor and 32 percent of the near poor have more than $50,000 in net home equity. (These and all succeeding figures are expressed in constant 1983 dollars.) The procedure we used to derive net home equity was as follows: First, we inflated 1980 housing prices to 1983 values using National Association of Realtors figures on the median sale prices of existing single-family homes. These calculations were done separately for each of four regions in the county. The Annual Housing Survey does not report net home equity as such. It provides an estimation of a home's value and an indication of whether the home is owned free and clear. To estimate the remaining debt for the fifth of homeowners who have some, we estimated a bivariate regression that predicted the outstanding mortgage debt/value ratio from the number of years since the owners had moved into the house, using data from the 1970 Survey of Residential Finance. We then applied this equation to the Annual Housing Survey data to estimate the remaining debt on the home, which was then subtracted from the home's value to derive net home equity. These estimates are for single-family homes on less than 10 acres without a commercial establishment or medical or dental office. Cooperatives, condominiums, mobile homes and trailers are excluded.

Though home equity is the major asset held by elderly homeowners, it has not typically been used to finance consumption. This has been true for a

EXHIBIT 12.1
Relationship between Poverty Status and Net Home Equity

	Income as a Percentage of the Poverty Line		
Net Home Equity*	Less than 100%	100% to 124%	125% or More
To $25,000	42	27	14
$25,001 to $50,000	36	41	36
$50,001 to $75,000	14	19	28
$75,001 to $100,000	5	7	12
More than $100,000	3	6	10
TOTAL	100	100	100

*Expressed in 1983 dollars. (See text.)
Source: Tabulations from the 1980 Annual Housing Survey. Unless otherwise indicated, all other results are derived from these data as well.

variety of reasons, of which perhaps the most important is that until recently the only way to unlock home equity was to sell one's home and move. The great majority of elderly homeowners, however, have been reluctant to do this, and the attachment of the elderly to their homes has been documented in several surveys and studies of housing choice (Jacobs, 1981; Rabushka and Jacobs, 1980; Jacobs, 1983). The home equity loans now frequently advertised in the media also have limited potential for the elderly, because they are amortized over a short time period and they require monthly payments from the owner. They impose both a financial barrier (because few elderly homeowners have enough other income to make those payments) and a psychological one (because the elderly have shown a substantial reluctance to accept major debt responsibilities).

To overcome these difficulties, some innovative plans have been developed that will unlock, or convert, home equity into income for the elderly without forcing them to move or make monthly payments on a loan. Popularly known by the generic term reverse annuity mortgage (or simply reverse mortgage), these plans have received increasing attention in a variety of print and electronic media. They include loans that are paid back only after the elderly move or die, and sales that allow the elderly to stay in their homes for as long as they wish and are able. There are currently a handful of private and public sector programs around the country that are converting home equity into income for the elderly (Guttentag, 1982; Scholen and Chen, 1980). More are being developed. (The best source of information about these programs is the National Center for Home Equity Conversion in Madison, Wisconsin.)

What is the possible impact of these new financial instruments? There have been a few attempts to estimate empirically the national potential of reverse mortgages (Jacobs, 1980 and 1982; Neubig, 1980). Jacobs has shown in previous research that a large number of elderly homeowners could convert their net home equity into a lifetime stream of supplementary income. To anticipate some of the results to be presented in later tables, we report in Exhibit 12.2 potential reverse annuity mortgage (RAM) payments for various elderly income groups. More than a quarter of the poor and more than a third of the near poor could receive RAM payments of at least $2,000 per year. These payments would increase at a yearly rate of 8.5 percent and continue for a lifetime.

A key finding in Jacob's earlier work was that single elderly homeowners are best able to convert home equity into a lifetime income supplement because their life expectancies are shorter than the joint and survivor life expectancies of couples. Data reported in Exhibit 12.3 reveal that those elderly homeowners who live alone have the greatest potential equity-based annuity. Within each family size group, those with low incomes would have only slightly lower RAM payments than would more affluent homeowners.

EXHIBIT 12.2
Size of Potential Yearly RAM Annuity by Poverty Status

Potential Annual RAM Payment	Income as a Percentage of the Poverty Line		
	Less than 100%	100% to 124%	125% or More
$1,000 or less	40	31	29
$1,001 to $2,000	32	31	36
$2,001 to $3,000	13	16	15
$3,001 to $5,000	9	13	12
More than $5,000	6	9	8
TOTAL	100	100	100

One reason that low-income elderly would not have smaller payments is that they tend to be older, often aged 75 or older (Jacobs, 1982). Like being single, very old age is accompanied by a shorter life expectancy, and spreading a given amount of home equity over fewer years produces larger yearly payments. Thus, while low-income aged have somewhat less home equity, their very old age often offsets this disadvantage when they convert home equity into income.

From these findings we can derive a profile of opportunity for home equity conversion. Those who are living alone, are quite old, or both, can best

EXHIBIT 12.3
Size of Potential RAM Annuity by Family Structure and Low-Income Status

Potential Annual RAM Payment	Singles		Couples	
	All	With low Income*	All	With low Income*
Up to $1,000	25	32	40	51
$1,001 to $2,000	31	31	39	34
$2,001 to $3,000	17	15	11	8
$3,001 to $5,000	15	12	6	5
More than $5,000	11	9	3	2
TOTAL	99**	99**	99**	100

*Income less than 125 percent of the poverty line.
**Not equal to 100 because of rounding off.

benefit from reverse mortgages. Yet, as we shall discuss later, Weissert has previously shown that these characteristics also tend to put elderly people at greater risk of need for institutional residency or other long-term care. Our central purpose in this study is to document the substantial overlap between the profile of opportunity (for home equity conversion) and the profile of need (for long-term care). To the extent that they match, a new way of financing long-term care becomes possible.

Estimating the Need for Long-Term Care

While long-term care has been variously defined, we have chosen to focus on that portion of the aged disabled population most likely to incur high costs either for substantial and frequent home care or for institutionalization to procure personal care (Weissert, 1983; Weissert, et al., 1983). This population is effectively described by the Katz Activities of Daily Living Scale, which defines and measures need for human assistance in six activities: bathing, dressing, toileting, continence, transferring, and eating. Four of these six categories are captured by the 1977, 1978, 1979 and 1980 National Health Interview Surveys, and analysis of both the scale's properties and its results in these surveys shows that these four items serve as excellent proxies for the remaining two items (Katz, et al., 1970; Weissert, 1983).

Weissert and Scanlon (1983) have also identified the determinants of nursing home residency using a data set that combined the 1977 National Nursing Home Survey and the 1977 National Health Interview Survey. They found that among the aged, personal care dependency was among the most important determinants of residency in a nursing home. Although those with lower-level dependencies (for example, in mobility or household activities) may also require some amount of long-term care, the intensity and hence the cost of these services are much lower than for those dependent in personal care. In this exploratory research it is appropriate to focus on those who are most at risk of accumulating catastrophic care costs.

To estimate the risk of dependency in personal care faced by elderly homeowners (both individuals and couples), we analyzed data from the 1977 National Health Interview Survey and the 1977 National Nursing Home Survey. The combined data set was representative of all living Americans aged 65 and over. First we split the sample randomly into two halves, each having over 6,000 observations. Then, using one part of the split sample, we estimated an equation predicting the probability that an elderly person would be dependent in personal care at a specific time in his or her life. Logistic regression was used for the estimation because of the low probability of dependency in the entire sample (8.7 percent). The variables we used included measures of a person's age, sex, marital status, and race, as well as various interaction terms and transformations of these measures.

The equation was then used to estimate the risk of dependency for each person in the second part of the split sample. We then compared the risk estimate with the actual prevalence of dependency in personal care. Exhibit 12.4, showing the results of this procedure, reveals that the risk estimates were very good measures of the actual likelihood of being dependent in personal care. Of those whose estimated risk was between 3 percent and 5 percent, for example, the actual prevalence was 4.5 percent.

The exact same procedure and model were used to estimate the risk of institutionalization. Overall, 4.6 percent of the subsample were residents of nursing homes. In Exhibit 12.5 we report the close match between estimated risk and actual institutionalization rates. These results suggest that the equations derived should provide reasonably reliable estimates of risk of dependency and risk of institutionalization.

In gauging an elderly person's capacity to pay for long-term care over a lifetime, we had to take into account the fact that the risk of need for such care increases with each year of age. We therefore estimated the relevant probabilities for each person as they aged and included these estimates in our analysis. We should note that while these probabilities were calculated for each year of life, they do not precisely measure the risk of dependency (or institutionalization) for an entire year. For example, some who were living in the community at the time of their interview might have entered a nursing

EXHIBIT 12.4
Comparison Between Estimated Risk and
Actual Dependency in Personal Care

Estimated Risk of Dependency (Percent)	Actual Percent Dependent	Percent of Elderly Population
Less than 3	2.9	30
3 to less than 5	4.5	26
5 to less than 10	8.4	19
10 to less than 15	10.9	9
15 to less than 20	19.3	5
20 to less than 25	21.0	3
25 to less than 35	25.7	4
35 or more	41.6	3
TOTAL	8.7	99

Source: Special tabulations from the 1977 National Health Interview Survey and the 1977 National Nursing Home Survey.

EXHIBIT 12.5
Comparison between Estimated Risk and Actual Rates of Institutionalization

Estimated Risk of Institutionalization (percent)	Actual Percent Institutionalized	Percent of Elderly Population
Less than 3	1.1	61
3 to less than 5	2.8	11
5 to less than 10	8.3	15
10 to less than 15	12.4	6
15 to less than 20	18.8	2
20 to less than 25	19.0	2
25 or more	37.2	2
TOTAL	4.6	99

Source: Special tabulations from 1977 National Health Interview Survey and the 1977 National Nursing Home Survey.

home later that year (or might have been in one earlier). Conversely, some who were found to be dependent in personal care might have become (or might have been) independent at another time that year.

The result of these (unmeasured) differences is that our estimates of yearly risk may be somewhat lower than they would have been had the appropriate data been available. Countering this bias, however, is the fact that in our subsequent analytical work we impute risk probabilities to elderly homeowners who are living in the community. The fact that they are not in institutions may be indicative of a level of physical independence beyond the estimates derived from their demographic characteristics. To the extent that this is true, we may be overestimating their risk.

To address the central research question of this study, we then turned to the 1980 Annual Housing Survey. We limited our analysis to those homeowners who lived alone or only with their spouses, who were 65 years old or older, and whose spouses, if present, were similarly aged. In 1980, there were eight million such households, 55 percent of which consisted of elderly individuals living alone. For each elderly homeowner, we used the derived equations separately to estimate risk of dependency and risk of institutionalization. For married couples the probability that at least one of the pair would be dependent was then calculated, as was the probability that at least one would be institutionalized. Each household was characterized with respect to its risk estimates, it poverty status, and its family structure (including age and sex).

Exhibit 12.6 uses the estimation model to predict risk of dependency in personal care by family structure: that is, for single people and for elderly cou-

EXHIBIT 12.6
Risk of Dependency in Personal Care by Family Structure

Risk of Dependency (Percent)	Singles	Couples*	All Households
Less than 5	25	27	26
5 to less than 10	47	50	49
More than 10	28	23	26
TOTAL	100	100	101**

* Probability that at least one spouse will be dependent in personal care.
** Not equal to 100 because of rounding.

ples. The Exhibit shows that household risk of dependency does not differ substantially by family structure, though couples are on average younger and have individually lower probabilities of dependency. Exhibit 12.7, however, shows a substantial difference in household risk of institutional residency. Singles are much more likely to be at high risk of eventually living in a nursing home. Our analysis shows that some small portion of the difference is due to the generally older age of singles, but most of the difference is explained by the availability of social support, in this case from the spouse.

These differences by family structure are very important for three reasons. First, singles have the greatest risk of institutional residency. Second, they are presumably much less likely to have informal care available to them when they become personal-care dependent. Third, because they are older, they are likely to die sooner than couple members. Because they have shorter life expectancies, they have more money available from their equity each year

EXHIBIT 12.7
Risk of Institutionalization by Family Structure

Risk of Institutionalization (Percent)	Singles	Couples*	All Households
Less than 5	56	84	69
5 to less than 10	24	12	19
10 or more	20	4	13
TOTAL	100	100	101**

* Probability that at least one spouse will be institutionalized.
** Not equal to 100 because of rounding.

assuming the money is paid out on a lifelong basis. This is true despite the fact that couples tend to have somewhat higher equity than singles.

Using Home Equity for Pay for Home Care

Previous research has shown that many institutionalized elderly persons could live in the community if they received adequate personal assistance in their daily activities. While subsequent studies have suggested that the size of this group may be smaller than originally thought, a growing industry now supplies such assistance, and this home care is partially financed by the public sector. However, many dependent elderly homeowners who desire care do not qualify for these programs. The first focus of our research is to determine whether home equity might help pay for the home care of people dependent in personal care.

A financial instrument to convert home equity into income for this purpose will ideally have several characteristics. First, it should allow the elderly to stay in their homes as long as they are physically able, without facing the threat of the cutoff of RAM payments or the forced sale of the home. Additionally, it should allow the homeowners to convert only that portion of home equity required to pay for home care (or other consumption deemed necessary by the owner). It should also be adjustable to price increases, to reflect the high inflation rate that has affected most health care services. Finally, it should be financially sound, able to make its payments and recover these and other costs upon the sale of the home or the death(s) of its owner(s).

Under a grant from the Robert Wood Johnson Foundation, which also funded the present study, Jack Guttentag of the University of Pennsylvania and Robert Garnett of Southwest Texas State University have modeled such an instrument, which would convert home equity into lifetime monthly loans to finance long-term health care (or other expenses). The model is not a blueprint for a home equity conversion plan per se; rather, it provides data on how large a RAM payment could be realized from each $1,000 of home equity available for conversion by an institution that had certain financial characteristics. These include some characteristics of private sector institutions (for example, a net positive real rate of return), and some characteristics of public sector programs (for example, the absence of tax liabilities). The model incorporates some assumptions about the economy in general, and the housing and health care markets in particular.

We are fairly conservative in the assumptions we make to utilize the model. Specifically, we assume that the general inflation rate will be about 6 percent, but that health service prices will rise at a rate 2.5 percentage points higher. This 8.5 percent rate is slightly higher than the inflation in nursing home costs during the last decade, and slightly lower than the increase in the cost of home service in that period. The RAM payments would thus rise 8.5 percent each year to offset price increases. We also assumed that housing prices would increase at the rate of general inflation. Home values increased faster than inflation during the two prior decades, but high interest rates suppressed appreciation rates in the early 1980s. Lower mortgage rates will undoubtedly increase home appreciation rates. We also require the home equity conversion instrument to net a real rate of return of 6 percent (that is, a nominal rate of 12.4 percent return). Finally, we allow elderly homeowners to convert a maximum of 91 percent of their equity. Thus, they (or their heirs) would retain a *minimum* of 9 percent of their home's value.

The size of the maximum RAM payment that could be derived from home equity is a function of the current value of the net equity, and the current age and the sex of the owner (and spouse when present). We calculated these potential payments (expressed in annual terms) for each household, using the 1980 Annual Housing Survey data. Exhibit 12.8 shows the distribution of these payments by family structure and current risk of dependence in personal

EXHIBIT 12.8
Potential Annual RAM Annuity by Family Structure and Risk of Dependency in Personal Care

Potential Annual RAM Payment	Estimated Risk of Dependency		
	Less than 5%	5% to Less than 10%	10% or More
	Singles		
Up to $2,000	86	56	29
$2,001 to $3,000	9	23	15
$3,001 to $5,000	4	14	28
More than $5,000	1	7	28
TOTAL	100	100	100
	Couples		
Up to $2,000	93	81	57
$2,001 to $3,000	4	13	17
$3,001 to $5,000	3	4	18
More than $5,000	0	2	9
TOTAL	100	100	101*

* Not equal to 100 because of rounding.
** Probability that either spouse is dependent in personal care.

care. Our major hypothesis was correct. Those who are at greatest risk are also in the best position to convert home equity into income. More than half (56 percent) of all high-risk, single elderly homeowners could generate more than $3,000 per year (to start) out of their home assets. This is a critical finding, because these individuals, most likely to require home assistance, do not have a spouse (or other relative) in the home and quite probably would need to receive some home care to continue living independently in the community.

Married homeowners are generally less likely to require personal assistance (other than that of their spouses) and are also less well suited to convert home equity into a lifetime income stream. Nevertheless, those couples who face at least a 10 percent probability that one or the other partner will need personal care have the highest potential RAM payments. More than a quarter (27 percent) could get more than $3,000 a year (to start).

To see how far these RAM payments could go in paying for home care, we used the research results of a major Medicare-financed homemaker services demonstration program. This study found that when offered home care free of charge, persons dependent in personal care consumed an average of 387 hours of formal care per patient year (Weissert, et al., 1980). We obtained a current charge quotation for homemaker services from the largest provider or homemaker services in that study, the San Francisco Home Health Agency. That agency is one of the nation's largest home health providers, and it operates in a very high cost area. The agency's average charge, and the one used in our annual cost estimates, is $9.25 per hour. From these data we derived an average yearly cost of home care of $3,580. We regard this as a conservatively high estimate of average charges for home care.

Exhibit 12.9 reveals what proportion of elderly homeowners could finance these services for the rest of their lives out of the proceeds of our home equity conversion instrument. As expected from the data displayed in the pre-

EXHIBIT 12.9
Percentage of Elderly Homeowners Who Could Purchase $3,580 (Plus Annual Increases for Inflation) Worth of Home Care Each Year by Family Structure and Risk of Dependence

	Risk of Dependence		
	Less Than 5%	5% to Less than 10%	10% or More
All Homeowners	2	8	30
Singles	3	15	48
Couples	0	1	3

vious table, we find that RAM payments would cover these costs for many of those at greatest risk of need, including nearly half of all high-risk singles.

Yet we have reason to believe that these figures underestimate the true potential of home equity conversion for home care. We have assumed here that those dependent in personal care would purchase the total package of formal services. That assumption ignores the fact that if elderly homeowners had to pay for these services themselves, some of them would undoubtedly spend less money on formal care and would endeavor to rely more on family, friends, or voluntary sector help, where available. For purposes of this analysis, however, we continue to assume that elderly homeowners would purchase the entire package. (Another conservative assumption is that where a couple purchases home services, both husband and wife need these services. In most cases, this will not be true, but for our purposes we assume that it is.)

Still another assumption we have made is extremely conservative. To estimate RAM payments we have been using the 1971 Individual Annuity Mortality (IAM) Table, which the insurance industry has used to price lifetime annuities. The mortality rates in this table are lower, and life expectancies are correspondingly higher, than for most of the elderly population. For example, a woman aged 75 had a lifetime expectancy of 11.5 years in 1978 (U.S. Dept. of Health and Human Services, 1978). The 1971 IAM table, however, lists her life expectancy as 12.3 years (American Council on Life Insurance, 1980).

In actuality, onset of dependency in personal care almost certainly is associated with reduced life expectancy. We know of no study that attempts to estimate the magnitude of this change. We did, however, make a modest adjustment to reflect this shift in expected mortality rates. By setting back the 1971 IAM mortality distribution a total of five years, we calculated RAM payments on the basis of life expectancies somewhat shorter than those of the general elderly population.[3] For example, we assumed that the 75-year old woman with a need for assistance in personal care would have a life expectancy of 9.1 years. In fact, it probably would be even less.

Exhibit 12.10 illustrates the impact of this adjustment for various segments of the single elderly homeowner population. More than a third of such homeowners could pay for home care using their RAM annuity. About three-fifths of those most likely to face a need for home care could finance this care with their home equity. More importantly, almost one-half of those who have very low income and who are at greatest risk of dependency could buy home care with their RAM payments. This finding is truly impressive and, we think, of great importance.

Still another conservative assumption we have made is that elderly homeowners would not touch their regular incomes to finance their home care. However, many aged people would undoubtedly spend some of this

EXHIBIT 12.10
Percentage of Single Elderly Homeowners Who Could Purchase Home Care Each Year Using Only the RAM Payment by Mortality Distribution, Income, and Risk

	Mortality Distribution	
	1971 IAM*	1971 IAM Set Back 5 Years
All Single Elderly Homeowners	22	35
High-Risk Singles**	48	61
Low-Income Singles***	17	28
Low-Income High-Risk Singles	35	48

* 1971 Individual Annuity Mortality.
** Risk of Dependence greater than or equal to 10 percent.
*** Income less than 125 percent of the poverty line.

income if that meant they could stay out of a nursing home or could relieve a relative of some of the burdens of informal care. Others might prefer to exhaust their regular income resources before they used their home assets.

To deal with this possibility, we developed estimates which assume that people might use as much as one-half of their discretionary income before they spend a RAM annuity. Again, we estimated discretionary income conservatively. First we eliminated all earned income since a person experiencing severe dependency would probably not have earnings, and a spouse's earning power might be lost if she or he had to remain home with the dependent person.[4] (Also, earnings in all cases would eventually cease.) Then we subtracted income equal to twice the poverty line for the individual person or couple. (This level of income for couples was 5 percent higher than the Bureau of Labor Statistics (BLS) "intermediate" budget for a retired couple in 1981. There was no BLS series of budgets for retired singles, and the couples budget budget series was discontinued after 1981.) In constant 1983 dollars, this amounted to $9,600 for an individual and $12,000 for couples. Remaining income above this amount was classified as discretionary.

Exhibit 12.11 reveals the impact of allowing elderly homeowners who are dependent in personal care to use some of their current discretionary income to help pay for home care. Still more homeowners could afford this care. Nearly one-half (47 percent) of all those at high risk of need could pay for it if they had to. For singles, this number increases to 63 percent. Most couples still could not afford the yearly service package, but remember that most couples would not need to purchase as many services as we are assuming in these calculations.

EXHIBIT 12.11
Percentage of Elderly Homeowners Who Could Purchase Home Care Each Year Using One-Half of Discretionary Income in Addition to RAM Payment by Mortality Distribution, Family Structure, and Risk

	Mortality Distribution	
	1971 IAM*	1971 IAM Set Back 5 Years
All Elderly Homeowners	23	31
High-Risk Homeowners	36	47
All Singles	31	42
High-Risk Singles	51	63
All Couples	13	16
High-Risk Couples	13	22

* 1971 Individual Annuity Mortality.
** Risk of Dependence equals or exceeds 10 percent.

Thus, home equity could potentially have a significant impact on elderly homeowners' capacity to pay for care in their homes. The conversion of home equity would enable some who might otherwise be institutionalized to remain in the community. It would also let some dependent homeowners relieve spouses or other relatives of some of the burdens of informal care.

How much equity an elderly homeowner would want to give up to obtain home care would be a matter of individual choice. However, home equity conversion would offer a financing option not now available to hundreds of thousands of people who might need such care.

Using Home Equity to Pay for Nursing Home Insurance

The probability that an elderly homeowner will eventually undergo a long-term nursing home stay is quite low, though it is almost certainly higher than the probability that his house will burn to the ground. Homeowners routinely insure against the latter catastrophe, but few of the elderly are insured against the financial impact of a very long stay in an institution. In part, this reflects a variety of difficulties faced (or imagined) by potential sellers of such insurance policies. But the lack of availability of catastrophic cost insurance is also reinforced by the demand limitations of some older widows and couples who might feel that they could not afford such insurance using their regular income. Most elderly people do pay for some health insurance privately

(Cafferata, in press), but they may perceive their capacity to finance still more insurance to be quite limited.

Home equity conversion could be used to pay for such an insurance policy. To explore this possibility, two steps are necessary. First, we must specify the stream of payments required over a lifetime to pay for nursing home or other long-term care insurance. Next we must determine the degree to which a home equity conversion instrument tailored to this purpose would cover the costs of this insurance. Without a fully developed market for long-term care insurance, we must of necessity make some judgments about what services would be covered and how payment schedules could be determined.

In what follows, we analyze two kinds of coverage and three kinds of payment from three home equity conversion instruments. One of the insurance plans has been put together as a prototype private sector insurance instrument. Another is a conceptual pooling of costs without the regulatory requirements of a private sector plan. One of the home equity conversion instruments is a private sector plan now actually available in one state. The others are derived from the home equity conversion model we used in the previous section. The reader is thus forewarned that our analysis is illustrative rather than definitive, and that the plans should not be compared directly because they have somewhat different objectives and are financed in different ways. Nevertheless, our results seem robust and the major findings are consistent across plans.

The first plan we model represents a simple pooling of costs for long-term nursing home care, with each participant required to pay a share equal to his expected cost of a long-term stay. While we call the plan an insurance plan, the reader should understand that it is not comparable to a private-sector instrument, which would have reserve requirements as well as a variety of other costs borne by insurance companies. It is, however, insurance in the sense that it pools the risk of catastrophic nursing home costs and as such represents most of the limited range of cost factors likely to be taken into account if such a plan were offered by a government agency.

We first calculated the expected cost of a long-term stay for each elderly homeowner (and for her spouse where present). We defined a long-term stay as one exceeding four months, and we specified that the plan would have a four-month deductible to be paid by the elderly homeowner. The expected cost of a long-term stay was set to equal the probability of a stay of more than four months (if institutionalized) multiplied by the expected length of stay beyond four months multiplied by the cost of a stay of this expected length. (The first probability—that of being institutionalized—was calculated for each homeowner as described earlier. The second and third values in the formula were obtained from the discharge file of the 1977 National Nursing Home Survey. To estimate the final value, the cost, we took the 1976 data on the average monthly costs of nursing home stays of one to three years and inflated these costs to 1983 dollars (compounding at a rate of 8.5 percent per year).

The cost of a long-term stay, as derived from this formula, would vary from one year to the next for each homeowner, in part because prices would rise, but also because the person would be older (and therefore at greater risk of institutionalization). Also, the married homeowner may lose a spouse (most often through death)[5] and hence also increase her probability of institutionalization. To provide an annual RAM payment to meet these increasing costs, the home equity conversion model described in the previous section was modified so that the annual payment increased at a rate sufficient to cover both health price increases and yearly increases in the probability of being institutionalized. This modification required that annual payments increase 20 percent each year for single men, 21 percent for single women, and 29 percent for married men and women. For couples, the insurance plan requires addition of the expected costs for each spouse. We again used the 1971 IAM table to reflect mortality rates in the general elderly population.

Exhibit 12.12 describes the annual RAM payments available from this plan. As with the first instrument, singles could realize greater payments than could couples. Within each group, households with greater risk of institutionaliza-

EXHIBIT 12.12
Potential Annual RAM Annuity Available for Catastrophic Nursing Home Cost Insurance by Family Structure and Risk of Institutionalization

Potential Annual RAM Payment	Estimated Risk of Institutionalization*		
	Less than 5%	5% to Less than 10%	10% or More
	Singles		
Up to $1,000	88	45	15
$1,001 to $2,000	10	34	27
$2,001 to $3,000	1	11	20
More than $3,000	1	10	38
TOTAL	100	100	100
	Couples		
Up to $1,000	99	87	43
$1,001 to $2,000	1	11	40
$2,001 to $3,000	0	1	8
More than $3,000	0	1	9
TOTAL	100	100	100

*For couples, the risk is the probability that either spouse will be institutionalized.

tion also have larger potential RAM payments. The reader will note that these payments are lower than those available from the first instrument (and reported in Exhibit 12.8). However, as we report below, the yearly premiums to support this insurance plan are much lower than the yearly costs of home care, so that more elderly homeowners could finance insurance costs than could pay for home care.

The next step in our analysis was to estimate the proportion of elderly homeowners whose annual RAM payments could cover the pooled costs of extended nursing home stays for the rest of their lives. (For these calculations, we returned to the 1971 IAM tables. Thus we assume life expectancies somewhat longer than the general population's. This should result in conservative estimates of annuity payments. As before, we allow homeowners to convert up to 91 percent of their equity.) Exhibit 12.13 reports these results for a variety of elderly homeowner groups. Slightly over half of all households could pay for this catastrophic nursing home cost insurance.

Nearly half of all homeowners with low income but high risk of institutionalization could use this method of payment. In contrast with the home care plan, a substantial number of couples could also pay for insurance out of their home equity, though not many in the high risk group could do so.

As in our analysis of the home care plan, we also estimated the percentage of elderly homeowners who could pay for catastrophic cost insurance if they used some of their discretionary income in addition to their RAM payments. Exhibit 12.14 reveals a substantial jump in the number of people who could make such a purchase. Nearly three-quarters of all elderly homeowners could buy insurance using no more than one-quarter of their discretionary income and their RAM payment. Surprisingly, a larger percentage of couples than

EXHIBIT 12.13
Percentage of Elderly Homeowners Who Could Purchase
Catastrophic Nursing Home Cost Insurance Using Only the
RAM Payment by Family Structure, Risk, and Income

	All Homeowners	Singles	Couples
All Homeowners	53	64	39
High Risk*	58	64	18
Low Income**	43	49	22
Low Income-High Risk	47	49	—

* Risk of institutionalization equals or exceeds 10 percent.
** Income less than 125 percent of the poverty line.
*** Sample too small for reliable estimate.

EXHIBIT 12.14
Percentage of Elderly Homeowners Who Could Purchase Catastrophic Nursing Home Cost Insurance Using One-Quarter of Discretionary Income in Addition to the RAM Payment by Family Structure, Risk, and Income

	All Homeowners	Singles	Couples
All Homeowners	72	67	77
High Risk*	64	65	59
Low Income**	43	49	22
Low Income-High Risk	47	49	***

*Risk of institutionalization equals or exceeds 10 percent.
**Income less than 125 percent of the poverty line.
***Sample too small for reliable estimate.

singles could do this. The difference lies in the much greater discretionary income enjoyed by many couples.

A second insurance plan for consideration here is that developed as a prototype private sector, long-term care insurance program by Mark Meiners and Gordon Trapnell (Meiners and Trapnell, 1983). This plan would pay a fixed amount per day ($50) for nursing home stays beyond three months. It also has a provision to pay for home health services as an alternative to institutionalization. As structured, the plan would have fixed premiums over a lifetime and fixed benefits whenever they are drawn. For purposes of our analysis, we varied the premiums, increasing them at 8.5 percent per year so that the benefits could increase at that rate.[6] The RAM plan previously considered for home care was then applied to these premium estimates. Exhibit 12.15 shows that a large portion of elderly homeowners (including four out of every five high risk homeowners) could also buy this long-term care insurance.

Finally, we applied to the original prototype insurance plan (with fixed premiums and fixed benefits) the reverse mortgage payments now actually available from a company in New Jersey. American Homestead Mortgage Corporation recently began to offer its Century Plan, which provides fixed reverse mortgage payments to elderly homeowners over a period up to 40 years (essentially for a lifetime). These loans are made with a below-market nominal interest rate in exchange for a share of future home appreciation. (More information about the plan is available from American Homestead at the Company's offices in Mount Laurel, New Jersey.) Using this reverse mortgage payment (and up to one-fourth of discretionary income) about half (52 percent) of all elderly homeowners (and 75 percent of all singles) could purchase the prototype long-term care insurance. About one in four couples do so.

EXHIBIT 12.15
Percentage of Elderly Homeowners Who Could Pay the Premium for a Prototype Long-Term Care Insurance Policy Using One-Quarter of Discretionary Income in Addition to the RAM Payment by Family Structure, Risk, and Income

	All Homeowners	Singles	Couples
All Homeownres	66	82	47
High Risk*	83	88	53
Low Income**	59	71	16
Low Income-High Risk	78	80	***

* Risk of institutionalization equals or exceeds 10 percent.
** Income less than 125 percent of the poverty line.
*** Sample too small for reliable estimate.

Thus, we see that for each combination of insurance instrument and RAM payment plan, a very high proportion of all older single homeowners, and a significant number of older couples, could finance long-term care out of their home equity (in some cases using a portion of their discretionary income). We should note as well that most people who could pay for these plans would not have to use all of their available home equity to do so. Restricting homeowner financing to no more than two-thirds of the potential RAM payment and one-quarter of discretionary income, we still find that about one-half of elderly homeowners could buy long-term care insurance.[7] Home equity can clearly help finance catastrophic long-term care insurance plans for many older Americans.

Discussion

Our analysis provides strong evidence that a large proportion of older Americans could use some of the assets that they have tied up in their homes to help finance their long-term health care needs. For some, this could mean gaining access to care not now available. Others could relieve family and friends of burdens of providing needed personal assistance or nursing home payments. All who participated in a home equity conversion program to provide home care would be able to stay in their homes as long as they were physically and mentally able. Those who used RAM payments to finance long-term care insurance would be protected against the improbable but devastating costs of a lengthy nursing home stay.

Throughout, we have tried to be judicious in the assumptions underlying our estimates of the private capacity to finance long-term care. We have not, for example, included the use of assets other than home equity. Moreover, our conservative definition of discretionary income and the limited partial use of it may underestimate both the capacity and the willingness of elderly homeowners to help pay their health bills. In California, we should note, participants in the Reverse Annuity Mortgage Program list health care as the primary reason for taking out a reverse mortgage, and a 1980 survey of elderly Wisconsin residents found that paying for health care would be the most important use to which RAM payments could be put (Sholen and Chen, 1980).

While home equity conversion facilitates the use of private resources, there are clearly public purposes that might be served in the process. Among these are:

- Increased access to health care services;
- Expansion of individual choice in health-care decisions;
- A more equitable and less arbitrary distribution of health-care financing burdens (through risk pooling); and,
- Support of the elderly's desire to remain in their homes.

The public-sector interest in encouraging the development of home equity conversion suggests that federal and state governments should remove those regulatory barriers that impede the development of home equity conversion plans and make other legislative changes that might facilitate that development. Some of this work has begun, while other steps remain to be taken. In the U.S. Senate, for example, there is currently a bill to clarify the tax consequences of sale-leaseback programs that allow elderly homeowners to sell their homes and still remain lifetime tenants in them. Last year the Secretary of Housing and Urban Development, Samuel Pierce, proposed a demonstration program that would insure up to 1,000 reverse mortgage loans, a step that would allow financial institutions some of the protection provided them under conventional mortgages. House and Senate action on reverse mortgage insurance would make a major contribution to the development of home equity conversion programs.

With respect to the use of home equity to finance long-term health care, more work should be done before large scale efforts are launched to convert home equity for this purpose. An effort to estimate the reduced life expectancies of those dependent in personal care would be invaluable, for these figures would allow institutions to provide higher yearly RAM payments on a financially sound basis to those who might use home care. Also needed are more precise estimates of the costs of long-term care for various groups of patients in different care settings. It will also be valuable to expand the definition of people who need assistance, in order to estimate the potential home equity financing of assistance only in mobility and instrumental daily living activities.

Another important research effort might consist of attempts to validate our estimates of risk, cost of service, and the home equity conversion potential for financing these services. Other extant data might be analyzed for validation purposes. However, it might be extremely valuable to assess directly what home equity resources are available to recipients of health-care assistance. Samples of Medicaid (or Medicare) patients at a national or state level could be analyzed for this purpose.

Based on this and other work, it should be possible to structure a demonstration program that would convert home equity for the purpose of financing long-term health care. But the design process would need to address a number of important policy questions. Among them are the following:

- Appropriateness and variety of public subsidy mechanisms to encourage participation;
- Identification and removal of federal and state legislative and regulatory barriers;
- Copayments, deductibles, scope of benefits, and other methods of addressing adverse selection and moral hazard problems;
- The potential role of various institutional participants, including state Medicaid programs, private insurance carriers, lending institutions, employers, investors, consumer organizations, and the Health Care Financing Administration;
- Demand and participation estimates and incentives;
- Cost estimation; and,
- Equity considerations.

Among the items on this list, equity considerations are the knottiest. Is it appropriate to call upon those who have earned and saved in the form of home equity to pay for their own care? Would a program of this type relieve the long-term care burden from one group but defuse pressure for public action to serve other politically less potent but needy groups, for example, renters and the poor? Should the availability of home equity be regarded as an excuse to cut off public support to those who have it?

These issues involve value judgments not amenable to research other than that which is involved in a careful weighing of costs and benefits from the perspective of the potential beneficiaries—elderly homeowners and renters. One benefit for homeowners is the potential for using finances other than income to protect one's assets against catastrophic loss in the event long-term care is needed. The payoff in terms of reduced anxiety could be profound for those who have assets and income to protect. The risk is that the opportunity to pay for some preferred care may be granted only at the cost of removing the special exemption now afforded home equity. As a protection against this possibility, homeowners are likely to support such a program only if participation—and the extent of participation—remains voluntary.

Renters, on the other hand, may support a program that offers no direct benefit to them if they anticipate the possibility that risk sharing by homeowners may benefit everyone. It could do so by expanding the total pool of public and private resources expended on long-term care during a period when there seems to be little likelihood of any major public-only benefit expansion. This could occur because homeowners protected from catastrophic loss would find no need to spend down to Medicaid eligibility, thus leaving more public funds available to share among those who already qualify. Governments may want to subsidize homeowners' insurance and home equity conversion costs with some of the savings, but total public expenditures on their behalf may nonetheless be lower.

Conclusion

This analysis shows that there is a substantial potential for using home equity to relieve financial and familial burdens of long-term care for hundreds of thousands of homeowners. More work needs to be done to validate our estimates and to explore further and crystallize some major public policy issues as well as to prepare the way for a demonstration of the feasibility of the concept. It is essential to consider future steps carefully and to weigh the merits of arguments for and against a major public policy effort to sponsor use of home equity to pay for long-term care. No one should believe that home equity conversion can simply replace public subsidy of the long-term health care needs of the aged. It may provide more care options to those who have both equity and needs beyond what is now publicly supported. Nor does home equity conversion deserve to be dismissed as an indulgence for the elite. A great many elderly poor are homeowners who could benefit from a conversion program. And, if made sufficiently attractive through public subsidy programs, it could ultimately benefit nonhomeowners by reducing the demand for Medicaid-supported care.

Some have taken the position that home equity should not be converted for the purpose of financing long-term care, because in their view the public sector should take all responsibility in this area. Yet this position may itself be destructive. If government takeover of all long-term care financing is not in fact a realistic prospect, a great many elderly people who could get relief from the burdens of long-term care will be denied.

The magnitude of the problem of long-term care financing suggests a great need for creative ideas. Home equity conversion merits careful consideration in this context.

Notes

1. The results reported in this paper are primarily part of a large research effort. Views expressed are those of the authors and do not necessarily represent the views of the University of Rochester, the University of North Carolina, the Urban Institute, or the Robert Wood Johnson Foundation, which supported this research. The authors wish to acknowledge the valuable assistance of Dr. James Firman of the Robert Wood Johnson Foundation; Kenneth Scholen of the National Center for Home Equity Conversion; Dr. Jack Guttentag of the University of Pennsylvania; Dr. Robert Garnett of Southwest Texas State University; Dr. Eric Hanuschek of the University of Rochester (currently with the U.S. Congressional Budget Office); Dr. Mark Meiners of the National Center for Health Services, Department of Health and Human Services; and James Burke, President, American Homestead Mortgage Corp.
2. The data supporting these observations are from the 1980 Annual Housing Survey, which we analyzed for this study.
3. That is, we assumed that a 75-year-old woman dependent in personal care would face a mortality rate equal to that faced by a nondependent 80-year-old.
4. This is also a conservative assumption. If a working spouse quit her job, there would presumably be less need for normal care. If she continued working, part of her earnings could be used to purchase such care.
5. In 1978 there were only 6,000 men aged 65 and older and 3,000 similarly aged women whose marriages ended in divorce or annulment (U.S. Dept. of Health and Human Services, 1978b).
6. The reader should note that we used the premium prices that Meiners and Trapnell have estimated for group plans, which would most closely approximate coverage of the general elderly public.
7. The precise figures are 56 percent for the pooled cost model; 49 percent for the rising benefit prototype private sector plan; and 46 percent for the fixed benefit plan purchased using Century Plan payments.

References

American Council on Life Insurance. *1979 Life Insurance Fact Book.* Washington, D.C.: American Council on Life Insurance, 1980.

Cafferata, G. L. *Private Health Insurance Coverage and Premiums of Persons 65 Years and Over Covered by Medicare. National Medical Care Expenditure Survey. National Center for Health Services Research.* Washington, D.C.: U.S. Department of Health and Human Services, in press.

Friedman, J., and Sjogren, J. "Assets of the Elderly as They Retire," *Social Security Bulletin* 44 (1), January 1981.

Guttentag, J. "Home Equity Conversion: A New Factor in Retirement Planning." In Cagan, P., *Saving for Retirement.* Washington, D.C.: American Council on Life Insurance, 1982.

Jacobs, B. "The Potential Antipoverty Impact of RAMs and Property Tax Deferral." In Scholen, K., and Chen, Y., *Unlocking Home Equity for the Elderly.* Cambridge, Mass: Ballinger Publishing Co., 1980.

Jacobs, B. "The Housing of Elderly Americans." Keynote address to the 1981 White House Conference on Aging. Washington, D.C., December 1981.

Jocobs, B. "An Overview of the National Potential for Home Equity Conversion into Income for the Elderly." University of Rochester Public Policy Analysis Program, Discussion Paper No. 8205. Rochester, NY, March 1982.

Jacobs, B. "Facts, Stereotypes and Politics: Decisions on Programs for the Elderly." University of Rochester Public Policy Analysis Program, Discussion Paper No. 8307. Rochester, NY, September 1983.

Katz, S., Downs, T. D., Cash, H. R., et al. "Progress in Development of the Index of ADL." *Gerontologist* 10, (1), Spring 1970, 20–30.

Meiners, M., and Trapnell, G. *Long-Term Care Insurance: Premium Estimates for Prototype Policies.* National Center for Health Services Research, 1983.

Neubig, T. "Reverse Annuity Mortgages: A Dissaving Mechanism for Older Homeowners." In Duncan, G. J., and Morgan, J. N. (eds.), *Five Thousand American Families—Patterns of Economic Progress,* Vol. VIII. Ann Arbor, Michigan: Institute for Social Research, University of Michigan, 1980.

Rabushka, A., and Jacobs, B. *Old Folks at Home.* New York: Free Press, 1980.

Scholen, K., and Chen, Y. (eds.). *Unlocking Home Equity for the Elderly.* Cambridge, Mass.: Ballinger Publishing Co., 1980.

Shanas, E. "The Family as a Social Support System in Old Age." *Gerontologist* 19 (2), April 1979.

U.S. Department of Health and Human Services. *Vital Statistics of the United States, 1978.* Vol. II—Mortality. Part A, Table 5-3, 1978a. Washington, D.C.: Government Printing Office, 1978.

U.S. Department of Health and Human Services. *Vital Statistics of the United States, 1978.* Vol. III—Marriage and Divorce. Section 2, Table 2-11. 1978b. Washington, D.C.: Government Printing Office, 1978.

Weissert, W. "Size and Characteristics of the Noninstitutional Long-Term Care Population." Working Paper No. 1466-20. Washington, D.C.: Urban Institute, Rev. December 1983.

Weissert, W., and Scanlon, W. "Determinants of Institutionalization of the Aged." Working Paper No. 1466-21. Washington, D.C.: Urban Institute, Rev. July 1983.

Weissert, W., et al. "Cost-Effectiveness of Homemaker Services for the Chronically Ill." *Inquiry* 17 (Fall 1980), 230-243.

Weissert, W., et al. "Encouraging Appropriate Care for the Chronically Ill: Design of the NCHSR Experiment in Nursing Home Incentive Payments." *HCFA Review,* December 1983.

13

Excluding Gain on the Sale of a Residence: When Should the Election Be Made?

Rolf Auster

Most homeowners over 55 who are considering selling their homes are faced with a difficult decision: Should they currently use their $125,000 gain exclusion (under Section 121) or save it for the future? The decision can be difficult because of the complex rules and many variables, such as age, health, amount of gain, plans for the future sale of the replacement home, the expected impact of inflation on future home values and the current use of the tax dollars saved by the election.

This paper reviews the basic requirements of Section 121, examines its quirks and traps, and explains its interplay with the rules for gain deferral. It also suggests planning techniques to prevent the loss of the exclusion and to maximize its benefits.

The Basic Requirements

For a seller to qualify for the $125,000 gain exclusion on the sale of his or her home,[1] the following requirements must be met:

The Practical Accountant, Vol. 15 (December 1982), 73–77. Reprinted by permission of the Practical Accountant. Copyright © 1982, Warren, Gorham & Lamont, Inc., 964 Third Avenue, New York, NY 10155. All rights reserved.

1. The seller must have attained age 55 by the date of sale or exchange (i.e., at the "closing").
2. The seller must have owned and used the home as a principal residence for at least three of the five years prior to sale (thus the home could be rented out for the last two years).
   Note: If the home is owned jointly (as community property, tenancy by the entirety or joint tenancy, but *not* as tenancy in common), it is sufficient that only *one* spouse meets the *age, use,* and *ownership* requirements. If a deceased spouse met the *use* and *ownership* requirements, the surviving spouse, if over age 55, may make the election.[2] If the residence being sold was acquired as the result of an involuntary conversion of a previous residence (with the basis carrying over under Section 1033(b)), the holding period of the previous residence can be tacked on to the holding period of the present residence for purposes of meeting the *use* and *ownership* requirements.[3]
3. If the seller is married on the date of sale, *both* spouses must join in the election—even though only one of them owns the residence.
4. If the seller is married on the date of sale, *neither* spouse could previously have elected the exclusion.[4]

The interaction of the last two rules can have far-reaching—and unexpected—effects where a spouse remarries.

EXAMPLE: Adam, who is married to Eve, sells a house that he owns *individually* and makes the Section 121 election *with Eve* (since they both must make the election). Adam dies and Eve later marries Ringo. Eve's previous election as to Adam's house prevents not only Eve but also Ringo from making a new election. However, if Ringo divorced Eve, his election would be restored. Similarly, if Eve and Ringo live together without remarrying, Ringo's election would remain intact.

Where two homeowners, each over 55, are planning to get married, the effects of these exclusions can vary greatly according to when they sell their houses:

1. If *neither* party sells prior to their marriage, only one exclusion may be claimed during the marriage.
2. If *one* party sells prior to their marriage (and elects the exclusion), neither may elect the exclusion during the marriage. However, after a divorce or the death of the selling party, the non-selling party may elect the exclusion.
3. If *both* parties sell their houses prior to their marriage (and both elect the exclusion), they will get both exclusions (up to a total of $250,000). And there would be no "recapture" of the double exclusion on their marriage.

In the case of a married couple filing separate returns, the exclusion is limited to $62,500 each—regardless of the form of ownership. Thus, if the home is owned in the name of only one spouse, and they file separately, the non-owner spouse's half of the exclusion is lost since only the owner realizes a gain from the sale.

Avoiding Property Settlement Traps

A property settlement in a divorce proceeding may result in realized gain to the spouse (say, the husband) giving up the property, even if the disposition is ordered by the court.[5] If the husband is not in a position to buy a replacement residence of equal or greater value, he may have to recognize a large gain. However, if he is close to 55 and otherwise meets the requirements for the Section 121 exclusion, there are a number of techniques available for avoiding this unwanted gain (assuming the relationship between the parties is sufficiently amicable[6] to allow their implementation):

1. The transfer can be delayed until the husband's 55th birthday.
2. The husband can gift the home to his wife. There would be no gain recognized, and there is no longer any gift tax on interspousal transfers.[7]
3. The husband can transfer to the wife a short-term interest in the home with the future interest (the remainder and title) not passing until he turns 55. This is a contract for deferred delivery, with the wife retaining the right to live in the home until title passes.
   Caution: The IRS may assert that, in substance, the complete transfer took place *initially.* How the courts would rule is unknown, since this issue has not yet arisen. A collateral consequence of this technique is that the husband's continued payments of taxes and mortgage installments would be treated as alimony, deductible by the husband and taxable to the wife.[8]
   Warning: If the husband moves out, he must be careful not to fail the three-out-of-five years "use" test. Thus, a husband *under* age 53 must continue to use the house as his principal residence until he is 53.

Of course, if the husband intends to buy a new residence after the divorce, none of the foregoing planning techniques would be necessary. The husband may presumably "roll over" his gain by buying the new residence, despite the absence of sales "proceeds."

The Interplay of Sections 121 and 1034

Under Section 1034 the seller of a house *must* exclude all or part of the gain if a replacement residence is purchased within two years before or after the sale. Gain is recognized only to the extent the cost of the new residence falls short of the "adjusted sales price" of the old residence.

If Section 121 is elected, the excluded gain, which is always 100 percent of the realized gain (up to the $125,000 maximum) reduces the "adjusted sales price" of the old residence. In other words, the exclusion reduces the amount required to be reinvested to postpone any remaining gain.

EXAMPLE: John sells his home with a $50,000 basis for an adjusted sales price of $300,000. Without the Section 121 election, he must reinvest the full $300,000 to defer the $250,000 gain. With the election, he need invest only $175,000 ($300,000–$125,000).

Moreover, the Section 121 exclusion does *not* reduce his basis in the replacement residence.[9] *Thus, if the replacement residence costs $225,000, the tax results are as follows:*

No election:
Gain recognized (300,000–$225,000)	$ 75,000
Gain deferred ($25,000–$75,000)	$175,000
Basis in new residence:	
Cost of new residence	$225,000
Less gain deferred	$175,000
Basis	$ 50,000

With election:
Gain recognized	–0–
Gain deferred ($250,000–$125,000)	$125,000
Basis in new residence:	
Cost of new residence	$225,000
Less remaining gain deferred	$125,000
Basis	$100,000

How Repossessions Are Handled

Where a house is repossessed by a seller who elected the Section 121 exclusion, the tax treatment upon the buyer's default depends on *when* the property is resold. If it is resold within one year of the repossession, the repossession is disregarded and a new realized gain is computed by adding collections on the original sale to the amount realized on the resale as if it were one transaction.[10] On the other hand, if the resale takes place *more* than one year after repossession, the original exclusion stands. The remaining gain, if any, is computed according to the general nonrecognition rules in Section 1038, which apply to all seller-creditor repossessions.

EXAMPLE: Sam elects the Section 121 exclusion on the sale of his home for $150,000 (basis $50,000) since he has no intention of replacing it. Consequently no gain is recognized. The buyer defaults (having built no equity in the home) after paying $40,000 plus interest.

If Sam repossesses the house and resells it within a year for $170,000, the tax result is as follows:

New sales price	$170,000
Plus: amounts collected	40,000
Amount realized	$210,000
Less: adjusted basis	50,000
Recomputed gain	$160,000
Recomputed exclusion	$125,000
Recognized gain	$ 35,000

If the resale takes place more than a year after repossession, the original exclusion of $100,000 would stand unless the original election is revoked and a new one is made (by filling an amended return within the period of limitations). Without a new election, the recognized gain would be $60,000 instead of $35,000.

Amount realized (as above)	$210,000
Adjusted basis	(50,000)
Original exclusion	(100,000)
Recognized gain	$ 60,000

When to Elect

When a taxpayer who is eligible for the Section 121 exclusion sells his residence at a gain, it is not always obvious whether he should elect the exclusion. Fortunately, he has the full three-year period of limitations in which to change his mind, whether or not he made the election.[11]

Here are some situations that may confront the taxpayer—and the planning possibilities:

Replacement Residence Purchased

Where a replacement residence is purchased, the decision as to the Section 121 election depends in large part on whether the *full* gain on the sale of the old residence is deferred under Section 1034.

Full Gain Deferred. If the full gain on the sale is deferred under Section 1034 because a new residence is purchased, the Section 121 election should obviously *not* be made. Since no tax is due whether the gain is excluded or postponed, the only effect of the Section 121 election would be to step up the basis of the replacement residence. During ownership, however, the basis in a residence is largely irrelevant, since the property is nondepreciable. (Of course, if the replacement residence is going to be used for business, then the Section 121 election is probably preferable, since ordinary deductions would be obtained at the cost of using up the exclusion, which would only be an offset against a possible capital gain in the future.)

The Section 121 election may be more advantageously used for the subsequent sale of the replacement residence because:

1. If the exclusion cannot be fully used on the current sale (because the gain is less than $125,000), a future sale will probably utilize the exclusion to a greater extent (since the property will probably appreciate).
2. The exclusion may be increased (it has already been increased three times as the box indicates).[12]

In short, a seller whose entire gain is deferred under Section 1034 usually has little or nothing to gain, and possibly something to lose, by making the election. This is true even if he dies before he can use the election because:

1. He paid no tax up front, regardless of whether the election was made; and
2. The basis is stepped up to fair market value upon his death, again regardless of whether the election was made, so that all accumulated appreciation evaporates for tax purposes.

Full Gain Not Deferred. If the full gain is *not* deferred under Section 1034 because the purchase price of the new home is less than the adjusted sale, the decision then depends on the taxpayer's age, health, and future plans:

- A taxpayer who is still young and in good health might consider saving the exclusion for use against the new house. If the recognized gain on the current sale is less than the $125,000 maximum, inflation alone may bring the gain up to the maximum by the time the new house is sold.

> ### How the Tax Break Developed
>
> Tax-free treatment for the sale of a residence has gone through four phases:
>
> 1. Starting in 1964, new Section 121 allowed taxpayers age 65 or older to elect to exclude any realized gain on the sale of their home which was attributable to the first $20,000 of the "adjusted sales price" (sales price net of selling expenses and less "fixing-up" expenses). The property must have been owned and used by the taxpayer as a personal residence for at least five of the eight years before the sale. If the adjusted sales price exceeded $20,000, the exclusion was partial and was based on the ratio that $20,000 bore to the adjusted sales price. The exclusion could be used only once.
>
> 2. In 1977, the $20,000 limitation was increased to $35,000.
>
> 3. For sales and exchanges after July 26, 1978, the exclusion was changed to a *flat* maximum of $100,000 of any realized gain. The age requirement was reduced by ten years to age 55. The ownership and use requirement also was reduced to three of the previous five years. The new election was made available notwithstanding any election in effect under prior law. For dispositions up to July 26, 1981, sellers could elect to use the old ownership and use requirement.
>
> 4. For sales and exchanges after July 20, 1981, the flat exclusion was increased to $125,000.

- A taxpayer who is elderly and in poor health, and intends to live in the replacement residence until his death, should probably elect the exclusion so as to avoid *any* tax currently. However, his surviving spouse can never make another election. This is of significance only if the spouse will sell the house. Even if she does sell it, her basis may have been stepped-up to the value at the date of her husband's death.

No Replacement Home Contemplated

When the seller does not expect to purchase a replacement home, the election should probably be made to avoid tax if the gain is significant, even though the seller is not completely sure that he will never buy another home. Should the situation change within three years, he can revoke the election.

No Replacement Home Possible

When the seller is "certain" that he will never buy another residence, the election obviously should be made, regardless of the size of the gain.

The Wastage Problem

The most difficult decision comes when the recognized gain is less than the maximum $125,000 exclusion, either because the realized gain is small or because of partial deferral under Section 1034, since the unused portion of the exclusion is lost once the election is made. If there is a possibility that a replacement residence will be purchased, the taxpayer has to decide whether the current tax savings will be greater than the *present value* of the estimated future tax savings. The answer is difficult, if not impossible, since there are several unknowns: the future gain, the future exclusion, the future tax rate, the discount rate and the number of years until the replacement residence is sold.

Conclusion

Section 121 is a significant tax benefit to large numbers of taxpayers. However, the rules are complex and they interplay with other Code sections. It is not always clear when the homeowner should make the election. It is therefore important that the taxpayer and his advisors are aware of all of the ramifications to get the maximum benefit from the exclusion.

Notes

1. The reason for the sale is irrelevant. Thus, an involuntary conversion (e.g., fire, flood and condemnation) also qualifies for the exclusion.
2. In fact, the taxpayer need not even be alive for the Section 121 election to be available. In *Rev. Rul.* 82-1, a taxpayer who met all of the Section 121 requirements entered into a binding executory contract to sell his residence and accepted a down payment. After substantial fulfillment of the prerequisites for the sale, the taxpayer died. His executor received the balance of the purchase price and delivered the deed. The ruling holds that the sale qualifies under Section 121.
3. Section 121(d)(8).
4. This applies to the predecessor $100,000 exclusion as well.
5. *Davis,* 62-2 USTC § 9509, 9 AFTR 2d 1625 (Sup. Ct., 1962). This assumes that the property settlement is not a division of property. Also, in some jurisdictions, property settlements will generally not result in realized gain because of legislation creating certain property rights for the non-owner spouse.
6. Clearly, a vindictive and uncooperative wife may not go along with her husband's plans to reduce *his* tax since she will wind up with the home in either case. She may even prefer that he winds up with a taxable gain.
7. Section 2523(a).
8. Reg. 1.71-1(c).
9. Reg. 1.121-5(g)(1).
10. Reg. 1.1038-2.
11. Section 121(e).
12. Of course, Congress also could restrict, reduce, suspend, or repeal the exclusion.

IV

The Elderly as a Political Force

14

The Elderly as a Political Force

Douglas Dobson

At the turn of the century, only 4 percent of this nation's citizens were sixty-five years of age or older. In the eight decades that have since passed, there have been rather sharp changes in the conditions that influence the age structure of the population. Rapid advances in health related technologies, for instance, have greatly extended life expectancy. Fertility rates, with the exception of the postwar "baby boom," have continued to decline. Immigration rates dropped sharply after the first two decades of this century and have remained relatively low. As a result, about one out of every ten persons in the United States is presently over the age of sixty-five.[1]

Projecting the age composition of the population into the future is risky, for estimates depend, among other things, on crucial assumptions about rates of fertility and mortality. Present indications suggest, however, that growth in the size of the elderly population is likely to continue unabated until well into the next century. Indeed, if current projections are accurate, we can anticipate rather sharp increases in both the absolute and relative size of the elderly population. By 2035, the U.S. population will have increased by about 40 percent relative to 1980. During the same period, the population sixty-five and older will have grown by more than 130 percent. Thus, at the end of the first third of the century,

---

From *Aging and Public Policy: The Politics of Growing Old in America,* edited by William P. Browne and Laura Katz Olson. Westport, Connecticut: Greenwood Press, 1983, pp. 123-44. Reprinted by permission of Greenwood Press.

over 18 percent of the population (some fifty-six million persons) will be aged sixty-five or older.[2]

Rapid changes in the age structure of the American population potentially could have significant economic, social, and political implications. Indeed, there is little doubt, given present federal policies, current inflation rates, and an increasing number of elderly beneficiaries, that economic effects will be significant. As Hudson has observed,

> Total outlays for the aging, survivors, and retirees under OASI, civilian and retirement insurance plans, railroad retirement, SSI, Medicare and Medicaid were $122 billion in 1977.... The corresponding figure for the FY1979 budget... [was] $148 billion, or 29.6 percent of the total [federal] budget. HEW Secretary Califano estimates that, if present trends continue, "real" spending on behalf of the elderly will triple by 2010.[3]

Reasoned speculation about the social and political implications of an aging population is somewhat more difficult. On the basis of sheer numbers, there is little doubt that the elderly have the *potential* to play a significant political role, just as laborers and blacks have done in this century. Moreover, recent years have seen the formulation and rapid growth of a number of interest groups concerned with aging policy.[4] Estimating the likelihood that these potentials will be realized as effective "senior power" in the political process is highly problematic, however, given our present state of knowledge. Neither our theories of social and political change nor our existing data bases have sufficient power to permit precise projections of current values, attitudes, and behaviors—to say nothing of contextual factors—into the distant future.

To say that we cannot provide definitive answers to long-range questions about the political implications of an aging population should not be cause for despair. The question is complex, and research that has been explicitly concerned with the relationships between age and political behavior is of rather recent vintage. Rigorous, empirically based research is even more recent. Thus we are just beginning to sort out some of the dynamic relationships between age and politics. As our understanding grows, so too will our ability to make informed judgments about the future.

In this chapter, we will explore the major lines of research relating age to political behavior. In addition, we will also consider some recent data that provide insight into the contemporary political implications of age consciousness. We will also briefly consider some of the political implications of aging as seen through the eyes of elected representatives. Our principal concern will focus on the question of whether elderly citizens constitute a distinctive political force in American politics.

Age and Political Behavior

Attempts to understand the relationship between age and political behavior must confront at least two major issues, both of which relate to the influence of age as an explanatory variable. The first issue revolves around the question of how observed differences between younger and older individuals should be interpreted. As a person ages, several processes are at work. There are physiological and psychological processes, which we would generally refer to as "maturation" or "aging." Those processes include changes in both individual body chemistry over time and the cumulative effects of life experiences such as familial socialization and formal education. There are also social, political, and economic circumstances that may be relatively unique to persons born within a particular span of time. For such a "cohort" or "generation," shared experiences *may* lead to shared responses to new social, political, or economic conditions. To the extent that different cohorts have radically different life experiences, such experiences may serve as a basis for explaining observed age-related differences in political attitudes and behavior. We must therefore consider what have been termed "period" effects or "history." Some cohorts may experience wars, depressions, technologoical developments, or other events that differ from those experienced by both younger and older cohorts. These experiences, no doubt, influence the responses of each succeeding cohort to new social, economic and political developments.[5]

Perhaps the most straightforward approach to understanding the ways in which these effects serve as competing explanations of age-based differences is to consider a hypothetical example.[6] Suppose that we sampled two groups of individuals—those aged eighteen to twenty-five, and those aged sixty-five and older. Suppose further that we asked each respondent to tell us whether they generally thought of themselves as a Democrat, an Independent, or a Republican, and assume that we found, after tabulating the results, that in the younger group 75 percent were Democrats, 15 percent were Independents, and 10 percent were Republicans. For the older group, assume that results were a mirror image, that is, 10 percent were Democrats, 15 percent were Independents, and 75 percent were Republicans. The question is, do these results support the argument that aging "causes" people to become more Republican in their outlook? Although one can find instances in which such interpretations have been made,[7] it appears that the answer is no.

To see why observed differences between age groups do not necessarily lead to the conclusion that those differences are due to age, we need only change the name of the variable under consideration. Suppose that instead of collecting data on partisan affiliation we had instead asked the same respondents to report their education as more than high school, high school graduate, or less than high school and that we obtained the same percentage distributions as above for the two groups. It is easy to see that interpreting such results to mean that an individual's age "causes" a decline in educational level is fallacious. Indeed, we would expect almost no variation in an individual's educational level after about the third decade of the life cycle. In no case would we expect that an individual's educational attainment would decline with increasing age.

Results such as these are more appropriately understood as cohort differences. With the expansion of the public school system, the enactment of compulsory attendance legislation, and the development of college loan programs, each succeeding generation has experienced higher levels of educational attainment. Thus, in any cross-sectional sample, older individuals are likely to report having completed fewer years of formal education than younger individuals. But such results are obviously independent of the aging process itself.

More recent research has confronted these difficulties by relying upon a series of data collected over the years rather than a single, cross-sectional sample. In this way, researchers have sought to observe changes in the behavior of the same-age cohort over time, thus permitting at least a rough estimate of the relative effects of maturation and generation. Although such an approach has not completely solved the problem of interpretation of age differences, it represents a significant advance over single-year, cross-sectional approaches. Ultimately, however, resolution will very likely require panel studies that observe the same individuals over relatively long periods of time.

A second major issue in the study of age and political behavior relates to the distinction between chronological and "subjective" age.[8] Chronologically, individuals age at the same rate. But it is unlikely that everyone of the same chronological age perceives themselves to be of the same age subjectively. Indeed, in a youth-oriented society such as that found in contemporary America, there are probably substantial inducements to resist psychologically the notion of "being old." Whether such considerations have significant implications for understanding the relationship between age and political behavior is presently unclear. It is clear, however, that substantially more research on the issue is needed.

With these interpretative problems as background, let us turn to an overview of current findings relating to age and political behavior. In so doing, we shall consider the effects of aging on political involvement, political interest, and political attitudes.

Age and Political Involvement

Although the politics of aging often has not been of primary concern, a number of scholars have considered the relationship between age and selected aspects of political involvement. Cross-sectional studies that have examined the relationship between age and political participation generally come to the same conclusion. Participation rates are lowest among citizens in their late teens and early twenties. From that point, the data typically suggest a pattern of increasing participation rates up through middle age with a decline beginning in the fifty- to sixty-year age range.[9] Norman Nie and his associates report that this general pattern holds not only in the United States but in Austria, India, Japan, and Nigeria as well:

> Patterns... are remarkably similar.... It would be difficult to imagine a more heterogeneous set of nations in terms of culture, location, or level of development. Each has its own historical sequence, exposing its citizens to different political experiences at different times... this heterogeneity... makes this similarity of pattern more convincing.[10]

While there is a general agreement about the overall pattern of political involvement as shown from cross-sectional studies, explaining why participation rates decline in later years appears to be more difficult. One potential explanation revolves around differences in the sociodemographic characteristics of various age cohorts. Previous research consistently has shown that political participation is related to a number of individual characteristics.[11] Males, persons with more education, higher income, and higher occupational status, tend to participate at relatively high rates. To the extent that cohorts differ with regard to these characteristics, such differences serve as one potential explanation of age-related variation in participation rates. This argument, of course, rejects the notion that the aging process itself leads to lower levels of involvement, suggesting, rather, that observed differences may be due to the fact that contemporary older cohorts are not likely to have characteristics associated with high levels of political involvement.

Nie and his associates addressed this question in their cross-national study by controlling for sex and level of educational attainment. They found that the "downturn in activity apparent in the uncorrected data was either substantially reduced... or completely eliminated."[12] Thus, there is some evidence for the argument that the lower participation rates observed in contemporary elderly cohorts are probably due, at least in part, to the unique sociodemographic composition of that group. Nie and his associates went on to suggest that there may be an additional factor related to the aging process itself that accounts for *residual* variation in elderly participation rates. They described the process as one of "slow down," when "old age brings sociological withdrawal as individuals retire from active employment... [as well as] physical infirmities and fatigue that lower the rate of political activity."[13] To examine this hypothesis, the authors used retirement from the active work force as an indicator of "slow down." Results were not fully consistent across all of the countries examined. In India,

Japan, and the United States, working older citizens participated at higher rates than their retired counterparts. In Austria, the results were reversed. Nonetheless, Nie and his associates concluded that "the data are consistent with the 'slow down' explanation of the decline in citizen activity in later years."[14]

A "slow down" interpretation has not been supported by cohort analyses focusing on other aspects of political involvement. Norval Glenn and Michael Grimes, for instance, analyzing some twenty-eight national surveys, examined the relationships among aging, voting, and political interest. With regard to voting, their cohort analysis yielded "no convincing evidence of a decline in voting as people age into their sixties and seventies."[15] Similarly, when they examined levels of political interest, they concluded that the "data [were] ... generally consistent with ... [the] hypothesis that political interest typically increases from young adulthood to old age."[16] They found no support for the idea that aging brings on an inevitable withdrawal.

From yet another perspective, Glenn tested the related hypothesis, suggested by Kenneth Gergen and Kurt Back,[17] that as people age they are less likely to hold or to express opinions.[18] Controlling for both sex and education, Glenn found no support for the hypothesis. In fact, he suggested that, although the data may be subject to differing interpretations, "they suggest that people slowly but steadily become more attuned to current events as they mature from young adulthood to old age."[19]

The ultimate resolution of the meaning of observed age-participation relationships has clear implications for our prognostications about the political roles of future elderly cohorts. If the existing downturn in participation in later life is, as most recent research suggests, primarily due to the unique characteristics of the contemporary elderly, then the gradual replacement of the present cohort with more highly educated individuals should work to increase rates of political participation by future elderly citizens.

Age and Political Attitudes

What political values do the elderly hold? Does the aging process inexorably lead to changes in political attitudes? If the elderly had more political power, would they seek to enact public policies that are more liberal or more conservative? These are some of the questions that have been posed by researchers concerned with the relationship between age and political attitudes. As late as 1974, Glenn characterized the study of age and opinions as a "virgin research area."[20] Thus, many questions remain unanswered.

The issue that has been investigated most intensely relates to the widely held belief that, as people age, they grow more conservative in their political outlook. According to this notion, socialization affects age cohorts as political culture changes in content. Attitudes, values, and ideologies vary from generation to generation as older cohorts reflect

> greater rigidity, cautiousness, and increasing resistance to change. Further pressures against the acceptance of social and political change become manifest with increasing integration into the social system, which leads to a greater stake in the status quo. Presumably, therefore, older cohorts are not only the bearers of the more traditional political culture, but their members increasingly adhere to the content of their political socialization as they age.[21]

Riley and Foner, in their monumental review of research findings relating to age, reported on several pre-1968 studies that support the above arguments.[22] Campbell and his colleagues, for instance, found that the elderly were more resistant to change.[23] Stouffer found older persons to be less tolerant of political and social nonconformists.[24] Early researchers also found elderly citizens to be less favorable toward racial integration in public schools,[25] more opposed to having either a black[26] or a Catholic[27] as president, and generally less favorable toward governmental intervention in social issues.[28] As Glenn concluded in 1974, "The preponderance of evidence from contemporary Western countries shows that at any point in time older people as a whole are more conservative than young adults."[29]

In recent years, these findings relating age to conservative opinions have been seriously questioned. Cutler and Kaufman, for example, pointed out that "much of the support for the aging-conservatism hypothesis has come from single cross-sectional studies."[30] The interpretation problems related to the relative import of maturational, cohort, and period effects once again come into play. Their research, which employed cohort analysis across two surveys completed in 1954 and 1973, focused on Stouffer's finding that older persons tend to be less tolerant of nonconformity. They found that in 1973 younger cohorts were, once again, more tolerant than older cohorts. All cohorts, however, shifted in the direction of higher tolerance; the younger cohorts appeared to have changed toward higher tolerance levels at a faster rate than older cohorts.[31] Thus, Cutler and Kaufman found no evidence for the simple aging-conservatism hypothesis. Their results suggesting that younger cohorts change more rapidly than older cohorts implies, however, that the elderly may always be conservative in a relative sense due to their slower rate of change.

Subsequent work by Cutler, which examined attitudes toward legalized abortion during the period from 1965 through 1977, casts some doubt on the finding that the elderly change their opinions at slower rates than younger citizens. On abortion issues, Cutler found that "older persons... change their attitudes over time in the same direction as younger persons," and, moreover, "older persons can change their attitudes to the same extent as younger persons."[32]

Other researchers have approached the aging-conservatism hypothesis from a partisanship perspective. Early cross-sectional studies by Campbell and his colleagues suggested that older persons were more likely than younger ones to identify themselves as Republicans.[33] Given the usual presumption that the Republican party is more conservative than the Democratic party, this finding was interpreted as additional support for the aging and conservatism hypothesis. Crittenden's analysis echoed these results.[34] Neal Cutler, however, analyzed Crittenden's data further, using a cohort design, and found no evidence for linear increases in Republican identification as cohorts aged.[35] More recently, Glenn and Hefner analyzed data from both Gallup and Roper polls between 1945 and 1969. They also found no support for an absolute increase in Republican identification as cohorts aged. They did note, however, that there was some evidence of an increase in the "relative Republicanism of aging cohorts." They interpreted such a finding to mean that "social definitions of the politics of people in the aging cohorts probably changed a great deal even though party identification changed little. . . . [T]his finding suggests that many young liberals have become old conservatives without experiencing appreciable changes in attitudes and values."[36] Thus, the original findings of Campbell and his associates are probably best understood as "intercohort rather than life stage differences."[37]

A final area in which there has been at least some research focuses on the attitudes of the elderly on issues in which they presumably have some degree of self-interest. Campbell, for instance, noted that the elderly are as likely as young people to support government guarantees of low-cost medical care.[38] More recently, Heilig examined support for increased government spending across several issue areas, some of which were presumed to be of particular interest to the elderly, such as health, welfare, cities, and crime.[39] The results were mixed and did not support consistently the hypothesis that the elderly were more "liberal" on issues involving self-interest. Similarly, Epstein and Browne found that older persons were less likely than the young to (1) agree that Social Security should be paid from general income taxes; (2) favor decreasing both Social Security taxes and benefits; and (3) indicate a desire to work beyond the age of sixty-five.[40] On the other three issues they examined, all of which pertained to mandatory retirement, differences between younger and older groups were quite small. Finally, Dobson and St. Angelo examined the relationship between age and a generalized measure of support for government intervention on behalf of the elderly. They found no essential differences between the responses of younger and older citizens.[41]

What, then, is the relationship between age and political attitudes? Earlier findings notwithstanding, recent work appears to lead to the conclusion that aging per se probably has no systematic impact on an individual's political outlook. Or, as Epstein and Browne have suggested, results seem to adhere to the "sometimes it's this way, sometimes it's that way principle," yielding no consistent patterns.[42] To be sure, cohort differences do exist, but there is little support for the hypothesis that those differences are due to maturational factors.

Toward a Political Movement?

A final set of issues that have concerned observers and scholars is whether, and under what conditions, we might expect to see the elderly coalesce into a unified political force. As Ragan and Dowd have posed the issue,

> Whether the notion is couched in the politico's language of a "voting bloc" or in the sociologist's vocabulary of political age group consciousness, the underlying assumption remains the same: The aged, because of prevailing demographic trends in society, will increasingly become aware of their common political and economic plight and will consequently attempt to parlay this awareness into a broad-based social movement.[43]

Some scholars view the development of age-based cleavages, pitting the young against the old, as quite likely. Leonard Cain, for instance, suggests at least two factors that may lead to age-based conflict.[44] First, the increased geographic mobility of both children and their elderly parents will continue to contribute to a weakening of kinship ties. Second, and perhaps more important, the increasing size of the elderly population is likely to create significant pressure on the economic system. According to Cain, as these pressures grow more intense, the tacit intergenerational commitment to provide support for those in a dependent status will be weakened. Indeed, he argues that both the young and the old will have to "struggl[e] for economic support from an intervening middle-aged group."[45] That struggle, in his view, probably will lead to political and social conflict.

In a similar vein, Arnold Rose has noted that there are a number of demographic and social forces that are likely to lead to the development of a "subculture of the aging."[46] Included among those forces are (1) increasing numbers of older persons; (2) the fact that the elderly are physically vigorous due to improved health care; (3) commonality of interest among the elderly in the provision of health-care services at reasonable cost; (4) development of "age-segregated" housing in retirement communities; (5) decreasing integration of the elderly into general society due to increases in early retirement; (6) older people's rising educational and economic levels; (7) development of social service programs providing vehicles for interaction among the elderly; and (8) the breakdown of the multigenerational family unit.[47] As a result of these developments, Rose concludes that "The elderly seem to be on their way to becoming a voting bloc with a leadership that acts like a political pressure group."[48]

Other scholars have come to more negative conclusions about the likelihood of an age-based political movement. Binstock, for one, argues that the case for an elderly voting bloc "is impressive only in the most superficial sense."[49] Binstock is drawn to this conclusion, in part, because of what he views as "critical limitations" on electoral politics as a vehicle for addressing the problems associated with aging. The first of these limitations revolves around a distinction between electoral outcomes and policy adoption. Certainly, the elderly have the potential to influence the outcomes of elections, given their share of the voting population. It is quite another matter, however, to translate electoral victory into concrete policy decisions. Second, Binstock points to the diversity of the elderly. Their partisan attachments, voting behavior, and political values are as diverse as their social, economic, and geographic backgrounds. Such diversity is clearly not conducive to the development of unified political action. Third, Binstock argues that the issues of American politics typically have not been "framed in terms of the special interests of the aged."[50] Thus, even if the elderly wished to vote on the basis of age-related interests, it would be quite difficult to do so.

Anne Foner also has assessed the possibility of age-based political conflict.[51] In large part, Foner views age as operating to structure social and political relations in much the same way that social class does. Such "age stratification" does not, however, necesssarily suggest the emergence of age-based conflicts. Age is but one of the many possible bases of stratification. Individuals in a given age stratum may identify with political and social groups on the basis of sex, social class, occupation, race, or religion rather than age per se. Such cross-pressures probably work to reduce the potential for age conflicts. Moreover, age is not static, it changes with the passage of time since there is a "continuous movement of individuals in and out of an age stratum."[52] The fact that membership in any given age group is transient has at least two implications. First, the perpetual influx of new members requires a continuous "rebuilding of solidarity." Second the inevitable movement of individuals out of a particular age stratum weakens their sense of identification with it.

At the same time, however, there are cross-cutting pressures that may work to heighten age solidarity and thereby increase the potential for age conflict. In Foner's words,

> Individuals of like age move together through a particular historical environment. Unlike members of a given social class or ethnic group who have lived varying periods of time and have been exposed to diverse historical experiences, age peers share a common past and face a common future, and this commonality cuts across other lines of staratification.[53]

This statement suggests that it is not age per se that provides a basis for group solidarity but rather a commonality of political orientation presumably derived from shared social and political experiences. Indeed, as Ragan and Dowd have argued, this distinction differentiates between a simple age cohort and a "political generation."[54] They note that only the latter will affect the possibility of age becoming a major factor in political conflict.

In sum, it appears that reasonable arguments can be marshaled on both sides of the question. The changing age structure of the population suggests a potential for the elderly to become a considerable force, a potential that may be reinforced by a number of social and economic developments. On the other hand, there are a large number of other cleavages that can foster political conflict. The transiency of age-stratum membership, along with competing group identifications, are continuing forces that undoubtedly will weaken the potential for age-based political conflict.

Age and Political Behavior: The Contemporary Cohort

In the final section of this chapter we shall turn our attention to the current cohort of elderly citizens. Our central concern is whether there is any evidence suggesting the existence of age-based political mobilization among the contemporary elderly. Specifically, we will consider the political implication of "age consciousness," and, in addition, we shall provide some evidence on the political impact of the contemporary elderly from the perspective of political leaders.

A common assumption underlying much of the discussion about the political potential of the elderly is that the development of "age consciousness" or "age-based identification" is necessary for the creation of an age-based political movement. Moreover, age consciousness must have political meaning. That is, age must become "a major referent in fixing sociopolitical beliefs," and in addition, the political system must "frame relevant policy issues in age-related terms."[55] What about the current generation of older Americans? Do they identify with each other on the basis of age? What social processes lead to the development of age consciousness? Does such an identification have implications for the politics of aging?

To provide at least some tentative answers to these questions, we shall rely upon data from a 1976 election survey completed by the University of Michigan's Center for Political Studies.[56] Since the primary concern here is with elderly citizens, we have included only persons age sixty or older in our analysis. These individuals were born between the turn of the century and the onset of World War I. In their youth, this cohort experienced a catastrophic economic depression, a major realignment of electoral politics from Republican to Democratic dominance, and the beginning of World War II. At the onset of the Great Depression, the bulk of this generation would have ranged in age from their mid-teens to perhaps their early thirties. In many respects, then, the elderly respondents to be discussed below may be characterized as the Depression era generation.

Our measure of group identification derives from a series of questions included in the 1976 survey. Respondents were provided a list of sixteen groups and asked to identify "those groups you feel particularly close to—people who are most like you in their ideas and interests and feelings about things." Having completed this task, the respondents were asked to review the list of groups they felt "close to" and to identify the one to which they felt "closest." The distribution of respondents is shown in Exhibit 14.1.

Foner's observation with respect to the existence of multiple lines of stratification among the elderly is borne out by these data.[57] Indeed, almost two-thirds of the respondents (63.4 percent) reported a primary identification with some group other than "older people," and an additional 11.3 percent reported feeling close to no group at all. Thus, one respondent in four felt a strong sense of group identification with the elderly. Class ("middle-class people" and "poor people") and occupation ("workingmen," "farmers," and "businessmen") accounted

EXHIBIT 14.1
Distribution of Group Identifications of Persons Age 60 or Over: 1976

Group to Which Respondent Felt Closest	Percent
Businessmen	2.6
Liberals	0.6
Southerners	1.1
Poor people	6.4
Catholics	2.4
Protestants	3.7
Jews	0.9
Young people	2.5
Whites	4.2
Blacks	2.4
Conservatives	3.2
Women	3.9
Middle-class people	15.2
Workingmen	8.7
Farmers	5.6
Older people	25.3
No group	11.3
Total	100.0
Total Number	(724)

Source: Compiled by author from 1976 election data. Center for Political Studies, University of Michigan.

for 21.6 percent and 16.9 percent of reported identifications, respectively. The remaining 24.9 percent of the elderly in this sample reported primary identification with a rather wide variety of groups.

Clearly, the present generation of elderly citizens is characterized by considerable heterogeneity. But the fact that about one-fourth of the respondents report a primary sense of identification with older persons should not be discounted as insignificant. Given a population base of roughly thirty-four million persons aged sixty or older,[58] the figures reported in Exhibit 14.1 suggest that perhaps as many as eight million elderly have some sense of age consciousness. If such identifications were linked directly to political behavior, the political impact would be quite significant.

As a first step toward understanding the political implications of age-based identification, we analyzed the types of elderly citizens who identified with other older persons. As the data in Exhibit 14.2 indicate, respondents who reported

EXHIBIT 14.2
Selected Background Characteristics of Persons Age 60 and Older by Identification with Older Persons: 1976

	Respondent Feels Closest to:	
Characteristic	Older Persons (percent)	Other Groups (percent)
Sex		
Male	29.8	42.4
Female	70.2	57.6
Total	100.0 (153)	100.0 (451)
Education		
Eighth grade or less	51.1	37.2
Ninth through eleventh grade	16.4	16.6
High school graduate	20.4	24.5
Some college	3.6	12.4
College graduate	8.5	9.3
Total	100.0 (153)	100.0 (447)
Employment status		
In labor force	9.5	25.2
Retired	54.8	43.1
Permanently disabled	3.9	4.4
Housewife	31.8	27.3
Total	100.0 (153)	100.0 (451)

Note: Parentheses indicate number.

Source: Compiled by author from 1976 election data. Center for Political Studies, University of Michigan.

feeling closest to other elderly people tended to have the following characteristics: (1) female (29.8 percent); (2) low levels of educational attainment (51.1 percent reported eighth grade or less); and (3) retired (54.8 percent) from the active work force. Elderly respondents reporting primary identification with groups other than older persons were significantly different with respect to these characteristics. Specifically, they were (1) less likely to be females; (2) less likely to report low levels of educational attainment, and more likely to have educational experiences beyond high school; and (3) less likely to be retired.

If the "age-conscious" have background characteristics that are significantly different from other elderly, do those differences have political significance? That is, do the age-conscious elderly approach politics with orientations differing from the elderly who are not age-conscious? The results shown in Exhibit 14.3 suggest that they do not, at least in terms of partisanship and self-perceived ideology. Both groups tend to be Democratic (43.7 percent for the age-conscious, and 45.4 percent for other elderly). The age-conscious group was slightly less likely than other elderly to report Republican affiliation and slightly more likely to identify themselves as Independents. The differences, however, were not statistically significant.

The same pattern emerged when self-perceived political ideology was considered. About 16 percent of both groups viewed themselves as having a liberal ideology. The age-conscious were slightly more likely to view themselves as conservatives. But, once again, those differences were not statistically significant.

Thus far, then, we have seen that the elderly who identified with older persons differ from other elderly with regard to selected personal characteristics, but the two groups approached politics with essentially the same political orientations. If age consciousness had political meaning among the contemporary elderly, we probably would not have found such similarities between our two groups. Rather we would have expected respondents identifying with the elderly to be different from and more homogeneous than other elderly citizens, irrespective of party affiliation or ideology. The data shown in Exhibit 14.3 lead us to wonder whether subjective identification with the elderly has political meaning.

Data provided in Exhibit 14.4, which shows the relationship between elderly identification and seven indicators of political involvement, are even more compelling. If age consciousness were to serve as a basis for mobilization, we would expect to find that age-conscious older persons would be involved in the political process to a greater extent than other elderly. However, the results shown in Exhibit 14.4 suggest just the opposite. Across all seven indicators of political involvement, those who reported primary identification with other elderly were *less* likely to be politically involved.[59]

These findings raise serious questions about the political relevance of age consciousness among the contemporary generation of older Americans. The lack of

EXHIBIT 14.3
Partisan Affiliation and Ideology of Persons Age 60 and Older by Identification with Older Persons: 1976

	Respondent Feels Closest to:	
Characteristic	Older Persons (percent)	Other Groups (percent)
Partisan affiliation		
Strong Democrat	25.0	20.0
Weak Democrat	18.7	25.3
Independent	28.9	20.2
Weak Republican	13.3	19.7
Strong Republican	11.8	13.8
Other	2.3	0.9
Total	100.0 (150)	100.0 (449)
Ideology		
Liberal	16.8	16.2
Moderate	28.8	38.4
Conservative	54.4	45.4
Total	100.0 (63)	100.0 (266)

Note: Parentheses indicate number.
Source: Compiled by author from 1976 election data. Center for Political Studies, University of Michigan.

EXHIBIT 14.4
Political Involvement of Respondents Age 60 and Older by Identification with Older Persons: 1976

| | Respondent Feels Closet to: | | | |
| | Older Persons | | Other Groups | |
Respondent Reported Having:	Percent	Number	Percent	Number
Voted in 1976 presidential election*	66.6	153	76.8	451
Tried to influence the votes of others*	22.0	153	31.4	451
Given money to a party or candidate*	3.0	150	9.7	450
Written to a public official	18.7	153	24.4	450
Attended political rallies/meetings	3.0	153	6.3	451
Worked for a party or candidate	3.0	153	5.1	451
Worn a campaign button or sticker	2.0	151	5.9	450

*Significant at .05 or less.
Source: Compiled by author from 1976 election data. Center for Political Studies, University of Michigan.

partisan or ideological homogeneity implies that even if those who identified with the elderly as a group were highly involved in politics, their "participation input," as Verba and Nie have called it, would probably be quite diverse. Certainly, it would be no less diverse than the input of elderly citizens who are less age-conscious. Some older individuals would be inclined to support Democratic candidates, while others would be more likely to support Republican ones. Similarly, the elderly would be as likely to support "conservative" as they would more "liberal" solutions to policy problems. In short, the findings on partisanship and ideology suggest that age has not supplanted more traditional lines of political cleavage among the contemporary elderly.

Such a conclusion is strongly reinforced by the findings on political involvement. A group's political success depends, at least in part, on the ability to maintain high levels of commitment and involvement among participants. Our findings that age-based identification is not associated with high levels of political involvement can be interpreted to mean that increasing levels of age consciousness would not necessarily foster a strong old-age political movement.[60] Indeed, if age consciousness is to serve as a basis for the development of an aging movement, the structure of these relationships will have to undergo a radical transformation.

The Politics of Age:
A Legislative Perspective

Given that we find little evidence for the existence of an age-based political movement among the contemporary generation of elderly, one may reasonably wonder at the relative success of aging advocates in the policy process. Indeed, programs for the elderly have served as legislative landmarks at both national and state levels. There are at least two explanations for these developments. First, it may be that legislators view the elderly as a unified and effective political force that they cannot afford to alienate. Undoubtedly, this is the picture that advocates have promoted to legislators. An alternative explanation is provided by Hudson's observation that "the political legitimacy of the aging has rested in the widespread belief that, as a class of persons, they are singularly disadvantaged by low incomes, poor health, and a particular vulnerability brought on by their place in the life cycle."[61] Thus, in his view, legislative successes in aging policy development have not necessarily been due to political power. Rather they have been due to the belief among elites that the elderly are worse off than most other population segments.

In a 1979 survey, Dobson and Karns asked state legislators to report on their perceptions of political involvement and the relative status of older persons.[62] They also measured legislators' support for an expanded state role in the provision of benefits to the elderly[63] and the relative importance which legislators attached to aging issues, in contrast to other types of state policies.[64] They found that state legislators do, in fact, view the elderly as being highly involved in politics. About 75 percent of the state legislators perceived the elderly as voting more regularly than other citizens. Just under one-third (29.3 percent) believed that many elderly were involved in political organizations, and another 60 percent believed that at least some were. Similarly, only 26 percent viewed elderly organization leaders as ineffective, while 74 percent saw them as effective in the policy process.

Legislators were less unanimous about the relative status of the elderly. Only a small fraction of the respondents (2.2 percent) viewed the elderly as "better off" than most other age groups. Just under half (45.1 percent), however, stated that the elderly were "about as well off" as most other citizens. Finally, a slight majority (52.6 percent) believed the elderly to be "worse off" than other citizens.

Exhibits 14.5 and 14.6 suggest some political consequences of legislators' beliefs about the political involvement and relative status of the elderly. Exhibit 14.6 relates legislators' perceptions to levels of support for state intervention. Exhibit 14.6 does the same for the level of importance that legislators attached to aging issues. In both instances, the results are quite clear. Beliefs about the well-being of older citizens tend to have strong effects on legislators' support for state intervention and the importance they attach to aging issues. Legislators who responded that the elderly were at least as well off as other age groups were considerably less likely to support a positive state role for, or to attach much importance to, aging policy issues.

In sharp contrast, legislators' perceptions about the political roles of the elderly had no impact upon either support for state intervention or the perceived importance of aging issues. Although legislators perceive the elderly as being involved in the political process and as having effective political leadership, such views do not appear to translate into policy support. Apparently, as Hudson's remarks suggest, legislators respond to the elderly on the basis of welfare concerns rather than on political considerations.

Conclusions

The findings presented here as well as those emerging from other research suggest that, although the elderly are an important and perhaps especially regarded group in contemporary American politics, there is little support for the notion that they are a distinctive, unified political force. To be sure, the current generation of elderly differ from the young. They are, for instance, more likely to be conservative in political orientation. Similarly, they are more likely to have partisan inclinations that favor the Republican party. But such findings do not imply that the elderly are a homogeneous political group. Their attitudes and po-

EXHIBIT 14.5
Support for an Expanding State Role in the Provision of Benefits to the Elderly and Perception of Elderly Status and Political Involvement among State Legislators: 1979

	Legislator's Level of Support			
Variable	Low (percent)	Moderate (percent)	High (percent)	Total Number
Elderly are:*				
Better off than most	43.4	44.2	12.4	23
As well off as most	54.2	30.4	15.4	458
Worse off than most	36.1	29.2	34.7	543
Elderly vote:				
More regularly than others	43.3	31.3	25.4	758
About as regularly as others	45.8	29.8	24.4	214
Less regularly than others	56.0	12.5	31.5	36
Elderly leaders are:				
Ineffective	42.9	30.2	26.9	271
Effective	44.2	30.5	25.3	741
How many elderly are politically involved?				
Few	46.1	27.1	26.8	109
Some	41.6	31.8	26.6	606
Many	47.7	28.8	23.5	297

*Significant at .05 or less.
Source: Compiled by the author.

litical orientations are about as diverse as the population at large. Such diversity serves to inhibit a realization of the political potential of the elderly, for success in the halls of Congress and the state legislatures depends, at least partially, on uniformity of articulated policy preferences.

Further, among the current generation of elderly it does not appear that "age consciousness" serves as a basis for political mobilization. In fact, it is doubtful that age consciousness has political meaning for *most* elderly citizens. The age-conscious elderly are not more homogeneous than other elderly in either political affiliation or ideological orientation. Perhaps more importantly, the age-conscious elderly are substantially less likely than other elderly to be involved in the political process. If the elderly are a distinctive political force in America, their impact probably derives from an ideology among many political elites supporting the notion that the elderly are uniquely disadvantaged.

EXHIBIT 14.6
Importance of Aging Issues and Perceptions of Elderly Status and Political Involvement among State Legislators: 1979

Variable	Importance of Aging Issues to Legislators			
	Low (percent)	Moderate (percent)	High (percent)	Total Number
Elderly are:				
Better off than most	51.8	35.1	13.1	23
As well off as most	48.6	31.5	19.9	458
Worse off than most	23.6	35.1	41.3	534
Elderly vote:				
More regularly than others	35.6	34.2	30.2	758
About as regularly as others	34.5	33.5	32.0	214
Less regularly than others	31.2	32.4	36.4	36
Elderly leaders are:				
Ineffective	31.6	36.4	32.0	271
Effective	36.0	33.3	30.7	741
How many elderly are politically involved?				
Few	37.1	31.5	31.3	109
Some	34.6	36.9	28.5	606
Many	34.7	29.4	36.0	297

* Significant at .05 or less.
Source: Compiled by the author.

It is difficult to say what lies beyond the horizon. There are indications that the elderly may be losing their especially favored political status in the face of staggering inflation and efforts to contain or reduce the size of government programs. This suggests that major political issues will include questions of old age in the coming decades, possibly with fewer benefits accruing to older people. It is unclear, however, whether such changes will foster political mobilization among the elderly. It is obvious, however, that the elderly of the early twenty-first century will be more highly educated, in better health, and perhaps more politically experienced than contemporary older Americans. As the present cohort is replaced by the politically active 1960s generation, it is certainly possible to visualize scenarios in which age could be a major source of cleavage in the American political system.

Notes

1. Matilda White Riley and Anne Foner, eds., *Aging and Society*, Vol. 1 (New York: Russell Sage, 1972), pp. 15-38.
2. Donald G.Fowles, *Statistical Reports on Older Americans: Some Prospects for the Future Aging Population* (Washington, D.C.: Department of Health, Education, and Welfare, 1978).
3. Robert B. Hudson, "The 'Graying' of the Federal Budget and Its Consequences for Old-Age Policy," in *The Aging in Politics: Process and Policy*, ed. Robert B. Hudson (Springfield, Ill.: Charles C. Thomas, 1981), p. 274.
4. Since aging interest groups are treated elsewhere in this volume, they will not be considered here. Rather we will focus upon the political behavior of the "mass" of elderly citizens, and our findings will reflect this restricted focus. Professor Pratt notes in Chapter 7 of *Aging and Public Policy: The Politics of Growing Old in America* (Westport, CT: Greenwood Press, 1983) that the development of stable aging interest groups is an important phenomenon. It is not really possible to comprehend the politics of aging without paying careful attention to the roles played by aging interest groups.
5. One of the best discussions of these issues may be found in Matilda White Riley, "Aging and Cohort Succession: Interpretations and Misinterpretations," *Public Opinion Quarterly* 37 (1973): 35-49.
6. This example is drawn from Neal E. Cutler and John R. Schmidhauser, "Age and Political Behavior," in *Aging: Scientific Perspectives and Social Issues*, ed. Diana S. Woodruff and James E. Birren (New York: D. Van Nostrand, 1975), pp. 374-406.
7. See, for instance, Angus Campbell, et al., *The American Voter* (New York: Wiley, 1960).
8. See Cutler and Schmidhauser, "Age and Political Behavior," pp. 387-90.
9. See Sidney Verba and Norman H. Nie, *Participation in America* (New York: Harper & Row, 1972), ch. 9; and Riley and Foner, *Aging and Society*, pp. 464-68.
10. Norman H. Nie, Sidney Verba, and Jae-on Kim, "Participation and the Life Cycle," *Comparative Politics* (1974): 326.
11. Verba and Nie, *Participation*, chs. 8-14. See also Lester Milbrath, *Political Participation* (Chicago: Rand McNally, 1965).
12. Nie, Verba, and Kim, "Participation and the Life Cycle," p. 329.
13. Ibid., p. 333.
14. Ibid., p. 335. Note also that the work by Verba and Nie, *Participation*, suggests that their "slow down" interpretation may vary across "modes" of participation. Specifically, while their measure of overall participation showed a residual downturn in elderly involvement after the socioeconomic status (SES) effects were removed, the same was not true for their measure of voting involvement. In addition, they found no age-related variation in rates of contacting public officials. Thus, while they do not fully acknowledge it, evidence for a "slow down" interpretation is probably limited to more costly political acts such as campaign involvement or communal activity.
15. Norval Glenn and Michael Grimes, "Aging, Voting and Political Interest," *American Sociological Reveiw* 33 (August 1968): 567.
16. Ibid., p. 572.
17. Kenneth Gergen and Kurt Bach, "Communication in the Interview and the Disengaged Respondent," *Public Opinion Quarterly* 30 (1966): 385-98.
18. Norval Glenn, "Aging, Disengagement and Opinionation, "*Public Opinion Quarterly* 33 (1969): 17-33.
19. Ibid., p. 27.
20. Norval D. Glenn,"Aging and Conservatism," *Annals* 415 (1974): 176-86.
21. Stephen J. Cutler and Robert L. Kaufman, "Cohort Changes in Political Attitudes: Tolerance of Ideological Nonconformity," *Public Opinion Quarterly* 39 (1975): 69-70.
22. Riley and Foner, *Aging and Society*, 473-75.
23. Campbell, et al., *American Voter*.
24. Samuel A. Stouffer, *Communism, Conformity and Civil Liberties* (New York: Doubleday, 1955).

25. Herbert H. Hyman and Paul B. Sheatsley, "Attitudes Toward Desegregation," *Scientific American* 211 (1964): 16-23.
26. Hazel Gaudet Erskine, "The Polls," *Public Opinion Quarterly* 26 (1962): 142-48.
27. Hazel Gaudet Erskine, "The Polls," *Public Opinion Quarterly* 29 (1965): 332-95.
28. H.J. Eysenck, *The Psychology of Politics* (London: Routledge, 1954).
29. Glenn, "Aging and Conservatism," p. 181.
30. Cutler and Kaufman, "Cohort Changes," p. 70.
31. Ibid., pp. 77ff.
32. Stephen J. Cutler et al., "Aging and Conservatism: Cohort Changes in Attitudes About Legalized Abortion," *Journal of Gerontology* 35 (1980): 115-23.
33. Campbell, et al., *American Voter*.
34. John Crittenden, "Aging and Party Affiliation," *Public Opinion Quarterly* 26 (1962): 648-57.
35. Neal E. Cutler, "Generation, Maturation, and Party Affiliation: A Cohort Analysis," *Public Opinion Quarterly* 33 (1969-70): 583-88.
36. Norval D. Glenn and Ted Hefner, "Further Evidence on Aging and Party Identification," *Public Opinion Quarterly* 36 (1972): 38.
37. Ibid., p. 44.
38. Angus Campbell, "Social and Psychological Determinants of Voting Behavior," in *Politics of Age*, ed. Wilma Donahue and Clark Tibbitts (Ann Arbor: University of Michigan Press, 1962) pp. 87-101.
39. Peggy Heilig, "Self Interest and Attitude Patterns Among the Elderly" (Paper presented at the Annual Meeting of Midwest Political Science Association, Chicago, 1979).
40. Laurily Keir Epstein and William P. Browne, "Public Opinion and the Elderly: An Explanation of the 'Sometimes It's This Way and Sometimes It's That Way Principle'" (Paper delivered at the Annual Meeting of the Midwest Political Science Association, Chicago, 1979).
41. Douglas Dobson and Douglas St. Angelo, *Politics and Senior Citizens: Advocacy and Policy Formation in a Local Context* (Washington, D.C.: Administration on Aging, 1980).
42. Epstein and Browne, "Public Opinion."
43. Pauline K. Ragan and James J. Dowd. "The Emerging Political Consciousness of the Aged: A Generational Interpretation," *Journal of Social Issues* 39 (1974): 137.
44. Leonard Cain, "The Young and the Old: Coalition or Conflict Ahead?" *American Behavioral Scientist* 19 (1975): 166-75.
45. Ibid., p. 172.
46. Arnold Rose, "The Subculture of Aging: A Framework for Research in Social Gerontology," in *Older People and Their Social World*, ed. Arnold M. Rose and Warren A. Peterson (Philadelphia: F. A. Davis, 1965), pp. 3-16.
47. Ibid., pp. 4-5.
48. Ibid., p. 14.
49. Robert H. Binstock, "Interest-Group Liberalism and the Politics of Aging," *Gerontologist* 12 (Autumn 1972): 265-280. See also Robert H. Binstock, "Aging and the Future of American Politics," *Annals* 415 (1974): 199-212.
50. Binstock, "Interest Group Liberalism," p. 118.
51. Anne Foner, "Age Stratification and Age Conflict in Political Life," *American Sociological Review* 39 (1974): 187-96; and Anne Foner, "Age and Society: Structure and Change," *American Behavioral Scientist* 19 (1975): 144-65.
52. Foner, "Age and Society," p. 152.
53. Ibid., p.153.
54. Ragan and Dowd, "Emerging Political Consciousness."
55. Ibid., p. 143.
56. The data utilized in this section were made available by the Inter-University Consortium for Political and Social Research. The data for the 1976 American National Election Study were collected by the Center for Political Studies of the Institute for Social Research, University of Michigan. Neither the original collectors nor the consortium bear any responsibility for the analyses or interpretation presented here.
57. This conclusion was also supported by inspection of responses to each of the sixteen items, taken independently. The percentage distribution of "feel close" responses for each group was as fol-

lows: businessmen, 19.6; liberals, 8.1; Southerners, 18.3; poor people, 38.8; Catholics, 20.3; Protestants, 40.1; Jews, 9.2; young people, 32.9; whites, 44.5; blacks, 12.7; conservatives, 20.0; women, 41.7; middle-class people, 59.9; workingmen, 52.1; farmers, 42.4; and older people, 72.1.
58. U.S. Department of Health and Human Services, Administration on Aging, *Statistical Notes* (Washington, D.C.: National Clearinghouse on Aging, April 1980).
59. The relationships reported in Exhibit 11.4 were controlled for both sex and education. Results did not differ substantially from those shown here.
60. E. Cumming and W.E. Henry, *Growing Old: The Process of Disengagement* (New York: Basic Books, 1961).
61. Robert B. Hudson, "'Graying,'" p. 274. For a related discussion, see Binstock, "Aging and the Future," pp. 212ff.
62. The state legislature data resulted from a mail survey of legislators in twenty-seven states. For a detailed description of the research, see Douglas Dobson and David A. Karns, *Public Policy and Senior Citizens: Policy Formation in the American States* (Washington, D.C.: Administration on Aging, 1979).
63. The measure of "support" utilized here resulted from a factor analysis of items asking state legislators whether they believed that the state should do much more, should do some more, has done about enough, should do some less, or should do much less across twelve contemporary aging policy issues: lowering cost of prescription drugs; elimination of age discrimination; funding senior centers; reducing crime against the elderly; enabling individuals to work past normal retirement age; providing transportation; reducing utility costs; relieving property taxes; providing alternatives to institutionalization; providing good housing; regulation of nursing homes; and providing adequate health care.
64. The importance of aging policy issues was determined by asking legislators to judge each of the policy issues as "important" or "not important" in contrast to other state issues. Responses were, once again, factor analyzed.

15

Setting the Elderly Housing Agenda

Jon Pynoos

Introduction

In a landmark study of federal housing policy-making in the late 1960s, Harold Wolman (1971) wrote that "the most striking fact about the housing political system was the degree to which the system's environment constrained the range of decisions open to the system." This paper will explore how the broader economic and political situation defines the nature of the housing problems that are dealt with and the extent to which input from organized groups influences major distributive housing decisions affecting the elderly. In particular, it will discuss the importance of housing for the elderly, describe the major actors in the policy arena, analyze the influence that elderly interest groups have had on policy, identify agenda items that have yet to be addressed, highlight emerging directions in housing policy, and suggest how current developments may influence the future agenda of elderly housing.

The Importance of Housing for the Elderly

Housing for the elderly is one of the most important yet unappreciated issues confronting our society. Housing for all age groups bears significantly on the

---

From *Policy Studies Journal*, Vol. 13, No. 1 (September 1984). Reprinted by permission of *Policy Studies Journal* and J. Pynoos.

quality of life, as it is a basic necessity relating to available neighborhood services, status and health, and consumes a high proportion of income. Older persons place special importance on housing because they are likely to spend more time in it, have more difficulty taking care of it, find that its physical structure no longer meets their needs, and have special psychological attachments to it. But compared with other areas such as income assistance and health care, housing has had a relatively low priority as a political issue for the elderly. That is because

1. the elderly have benefited de facto proportionally more than other groups from federal housing assistance programs;
2. most elderly own their homes, aided by homeowner deductions for mortgage interest and property taxes—the largest unrecognized housing subsidy program;
3. the housing arena is dominated by much stronger and better organized producer groups;
4. the elderly have had difficulty generating enough political support to help create a national housing policy, especially at a time when the federal government is rapidly moving away from housing as a priority; and
5. the parameters of federal support for housing itself are somewhat outside the influence of housing interest groups.

Most recent agenda setting efforts in the elderly housing arena at the federal level have been directed toward trying to maintain what has already been achieved, modify existing programs to serve a larger number of older persons, and adapt to a strategy of making better use of existing housing resources rather than toward producing new units.

Political Actors in the Elderly Housing Field

Housing policy in the United States has been set primarily at the national level, where federal programs have formed the basis for state and local activity. Federal housing policy is made through the "iron triangle"—the interaction of administration, Congress, and a variety of nationally organized interest groups. The Department of Housing and Urban Development (HUD) generally represents the administration. But because services are necessary for supporting frail elderly, the Department of Health and Human Services (HHS) also can play a role. Moreover, the Office of Management and Budget attempts to set the parameters of housing policy, given the importance of housing in the national economy and the cost of housing assistance programs. On the congressional side, policy-making is fragmented: the Subcommittee on Housing and Consumer Interests of the Select Committee on Aging and the Senate Committee on Aging are focal points for raising agenda issues related to the elderly; Housing Subcommittees of the Senate and House Banking Committees hammer out legislative language; and House and Senate Appropriations Committees deal primarily with the housing budget.

Interest group lobbying efforts in the general housing field have long been dominated by materials producers, builders, real estate developers, financiers, housing officials, and labor unions. Two of the most powerful organizations, the National Association of Home Builders and the National Association of Realtors, have large, well-paid staffs and strong political connections at the national and local levels (Lilley, 1980). Like the business interests they represent, the housing industry lobby groups are organized along narrow lines. Partly as a result of major financial contributions they make to campaigns of key members of congressional housing committees, these groups are highly influential in developing policies, laws, and regulations (Hartman, 1983). They generally have opposed regulation of the housing industry. Although some groups have also attempted to restrict government programs to only the poorest to avoid competition with the private sector, developers and builders have supported programs such as Section 8 new construction. The heart of their efforts has been an attempt to keep the production of housing high and stable by keeping interest rates low. Recently this philosophy has translated into attempts, especially on the part of the realtors, to reduce expenditures for programs, including housing, that contribute to the large federal budget deficit.

In contrast to the major business-related housing interest groups, those representing housing consumers, especially lower-income housing consumers, seem extremely weak. None of the major organizations involved in elderly housing has had more than one or two staff persons assigned to housing as a specialty. This is a clear disadvantage in a field where there are dozens of complex individual programs and in which the private profit-making sector is extremely active. In the field of elderly housing, those interests generally have been represented by a small but active nucleus of three types of groups: multi-mission national organizations, non-profit sponsors, and coalitions (National Policy Center on Housing and Living Arrangements for Older Americans, 1981).

Multi-mission national organizations such as the American Association of Retired Persons (AARP) and the National Council on Aging (NCOA) play an active role in trying to promote housing assistance programs for the elderly and in protecting the interests of consumers. However, in contrast to the business-oriented lobby groups, housing is only one of many issues with which these organizations are concerned. Housing has not been a high-priority item, compared with income security and health issues.

Many non-profit sponsors are represented by the American Association of Homes for the Aged (AAHA), composed of 2,200 providers of housing, health care, and community services. This association is closest in nature to the private sector organizations that lobby for housing. Although its major efforts in the past have focused on nursing and health care, it has been extremely active in protecting and modifying Section 202, the housing program in which many of its members have a special stake and expertise owing to their sponsorship of projects.

The Ad Hoc Coalition for Elderly Housing consists of such groups as AAHA, AARP, B'nai B'rith, the National Council of Senior Citizens, the Jewish Federation, the National Catholic Charities, the National Caucus on Black Aged, and the Volunteers of America. In spite of the fact that it has no permanent staff and meets irregularly, the coalition members share information and work together to influence policy. Most of its efforts are focused on defending the level of Section 202 housing and fighting potentially damaging technical changes which individual organizations have neither the expertise nor the staff time to pursue. The Ad Hoc Coalition for Elderly Housing and many of its member groups also belong to the National Low-Income Housing Coalition, the principal national lobbying group for low-income housing legislation.

The Influence of Elderly Interest Groups

In spite of the limited resources of their interest groups, it is clear that the elderly have been a prime beneficiary of federally subsidized housing programs. According to a recent analysis of Housing and Urban Development data (Zais et al., 1982), roughly 1.2 million households headed by the elderly were assisted in 1980 through HUD's housing assistance programs (e.g., public housing, Section 8, Section 202, Section 236). The elderly constituted about 39 percent of all assisted households, even though they represented a smaller proportion of the eligible population and there was significant variation in how well individual programs served the elderly. The elderly benefited proportionally more than the non-elderly from programs that created new construction, such as Section 202, public housing, and those parts of Section 8 related to new units.

Section 202

Section 202 is the program in which it is easiest to see the influence of elderly interest groups. It was created by the Housing Act of 1959 to construct housing units for moderate-income older Americans. In contrast to other federal programs open only to public housing authorities or including the profit sector as major participants, Section 202 has been available only to non-profit sponsors. By the end of 1980, Section 202 accounted for approximately 120,000 units of housing. In many ways it has been the flagship of HUD's production-oriented programs having had few management problems, almost no defaults, and being judged by its residents as very high quality. Nevertheless, it has been the subject of much political controversy around its alleged high costs of production, the tendency of early projects to house primarily moderate- and middle-income whites, the exclusion of limited profit and profit-making groups as sponsors, and the drain that the program makes annually on the federal budget because of its use of direct loans from the federal government at reduced interest rates. Private sector housing groups have particularly objected to the program's use of federal funds at below market interest rates and the construction of government subsidized housing that competes with their own activities (Olson, 1982).

The lobbying of elderly groups for Section 202 has been much more intense than for any other federal housing program and has included testimony, letter-writing campaigns, and even an unheard of demonstration at the HUD Secretary's office in support of the program. Several administrations have attempted to end or significantly reduce the program, and in fact, there was a six year lapse during which no new units were added to the stock. Nevertheless, the program has persisted, even though its reappearance in 1974 included major modifications such as reducing the mortgage period from 50 to 40 years and tying Section 8 housing subsidies to the program so that lower-income persons can live in the housing.

The lobbying efforts for Section 202 housing seem to have been successful for a number of reasons:

1. they have created their own constituency of religious, fraternal, and non-sectarian sponsors, all of whom have a stake in the program but are viewed by legislators as altruistic because they provide services that otherwise would be unavailable and do not derive profits or tax benefits from projects;
2. the residents who live in the housing tend to be representative of the members of larger consumer-oriented organizations such as AARP, which has consistently supported the program;
3. Section 202's management record and high quality distinguish it from many other HUD programs, which have also included non-elderly;
4. even though Section 202 has not produced a large number of total units, the small-scale nature of the projects has resulted in the program's availability in a large number of congressional districts, making it a popular program for representatives and senators who can point to the projects as clear evidence of their ability to bring resources to communities and serve the elderly;
5. the non-profit sponsors and their representative organizations have developed an expertise in Section 202 operations and often have been called upon by congressional committees and the executive branch to provide information, draft pieces of legislation and demonstrate the support of their members for or against particular policy initiatives;
6. there has been an exchange of personnel among HUD, the congressional committees and interest groups, reinforcing both their working relationships and support for the program; and

7. because Section 202 is the only federal housing program earmarked specifically for the elderly and handicapped, it is the focal point for elderly organizations which have limited staff, expertise and resources to expend in the housing field.

Although there is little question about the success of elderly groups around Section 202 housing, it is important to note that the size of the program itself has made it a smaller target for groups that oppose federally supported housing production programs.

Public Housing

While the influence of elderly organizations is clear in the case of Section 202 housing, it is less evident in major programs such as public housing. Nevertheless, this program has actually benefited a much larger number of elderly persons. In this case, it might be said that the elderly have benefited from a program initially supported and designed for other groups because the elderly have been viewed as a more socially desirable group. Public housing, the oldest and largest federal program to build new housing for low-income persons, had its origins in the Housing Act of 1937. Public housing projects constructed before the mid-1950s had very few elderly residents. Built initially to stimulate employment in the construction industry and to improve central cities, public housing was supported by trade unions, liberal political groups connected to the housing movement, and central city politicians interested in slum clearance. The early projects housed families considered to be the submerged middle class who were prevented by unfortunate economic circumstances from occupying decent housing in the private sector (Friedman, 1968). Public housing's proponents assumed that a move from overcrowded, unsafe, and unsanitary conditions to better housing would improve a family's physical and psychological health. As the general economic situation eased after the depression, many of the early public housing tenants purchased their own housing, aided by government-backed low interest loans and tax deductions for interest on mortgages, or moved into private rental housing.

By the mid-1950s, public housing—already a somewhat unpopular program because of its socialist connotation and potential competition with the private sector—increasingly became occupied by permanently poor and predominantly black families. At a time when opposition to housing projects began to result in their defeat at the local level, a new interest in the program was sparked by legislative and administrative changes that provided incentives for elderly participation in the program. For example, legislative amendments eased qualification requirements (e.g., single older persons were made eligible), and provided increased financial assistance for housing designed especially for the elderly

(Meehan, 1979). As a result, elderly projects proliferated, especially in the suburbs, where family public housing was less welcome. This experience has led several commentators to suggest that the success of the elderly in federal housing programs has come at the expense of younger families. Unfortunately, elderly housing interest groups have not advocated as strongly for public housing as they have for the smaller Section 202 program. As one congressional staff aide pointed out, elderly organizations have not commonly recognized that public housing, and both the new construction and rent subsidy parts of Section 8 housing, have served older persons well; and in fact, the organizations have not seen these programs as elderly related. That has added to public housing's jeopardy, as the administration attempts to move away from production programs and reduce its outlays for housing in general.

An Unfinished Agenda

Whether due to the advocacy efforts of elderly housing interest groups or simply to the desirability of elderly as program participants, there is little doubt that the elderly have won more than their share of federally funded housing assistance programs. Still, it is important to note that only three percent of the elderly have benefited from these programs and that the needs of several million elderly for housing that is affordable, safe, accessible, and suitable in terms of neighborhood amenities and services have gone unaddressed. For example, an analysis by the author of HUD data indicates that in 1979 approximately 2.3 million elderly paid excessive housing costs (over 30 percent of income for housing), and 1 million older persons still lived in physically inadequate housing. Countless others still reside in neighborhoods that could be categorized as inadequate or unsafe.

Moreover, despite the passage of a congregate housing services demonstration program in 1978, after ten years of efforts, congregate housing is barely beyond the starting blocks. There is still virtually no congregate housing available for frail persons who need personal and health care services other than the skilled nursing care found in more institutional settings. Previous efforts have been thwarted by the "39-year-old gap"—HUD loan program such as Section 202 support 40-year mortgages while services through HHS are generally funded on a yearly basis—as well as HUD's reluctance to go beyond shelter into services. In addition, both Congress and the administration are hesitant to launch an expanded program without evidence that congregate housing is cost-effective in preventing or delaying institutionalization in intermediate or skilled nursing facilities, data which will not be readily available from the current demonstration.

Elderly organizations have been effective in getting these issues on the housing agenda of the House Select Committee on Aging and the Senate Special Committee on Aging where they have relatively easy access and most of their attention has been placed. Over the last several years these committees have held hearings on topics such as Section 202, the impact of the administration's housing proposals on older Americans, alternative housing options for the elderly, congregate housing services, shared housing and home-equity conversions. The Committees on Aging, however, have very little direct power themselves as they neither propose legislation nor appropriate funds. Moreover, given the current political climate in Washington, there has been very little progressive action on these programs.

New Directions in Housing Policy

Several major policy shifts have recently occurred that are affecting the direction of elderly housing. First, there has been a reconceptualization of what constitutes housing problems. In the mid-1970s, once the great majority of the housing stock met minimum standards (lack of indoor plumbing, hot and cold running water, complete kitchens, and overcrowding had been greatly reduced), housing quality problems began to be viewed as residual, affecting certain pockets of the population, such as those persons living in rural areas and inner-city slums. The gradual improvement in the quality of most of the stock also lessened the strength of the argument that new construction was necessary to improve mental and physical health. During this period, policy analysts began to redefine housing problems of low-income persons less in terms of dwelling quality and more in terms of how much of a person's income was spent on housing, an issue especially relevant to elderly living on fixed income.

Second, housing solutions for the elderly have begun to focus on making better use of the existing stock, given the preference of most older persons to stay in their own homes. As a result, there has been an increased emphasis on programs such as house sharing, accessory apartments, and home-equity conversions in which elderly have to rely more on their own housing resources rather than government programs to improve their income and housing situations. Such approaches received the strong endorsement of the President's Commission on Housing, a conservative group of advisors appointed by President Reagan in 1981 to chart the future of housing policy. Using data from the annual housing survey, the Commission pointed out the potential for house-sharing. In 1979, there were 12.2 million one- or two-person homeowner households headed by persons 55 or older living in homes of five rooms or more, far above the standard of one person per room. The Commission also referred to the $30 billion to $40 billion potential market for home equity. The Commission assumed that both shared housing and home equity conversion programs would require little federal intervention or expenditures (President's Commission on Housing, 1982).

Third, the administration is downgrading government assistance in housing as a national priority. One analyst has estimated that one-half of the administration's first-year budget cuts came from the housing assistance program (Stegman, 1984). The administration's housing reductions are motivated not only by costs, but also by a philosophy that the private sector working through the market economy "can provide for housing far better than federal programs" (President's Commission on Housing, 1982).

Fourth, in spite of the concern over how much of their income poor persons spend on housing, the cost for participants in government-assisted housing programs is rising, and eligibility requirements are becoming increasingly restricted. In 1981, Congress enacted legislation intended to increase over a five year period the percentage of income residents have to pay for housing from 25 percent to 30 percent, while it reduced the income limits for eligibility.

Fifth, the federal government is moving away from what it considers a relatively expensive housing production program to a limited, direct cash housing assistance payments program. The latter type aims to reduce the gap between existing rent and the 30 percent of income that a lower-income household will be expected to pay for housing. Housing subsidies that are provided to participants who live in existing housing in the private sector also received support from the President's Commission on Housing. The movement towards such a voucher-type program is based on a decade of policy analysis, culminating in the Housing Allowance Experiment, the results of which indicated that it costs about twice as much to provide a unit-month of housing services from a federally assisted, newly built unit than it did to lease a privately owned existing unit (Mayo, Manfield, Warner, and Zwetchkenbaum, 1979). The elderly clearly have done well in production-oriented programs, but their success in direct payment programs is still unclear. Because this demand-oriented program requires a participant to live in a unit that meets certain housing standards, elderly persons who generally live in older housing units may not qualify unless they move, a disincentive for the elderly, who move less often than the rest of the population, to participate in the program. These programs do have the advantage of potentially allowing persons greater freedom of choice, especially to stay in their own residences, and could be applied to homeowners as well as renters. But the currently proposed housing assistance payment program, sometimes referred to as the voucher program, will subsidize only the difference between 30 percent of a person's rent and what is considered to be the payment standard or fair-market rent in an area. If this payment standard is low and if it is adjusted only two times over a period of five years as proposed, then participants will find themselves paying an excessive proportion of their income for housing, even by the 30 percent criteria.

The Continuing Dynamics in Setting the Elderly Housing Agenda

Faced with the stark realities of decreased federal funding for housing, a change of emphasis towards income-related housing problems and reliance on the existing stock, elderly interest groups have found themselves in a very different political environment than in previous administrations. As a result, a number of new developments have recently occurred that may influence the agenda for elderly housing in the future.

The Entrance of New Housing Groups

The shift in direction away from production-oriented programs towards shared housing and reverse annuity mortgages has begun to draw a new group of players into the elderly housing field. Two national organizations that serve as clearinghouses for information as well as program advocates have been formed around these concepts: the National Shared Housing Resource Center in Philadelphia and the National Center for Home Equity Conversion in Madison, Wisconsin. Both of these centers have received some federal funding over the last several years but continue to operate independently on relatively small budgets. Nevertheless, they have begun to influence federal policy, aided by the administration's endorsement of their approaches. For example, in November 1983, Congress included in the Omnibus Federal Housing Bill a section authorizing the use of Section 8 rental subsidies for shared housing. Support for this bill came not only from a number of the approximately 100 grass-roots shared housing groups that have sprouted up around the country, but also from major national organizations such as AARP. One such home equity conversion bill proposed to solve a tax problem in a type of a plan whereby the original owner sells his home and then leases it back. It received a fair amount of support but failed because of opposition from the Treasury, which objected to its potential budgetary and tax implications. Overall, however, it is clear that these new groups are riding the wave of a new trend and have received considerable support from Congress, the administration, and various national organizations. It is yet to be seen how these new organizations will integrate themselves with more traditional organizations such as AAHA to form a broader movement for more elderly housing, or whether they will view themselves as competitors for scarce resources.

At the same time that new groups are forming around housing options, proprietary organizations are also demonstrating more active interest in elderly housing. For example, the National Association of Home Builders, the American Institute of Architects, and the National Leased Housing Association have recently established elderly housing committees. In addition, developers who used to build Section 8 new construction have also discovered the elderly housing market, and a new association of elderly housing producers has been formed. While such groups represent potential support for elderly housing, non-profit Section 202 sponsors are likely to view them as threats.

Competition for Scarce Resources Among the Elderly and Non-Elderly

The House and Senate appropriations committees now allocate a fixed amount of money for housing which is then divided among various programs. The federal budgetary system has adopted an accounting system that calls for full disclosure of a program's costs over the entire period of the existing contract. Housing programs, which in the case of new construction are often assumed to have a forty-year life, are particularly vulnerable in budget deliberations because the expenditures seems so large. For example, the House appropriations for the most recent housing bill provided for over $58 billion in new budget authority, although the amount authorized for the first year amounted to just under $10 billion. These circumstances, combined with the administration's low priority for housing in general, have given low-income housing interest groups a strong incentive to lobby together for housing appropriations.

The most recent evidence of such joint lobbying were the successful efforts of groups such as the National Low-Income Housing Coalition and Ad Hoc Coalition for Elderly Housing to help pass the Housing and Urban-Rural Recovery Act of 1983. The first housing bill since 1980, this piece of legislation included funds for new construction and vouchers, although the number of vouchers (38,500) fell far below the 91,000 requested by the administration. Instead of offering its unqualified support for the vouchers, Congress reserved funding for some new construction and other housing programs. The bill also maintains rent levels in government-assisted housing at 27 percent of household income. While the administration refused to restore the 25 percent income/rent ratio, it agreed to allow a $480 deduction from gross income for every household member other than head of household and $400 for each elderly member. Therefore, even though the bill provided only a modest $9.9 billion in new funds for federally assisted housing programs, it did provide additional security for participants in federal programs. This suggests that while organized interest groups had little influence over major housing appropriations, they could have an effect on specific provisions of particular programs, general eligibility requirements, and the division of funds among various programs.

The Act itself was attached as a rider to the International Monetary Fund contribution bill; therefore many conservative legislators, who otherwise would have been opposed, voted for it in order to have the full bill passed, indicating the difficulty that housing proposals are having in Congress. Congressman Roybal commented about efforts to write legislation which addresses the housing needs of the elderly: "It is becoming more difficult to even try."

While low-income housing groups have generally pulled together in support of overall housing budgets, given that federal housing policy is a patchwork of ad hoc programs, interest groups have a tendency to try to divide the pie after the appropriations battle so that their particular programs get as large a piece as possible. However, at least until recently, there has not been an overt struggle between elderly and non-elderly groups. Although their major interest has been Section 202 housing, elderly interest groups have begun to recognize the importance of other programs and non-elderly groups want their support. Nevertheless, the 1984 House and Senate budget negotiations indicate potentially increasing direct competition. For example, the 1983 housing bill included 14,000 Section 202 housing units for the elderly, far below the 1979 level of approximately 20,000 units. In the debates over the 1984 bill, Congressman Bolan indicated that the House would keep the administration's proposal of 10,000 units of Section 202 housing and add 10,000 units of public housing, because the Senate side was expected to propose a higher level of Section 202 housing but no new public housing construction. He suggested that the House was willing to trade off additional units of Section 202 housing for the Senate's concession to fund units of public housing. In this way, the needs of elderly and handicapped would be balanced against those of lower-income families, the latter having been the most severely affected by the deep cuts in public housing. The compromise reached resulted in approximately 14,000 units of Section 202 housing and 6,000 units of new public housing. Such clear congressional trade-offs could set a dangerous precedent of playing 202 against public housing, thereby disrupting the attempts at coalition building between elderly and non-elderly interest groups.

The Broadening Agenda of Elderly Housing Interest Groups

Up until the mid-to-late 1970s, elderly housing interest groups, including the Ad Hoc Coalition for Elderly Housing, focused solely on Section 202 housing. Gradually, however, in response to the changing federal agenda as well as their participation in organizations such as the Low-Income Housing Coalition, elderly housing interest groups have begun to broaden their housing perspective. For example, AAHA's 1983 federal housing policy objectives include federal mortgage insurance to help finance a continuum of care, loan authority to finance an additional 25,000 units of Section 202 housing, financing for the construction and rehabilitation of housing facilities specifically designed for low-income elderly, congregate housing, standards for board-and-care homes, and a number of more detailed recommendations related to HUD operations and administrative policies (American Association of Homes for the Aging, 1983).

The 1984 Federal Legislative Policy Statement of AARP is even broader than that of AAHA, indicating the difference between a mass membership, consumer-oriented organization and a provider group. AARP's housing agenda includes support not only for Section 202 housing, but also housing construction for low-income persons, full funding for public housing maintenance and operating subsidies, congregate housing, and opposition to HUD's divestment policies of existing public housing. In regard to administration proposals to convert Section

8 rental assistance program to vouchers, the policy statement suggests that such a strategy is shortsighted because it is made in a context which ends most new construction and focuses nearly all housing-aid resources on existing housing. AARP does not oppose the voucher approach in principle, but argues that proposals must also "address the need for adequate authorizations and benefit levels and for adequate supplies of suitable, affordable housing" (American Association of Retired Persons, 1984).

Such a broadening of their housing agenda beyond Section 202 still has not greatly affected where elderly interest groups put their energies. Even though Section 202 is the only new construction program that elicits support from Democrats and Republicans in both houses, elderly housing advocates feel they must be vigilant in its defense. For example, early in the Reagan administration, when Office of Budget and Management Director David Stockman's trial balloon federal budget eliminated Section 202 housing, there was an immediate outcry by both elderly housing interest groups and Congress. Subsequent administration budgets reduced the number of units from those of the Carter administration and regulations have also reduced the size of units and amount of common space. The administration has recently also proposed competitive bidding and changes in the interest-rate subsidy formula. As one Section 202 advocate indicated, such issues can "eat you alive" in terms of time and energy. Therefore, on housing issues that pertain to all low-income persons, elderly organizations tend to be followers rather than leaders. Nevertheless, at least now, traditional elderly interest groups give lip service to other programs such that when, for example, the Low-Income Housing Coalition has a sign-off letter, the Ad Hoc Coalition for Elderly Housing and the major elderly organizations lend their support. Moreover, in the last two years, AARP and the National Council of Senior Citizens have moved beyond working with the aging committees and have begun testifying at the all-important HUD appropriations hearings. How far such efforts can go without stretching the credibility and the limited resources that elderly organizations devote to housing advocacy is yet to be seen.

Setting the Future Agenda

For elderly interest groups to increase and expand their advocacy efforts beyond their current efforts, housing itself will have to rise in priority. Thus far, as noted earlier, unlike income and health issues, housing problems have not appeared to crosscut all elderly, dividing in particular homeowners from renters or, as one policy analyst has put it, the "haves from the have-nots" (Struyk, 1983). In a recent Harris poll commissioned by NCOA in which the elderly were asked to rank-order their ten most serious problems, poor housing ranked last. However, two problems closely associated with housing, the high cost of energy such as heating oil, gas and electricity, and fear of crime, ranked first and second respectively (National Council on Aging, 1982). If housing is redefined to include the amount of income spent on shelter, services necessary to stay in the community and neighborhood amenities like safety and transportation, then its recognition as a more important issue might rise. A policy statement by major elderly organizations that affordable and suitable housing in good condition should be a right or entitlement might begin to raise the political consciousness of the elderly. Unless housing becomes a more universal consumer as well as a producer issue, it will be difficult to generate the kind of political support needed to affect a major change in policy, such as in the case of Social Security, assuming that popular support is a necessary ingredient for social change. But for such a strategy to succeed, housing will have to become a high priority for other age cohorts as well as the elderly, which may be precipitated if a long period of high interest rates and inadequate supply of new housing drive up the price of housing and make it unavailable for families as well.

In the absence of a reconceptualization of the housing problem, given the technical nature of housing programs and the lack of power that organized elderly interest groups have to influence housing appropriations, the likely outcome will be that elderly housing will receive only limited attention at the federal level. In this case much of the action will shift to state and local arenas where more attempts will be made to pass bonds to construct new housing and to use community development block grants for programs such as shared housing, home-equity conversions, home repair and home maintenance. This is particularly likely in a period when upcoming federal battles are expected over major universal entitlement programs such as Medicare and Medicaid. It can be expected, however, that elderly interest groups will continue their efforts at the federal level on behalf of Section 202 housing. Moreover, if supportive housing for frail older persons comes to be viewed as the missing link in the long-term care system, the next several years may find elderly housing advocates joining with their long-term care colleagues to pressure for an expanded congregate housing program given the expected dramatic increase in elderly persons over 75 years of age. Such an effort, if successful, would continue their recent history of limited, piecemeal approaches to specific housing problems rather than attempts to overhaul the system.

References

American Association of Homes for the Aging. 1983. *Public Policy Objectives for the 98th Congress* (Washington, D.C.), mimeo.

American Association of Retired Persons. 1984. *1984 Federal Legislative Policy* (Washington, D.C.), mimeo.

Friedman, Lawrence. 1968. *Government and Slum Housing: A Century of Frustration* (Chicago: Rand McNally).

Hartman, Chester (ed.). 1983. *America's Housing Crisis: What Is To Be Done?* (Boston: Routledge and Kegan Paul).

Heskin, Alan. 1983. *Tenants and the American Dream: Ideology and the Tenant Movement* (New York: Praeger).
Lilley, W. 1980. "The Homebuilders Lobby," in J. Pynoos, R. Schafer, and C. Hartman (eds.), *Housing Urban American,* 2nd ed. (New York: Aldine).
Mayo, S., S. Mansfield, D. Warner, and R. Zwetchkenbaum. 1979. *Housing Allowances and Other Rental Housing Assistance Programs, Part 2: Costs and Efficiency* (Cambridge: Abt Associates).
Meehan, Eugene. 1979. *The Quality of Federal Policymaking: Programmed Failure in Public Housing* (Columbia: University of Missouri Press).
National Council of Older Americans. 1982. *The Myth and Reality of Aging in America,* mimeo.
National Policy Center on Housing and Living Arrangements for Older Americans. 1981. *Housing Policies and Programs for the Elderly, 1970-1980* (Ann Arbor: University of Michigan), mimeo.
Olson, Laura. 1982. *The Political Economy of Aging* (New York: Columbia).
President's Commission on Housing. 1982. *Report of the President's Commission on Housing* (Washington, D.C.).
Stegman, M. 1984. "The States Chip In," *Planning* (January).
Struyk, R. 1983. "Future Housing Assistance for the Elderly," paper presented at the Gerontological Society of America, 36th Annual Scientific Meeting.
Wolman, Harold. 1971. *The Politics of Federal Housing* (New York: Dodd, Mead, and Co.).
Zais, James, Raymond Struyk, and Thomas Thibodeau. 1982. *Housing Assistance for Older Americans* (Washington, D.C.: Urban Institute).

V

Current Programs and Emerging Issues

16

Housing Options for the Elderly

Linda Daily

Many families today must face the difficult decision of how to help care for elderly parents or other relatives. But choices are no longer limited to nursing homes or living together under one roof. Older Americans have more housing options than ever before. Contrary to popular belief, only 5 percent of those over 65 live in nursing homes, while 70 percent own their own homes. Others select "continuing care" communities where they live independently with the assurance that all health needs will be taken care of in the future. Those who can afford it often opt for the social/recreational lifestyle found in the retirement havens that have sprung up in the western and southern states.

Choosing where to live is not always a simple matter of preference, however, because of health needs, income limitations and the supply of housing. Innovative living arrangements are emerging as more elderly persons move in with their families or non-relatives to cut down on housing costs and maintain independence. Options include building apartments within existing homes, renting individual rooms or purchasing a separate unit known as an elder cottage or "granny flat." Home and health support services and adult day-care programs help keep more dependent elderly in their own homes or living with family members. Federal projects provide affordable housing for some low-income elderly.

From *Editorial Research Reports*, 2, 5 (August 6, 1982), pp. 571-88. Reprinted with permission, Congressional Quarterly Inc.

Retirement living is an issue of growing importance. The number of older Americans is rapidly increasing and is expected to grow from 11 percent of the population in 1980 to a projected 20.4 percent by 2030. By comparison, the elderly comprised only 4 percent of the population in 1900. Estimates of the number of elderly living in substandard housing run as high as 30 percent.[1] Budget constraints are forcing a reconsideration of federal housing and other support programs. Elderly homeowners are finding it increasingly difficult to manage the costs of big, older homes. The rental shortage is intensifying.

Health needs and income are closely linked to housing choices. As Dr. Robert Butler, director of the National Institute on Aging (NIA), observed: "The No. 1 cause of distress for most retired Americans is their income. The second is probably their health. The third is their housing."[2] Older Americans generally have greater health needs than the rest of the population because they are more likely to suffer from one or more chronic afflictions, such as heart conditions. Despite disabilites, most elderly are able to live independently. In 1980, more than 30 percent of the older population lived alone. But the need for help with daily activ-

EXHIBIT 16.1
U.S. Population, Age 65 and Older, 1900 to 2030

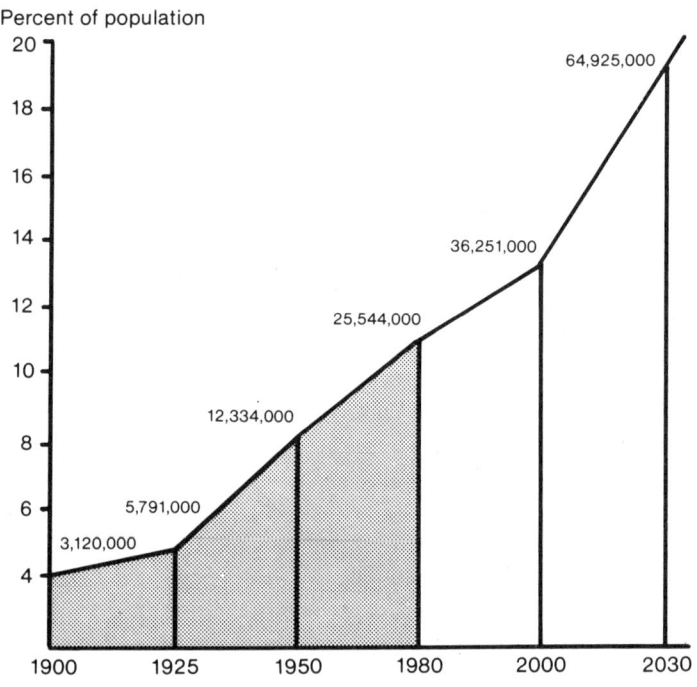

Housing Options for the Elderly

ities—such as dressing and bathing—increases with age. Families and friends provide most supportive care. But social and population changes may affect the availability of these informal supports, creating a more dependent elderly population.

The presence of a spouse and the availability of children are perhaps the two most important factors in keeping elderly persons out of nursing homes. But more women than ever now work outside the home, and some families are separated by long distances. More than 70 percent of nursing home residents are female, most are widows or single, and nearly half are childless.[3] Age is another factor. More than 20 percent of those 85 and older live in nursing homes. This predominantly female, "old, old" sector or the elderly population is expected to triple in the next 50 years.

Although only 5 percent of the elderly now live in nursing homes, utilization of nursing homes is expected to increase more than 50 percent in the next 20 years. And by 2030, the number of nursing home residents is expected to be almost 3 million, compared to 1.3 million today.[4] Total cost of nursing home care is expected to increase from $24.5 billion in 1981 to more than $75 billion by 1990, compared to only $2.1 billion in 1965.[5]

Improved Conditions in Nursing Homes

Congressional investigations in the 1970s uncovered widespread deficiencies in nursing homes: unsanitary conditions, inadequate nutrition, a high percentage of errors in administering drugs, misappropriation of residents' funds, and negligence and abuse of residents causing death and injury. "To the average older American, nursing homes have become almost synonymous with death and protracted suffering before death," the Senate Special Committee on Aging reported in a 1975 study.[6]

Today, the quality of care in nursing homes has generally improved for a variety of reasons. Some point to stronger enforcement of state and federal regulations, others to increased public awareness, improvements in geriatric training, and recognition of residents' rights. Many homes encourage self-development by offering educational classes and other programs. Others form activities with the community. Many residents organize resident councils to become more involved in issues affecting their lives.[7]

Challenges remain, however, in upgrading care. One of the most serious problems according to government studies is the lack of training for nurses' aides, who provide 90 percent of the "hands on" care of nursing home residents. Demanding work and low pay are cited as reasons for an annual turnover rate as high as 75 percent.[8] There are other problems, as well, including "a lack of rehabilitative services and specialized mental health services, both of which, if provided, would help people to move on to other housing situations," said Elma Griesel of the National Citizens' Coalition for Nursing Home Reform.

Residents often complain about regimented schedules, lack of privacy and other problems associated with the institutional character of nursing homes, 90 percent of which are operated for profit. Horror stories still surface on occasion. An 80-year-old Virginia nursing home resident died late in 1981 after being scalded in a whirlpool bath. In the spring of 1981, a grand jury indicted a Houston, Texas, nursing home corporation and six employees in the deaths of eight patients allegedly caused by neglect and abuse.

New Debate Over Government Regulation

Regulation of nursing homes is a continuing controversy. Last March [1982], Secretary of Health and Human Services Richard S. Schweiker rejected proposed changes in nursing home regulations that had been drafted by his staff. The proposals, which produced an outpouring of congressional and consumer protests, would, among other things, have dropped a requirement that the medical directors of nursing homes be physicians. The department is proceeding, however, with proposals to change the way nursing homes are inspected. The effort is one of the goals of the Vice President's Task Force on Regulatory Relief.

HHS wants to end annual inspections of all nursing homes to concentrate its resources on facilities with poor records of compliance with federal standards. Homes with good records would be inspected every two years. Other changes would eliminate follow-up visits to substantiate correction of problems, and allow a non-governmental commission to inspect nursing homes rather than require state agencies to determine if facilities meet federal standards. Agency officials will review public comments on the proposed regulations before deciding whether to make the changes permanent. The final decision, which could come at any time, rests with Schweiker.

Critics contend the revised inspection rules would cause the quality of care given residents to deteriorate since there would be less oversight at a time when federal funds provided states to enforce standards are being reduced.[9] A new study by the General Accounting Office found that more nursing home residents than ever before are infirm and require more intensive care. At the same time, GAO said, the states are seeking ways to reduce nursing home expenditures. Under these conditions, inspection procedures were seen as being particularly important to assure that residents receive quality care.[10]

The skyrocketing expense of nursing home care is hardly good news for federal and state governments struggling to trim already lean budgets. Government funds paid for more than 55 percent of nursing home costs in 1979, with private payments accounting for the rest.[11] Many nursing home residents originally paid for their care, but the high costs—now about $17,000 a year—depleted their savings.[12] Those without adequate personal resources often turn to Medicaid, the federal health care program for the poor, which accounts for 87 percent of government expenditures for nursing home care. Medicaid rules generally make it easier to qualify for care in a nursing home than in a private residence. On the other hand, Medicare, the federal health insurance program for the elderly, pays very little in nursing home benefits because coverage has a 100-day time limit and requires pre-hospitalization.

Congressional studies estimate that 20 to 40 percent of nursing home residents could live in the community if adequate support services were available.[13] Yet the health care system provides far greater support for institutional and medically oriented care. For every $10 spent on nursing home care, the federal government spends only $1 on home health care.[14]

Providing more alternative services, however, is on the agenda of nursing homes across the country, several industry spokesmen told Editorial Research Reports. Because of high construction costs, companies are not planning to build many new nursing homes despite a projected need for 300,000 to 400,000 new beds over the next decade. "We're beginning to see our companies getting into outpatient, home health, day care and retirement communities," said Jack MacDonald, executive vice president of the National Council of Health Centers, which represents chain or investor-owned nursing homes. MacDonald said the number of people coming in and out of nursing homes will increase, but the length of stay will decrease because other services will meet patients' needs.

Non-Institutional Options

Most older people want to stay in their own homes for as long as possible, despite the burden of high utility and maintenance costs. "If I lose my house, I lose the only important thing in my life," one 88-year-old homeowner recently told the House Select Committee on Aging. New financial arrangements allowing older homeowners to convert home equity into cash are being developed to make that decision easier to afford. Some states also allow elderly homeowners to defer property tax payments until they sell their homes or die.

Under one type of equity conversion plan, an investor purchases an elderly homeowner's residence and agrees to lease it back. The monthly payments the buyer makes to the seller exceed the monthly rent, giving the former homeowner a steady income. In reverse annuity mortgages, homeowners take out a bank loan borrowed against the value of their homes, providing a lump sum or monthly payments for a certain period after which the loan must be refinanced or repaid. High interest rates and financial risks associated with such programs have limited their appeal and growth, but several plans are now in existence.[15] Leo Baldwin, housing consultant for the American Association of Retired Persons—National Retired Teachers Association, said in a recent interview that such plans must have strong consumer protections providing legal services, counseling, and guaranteeing lifelong occupancy to prevent exploitation of the elderly.

In-home and community-based services also help older Americans live in their own homes or with others. The range and availability of public and private support programs depends on the community, but services often include homemaker assistance, home health aid, personal care, nursing care, medical equipment rental, home-delivered and group-site meals, and home maintenance. A variety of federal and state programs—each with its own eligibility criteria—fund community care services, which are managed by government agencies and non-profit and private organizations.

The complexity and fragmentation inherent in the system make it difficult— some say impossible—for elderly persons to get services they need. Information and referral systems are "the only way to serve the public without duplication of services, which we can't afford," Baldwin said. Some cities are taking steps to improve senior citizens' knowledge about programs. Boston, for example, publishes neighborhood service directories. Other cities publish newspapers or newsletters that focus on elderly issues and programs, or operate an "elderly hotline."[16]

Several states, some with the help of federal funds, also are trying to improve coordination of services and upgrade assessments of needs to prevent premature institutionalization. Florida's Community Care for the Elderly Program provides several "core" services to functionally impaired adults 60 and over. Under Connecticut's Promotion of Independent Living Program, staff members assess the needs of elderly clients, develop a plan of care and coordinate and monitor services.[17]

On the federal level, Congress in 1981 approved a provision that allows states to use Medicaid funds for certain home and community-based services if such care is cost-effective for persons who would otherwise be in nursing homes. Legislation has been proposed to establish a coordinated system of non-institutional services (S 861) and to promote development of home health programs and agencies and expand coverage of such services under Medicare and Medicaid (S 234). But neither bill is expected to be acted upon this year. Medicare and Medicaid generally limit coverage of home health services to instances when care is medically necessary, such as after an operation. The Congressional Budget Office estimated in 1977 that 1.7 to 2.7 million people needed in-home services, but only 300,000 to 500,000 were receiving them.[18]

Adult Day Care: Needed Help for Families

Families seeking support in day-to-day care of elderly relatives sometimes turn to adult day-care centers for help. In 1982, there were more than 800 programs serving 20,000 people[19] compared to 15 in 1974.[20] Some centers, often attached to hospitals and nursing homes, provide medical, rehabilitative and/or therapeutic services, while others combine minimal health monitoring with social activities. One of the most well-known programs is On Lok Senior Health Services in San Francisco, California, which was launched in 1972 as a day health center under an Administration on Aging grant. On Lok has since expanded its community care services to include home health services and a specially designed housing center.[21]

Another alternative is respite programs that offer temporary care for elderly persons whose families cannot provide their usual support because of vacation, illness or other problems. The Visiting Resident Program, run by the Metropolitan Jewish Geriatric Center in Brooklyn, New York, allows elderly persons living in the community to stay in a nursing home from one to six weeks.

As with in-home services, the issue of whether adult day care prevents premature institutionalization is controversial. A 1979 study by the National Center for Health Services Research concluded that day care was not a substitute for nursing home care, but a costly additional service. Critics disputed the study's findings and research methods.[22] Kay Larmer, director of the Annandale (Va.) Elderly Day Care Center, told Editorial Research Reports that when a vacancy does open on her average waiting list of 25 to 50 people, many people already have gone into nursing homes. "Families are willing to share the burden of care for impaired adults if they get support," she said.

According to Betty Shepherd, coordinator of the National Institute on Adult Daycare established by the National Council on the Aging, centers provide services to an average of 25 people a day for an average daily cost of about $20. Most programs are non-profit and base fees on ability to pay. Funding comes from several sources. In 1980, more than 300 programs relied on Title XX, the Social Services Amendments to the Social Security Act. The program was turned into a social services block grant in 1981 with a 25 percent reduction in funds. A March 1982 study by the Subcommittee on Human Services of the House Select Committee on Aging found that 10 states were reducing adult day-care services. Other funding sources include Title III of the Older Americans Act (also reduced in 1981), state and local governments and private donations. Medicare and private insurance rarely cover adult day-care services and only 14 states and the District of Columbia provide Medicaid reimbursement for the services.[23]

Although the funding situation is serious, "a majority [of programs] will survive—maybe on a shoestring—by turning to their communities for support," Shepherd said. More programs probably will rely on client fees to a greater extent, which could limit their use by the poor. The new Medicaid waiver provision that allows funding for community-based care will help adult day care, Shepherd said, as will a new tax credit enacted in 1981. The credit, which ranges between 20 to 30 percent of day-care costs, depending upon adjusted gross income, applies only to dependent elderly living with their families.

Innovative Shared-Housing Arrangements

Housing pressures also have led to the development of innovative living arrangements—such as shared housing, accessory apartments and elder cottages—that some observers say will revive the concept of the extended family. Shared households range from two unrelated persons sharing an apartment or home to group residences. The Boston chapter of the Volunteers of America opened an elderly group home in 1976. Called McCroham House, it offers residents the help of a house manager and various social services. The Shared Living House, which opened in Boston in 1979, houses 16 men and women, with ages ranging from 24 to 84, although most are over 55. Residents have to be self-sufficient since they share in the upkeep of the home.

The trend toward shared living quarters has spurred the growth of matching programs usually provided without charge by social service agencies. Homesharing for Seniors, which operated in several cities including Seattle and Philadelphia, interviews candidates and coordinates elderly and intergenerational matchups and "barter" arrangements where services are exchanged for room and board. While home sharing is often not ideal because of inevitable conflicts, the greater economic and personal security it provides usually outweighs the drawbacks.

Senior citizens living in homes they have outgrown, but want to keep, sometimes convert their houses into two-family residences. The Census Bureau estimates there are 2.5 million of these so-called accessory apartments, bringing in average monthly rents of $300 to $400. Another innovation is "echo" housing (elder cottage housing opportunity), an idea imported from Australia where it is known as the "granny flat." Energy-efficient, compact, removable homes are designed to be installed in the backyard of the family home for use by aging relatives.

Ed Guion, a housing manufacturer in Lancaster County, Pennsylvania, became interested in the concept when a local official tried to launch an elder cottage rental project that never materialized because of funding obstacles. Guion decided to use his own money to build a model unit. With the help of a private investor, he has built three homes and sold two at an average cost of $18,000. According to Guion, echo housing also could be located in clusters, for a village setting, or adjacent to nursing homes.

Although shared housing, accessory apartments, and echo housing help the elderly live independently and promote usage of underutilized housing in a tight market, they face significant obstacles in local zoning laws. Most municipal codes restrict the number of unrelated people who can live together. Restrictions in public welfare programs and federal rent subsidies also discourage shared housing arrangements. Single-family zoning regulations usually prohibit echo housing and accessory apartments.

Courtesy of Brooks Trubee
Princeton Community Housing, Princeton, New Jersey

Courtesy of Brooks Trubee
Princeton Community Housing, Princeton, New Jersey

Community opposition to zoning changes legalizing these living arrangements stems from concern that neighborhoods will deteriorate, causing property values to drop. Ignoring illegal conversions of single-family homes, however, could cause even more problems. "We have no way of knowing whether plumbing or electrical work was done properly, whether there are fire exits. We're going to have some fires, people trapped in buildings, see some neighborhoods deteriorating and all hell is going to break loose," said Leo Baldwin. "The answer is to legalize them [accessory apartments]—make it an appropriate way for people to retool existing housing."

There are signs of change. Several communities, including Babylon, New York, and Portland, Oregon, have legalized accessory apartments. Lancaster County, Pennsylvania, has approved zoning waivers for individual elder cottages. Proponents predict other communities will follow. According to Patrick Hare, a housing and planning consultant in Washington, D.C., who has conducted several studies on innovative living arrangements, local planners can change zoning laws without inviting the wrath of property owners by implementing certain restrictions. To legalize accessory apartments, for example, Hare recommends prohibiting any visual changes in the home and allowing only owner-occupiers to install or rent the units.

Attraction of Retirement Communities

More affluent older Americans often choose to live in retirement communities. A new study conducted by the Institute of Gerontology at the University of

Michigan estimates there are 970,000 people living in 2,300 retirement communities nationwide.[24] Traditionally located in the Sun Belt, communities such as Sun City, Arizona, are usually age-segregated and emphasize an active, leisure lifestyle. Some experts, like Leo Baldwin, doubt whether large communities like Sun City, with several golf courses, fancy recreation centers and a population of 100,000, will continue to be developed because of economic conditions. Smaller, less elaborate retirement villages may instead become more common.

Leisure World in Silver Spring, Maryland, for example, has 4,000 residents living in 2,800 single homes, apartments and semi-detached units. Residents have to be at least 50 years old; the median age is 73. Prices of homes start at $60,000 with maintenance fees averaging $150 a month. A variety of educational and recreational programs are offered and a medical center provides routine services.

In multi-level care centers, meals, social support services and nursing care are provided to elderly persons living in independent housing units. Operated by churches, universities or private companies, these communities vary from a single building to a campus-like setting of individual homes, apartment highrises and nursing facilities. Those concerned about future health needs and medical expenses often seek the security that continuing care communities offer.

Residents of Goodwin House in Alexandria, Virginia, a single-building facility sponsored by the Virginia diocese of the Episcopal Church, make a down payment ranging from $37,000 for an efficiency apartment to $60,000 for a one-bedroom unit. A monthly fee of about $700 for a single person and about $1,400 for a couple covers meals, personal assistance, maid service, various educational and recreational programs and all nursing care. Contributions from the church support residents who have exhausted personal funds. Administrator James K. Meharg, Jr., said in an interview that if inflation remains high, new residents might have to be limited to ensure that the program can pay for the needs of those already in residence. He said a waiting period of three years is common at Goodwin House.

Attempts to Regulate Boarding Home Care

Increasing attention is being focused on the nation's estimated 300,000 boarding homes as safety and financial fraud problems come to light.[25] Also known as rest homes, foster, adult or domiciliary care facilities, boarding homes provide room and board to more than 1 million people. Residents are usually elderly, disabled, or former mental patients who receive Supplemental Security Income (SSI) payments or other public assistance. In the last five years, 143 persons have died in 14 boarding home fires.[26] An investigation of 10 boarding homes conducted by the General Accounting Office in 1980 found operators abusing residents' funds and cheating the government to pad their own pockets. Boarding home residents also have been subjected to poor care and abuse. A

101-year-old woman was locked in a closet and two other elderly residents were told to spend the night in a park by a boarding home operator in Florida who did not want the city inspector to know she had too many boarders.[27]

Public concern about boarding home deficiencies prompted Congress in 1976 to enact an amendment to the Social Security Act that required states to license and regulate the facilities. The federal law, however, had no enforcement muscle since the only penalty was to withhold SSI payments from boarding home residents to encourage them to move to a licensed facility. The reasoning ignored the physical and mental limitations of many residents and the lack of adequate housing.

The Department of Health and Human Services is implementing a new plan to strengthen protections for residents in "board-and-care homes," which offer minimal medical and other supervision in addition to room and board. To help carry out its program, the department has established an inter-agency coordination unit, has provided the National Bureau of Standards with $400,000 to complete development of fire safety standards, and is implementing plans to develop a model state statute.

Under the department's new requirements, board and care operators who receive tenants' SSI payments directly will have to prove that their facilities comply with state regulations. States that want to use Medicaid funds for board and care homes also will have to prove they are enforcing standards. The program has been criticized for not including federal aid to states for upgrading enforcement activities, and for proposing to withhold Older American Act funds, which pay for nutrition and other support programs for the elderly, from states that fail to enforce regulations.

Federal Housing Policies Under Reagan

The federal government's involvement in housing efforts for the poor dates back to 1937 when the low-rent public housing program was established. Under the program, construction, financing and some operating costs are paid by the Department of Housing and Urban Development (HUD), although units are managed by state and local agencies. Since then, other housing programs have been launched.

Under Section 8, HUD pays rent subsidies to owners of existing, private rental housing or to developers of new or substantially rehabilitated housing for low-income persons. The subsidies equal the difference between what HUD has determined to be the fair market rent for the dwelling and the tenants' share, which is 25 to 30 percent of their income.

Under the Section 202 program, HUD provides direct, below market loans to non-profit sponsors to build rental housing specially designed for independent elderly and handicapped persons with very low incomes. Residents who meet Section 8 requirements pay no more than 30 percent of their income for rent. In 1978, Congress approved the Congregate Housing Services Act making funds available to Section 202 sponsors and public housing agencies to provide meals in a central dining area and personal and housekeeping services to partially impaired elderly and handicapped residents with the goal of preventing premature institutionalization. (Congregate housing programs, which provide an independent group living environment with the help of non-medical support services, have existed for many years through non-governmental agencies.)

Although Section 202 is the federal government's primary building program for the elderly, 202 units represent only a fraction of federal housing units occupied by the elderly because relatively few have been built. Nearly half of the 1.2 million public housing units are occupied by elderly persons. Most new public housing construction in the last 10 years has been for elderly projects, in part because of community resistance to programs for low-income families.[28] Nearly 40 percent of Section 8 units also are occupied by elderly persons.[29]

A redirection in federal housing policy is occurring under the Reagan administration. The private market and local initiative are viewed as the major sources in meeting needs. According to a report by the President's Commission on Housing, affordability—not supply—is the greatest housing problem faced by low-income people.[30] Opposition to federal housing programs stems in part from their long-term financial commitments. For example, the Section 8 existing housing programs involve 15-year contracts for assistance payments.

To carry out its philosophies, the administration has proposed using a voucher system to replace all federally assisted housing programs, with the exception of Section 202. Under this system, qualified recipients would receive cash assistance to help pay for private housing in the community. Critics argue that federal incentives for new construction are crucial because the present housing supply—both public and private—is inadequate and the demand is increasing. The average waiting time to get into public housing programs is several years. One critic also observed that if you increase the amount of money to pay for housing, but do not increase the supply, prices will rise.

Section 202 is up for renewal this year, but most congressional observers believe the popularity of the program and its good reputation will help ensure its survival. But the congregate housing services program has been put on hold until HUD completes an evaluation due in 1984, despite congressional efforts to continue funding new projects. The 202 budget for fiscal 1983 will fund 10,000 units. Recommendations approved at the 1981 White House Conference on Aging called for the production of 20,000 units annually. Philip Abrams, a HUD deputy assistant secretary, said additional monies will be available from cancellation of 202 projects that have been in the planning stages for more than two years. New design restrictions on 202 projects soon to take effect also will reduce

Courtesy of Louis A. Sapienze for the New Jersey Housing & Mortgage Finance Agency
Park Place in Ewing Township was the first apartment building financed by the New Jersey Housing & Mortgage Finance Agency to be constructed from premanufactured, modular units. Premanufactured construction helped to reduce building time and cut costs. Today, Park Place houses 126 senior individuals and couples.

costs. Such policies have met strong criticism from aging and other groups, who stress that 202 programs sometimes incur greater costs in design features and encounter more time delays in construction because of the special needs of the elderly and handicapped people being served.

Economic and Social Issues

While older Americans have more choices in living arrangements than ever before, the need for a broader range of housing and care options is generating increasing attention and support. This is especially true for the frail elderly population. The ideal is to keep people living independently by providing a sequence or continuum of housing arrangements and support services that meet the aging individual's needs for progressively greater care. "For older people, housing and services must be treated as an integral set of concerns. An overriding necessity in meeting the housing-related needs of older people is to promote the development of a continuum of appropriate housing types," concluded a 1980 housing forum held in preparation for the December 1981 White House Conference on Aging.[31]

Delegates to the White House Conference did approve several recommendations urging development of coordinated, community-based services to help impaired elderly live in the least restrictive setting, with nursing homes viewed as the "last resort." Whether a well-developed plan of housing and care options will become a reality is a matter of conjecture. "It's a question of social values," M. Powell Lawton, director of behavioral research at the Philadelphia Geriatric Center, told Editorial Research Reports. "In-home health services are a glaring lack, that cost or no cost, need to be funded. If we're going to serve people in need, we've got to pay for it."[32]

Long-Term Public Policy Challenges

Many issues remain to be resolved that will have a significant impact on housing options for older Americans. The growth of the elderly population presents serious challenges for individuals and for government at all levels, especially in a constrained economy. Planning and saving for retirement will become increasingly important. Inflation already is causing some older workers to postpone retirement. Public skepticism about the durability of the Social Security system also remains high. While reform initiatives, such as raising the retirement age or reducing annual cost-of-living adjustments, have met political defeat in recent months, pressure is building for changes because of predicted shortages in trust funds and a reduced work force in future years that will have to support a larger retired population.[33]

Budget pressures are a continuing concern. Even with significant cutbacks in domestic programs such as Medicare and Medicaid and new tax increases, a federal budget deficit of well over $100 billion is expected in 1983. Many states have reduced spending and/or increased taxes to try to reduce multimillion-dollar deficits. More than 25 states are reporting problems in funding Medicaid, with some deciding to limit nursing home payments or freeze new bed construction.[34] Expansion of services and programs under such conditions will become increasingly difficult. And yet, because of the issue's importance, meeting the housing and support needs of the elderly is on the agenda of many local governments. The U.S. Conference of Mayors, at its July 1982 conference, approved a recommendation supporting greater use of alternative living arrangements for the elderly and continued federal support of innovative local programs.

Imaginative, cost-effective approaches to meeting the elderly's housing needs by combining government, business, community and volunteer resources will be much in demand. The National Association of Counties and the U.S. Conference of Mayors help local governments determine needs and develop policies through exchange of information, including innovative programs. Denver, Colorado, for example, provides a telephone hotline service through public and private funds to help low-income senior citizens find affordable housing. Jacksonville, Florida, has launched a "Corporate Caring" program where private companies "adopt" elderly congregate living facilities, taking responsibility for both the building and the residents. A new study has found a wide array of successful local strategies that help elderly persons "age in place."[35]

Politics will play the lead role in determining the degree of support for innovative living arrangements and other housing related needs, according to Leo Baldwin. Local governments will respond with a commitment to older Americans, if they are viewed as an important political constituency.

Notes

1. Robert N. Butler and Myrna I. Lewis, *Aging and Mental Health* (1982), p. 14.
2. Quoted in *U.S. News & World Report*, Feb. 26, 1979, p. 66. Butler is leaving NIA on Sept. 1, 1982, for New York's Mount Sinai Medical Center, where he will head the geriatric department.
3. See "Long Term Care: Background and Future Directions," Health Care Financing Administration, January 1981, pp. 9-10. Also see "Women and Aging," *E.R.R.*, 1981 Vol. II, pp. 713-732.
4. Ibid., p. 12.
5. Figures from Butler and Lewis, *op. cit.*, p. 283 and U.S. Department of Commerce, "U.S. Industrial Outlook, 1982," p. 406.
6. See "Nursing Home Care in the United States: Failure in Public Policy," Supporting Paper No. 6, U.S. Senate Special Committee on Aging, 1975, pp. xiv-xv.
7. See *Long Term Care of the Aging–A Socially Responsible Approach*, American Association of Homes For the Aging (1979), p. 17.
8. See "Long Term Care: Background and Future Directions," *op. cit.*, p. 28.
9. The federal budget allocation for inspecting Medicare facilities dropped to $13.6 million in 1982 from $24.7 million in 1981. Inspection funds for Medicaid facilities fell to $31.8 million in 1982, compared to $42 million in 1980.
10. General Accounting Office, "Preliminary Findings on Patient Characteristics and State Medicaid Expenditures for Nursing Home Care," July 15, 1982.
11. See "Long Term Care: Background and Future Directions," *op. cit.*, p. 15.
12. See Butler and Lewis, *op. cit.*, p. 283.
13. See "Developments in Aging: 1981," U.S. Senate Special Committee on Aging, 1982, p. 359.
14. See "Working Papers on Long-Term Care," Office of the Assistant Secretary For Planning and Evaluation, Department of Health and Human Services, October 1981, p. 7.
15. See "Developments in Aging: 1981," *op cit.,* p. 226, and Diana Shaman, "New Hope for the Elderly: Home Equity Conversion," *Real Estate Today,* May 1982, p. 36.
16. See "Administering Aging Programs, Vol. VI: Serving the Urban Elderly—Issues and Programs," U.S. Conference of Mayors, 1982, p. 39.
17. See Gail Toff, "Alternatives To Institutional Care For the Elderly: An Analysis of State Initiatives," Intergovernmental Health Policy Project, George Washington University, September 1981, pp. 18-21.
18. See "Long-Term Care for the Elderly and Disabled," Congressional Budget Office, February 1977, p. x.
19. Data from interview with Betty Shepherd, coordinator, National Institute on Adult Daycare.
20. Speech by Edith G. Robins, Special Assistant for Adult Day Health Services, Health Care Financing Administration, Oct. 22, 1980.
21. See "Adult Day Care Programs," U.S. House Select Committee on Aging, Subcommittee on Health and Long-Term Care, April 23, 1980, p. 88.
22. Ibid., pp. 18-24.
23. The 14 states are California, Colorado, Florida, Georgia, Kansas, Maryland, Massachusetts, Minnesota, Nebraska, North Dakota, New Jersey, New York, Texas and Washington. The Older Americans Act was enacted in 1965 to develop new or improved programs for older persons through grants to the states.

24. Data from interview with Robert Marans, whose study, "Changing Properties of Retirement Communities," will soon be published by the Institute of Gerontology at the University of Michigan.
25. See "Board and Care Homes—A Study of Federal and State Actions To Safeguard the Health and Safety of Board and Care Home Residents," Department of Health and Human Services, Office of the Inspector General, April 1982, p. iv.
26. See story by Sandra Sugawara in *The Washington Post*, April 23, 1982.
27. See "Fraud and Abuse in Boarding Homes," U.S. House Select Committee on Aging, June 25, 1981, pp. 2-3.
28. See "Working Papers on Long Term Care," *op. cit.*, p. 56.
29. See "Developments in Aging: 1981," *op. cit.*, p. 214.
30. President's Commission on Housing, "Interim Report," Oct. 30, 1981, p. 8.
31. See "Report of the Mini-Conference on Housing for the Elderly," Oct. 22-24, 1980, convened by the National Council of Senior Citizens.
32. The Philadelphia center includes a hospital, nursing home, research institute, two apartment buildings and several small boarding homes on one city block, with a day-care center operating in another part of the city.
33. See "Retirement Income in Jeopardy," *E.R.R.*, 1981 Vol. I, pp. 169-188.
34. See "Development in Aging: 1981," *op. cit.*, p. 382.
35. See Phyllis Myers, "Aging in Place: Strategies To Help The Elderly Stay In Revitalizing Neighborhoods," The Conservation Foundation in collaboration with The Urban Institute, 1982.

References

Books

Butler, Robert, *Why Survive? Being Old in America*, Harper & Row, 1976.
———, and Myrna Lewis, *Aging & Mental Health*, The C.V. Mosby Co., 1982.
Percy, Charles H., *Growing Old in the Country of the Young*, McGraw-Hill, 1974.
Powell, M. Lawton and S.L. Hoover, *Community Housing: Choices for Older Americans*, Springer Publishing Co., 1981.

Articles

"Granny Flats: Easing the Housing Crunch for the Elderly," *The Futurist*, February 1982.
Hare, Patrick H., "Carving up the American Dream," *Planning*, July 1981.
"Housing Needs: The Choices Increase," *U.S. News & World Report*, Sept. 1, 1980.
"The Aging of America," *Congressional Quarterly Weekly Report*, Nov. 28, 1981.
Trunzo, Candace E., "Health Costs—Solving The Age-Old Problem," *Money*, January 1982.
Wallis, Claudia, "Day Care Centers for the Old," *Time*, Jan. 18, 1982.

Reports and Studies

Editorial Research Reports: "Retirement Income In Jeopardy," 1981 Vol. I, p. 169; "Plight of the Aged," 1971 Vol. II, p 863.
Hare, Patrick H., "Accessory Apartments: Surplus Space in Single Family Homes," American Planning Association, Planning Advisory Service Report No. 365, 1981.
Health Care Financing Administration, "Directory of Adult Day Care Centers," September 1980.
House Select Committee on Aging, Subcommittee on Housing and Consumer Interests, "Congregate Housing Services," May 19, 1981; "Housing The Elderly: Present Problems and Future Considerations," July 29, 1981; "Shared Housing," Nov. 17, 1981.
Myers, Phyllis, "Aging In Place: Strategies To Help The Elderly Stay In Revitalizing Neighborhoods," The Conservation Foundation in collaboration with The Urban Institute, 1982.
National Conference on Social Welfare, "Long Term Care—In Search of Solutions: The Need for Long Term Care; Alternative Directions For Change in Long Term Care; Informal Supports in Long Term Care," 1981.

Toff, Gail, "Alternatives To Institutional Care: An Analysis of State Initiatives," Intergovernmental Health Policy Project, George Washington University, September 1981.
U.S. Conference of Mayors, "Administering Aging Programs, Vol. VI: Serving the Urban Elderly—Issues and Programs," 1982.

17

Housing Policy for Older Americans in the 1980s: An Overview

Jerold S. Nachison and Morton H. Leeds

Introduction

As evidenced by the concerns of the current administration and the Congress, this country's approach to housing the elderly in the 1980s will be reformulated. We are questioning the validity of the current approach to providing elderly housing, and services where appropriate. Examples of problems include:

1. the extremely high unit cost of building new or renovating housing;
2. the growing numbers of poor elderly who still live in the family home, are "cash poor," but have quite an amount of equity in their homes;
3. the numbers of elderly living in substandard housing;
4. the increasing numbers of frail elderly needing social and other supportive services to remain independent;

From *Journal of Housing for the Elderly*, Vol. 1, No. 1 (Spring/Summer 1983), pp. 3-13. Reprinted by permission of The Haworth Press, Inc., 28 East 22nd Street, New York, NY.
  This paper was submitted, by request, to the U.S. Department of State for adaptation for use at the World Congress on Aging, Vienna, Austria, in August 1982. While the authors are senior HUD staff, the paper does not necessarily reflect the views of the Department of Housing and Urban Development or the Federal Government.

5. the lack of coordination among public and private sector providers of housing and social services serving the frail; and,
6. the inability of existing mechanisms and procedures to assure owners of elderly housing that services for the frail poor can be paid for over the long term.

Yet, despite the production of over 300,000 units of new housing for the elderly in the 1970s, and the provision of rent subsidies for nearly 600,000 others, the housing problem for elder Americans remains, especially for those with low to moderate incomes. This is demonstrated clearly by: (a) the three-to-ten-year waiting lists at most subsidized elderly housing developments; (b) the fact that more than one-third of all the substandard housing in this country has elderly occupants; and (c) that construction costs are rising as is the demand for building new, or highly renovated, housing. Perhaps most important, construction of all housing for the elderly is slackening because of high interest rates and the slowing of general economic conditions.

To provide a context for further national and international discussion, this chapter briefly describes the current status of housing for the elderly in this country through an overview of the present situation and a discussion of emerging policy issues. While the focus of this paper is on federal policy, a large number of elderly are also served by the private sector; their housing needs are not necessarily affected by government action.

The Housing Issue

There is no question that the general condition of the housing stock, and of elderly housing in particular, has dramatically improved in the past forty years. General housing inadequacy has dropped from nearly 50 percent of all units in 1940 to about 7 percent currently, with about 8 percent of the units occupied by the elderly as substandard (President's Commission on Housing, 1981). Such housing is generally associated with elderly blacks and rural elderly—those with the lowest incomes of all (Struyk and Soldo, 1980). Thus, while the elderly as a whole are reasonably well housed by government policy, there is an acute and growing problem among those who are poor and minority—who tend to be in the lowest 15 percent of the elderly population (though this number has been argued to be as high as 30 percent) (Ibid). This problem has been highlighted by the much higher (up to double) housing costs borne by the elderly population as compared with the general population. The National Council of Senior Citizens (NCSC) estimates that the elderly 75+ pay more than 45 percent of their budgets for housing alone. Those in this age bracket make up 30 percent of the elderly population and this percentage is growing (Struyk and Soldo, 1980). There is also a body of information that shows a great number of elderly homeowners are "overhoused," that is, remain in their paid-for older homes long after their children grow up and move out, leaving the elderly person(s) with much more space than is needed. Thus, even with low housing costs, there may not be enough income to pay for necessary repairs and keep the house heated in winter or cooled in the summer.

Federal Sector Housing

The public sector has responded to the housing need of the poor through the Housing Act of 1937 and its many amendments, plus counterpart statutes at the state level. Most activity for housing for the elderly, however, has taken place since 1959. Under the federal statutes, about 1.35 million units of elderly housing either have been built, or have had rental subsidies made available to owners, mostly in the last twelve years (HUD *Challenge,* 1980), The prime focus since about 1950 has been on new construction programs, generally in low-income public housing, though the Section 202 program for moderate-income elderly has been popular and very prominent. These have been matched, additionally, through nearly 150,000 beds in nursing homes whose mortgages have been insured by federal programs. Finally, nearly 600,000 rehabilitated and existing units have been provided rental assistance (Ibid).

In addition to direct mortgage support, the federal government has also guaranteed construction loans through several programs. Also, extensive rental assistance has been made available to owners, and in the case of non-profit sponsors, further subsidy through direct loans at well below the market rate. Because of inflation and the resultant rise in the cost of building, however, the new construction market has nearly dried up. Housing programs in the near future will now stress rental subsidies which remain much cheaper on a per-unit basis than building. Some housing will, however, be rehabilitated, at least under current plans.

Private Sector Housing

There has been a large expansion of middle- and upper-income rental and condominium housing built since the early 1960s, mostly without government assistance, except for mortgage insurance. There have been a number of large residential communities, funded through the private market, built throughout the southwest and scattered through the northeast. These are targeted for the well and middle/upper income elderly, with the chief criterion for admission/purchase (other than ability to pay) being that one be over 55 and not have minor children. Also, the "life care" concept, after a disastrous start in the late 1960s, is now undergoing a renaissance for those wealthy elderly who can afford to pay the charges. Under this concept, the individual pays a large "founder's" fee, e.g., $20,000 or so, and high monthly costs for life, e.g., $1,500 or so at present rates. In return, the person receives housecleaning, personal assistance, meals and medical care when needed until he/she dies. Such arrangements as these serve well under 10 percent of the elderly overall, but are significant investments of capital for the private market to expend.

There have been some limited attempts to deal with the question of releasing home equity for elders who are poor, and dealing with the question of helping others to remain in their own, or a similar home, generally by sharing the costs of payment and maintenance. The private sector has come up with a number of "shared housing" experiments, with state support in a few cases. These experiments have involved both the rental and the cooperative markets. There have been a number of "reverse mortgage" programs started also, notably in California, Wisconsin and New Jersey.

Trends and Issues

Introduction

Currently, housing policy for the elderly is in a state of flux, in reaction to conflicts and pressures from other areas of the economy. Rising demand for more elderly housing is offset by the very high per unit costs, the current emphasis on use of the existing stock, and a shift away from construction and further subsidy to local housing agencies for operating costs. Growth of the frail population will be affected by cutbacks in the services sectors of the economy, both public and private. General interest rates have retarded construction growth in all sectors, and inflation continues. Yet, many elderly are overhoused (albeit perhaps in substandard buildings), and have large amounts of equity in their homes but little or no cash flow. They want to stay in their homes, or cannot afford to move out. However, there is little housing available for them even if they could afford to move.

Growth of Frail Elderly

As noted earlier, the growing numbers of very frail elderly has serious implications for housing policy in the future. The population of elderly 85+ is now expected to be more than 3 million in the year 2000—a great number of whom will be poor. There is a great need for financers, housing planners and service providers to understand the "continuum of living" concept covering the span from independent housing to hospitals. Ideally, an individual, with appropriate supports, could remain at home until 24-hour medical care is needed. A multiple response to this problem is needed as the multi-faceted housing and services delivery structure developed by public and private agencies reflects the overlapping and interconnected character of the human problems encountered.

Exhibit 17.1 graphically abstracts the outline of the complexity. Each side of the Exhibit captures a dimension of the problem: age/frailty, costs, and type of facility that comes into play.

As Exhibit 17.1 suggests, with aging there is a shift in the distribution of needs. Shelter comes to occupy a relatively small part of the individual's perception of need, while needs for supportive social and medical services increase substantially. As needs shift toward semi-independent living, there is a related increase in the total cost per day. Further, it is likely that the money added will go to support social and medical services rather than to housing.

As needs and costs change, the type of facility one requires changes as well. From the independence of the single-family dwelling, one moves to forms of congregate housing (HUD *Challenge*, 1980), then to the final dependency of an institution. While one can argue about the exact location of a facility in the continuum, those shown fit the normative progression.

With the rise of inflation in America, the search began for additional sources of income for the older person. As noted earlier, two of the major possible options ("a" and "b" below) are already under study, and both utilize the

EXHIBIT 17.1
The Continuum of Living

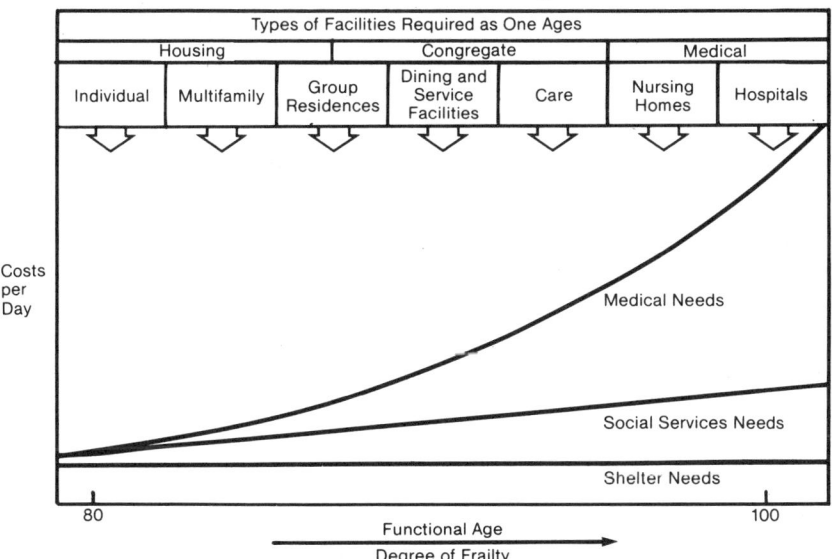

Note: This figure applies to handicapped as well as older persons. In this regard, it should be noted that the baseline represents functional and not chronological age.

older person's home. This occurs because between three-quarters and four-fifths of the elder population own their own homes, largely paid for.

a. Shared Housing. One source of income is based around existing but unused space. For those who are amenable to such, empty bedrooms could be rented to the young or other elderly themselves. Social support networks then can be developed internally. Other elderly can also band together and purchase larger homes using the cooperative form of ownership. Both of these have been attempted, some with state assistance. Early reports indicate success, especially where the human factor is clearly planned for in the beginning.

b. Reverse mortgages. In this concept, a bank or mortgage company purchases the property from the elder person and pays out the equity on a monthly basis, with the proviso that the individual could not be "evicted" during his/her lifetime. At death, the remainder of the equity would revert to the estate. While the few of these mortgages negotiated so far have had some success, generally this generation of elderly continues to want to leave property and other like valuables to family and heirs.

c. Families. Another source of income would be the immediate family of the elder person. While income sources other than the family have grown in recent years, a change may be shaping that would more directly involve the family again. Such changes would have the family provide more direct support from children and other relatives, whether the older person is living at home, in a rented apartment, or in the house of a child or other relative. Variations on this theme could involve direct payments to the family to assist in paying for care, where appropriate. This is especially necessary in cases of extreme frailty, when outside help is brought in.

How to Link Housing and Services

As long as there were few elderly, the family provided services and food, usually in the home. As the three-generation family weakened, today's pattern emerged: the older person lives near a key member of the family, often a daughter, who provides him/her with shopping, transportation, personal assistance and quasi-medical care.

During the past two decades or so, a complex of services has emerged to replace the role the family played in the past. These services, usually provided in the home, range from shopping escort or mailing letters, to the most elaborate, including 24-hour home-health care. Many difficulties arise when different sources and agencies provide similar services; when different forms of payment arise for these services; when duplication occurs among agencies (some of which are federal, state or local) in the same jurisdiction; when conflicts of judgment occur with very specialized case needs in order to provide a service; and when the cost of services at home rises above "reasonable" levels.

Courtesy of Louis A. Sapienze for the New Jersey Housing & Mortgage Finance Agency
Highland Plaza, financed by the New Jersey Housing & Mortgage Finance Agency, provides attractive and affordable housing for 111 senior citizen households. HMFA also secured federal rental subsidies, meaning that all residents pay no more than 30% of their incomes for rent.

Possibly most damaging is the fact that the entire housing and services system for the frail elderly is seldom perceived as a continuum ranging from the autonomous person or couple to the most dependent. Market forces are presumed to provide the services where needed, as long as the person is able to pay, and a limited "safety net" of programs exists for these poorer persons unable to pay for services at cost. Yet, the critical link between housing and services, the appropriate "targeting" of services with assured funding of the services for those people most in need, is not in place.

Currently, several approaches to comprehensive case management for congregate housing or levels of care, as a substitute for or enhancement of the family, are being tested in different localities. These all assume an overriding local structure of case findings which will maximize service availability to those most in need while minimizing costs. Case management—the professional assessment of needs jointly tied to both the housing and services systems—for the elder individual or couple provides an overall structure for "targeting." A general system of case management tying housing and services effectively together should arise in this decade.

Financing Housing for the Elderly

As one of the more popular federal programs of the last twenty years, elderly housing has grown steadily in terms of both investment and ongoing support through various subsidy processes. Historically, the private home predominated as it does today. But, with the shift from three-generational (grandparent, parent, child) to the two-generational (parent, child) households, changing life-styles and increasing numbers of very elderly persons, there has been a corresponding shift of elderly people away from their larger homes to both subsidized and unsubsidized apartments. In the 1960s, federal mortgage insurance of private construction loans was augmented by direct loans to owners of federal underwriting of a local community bond. Both of these have more recently been replaced by rent-supplement and rental assistance programs under the "fair market rent" concept which guarantees rent payments to the owners of buildings for low- and moderate-income renters. The owner, of course, has to build the structure using conventional market financing.

The cost of building new units, however, has nearly doubled in the last four years, and the cost of rehabilitating a building has also gone up significantly because of inflation. With the cost of housing for the elderly now running nearly $3 billion yearly, questions are being raised regarding more adequate and cheaper ways for the federal government to play a role in housing the elderly. These are now under review as part of the greater study of the role of the federal government in social programs. These issues can be looked at in a number of ways, summarized as follows: What is the cheapest and most effective way for the federal government to play a positive role in providing housing for the elderly? And, what are the appropriate roles for state/local governments and the private sector in the provision of housing for the elderly? A number of approaches are stated below:

a. Housing vouchers. A major interest of the current administration is to replace all construction programs with a system of cash vouchers. Under this approach the very low income elder person gets a voucher for a certain number of dollars, based upon some formula. With this voucher he/she could then go out and procure housing. While some advocates for construction programs point to prior research in this area and note that vouchers only seem to stretch the existing housing stock further without stimulating new construction or providing housing specifically for the elderly, the administration feels that a sufficient number of vouchers in circulation would stimulate private construction without further federal involvement.

b. Revision of construction programs. One approach would be to simplify current mortgage insurance and rent assistance programs into a standardized elderly housing stature. Another is to simplify further consolidation of statutes into a block grant for state/local government with the stress on rehabilitation to

Courtesy of Louis A. Sapienze for the New Jersey Housing & Mortgage Finance Agency
Ballantyne House in Newark, a 170-unit senior housing development, was built with an $8 million mortgage loan from the New Jersey Housing & Mortgage Finance Agency.

code rather than new construction. Inflation, however, would affect costs in this approach also, and it would have to be coupled with assistance for low- and moderate-income renters. Also, two other questions need more study: (a) To what extent can federal minimum property standards and local building codes be simplified and standardized; and (b) What are the appropriate roles best played by for-profit, limited dividend, and non-profit owners of housing for the elderly under either federal or local government aegis?

A useful corollary question is raised: How can state/local government pick up a larger share, or total cost when appropriate, of financing housing for the elderly? One method is by the sale of tax-exempt bonds. Another is by using the "revolving fund" approach. Under this concept, after an initial number of years of loans are made, any future loans are made from the repayments to the fund on the first loans. Thus, after a certain point, no new state/local (or federal) funds need enter the system. The drawback, though, is the large amount of "revolving" capital fund commitments which are carried annually on the budget.

c. *"Cashing out" all welfare and related programs.* Finally, there is another variant on the question of approach, one which surely will get some attention, if not much support: Should all welfare, housing and supportive services programs be "cashed out" in the form of a single payment to the recipient covering a multiplicity of needs? Under this approach an elderly individual or couple would receive one cash payment to cover all food, shelter, medical, and other needs. He/she then would have the responsibility for getting whatever goods or services are needed—a logical extension of the idea noted under the voucher concept above. But, again, opinions vary on whether or not this type of approach would necessarily stimulate the building industry.

All of these variations assume that there will remain a role for government, whether federal/state or local, in providing some measure of support for the housing industry to insure that the supply of housing for the elderly continues to expand for this growing population. While it is questionable if this nation, even using a combination of these or other new ideas, can achieve the recommendation of the 1981 White House Conference on Aging in the near future—200,000 units annually—this is certainly a goal worth attempting.

Conclusion

Substantial federal government involvement in housing for the elderly has been a relatively recent phenomenon. It is clear, additionally, that Americans generally support continued housing programs for the elderly. Given inflation, rising costs, growing demand and disparate approaches to providing housing for the elderly, the Congress and the administration must face the question of how to best provide the housing needed, especially for low- and moderate-income elderly—those most in need. In view of all the above, especially the disparity between the views of the administration and the recommendations of the White House conferees, housing for the elderly will certainly be a major discussion topic for the decade.

References

1. HUD *Challenge,* Vol. X, No. 8, August 1979, pp. 11-13, 18-19.
2. HUD *Challenge,* Vol. XI, No. 9, September 1980, p. 29.
3. National Association of Retired Teachers/American Association of Retired Persons, *Statement Prepared for the President's Commission on Housing,* October 1981, Washington, D.C., p. 2.
4. President's Commission on Housing, *Interim Report,* October 1981, Washington, D.C., pp. 13, 17.
5. Struyk, R. J., and Soldo, B. J., *Improving the Elderly's Housing,* 1980, Ballinger Publishing Company, Cambridge, Mass., pp. 18, 21, 26, 38.

18

Future Housing Assistance Policy for the Elderly

Raymond J. Struyk

Housing policy in the United States for both the elderly and the non-elderly has been changing rapidly under the spur of dramatic reductions in the level of resources the country believes it can allocate to federally supported social programs. This paper hazards a look into the future for government housing policy and, hence, programs for elderly Americans from the vantage point of what these interventions could be. It looks beyond the immediate federal budget woes, although its speculations are tempered by the probable realities of the 1980s. Judging from the manifest disenchantment of Americans in the late 1970s with high taxes and activist government, fewer federal resources are likely to be available regardless of which party is in the White House (Palmer and Sawhill, 1982).

This presentation takes four objectives of an enlightened housing policy as its starting point. Policies should be designed to

1. provide the elderly with a range of choice in their living arrangements. Hence, equivalent assistance should be provided to households with similar characteristics even though they choose different living arrangements.

2. facilitate timely adjustments in housing consumption and living arrangements as they become necessary and the household wishes to make them. So, for example, impediments to living in single-family units such as taking in boarders should be removed.
3. improve the housing circumstances of those receiving assistance—both upgrading housing quality to a minimum standard and reducing housing expenditures to a reasonable level—at the lowest cost possible.
4. treat all similarly situated households in the same way. This implies moving toward making housing assistance available on an entitlement basis for at least some segment of the population.

Observers of federal housing policy over the years are well aware that housing policy to date has not been formulated in such a way that these objectives could be achieved. Thus, the gap yawns wide between where we are and where we should be.

The next section of the paper summarizes recent federal initiatives—those of the Reagan administration—and comments briefly on whether they are consistent with the objectives stated above. The following section then deals with preferred government interventions through housing assistance to elderly renters and home-owners, concentrating on major policy thrusts.

Because of space constraints important but less pervasive areas such as shared housing and reverse annuity mortgages are not discussed. For the same reason, important background data on the present housing circumstances of the elderly are not included, but information on housing alternatives and on housing conditions may be found elsewhere (Myers, 1982; Struyk and Turner, 1984).

The Reagan Initiatives in Housing Assistance

A number of legislative actions taken in 1981–1983 based on the administration's budget proposals and the proposals themselves provide a pellucid picture of the administration's philosophy about housing assistance. In short, it has sought to halt the growth in the number of households receiving assistance, target the available assistance to poorer households, reduce benefits, and emphasize use of the existing stock over building new housing projects (for details, see Struyk et al., 1983).

Program Size

The administration took the position in its FY1983 budget that holding the number of households receiving housing assistance to 3.8 million—the number that would be receiving assistance at the end of FY1985 if its program were followed—is "essential to the administration's effort to control long-term federal government spending'' (Office of Management and Budget, 1982, p. 110). The administration began moving toward its objective by convincing Congress to appropriate funds sufficient to add only 52,000 units to the stock of assisted housing for FY1982, compared with the 100,000 unit program that had been proposed by the Carter administration. For FY1983 the figure was 62,000; the small increase over the FY1982 total was due to Congressional action since the administration has proposed net reductions in the number of assisted units. For FY1984, 85,000 incremental units were proposed, and Congress appropriated funds for approximately that number.

Sharper Targeting and Reducing Benefits

In 1981, Congress enacted three important changes in housing assistance programs. The purposes of these changes were better targeting of limited resources, greater equity among participants in public housing and other housing assistance programs, and greater equity between participants in housing programs and non-participants. The changes were the following:

1. The contribution by a tenant receiving housing assistance was increased from 25 to 30 percent of his or her income.
2. Eligibility for assistance was restricted by limiting the share of all recipient households with incomes between 50 to 80 percent of area median incomes (adjusted for family size) to 10 percent of the units available for occupancy; other recipients must have incomes below 50 percent of area median (about 133 percent of the poverty line on a national basis).
3. The definition of income used in computing the tenant's contribution was made uniform for the Section 8 and public housing programs. Traditionally, local authorities had wide latitude in defining incomes; now more of a household's gross income would be counted by some authorities in computing benefits.

There is no doubt that "very low-income households" (i.e., those with incomes below 50 percent of local median income) have more severe housing problems than other households. In 1977, renter-households with very low incomes spent 40 percent of their incomes, on the average, for housing compared with 25 percent for households in the 50 to 80 percent of median group. Likewise, 20 percent of very low-income renters live in units classified as needing rehabilitation, compared with 12 percent of those in the 50 to 80 percent of median income group (Levine, 1982).

Changes enacted to achieve greater equity among participants in the different housing programs and between participants and non-participants are, by themselves, on the mark. Participants have had the share of their incomes devoted to housing lowered dramatically by subsidies compared to non-recipients, some of whom would participate under an entitlement program. In 1977, for example, about 80 percent of unsubsidized very low-income renter housholders spent over 30 percent of their incomes on housing. Subsidized renters, on the other hand, were required to contribute only a quarter of their incomes for the housing they consumed.

Emphasizing Use of the Existing Stock

Extending a pattern initiated by Congress in 1980, both the executive and legislative branches of the federal government have continued to deemphasize new construction. The FY1982 housing budget had a mix of 88 percent existing and 12 percent new construction and substantial rehabilitation. The FY1983 budget, after taking into account the recision of funds already appropriated for new construction units, incorporated a net reduction in such units committed for funding. The main justification for building fewer new units to house low-income households is the greater expense of these units. In the early 1970s it cost about twice as much to provide a unit-month of housing services from a federally assisted, newly built unit than it did to lease a privately owned existing unit, according to very careful analysis carried out as part of the Experimental Housing Allowance program (Mayo et al., 1979). On the grounds of efficiency, existing housing dominates as long as it is in adequate supply.

In addition to emphasizing the use of existing units, significant changes in the administration of the Section 8 existing program were proposed. The resulting "housing voucher" program embodies two types of change. One type will make the program more efficient; changes are based on favorable experience in the Experimental Housing Allowance Program. The effects of the second type are less clear, but they may make the program less successful. These modifications would reduce the fair market rent, the rent upon which the government's subsidy is based. Coupled with the increase in the first year's tenant contribution to 30 percent of income and the proposed counting of the subsidy value of food stamps in income, these provisions probably would have made the benefits insufficient to induce families living in dwellings failing the program's physical standards to relocate to units that would meet these standards. In short, the program may not be capable of achieving the objectives of housing policy as they have been articulated. Congress rejected some of these changes in drafting its legislation, but, because the two houses failed to agree on a legislative package, no housing authorization bill was passed in the 1982 and 1983 sessions.

Initiatives Versus Objectives

On the positive side, some of the actions described above do move toward focusing aid on recipients most in need and toward creating greater equity in the treatment of persons participating in rental programs. They also move toward decreasing the differences between participants and non-participants and shifting housing assistance to a more efficient mode by stressing use of the existing stock.

The negative side of the ledger is longer. By capping or severely limiting the incremental number of participants, differences between the "haves" and the "have nots" are perpetuated. By continuing the separate forms of assistance to renters and homeowners, inequities will persist as well. Indeed, aid to elderly homeowners through forgiveness of up to $125,000 in gains on home equity at the time of sale is quite likely an inefficient way to provide assistance. Benefits to participants in the rental programs are sharply cut.

Finally, only limited choice is provided in these policies. Housing vouchers provide considerably more choice among dwellings than do project options, and forgiveness of the capital gains tax cuts the penalty of shifting to renter status, but limited entitlements restrict participants' mobility so they must remain within the jurisdiction where they first received their vouchers, and poor owners who become renters have no assurance of being able to receive aid as renters.

Housing Assistance Policy in the Future

It is sensible to begin a look at the future by considering the implications of housing assistance being available on an entitlement basis to qualifying renters and home-owners because this focus provides a sense of the magnitude of need. After a discussion of a general entitlement program, the analysis will turn to specific issues in program design for renters and home-owners.

The arguments in favor of entitlement are formidable. First, an entitlement approach ends the inequities in treatment that presently exist between recipients and would-be recipients. Second, it removes impediments to housing adjustments that may exist because those receiving assistance in a particular unit or jurisdiction fear that in relocating they risk losing them. Third, for poor elderly homeowners, the specter of encountering uncontrollable rents if they move from their unmortgaged home will dissolve. Fourth, the general availability of housing assistance would permit that assistance to be merged with the balance of the social welfare system to help limit the broader inequities in the system; this, in turn, would enormously facilitate thoroughgoing reform. Finally, housing assistance could be viewed as an integral element in the system of long-term care that must be developed in the next few years to handle the ballooning numbers of elderly in the United States.

Who could participate and what would the program be? Very briefly, the program is a housing voucher program—a program quite similar to the Section 8 existing program—in which the income cutoff for eligibility for a family of four is set at 50 percent of local area median income. Participants contribute 30 percent of their adjusted income for housing. (These are the current Section 8 program provisions.) Renters and home-owners may participate; the return on most assets, actual or imputed, is counted as income, including the return on home equity (Lowry, 1974). Subsidies for both homeowners and renters are calculated using the same rent levels as an estimate of reasonable housing costs in local areas based on the size of the rental unit needed. Thus, equity between the two tenure groups is achieved.

Three questions immediately come to mind when considering an entitlement program: (1) How many households will participate? (2) What will it cost? (3) How will it be financed?

The figures in Exhibit 18.1 constitute a rough estimate of participation, based on the open-enrollment portion of the Experimental Housing Allowance program (EHAP) (see Struyk and Bendick, 1981, for details). Greater precision is not possible because the income cutoff was higher in EHAP than in the proposed program, meaning that participation rates are somewhat downwardly biased. On the other hand, benefit levels were higher in EHAP than those likely to be in effect in a voucher program in the future, judging from 1981 Congressional action and the Reagan initiatives. Among the elderly about 2.3

EXHIBIT 18.1
Estimated Participation in an Open-Enrollment Housing Voucher Program (Millions of Households)

Households	Elderly Headed Households		Non-Elderly Headed Households		Total
	Owners	Renters	Owners	Renters	
Eligible to receive housing assistance (1979)	5.0	2.9	4.7	8.4	21.0
Currently receiving assistance (1983)	—	1.5†	0.7*	2.4†	4.6
Eligible but not receiving assistance	5.0	1.4	4.0	6.0	16.4
Likely to participate in voucher entitlement program‡	1.6	0.7	0.7	2.3	5.3

* HUD programs plus Farmers's Home Administration Section 502; no assistance in these programs to the elderly is assumed since data on the actual elderly/non-elderly split were not available.

† Estimates of eligibles are from Zais, Struyk, and Thibodeau (1982); estimates of current participants are from the same source applied to figures in the HUD FY 1983 budget (U.S. Department of Housing and Urban Development, 1982, p. H-20). The same elderly/non-elderly split as for HUD programs is applied to aggregate figures for the Farmers' Home Section 515 program (exclusive of Section 515/Section 8); figures on FmHA programs are from Drews (1982), p. 8.

‡ Participation rates are from the Housing Allowance Supply Experiment: Kingsley and Schlegel (1982), Table 5.1.

million additional households—70 percent of them owner-occupants—would participate if they could; another 3.0 million additional non-elderly would participate as well.

Judging program costs in the future is extremely difficult. It is estimated that under the 50 percent of median income eligibility rules the average annual subsidy payment under Section 8 existing program in 1983 would be about $2,400 if the program continued as it was in 1981. However, for purposes of these calculations, a total cost of about $2,200 per household per year in 1983 is a realistic figure, in light of the mix of owners and renters. Using this figure, the incremental cost of assisting all the additional elderly participants is about $5.1 billion in 1983; note that in federal budget parlance these are outlays. Assisting all of the incremental non-elderly participants would cost about another $6.6 billion. To start with all renters would require about $7.2 billion

An additional $11.6 billion in government expenditures (to serve everyone) in the current environment appears at first encounter to be a ludicrous suggestion because it would double current federal housing assistance payments. But these need not be additional expenditures; in fact, the costs should be met through reductions elsewhere in the budget. Of course, making cuts is difficult because of the competing interests of Congressional committees. Nevertheless, three sources in particular can be identified. First, the $1.3 billion budgeted for weatherization and heating assistance could be replaced with vouchers. Recipients could use voucher payments for these purposes, if they wish, or to meet other more urgent needs. Second, the $550 million in forgiveness of capital gains tax on home equity for those over age 55 could be repealed; the largest beneficiaries of this provision are households that need it least. Third, mortgage interest deductions from the federal income tax should be contained. The tax losses from such deductions are expected to double from 1982 to 1987 to a staggering $44.4 billion. It is well-known these benefits accrue disproportionately to high-income families (Greene, 1981). A reduction of only 35 percent in the 1983 tax losses, combined with the other cuts, would finance vouchers. The overall effect of substituting vouchers for the other expenditures would be a dramatically improved targeting of housing assistance toward the poor.

It is acknowledged that the enactment (or even consideration) of any new entitlement is unlikely. Therefore, the remainder of the paper turns to an examination of two salient issues in federal housing assistance for the elderly: constructing new rental units to serve poor elderly and reasonable means of assisting needy homeowners.

Renters: Do We Need New Construction?

The traditional bellwether of the federal government's concern for housing for the elderly has been size of the appropriation for the construction of housing projects by nonprofit sponsors for exclusive occupancy by the elderly and by the non-elderly handicapped under the provisions of the Section 202 program. Among all programs, elderly-designated projects, including public housing, now house over half of all elderly-assisted households and are widely thought of as the primary approach to aiding the elderly. A radical transformation to emphasizing leasing existing units is in the offing, driven by the high cost of new construction projects. In the past three years only token amounts of housing under the Section 202 and public housing programs for the elderly have been funded by the Congress.

In the years ahead the construction of new projects for the elderly beyond these low levels will occur only if newly built projects have a well-defined role in the long-term care system. In short, they will probably have to be congregate housing facilities (i.e., housing offering a number of services in addition to shelter) that can be demonstrated to be cost-effective alternatives to intermedite care facilities *and* to providing support services to the elderly in the dwelling units they would otherwise be inhabiting. If proven to be cost competitive, one can imagine a voucher program for congregate housing in which private developers would offer units developed without HUD assistance. Participants would be the frail elderly. Contributions by participants could be a much higher share of their incomes than the 30 percent specified for the pure housing programs since persons in congregate facilities would receive meals and other services in addition to housing. (On the provision of support services, see Stassen and Holahan, 1980.)

Unfortunately, the evidence upon which to base an argument for a vastly expanded congregate program is not presently at hand. Under a Congressional mandate HUD has been conducting a demonstration to determine whether the provision of support services in housing projects has a significant impact on the rate of institutionalization and mortality. The evaluation of these effects is scheduled for completion in early 1985, but it does not include detailed comprehensive analyses of cost-effectiveness compared to intermediate care facilities or a comparison of congregate facilities with the alternative of providing services to those living in the community. Thus, the requisite knowledge base for informed decision-making is at least several years distant.

Homeowners: Options for Assistance

The issue addressed here is the choice of strategy in assisting elderly homeowners. It was suggested earlier that the forgiveness of capital gains tax on home equity at the time of sale embodies problems of targeting and program integration and that it would be better to replace expenditures for this purpose with help to owners while they are living in their homes. The $500 million in annual tax losses could assist about 250,000 elderly homeowners under a voucher approach, or one-sixth of all of those likely to participate in such a program.

This section examines the two front-running options: housing vouchers and the provision of in-kind maintenance services. Vouchers provide cash grants to income-eligible homeowners on the condition that their dwellings meet minimum physical standards. The grants may be spent on housing or for any other purpose. Under the in-kind maintenance services approach, by contrast, an agency provides services directly to the household. The household, which typically is required to pay a small fixed fee (e.g., $25) to join the program, can spend the money (or time and effort) it would have otherwise devoted to dwelling upkeep on other items.

Thus, both approaches make it possible for the household to substitute publicly provided resources for its own, and the extent of such substitution is one important criterion for assessing the two approaches. That is, policy should favor the approach that transforms more of the federal expenditure into additional services of the type being explicitly supported, in this case housing. A second criterion is the administrative cost and simplicity of the approaches. The final criterion is the likelihood of participation of households in the two programs. The following paragraphs present the evidence for these three areas available from the Housing Allowance Supply Experiment (HASE) and a HUD demonstration of the in-kind services approach in seven cities (Ferguson and Moss, 1982; Lowry, 1981). The reader is warned that the data on the two approaches are not very comparable and that the comparison is therefore more suggestive than definitive.

The evidence on the amount of repair activity induced by housing vouchers—that is, above-normal activity—is quite convincing. Homeowners in Green Bay, Wisconsin, and South Bend, Indiana, in the mid-1970s spent $178 and $153 more per year on repairs, respectively, due to vouchers (Lowry, 1981). These expenditures represent about a 60 percent increase in repairs. Another way to express the effect is to say that the elasticity of voucher-induced repairs with respect to allowance payments (i.e., the percentage change in repairs divided by the percentage change in income) was 4.8 and 2.9, respectively, in Green Bay and South Bend. These are large increases.

The figures for in-kind services are less easily dealt with. On the average, the program delivered $208 per client in repair services (Ferguson & Moss, 1982). Some of these expenditures probably substituted for work that would have been done in the absence of assistance; alternatively, they may have induced some additional repairs. The $208 can be interpreted realistically as an upper bound. As such, it is certainly no more than the voucher figures which, when adjusted for inflation to allow comparability with the figures for in-kind services, are $247 and $213, respectively, for the two sites. Hence, the amounts for induced repairs are roughly comparable, with vouchers having a modest edge. Another important point about in-kind services is that the variance among the seven sites in the level of services provided under the in-kind program was very large indeed, with a range of $108 to $337 per year. Different levels of services were provided by the agencies despite quite strong guidelines from HUD. This raises the issue of equitable treatment of participants in such a program.

The comparison of administrative simplicity and cost for the two approaches is more conclusive. Vouchers are certainly easier to administer since they do not involve the direct provision of services. Both approaches require the standard tenant intake functions: outreach, screening for eligibility, etc. The greater administrative simplicity of vouchers is borne out in the cost figures. In the Supply Experiment 16 cents of every program dollar went for administration (Kingsley and Schlegel, 1982); the average for the seven sites providing in-kind services was about 35 cents (Ferguson and Moss, 1982, and author's computations). Beyond expense costs it seems probable that the in-kind services approach would require more HUD oversight, meaning higher costs in that quarter as well.

On the other hand, total costs are important; in 1981 a year of allowances would cost about $1,200 compared to about $800 for in-kind services. (The difference between the $800 figure and the costs of actual repairs and narrowly defined overhead is attributable to the provision of other services to clients (e.g., referrals and full overhead). Much of the allowances are spent on items besides housing, even though vouchers result in substantial repairs and are cheap to administer. By contrast, in-kind services are cheaper, but much of the total cost goes for administration.

Participation is more difficult to judge because of the lack of any information on an open-enrollment in-kind services program and because of the general differences in outreach. Using a variety of means, but emphasizing the media, the voucher program (HASE) was able to notify the vast majority of eligible elderly households about the program. Households had to apply for the program and qualify their homes with little or no aid from the administering agency. Under these conditions, one-third of the income-eligible elderly home-owners participated in the program (Kingsley and Schlegel, 1982).

In contrast, the typical pattern of outreach and enrollment for the provision of in-kind services has been much more intense. Neighborhoods are generally the target area, and outreach has even included door-to-door canvassing. Enrollment interviews are often conducted in the client's home. All of this means that more households may participate and that some "hard to reach" elderly may join this program who would not have attempted to enroll in a voucher program. Likewise, participation should be higher under the in-kind services approach because generally there has been no minimum physical standard that the home must pass in order for the household to receive in-kind maintenance services. (Of course, this means that some assisted units will not conform to society's definition of a "decent" home.) On the other hand, the small area approach may make comprehensive spatial coverage problematic; if so, clear inequities will arise between persons with and without access to the services.

An examination of the two approaches for assisting elderly homeowners comprehensively yields no clear "winner." Housing allowances do at least as well as in-kind assistance in inducing dwelling upkeep, and they are dramatically less complex and administratively costly. Low participation is a problem, but more detailed analyses indicate that more needy households participate at higher rates. Yet they are expensive compared to in-kind services. Still, *if* national policy were being made today on the basis of the available analyses, vouchers would seem to be the better choice.

Conclusion

At least the first half of the decade of the 1980s will be characterized by great tumult and probably fundamental change in federal housing assistance for the elderly. In the present environment of stringent budget constraints, any successful initiative in this area will have to possess three characteristics.

1. It must be largely "self-financing" in the sense that the initiative replaces a less efficient approach to addressing the same or related problem.
2. It must be convincingly cost-effective; a proven track record on cost will be essential.
3. It must move housing assistance toward greater cohesion and integration with the welfare and long-term care systems.

Under these conditions the trend will very likely include a greater reliance on housing vouchers to serve elderly renters and, possibly, homeowners. Their cost-effectiveness is proven, and their integration with the long-term care system seems quite straightforward.

The major impediment to their expansion will be finding the funds somewhere else in the federal budget. As noted earlier, however, the housing-related weatherization and energy assistance program and the tax expenditures on home equity capital gains forgiveness would provide a portion of the funds, with the balance coming from reductions in the generosity of mortgage interest tax deductions for higher-income households.

At the same time, tighter targeting of vouchers should be advocated. In particular, assistance should be concentrated on the long-term or permanently poor and not used as supplemental unemployment compensation (Newman and Struyk, 1983). Tighter targeting of this type would disproportionately favor the elderly. Indeed, one might begin the move to entitlement by enfranchising the elderly first.

To be sure, the choices ahead are difficult. Each produces losers as well as beneficiaries. Above all, the overriding goal must be greater equity in the treatment of similar households and a greater use of housing assistance to expand the choices available to elderly Americans.

Note

Work on this paper was supported by a grant from the Aetna Life and Casualty Foundation. The author received very useful comments on a previous draft from Jill Khadduri, Martin Levine, Sandra Newman, and James Zais. A different version of the paper is to appear in *Housing an Aging Society*, edited by Robert J. Newcomer, M. Powell Lawton, and Thomas O. Byerts and published by Van Nostrand Reinhold.

References

Drews, R. (1982). *Rural Housing Programs: Long-Term Costs and Their Treatment in the Federal Budget*. Washington, D.C.: Congressional Budget Office.
Ferguson, G.D., and Moss, W. (1982). *The Seven City Home Maintenance Demonstration for the Elderly: Preliminary Findings Report*. Cambridge, MA: Urban Systems Research and Engineering.
Greene, J.M. (1981). *The Tax Treatment of Homeownership: Issues and Options*. Washington, D.C.: Congressional Budget Office.
Kingsley, G.T., and Schlegel, P.M. (1982). *Housing Allowances and Administrative Efficiency*. Santa Monica, CA: The Rand Corporation.
Levine, M. (1982). *Housing Assistance Program Options*. Washington, D.C.: Congressional Budget Office.
Lowry, I. (1974). *Equity and Housing Objectives in Homeowner Assistance*. Santa Monica, CA: The Rand Corporation.
_____. (1981). *Experimenting with Housing Allowances*. Santa Monica, CA: The Rand Corporation.
Mayo, S., Mansfield, S., Warner, D., and Zwetchkenbaum, R. (1979). *Housing Allowances and Other Rental Housing Assistance Programs, Part 2: Costs and Efficiency*. Cambridge, MA: Abt Associates.
Myers, P. (1982). *Aging in Place*. Washington, D.C.: The Conservation Foundation.
Newman, S., and Struyk, R. (1983). "Housing and Poverty." *Review of Economics and Statistics*, 50, 243-253.
Office of Management and Budget (1982). *Major Themes and Additional Details, Fiscal year 1983*. Washington, D.C.: U.S. Government Printing Office.
Palmer, J., and Sawhill, B. (1982). *The Reagan Experiment*. Washington, D.C.: The Urban Institute Press.
Stassen, M., and Holahan, J. (1980). *A Comparative Analysis of Long-Term Care Demonstrations and Evaluations* (draft). Washington, D.C.: The Urban Institute.
Struyk, R., and Bendick, M., Jr. (1981). *Housing Vouchers for the Poor*. Washington, D.C.: The Urban Institute Press.
Struyk, R., Mayer, N., and Tuccillo, J. (1983). *Housing Policy at President Reagan's Mid-Term*. Washington, D.C.: The Urban Institute Press.
Struyk, R., and Turner, M. (1984). "Changes in the Housing Situation of the Elderly: 1974-79." *Journal of Housing for the Elderly*, 2, 3-20.
U.S. Department of Housing and Urban Development (1982). *FY1983 Budget*. Washington, D.C.: U.S. Department of Housing and Urban Development.
Zais, J., Struyk, R., and Thibodeau, T. (1982). *Housing Assistance for Older Americans: The Reagan Prescription*. Washington, D.C.: The Urban Institute Press.

APPENDIX A

Major Programs of the Department of Housing and Urban Development (HUD) to Assist the Elderly and Federal Outlays Benefiting the Elderly: FY 1981-FY 1983

Major Programs of HUD

Rental Assistance Programs

Section 8 helps lower-income families afford housing by paying the difference between what they can afford and the fair market rent for an adequate unit. Based on a formula, the tenant pays a percentage of income for rent. Through mid-1983, 41 percent of the nearly two million units under this program were occupied by the elderly.

Section 202 provides direct, low-interest loans to sponsors to finance the construction or rehabilitation of residential projects and related facilities for the elderly and handicapped. Projects may be sponsored by private, nonprofit organizations or consumer co-operatives. At the end of Fiscal Year 1983, more than 2,600 projects with approximately 161,400 units had been built or had funds reserved. The residents of nearly all these units receive Section 8 rental assistance.

Recent legislation permits shared housing for the elderly in the HUD-assisted programs. Shared housing benefits include companionship, security, and reduced housing costs.

Public Housing programs received federal aid for housing for lower income families. Tenants pay rent based on the same formula used for Section 8. Public housing has always included the elderly as eligible residents. At the end of Fiscal year 1983, over 514,000 units of low-income public housing, or 43 percent of the total, were occupied by the elderly.

Congregate Housing Services Program Demonstration operates in 60 projects and serves over 2,200 residents. Through a grant from HUD, partially impaired elderly persons in selected public housing and Section 202 projects receive meals and supportive services. The effectiveness of this program is being evaluated with a report of evaluation findings due in December 1984.

Rental Housing (Unassisted)

Section 231 Mortgage Insurance for Elderly Housing is HUD's principal program designed solely for unsubsidized apartment rental housing for the elderly. HUD insures mortgage loans to nonprofit or profit motivated entities and public agencies for construction or rehabilitation of rental accommodations for older presons. At the end of Fiscal Year 1983, 513 projects with a total of 67,936 units, were insured.

Sections 221(d)(3) and (4) are mortgage insurance programs similar to Section 231. The major difference is that the projects are planned to be affordable to low and moderate income families, including the elderly. Special projects for the elderly may be insured under this program, and they may include special features such as congregate facilities. Of the nearly 1.2 million units insured through the end of Fiscal year 1983, 10 percent have elderly occupants.

A recently authorized Retirement Service Center Program uses 221(d)(4) mortgage insurance. Projects developed under this alternative will have apartment units with meals, services, and an amenities package. The facilities are designed to bridge the gap between totally independent living arrangements and the health-care-oriented nursing home. Residency will be limited to elderly occupants paying market rate rents.

Section 232 Mortgage Insurance for Nursing Homes/Intermediate Care Facilities insures mortgages for the construction and rehabilitation of long-term care facilities. A state agency must certify the need for a facility. Eligible residents are those needing skilled nursing care and related medical services or those needing minimum but continuous care by trained or licensed personnel. Through the end of 1983 the vast majority of the residents in the 1,435 facilities (offering 171,902 beds) were elderly.

Recently enacted legislation allows insurance of residential facilities called board and care homes under Section 232. These facilities will not have medical services but will have 24-hour staff for continuous protective oversight of residents.

Section 242 Mortgage Insurance for Hospitals finances construction or rehabilitation of nonprofit and proprietary hospitals. The housing authorization legislation of 1983 amended this section to include public facilities as well, and regulations are being developed to implement the amendment. Through the end of Fiscal Year 1983, 209 hospitals with 56,418 beds have been insured.

Mortgage Insurance

Manufactured home parks exclusively for the elderly may be insured by HUD under legislation enacted in 1983.

Retirement Villages designed exclusively for the elderly are eligible for HUD/FHA single-family mortgage insurance. Subdivisions and planned communities which restrict ownership to those above a certain age, and which restrict the occupancy and the duration of visits by children, can be insured by HUD.

Home Equity Conversion Mortgages for the elderly are to be evaluated. A HUD proposal for a home equity conversion mortgage demonstration was turned down, and under housing authorization legislation an evaluation is to be conducted of the existing use of such mortgages. These mortgages, also called reverse annuity mortgages, are designed to help elderly homeowners who wish to remain in their homes to convert some of their equity into income to meet increased living and housing expenses.

Community Planning and Development

Community Development Block Grant (CDBG) program funds must be used to help low and moderate income households, eliminate slums and blight, or meet other urgent community development needs. Examples of CDBG funded projects that address the needs and problems of the elderly are: senior citizen centers; housing rehabilitation; weatherization services to promote energy efficiently; neighborhood improvements; neighborhood facilities; and public and social services.

Urban Development Action Grants (UDAG) are competitive grant awards to cities and urban counties which meet standards of physical economic distress to assist economic development projects in their community. UDAG awards have helped communities develop downtown and suburban shopping areas, community centers, and other public facilities that have indirectly benefited the elderly. Specific use of UDAG for elderly include: geriatric centers; elderly apartments; and nursing homes.

Research. HUD conducts and supports research, studies, testing and demonstration projects, findings from which can improve housing conditions and related housing and community services for the elderly and other members of special groups. Current focus of these activities center on congregate housing, self-sufficient businesses, and a guide book on retirement housing.

Source: U.S. Department of Housing and Urban Development, Office of the Deputy Under Secretary for Intergovernmental Relations, January 1985. In addition to the source indicated, the information for this Appendix was taken from United States Conference of Mayors, *Assessing Elderly Housing. A Planning Guide for Mayors and Local Officials* (Washington, D.C.: United States Conference on Mayors, 1985), pp. 58 and 9.

Summary of HUD Elderly Housing Program Activities

Sections	Program	Status of Program	No. of Projects	Mortgages	Units	Elderly Units	% Elderly Units	Cum.
		Unassisted Programs						
231	Mortgage insurance of housing for elderly	Active	497	66,145	1,154,003,727	66,145	100.0	12/31/84
221(d)(3)	Multifamily rental housing for low- and moderate-income families	Active	3,611	364,733	6,064,514,303	26,373	7.2	
221(d)(4)		Active	6,809	737,750	19,594,056,632	104,378	14.1	
207	Multifamily rental housing	Active	1,893	244,127	3,645,471,074	3,879	1.6	
232	Nursing home and intermediate care facilities	Active	1,488	178,558	2,491,653,517	178,558	100.0	
		Assisted Programs						
Title II	Low-income housing	Active	14,994	1,469,008	N/A	384,948		6/30/84
202	Direct loans for housing of elderly and handicapped	Active	2,537	180,752	6,081,449,912	154,865	85.7	
235[2]	Homeownership assistance for low- and moderate-income families	Inactive[3]	N/A	473,033	8,456,660,790	66,224	14.0	
		Active	N/A	117,089	4,409,450,088	3,981	3.4	
236	Rental and Co-op assistance for low- and moderate-income families	Inactive	4,058	435,891	7,557,614,685	56,128	12.9	
202/236	202/236 conversion	Inactive	182	28,591	487,075,452	28,591	100.0	
8[4]	Low income rental assistance:							
	Existing	Active	17,163	1,226,880	3,454,920,013	342,186	27.9	
	New construction	Active	8,339	534,536	2,717,369,316	299,192	56.0	
	Substantial rehab	Active	1,663	122,612	768,341,253	46,273	37.7	
23	Low Rent Leased Housing	Inactive	N/A	163,267	N/A	54,000+	35.0	6/85

Figures obtained from Management Information Systems Division, Housing, Department of Housing and Urban Development, April, 1985.

[1] 235 figures are based on CY 1982 recertifications.
[2] Figures on inactive line are for original program; figures on active line are for revised program.
[3] Excludes 202/8 reservations.

Federal Outlays Benefiting the Elderly*: FY1981-FY1983

Program	FY 1981 (Actual)			FY 1982 (Estimate)			FY 1983 (Estimate)		
	$ (Millions)	Percent of Elderly Budget	Percent of Total Budget	$ (Millions)	Percent of Elderly Budget	Percent of Total Budget	$ (Millions)	Percent of Elderly Budget	Percent of Total Budget
Total†	173,345	100.0	26.4	195,150	100.0	26.9	209,585	100.0	22.7
OASDI (Social Security)	97,096	56.0	14.8	109,708	56.2	15.1	121,221	57.8	16.0
Medicare	35,752	20.6	5.4	41,833	21.4	5.8	46,916	22.4	6.2
Other Retired, Disabled and Survivors Benefits‡	22,847	13.2	3.5	24,562	12.6	3.4	22,197	10.6	2.9
Medicaid	5,967	3.4	0.9	6,345	3.3	0.9	6,365	3.0	0.8
Housing	3,562	2.1	0.5	4,087	2.1	0.6	4,293	2.1	0.6
Supplemental Security Income	2,598	1.5	0.4	2,654	1.4	0.4	3,069	1.5	0.4
Other Federal Health Care	2,229	1.3	0.3	2,516	1.3	0.4	2,741	1.3	0.4
Older Americans Act Programs	993	0.6	0.2	905	0.5	0.1	758	0.4	0.1
Food Stamps	906	0.5	0.1	899	0.5	0.1	660	0.3	0.1
Miscellaneous	701	0.4	0.1	829	0.4	0.1	751	0.3	0.1
Title XX Social Services§	595	0.3	0.1	647	0.3	0.1	445	0.2	0.1
ACTION	85	0.1	0.0	87	0.0	0.0	88	0.0	0.0
National Institute on Aging	70	0.0	0.0	76	0.0	0.0	81	0.0	0.0
White House Conference on Aging	4	0.0	0.0	2	0.0	0.0	0	0.0	0.0

*Reflects outlays, including effects of proposed legislation, for recipients aged 65 and over in most cases. These are estimates based on federal agency information—which may be administrative counts, samples, or less accurate estimates from federal, state and program staff. Other federal programs that assist the elderly (e.g., consumer activities, USDA extension services, National Park Services) have been excluded due to data limitations.
† Totals may not add due to rounding.
‡ Includes Veterans Compensation and Pensions.
§ Includes Energy Assistance.
Source: Office of Management and Budget, Health and Income Maintenance Division.

APPENDIX B

Pending Congressional Legislation: June 1985

HOUSE OF REPRESENTATIVES

Resolution 37
SPONSOR: Biaggi
DATE INTRODUCED: January 30, 1985
HOUSE COMMITTEE: Banking, Finance and Urban Affairs
OFFICIAL TITLE: A resolution expressing the opposition of the House of Representatives to efforts to reduce the availability of housing provided by the Section 202 assistance program for the elderly and handicapped.
CO-SPONSORS: 49 Current Co-Sponsors
BILL DIGEST: Expresses the opposition of the House of Representatives to efforts to reduce the availability of housing under the section 202 assistance program operated by the Department of Housing and Urban Development for the elderly and handicapped.

Bill H.R. 1
BRIEF TITLE: Housing Act of 1985
SPONSOR: Gonzalez
DATE INTRODUCED: January 3, 1985
HOUSE COMMITTEE: Banking, Finance and Urban Affairs
OFFICIAL TITLE: A bill to amend and extend certain laws relating to housing, and for other purposes.
BILL DIGEST: Housing Act of 1985 - Sets forth specified regulatory authority of the Secretary of Housing and Urban Development regarding the

Department of Housing and Urban Development and the Farmers Home Administration.

TITLE I: Housing Assistance - Amends the United States Housing Act of 1937 to increase on October 1, 1985, the aggregate amount of budget authority available for lower-income housing rental rehabilitation and development grants. Extends budget authority utilization provisions through FY 1986. Authorizes additional development grant appropriations for FY 1986.

Authorizes public housing agencies to determine (with the Secretary's approval) monthly rents (as an alternative to the existing schedule) based on specified factors. Excludes from the definition of "adjusted income" ten percent of a family's income if any member of such family pays either Federal self-employment or FICA taxes.

Requires Federal housing assistance contracts with public housing agencies to be for 15-year periods.

Repeals the provision prohibiting new rental unit construction unless such costs are less than comparative acquisition or rehabilitation costs.

Directs the Secretary within six months to: (1) issue regulations that establish a comprehensive improvement assistance program allocation and distribution system; and (2) report to the Congress regarding such program. Requires such information to be included in the Housing and Urban Development Act annual report.

Amends the Housing Act of 1959 to authorize budget authority through FY 1986 for housing for the elderly and the handicapped. Limits FY 1986 loan appropriations. Prohibits a housing sponsor from requiring mandatory meal participation as a condition for occupancy.

Amends the Housing and Urban-Rural Recovery Act of 1983 to extend the interest ceiling on loans for housing for the elderly and disabled through October 1, 1986.

Authorizes FY 1986 appropriations under the Congregate Housing Service Act of 1978.

Amends the National Housing Act to: (1) limit aggregate amounts for contracts entered into with the budget authority provided on October 1, 1985; and (2) extend assistance payments and housing stimulus authorities through FY 1986.

Amends the United States Housing Act of 1937 to direct the Secretary to use a performance funding system to allocate lower-income housing project payments. Sets forth system factors, including: (1) annual inflation adjustments; (2) operating cost sharing between the Department of Housing and Urban Development and public housing agencies; (3) public housing agency reimbursement for unexpected costs; and (4) treatment of excess revenues and vacant units. Authorizes FY 1986 appropriations. Requires assistance to be paid in monthly installments, beginning by the first month of the fiscal year. Repeals income elegibility provisions.

Establishes the Task Force on Family Housing Needs in Assisted Housing to examine: (1) the problems of families with children living in federally-assisted highrise buildings, or on housing waiting lists; and (2) the need for additional housing construction. Requires a report to the Congress and the Secretary within one year.

States that specified assisted housing shall be developed in accordance with energy conservation standards (to be developed by the Secretary) with regard to cost-effective construction and operating costs.

Amends the United States Housing Act of 1937 to direct the Secretary to prepare and submit to the Congress a comparative study of the impact of assistance under the rent subsidy and payment standard (voucher) programs.

Requires the Secretary to: (1) include in the Housing and Urban Development Act annual report descriptions of specified characteristics of families in assisted housing; (2) and submit to the Congress a public housing management and funding report.

TITLE II: Rural Housing - Amends the Housing Act of 1949 to authorize FY 1986 programs for: (1) elderly housing loan insurance; (2) mutual and self-help housing; and (3) specified rural housing loan insurance and guarantee authority.

Authorizes FY 1986 appropriations for: (1) rehabilitation grants and loans; (2) structural repairs under the Rural Housing Insurance Fund; (3) farm labor housing; (4) multi-family unit rental assistance; (5) mutual and self-help housing; (6) site loans; (7) housing preservation; (8) rural housing loan funds; (9) low-income housing assistance; and (10) low-income homeownership and rental or cooperative housing.

Requires the Secretary to issue rural housing preservation grant program implementing regulations within 90 days.

TITLE III: Program Amendments and Extensions - Part A: Federal Housing Administration Mortgage Insurance Programs - Amends the National Housing Act to authorize FY 1986 programs for: (1) Title I insurance; (2) general insurance; (3) low and moderate income housing insurance; (4) co-insurance; (5) graduated payment and indexed mortgage insurance; (6) armed services housing insurance; (7)

land development insurance; and (8) group practice facilities insurance.

Directs the Secretary to: (1) establish maximum interest rates for insured mortgages and obligations; and (2) prepare and submit to the Congress a study of voluntary standards for modular homes.

Part B: Flood and Crime Insurance Programs - Amends the National Flood Insurance Act of 1968 to extend flood insurance and emergency implementation of flood insurance program authority through FY 1986.

Amends the National Housing Act to extend crime and riot insurance program authority through FY 1986. Extends contract authority through FY 1987.

Part C: Secondary Mortgage Market Programs - Amends the Federal National Mortgage Association Charter Act to extend the Government national mortgage association mortgage-backed securities program through FY 1986.

Prohibits the imposition of fees on Federal National Mortgage Association and Federal Home Loan Mortgage Corporation transactions. Limits fees on Government National Mortgage Association transactions.

Part D: Regulatory and Other Programs - Amends the Housing and Community Development Act of 1974 to authorize FY 1986 appropriations for urban homesteading.

Amends the Housing Act of 1964 to extend rehabilitation loan authority through FY 1986.

Amends the Neighborhood Reinvestment Corporation Act to authorize FY 1986 appropriations.

Amends the Solar Energy and Energy Conservation Bank Act to authorize FY 1986 appropriations.

Amends the Housing and Urban Development Act of 1968 to authorize FY 1986 counseling appropriations.

Amends the Home Mortgage Disclosure Act of 1975 to repeal the October 1, 1985, termination of authority date.

Amends the Energy Conservation in Existing Buildings Act of 1976 to authorize FY 1986 weatherization program appropriations.

Amends the Housing and Urban Development of 1970 to authorize FY 1986 research appropriations.

Authorizes FY 1986 appropriations for the neighborhood development demonstration program.

TITLE IV: Shelter Assistance for the Homeless and Displaced - Part A: Emergency Shelter Program - Authorizes FY 1986 emergency shelter program appropriations.

Part B: Second Stage Housing for the Homeless and Displaced - Directs the Secretary to: (1) carry out a demonstration program to determine the effectiveness of assisting nonprofit organizations in providing housing and supportive services for homeless persons; and (2) submit to the Congress an interim and a final report. Sets forth program requirements and FY 1986 budget authority.

TITLE V: Nehemiah Housing Opportunity Grants - Authorizes the Secretary to provide grants to nonprofit organizations to carry out a Nehemiah housing opportunity program to provide loans to families purchasing approved constructed or rehabilitated homes. Requires an annual report to the Congress.

Requires that each loan: (1) be secured by a second mortgage held by the Secretary; (2) not exceed $15,000; (3) be interest-free; and (4) be repayable to the Secretary upon the transfer of such property to an ineligible family under specified circumstances. Sets forth related program requirements, conditions of assistance, and selection criteria.

Establishes in the Treasury the Nehemiah Housing Opportunity Fund. Authorizes FY 1986 appropriations.

Bill H.R.167

BRIEF TITLE: National Home Health Clearinghouse Act of 1985
SPONSOR: Roe
DATE INTRODUCED: January 3, 1985
HOUSE COMMITTEE: Energy and Commerce
OFFICIAL TITLE: A bill to establish within the Department of Health and Human Services a Home Health Clearinghouse to provide elderly persons with a single place where they can obtain complete information on the Federal home health programs available to them.
BILL DIGEST: National Home Health Clearinghouse Act of 1985 - Establishes in the Department of Health and Human Services a Home Health Clearinghouse to gather and disseminate information concerning the various public and private agencies providing home health care and related services to the elderly. Directs the Clearinghouse to: (1) establish a computerized system for such purposes; and (2) publish current descriptions of Federal Services and benefits available to the elderly under the Social Security Act, the Older Americans Act of 1965, and other related laws.

Requires a cost report to Congress within one year. Authorizes appropriations.

Bill H.R.406

SPONSOR: Quillen
DATE INTRODUCED: January 3, 1985
HOUSE COMMITTEE: Ways and Means
OFFICIAL TITLE: A bill to amend the Internal Revenue Code of 1954 to provide a refundable tax credit for taxpayers who maintain households which include elderly persons who are determined by a physician to be disabled.
BILL DIGEST: Amends the Internal Revenue Code to allow a refundable income tax credit to any individual who maintains a household which includes one or more elderly qualified persons. Sets the amount of such credit at $1,000 for each such elderly person living in the household. Limits the aggregate amount creditable to $2,000 on any return for the taxable year.

Defines "qualified elderly person" as any individual who: (1) has attained age 65; (2) has an impairment which, as determined by a physician, renders such individual physically or mentally incapable of caring for himself and has lasted or is expected to last six months or longer; and (3) has as a principal place of abode for more than half of the taxable year the home of the taxpayer.

Bill H.R.505

BRIEF TITLE: Older Veterans' Health Care Amendments of 1985
SPONSOR: Edgar
DATE INTRODUCED: January 7, 1985
HOUSE COMMITTEE: Veterans' Affairs
OFFICIAL TITLE: A bill to amend title 38, United States Code, to improve the delivery of health care services by the Veterans' Administration.
CO-SPONSORS: 39 Current Co-Sponsors
BILL DIGEST: Older Veterans' Health Care Amendments of 1985 - Amends Federal law concerning veterans' medical care to define "respite care" for purposes of included coverage. Eliminates the requirement of the presence of a service-connected disability for purposes of eligibility for domiciliary care. Increases eligibility for outpatient and ambulatory services to include those veterans who have received nursing home care or domiciliary care. Makes similar changes to increase eligibility for transfers for nursing home care. Authorizes the Administrator of Veterans Affairs to provide direct admission to a veteran for treatment at an institution not under the jurisdiction of the Administrator if: (1) the veteran has been discharged from a Veterans Administration (VA) hospital; and (2) the veteran is currently receiving home health services under a VA hospital-based home care program.

Increase the number of VA centers of geriatric reasearch, education, and clinical centers from 15 to 25.

Bill H.R.644
SPONSOR: Conte
DATE INTRODUCED: January 24, 1985
HOUSE COMMITTEE: Ways and Means
OFFICIAL TITLE: A bill to amend the Internal Revenue Code of 1954 to allow a credit against income tax for expenses incurred in the care of certain elderly family members.
CO-SPONSORS: 38 Current Co-Sponsors
BILL DIGEST: Amends the Internal Revenue Code to allow a refundable income tax credit for expenses incurred in the care of elderly family members. Sets such credit at 30 percent of the expenses incurred for taxpayers with incomes of $25,000 or less. Reduces the rate of such credit, but not below 20 percent, by one percent for each $2,000 of taxpayer income in excess of $25,000.

Limits such credit to taxpayers with an adjusted gross income of less than $75,000. Imposes a maximum $10,000 limit on the amount of elderly care expenses that can be taken into account.

Defines "qualified family member" as any individual who: (1) is related to the taxpayer by blood or marriage; (2) is at least 70 years of age, is diagnosed with senile dementia of the Alzheimer type, or is disabled; and (3) has a family income of $15,000 or less.

Defines "qualified elderly care expenses" as payments for: (1) home health agency services; (2) homemaker services; (3) adult day care; (4) respite care; or (5) certain health care equipment and supplies.

Bill H.R.1192
BRIEF TITLE: Older Americans Alternative Care Act of 1985
SPONSOR: Panetta
DATE INTRODUCED: February 21, 1985
HOUSE COMMITTEE: Education and Labor. Energy and Commerce. Ways and Means
OFFICIAL TITLE: A bill to amend TitleXVIII of the Social Security Act to remove the homebound requirement for home health services and to include additional types of services as home health services, to amend the Domestic Volunteer Service Act of 1973 to clarify the purposes, goals, and administration of the senior companion program, and to amend the Internal Revenue Code of 1954 to establish an income tax credit for maintaining a household for dependents who are sixty-five years of age or older.

BILL DIGEST: Older Americans Alternative Care Act of 1985 - TITLE I: Medicare Amendments - Amends Title XVIII (Medicare) of the Social Security Act to remove the homebound requirement for home health services. Includes periodic chore and respite care services as home health services. Permits home health services to be provided in an adult day care center.

TITLE II: Senior Companions Program - Amends the Domestic Volunteer Service Act to authorize the Director of the Action Agency to make grants or contracts under the National Older Americans Volunteer Program to establish senior companion programs. Authorizes appropriations for FY 1985 for such programs.

TITLE III: Income Tax Credit for Maintaining Households Which Include Dependents Who Have Attained Age 65 - Amends the Internal Revenue Code to authorize an income tax credit for an individual who maintains in his or her home a household for a dependent over age 65.

Bill H.R.1774

BRIEF TITLE: Housing for the Handicapped Act of 1985
SPONSOR: McKinney
DATE INTRODUCED: March 27, 1985
HOUSE COMMITTEE: Banking, Finance and Urban Affairs
OFFICIAL TITLE: A bill to amend section 202 of the Housing Act of 1959 to ensure that the direct loan program under such section meets the special housing and related needs of nonelderly handicapped families.
BILL DIGEST: Housing for the Handicapped Act of 1985 - Amends the Housing Act of 1959 to require that at least 15 percent of loan funds appropriated under the housing for the elderly and the handicapped (Section 202) program be available for housing for (primarily nonelderly) handicapped families.

Limits rental subsidies to: (1) 90 percent of the initial rental (and utility) costs; and (2) 20 years. Requires participating families to pay a rent contribution of at least 25 percent, with any such amount requiring approval by the Secretary of Housing and Urban Development.

Exempts such housing projects from specified prevailing wage requirements.

Requires loan applicants to submit a service benefit plan describing support services for elderly and handicapped families.

Bill H.R.2292
BRIEF TITLE: Home Equity Conversion Mortgage Insurance Act
SPONSOR: Wortley
DATE INTRODUCED: April 30, 1985
HOUSE COMMITTEE: Banking, Finance and Urban Affairs
OFFICIAL TITLE: A bill to amend the National Housing Act to authorize the Secretary of Housing and Urban Development to carry out a demonstration program of insurance of home equity conversion mortgages for elderly homeowners.
BILL DIGEST: Home Equity Conversion Mortgage Insurance Act - Amends the National Housing Act to authorize the Secretary of Housing and Urban Development to insure a home equity conversion mortgage and to make commitments for the insurance of such mortgages prior to the date of their execution or disbursement if such mortgages: (1) may improve the financial situation or otherwise meet the needs of elderly homeowners; (2) can be developed to include safeguards for mortgagors to offset the special risks of such mortgages; and (3) have a potential for acceptance in the private market.

Includes among eligibility requirements for such insurance requirements that the mortgage shall: (1) have been made and held by a mortgage approved by the Secretary; (2) have been executed by an elderly homeowner; and (3) be secured by a one-family residential dwelling occupied by the mortgagor.

Provides that each mortgagee of a mortgage insured under this Act shall be required to give the homeowner, at the time of a loan application, a written explanation of the features of the home equity conversion mortgage.

Prohibits the Secretary from insuring a mortgage pursuant to this Act after September 30, 1988. Sets the total number of mortgages which may be insured under this Act at 1,000.

Permits the Secretary to take any action necessary to provide a mortgagor with funds due pursuant to an insured mortgage or ancillary contract which have not been paid by the party responsible and to obtain reimbursement of such payments for any source.

Requires the Secretary to evaluate and report to Congress by March 1, 1988, on the program authorized under this Act.

U.S. SENATE

Bill S.752
BRIEF TITLE: National Home Health Care Clearinghouse Act of 1985
SPONSOR: D'Amato

DATE INTRODUCED: March 26, 1985
SENATE COMMITTEE: Labor and Human Resources
OFFICIAL TITLE: A bill to establish in the Department of Health and Human Services a Home Health Care Clearinghouse to provide elderly individuals with a single place where they can obtain complete information on available Federal home health care programs.
CO-SPONSORS: 3 Current Co-sponsors
BILL DIGEST: National Home Health Care Clearinghouse Act of 1985 - Establishes in the Department of Health and Human Services a Home Health Care Clearinghouse to gather and disseminate information concerning the various public and private agencies providing home health care and related services to the elderly. Directs the Clearinghouse to: (1) establish a computerized system for such purposes; and (2) publish current descriptions of home health care services and benefits available to the elderly under the Social Security Act, the Older Americans Act of 1965, and other related laws.

Requires a cost report to Congress within one year.

Authorizes appropriations.

Bill S.779

BRIEF TITLE: Family Care Act of 1985
SPONSOR: Heinz
DATE INTRODUCED: March 28, 1985
SENATE COMMITTEE: Finance
OFFICIAL TITLE: A bill to amend the Internal Revenue Code of 1954 to allow a credit against tax for expenses incurred in the care of elderly family members.
CO-SPONSORS: 2 Current co-sponsors
BILL DIGEST: Family Care Act of 1985 - Amends the Internal Revenue Code to allow a refundable income tax credit for expenses incurred for qualified elderly care expenses for a qualifying family member.

Allows an income tax credit of 30 percent of the expenses incurred for taxpayers with incomes of $10,000 or less. Reduces the rate of such credit, but not below 20 percent, by one percent for each $2,000 of taxpayer income in excess of $10,000.

Limits such credit to taxpayers with an adjusted gross income of less than $50,000. Imposes a maximum $7,000 limit on the amount of elderly care expenses taken into account.

Defines "qualified family member" as any individual who: (1) is related to the taxpayer by blood or marriage; (2) is at least 75 years of age (or diagnosed with senile dementia of the Alzheimer type); and (3) has a family income of $15,000 or less.

Defines "qualified elderly care expenses" as payments for: (1) home health agency services; (2) homemaker services; (3) adult day care; (4) respite care; or (5) certain health care equipment and supplies.

Bill S.1007

BRIEF TITLE: Veterans Health Care Promotion Act of 1985
SPONSOR: Boschwitz
DATE INTRODUCED: April 25, 1985
SENATE COMMITTEE: Veteran's Affairs
OFFICIAL TITLE: A bill to amend Title 38, United States Code, to direct the Administrator of Veterans Affairs to develop and carry out a pilot program to determine the most cost effective methods of acquiring medical facilities to meet the needs of the Veterans' Administration and otherwise to promote additional health care for eligible veterans, and for other purposes.
CO-SPONSORS: 3 Current Co-sponsors
BILL DIGEST: Veterans' Health Care Promotion Act of 1985 - Directs the Administrator of Veterans Affairs to carry out a pilot program to determine the most cost-effective method of acquiring medical facilities for the Veterans Administration (VA) using certain specified methods. Requires the Administrator, not later than January 1, 1987, to enter into contracts to carry out the pilot program. Requires such contracts to be with an appropriate entity to construct and operate a nursing home for the VA.

Requires the Administrator to enter into a contract with an appropriate entity to plan for, design, and construct a medical facility for the VA and to lease or sell such facility to the VA as directed by the administrator. Directs the Administrator to also acquire two existing medical facilities.

Requires the Administrator to provide the Committees on Veterans' Affairs of the Senate and the House of Representatives an annual report on the administration of the pilot program and a final report promptly after the termination of such program.

Requires the administrator, within 90 days after enactment of this Act, to report to the same such Committees on: (1) the extent to which the VA furnishes respite care to elderly veterans and disabled veterans; (2) the VA's plans for furnishing such care in the future; and (3) an estimate of the cost of increasing community-based nursing home beds available to the VA by specified percentages.

Limits the amount of working reserve funds available to the VA for FY 1986 for the purchase of an urban medical facility.

Directs the President to include in the budget submitted to the Congress a statement of the estimated expenditures and appropriations required to carry out the pilot program.

Bill S.1074

BRIEF TITLE: Immigrant Repatriation Study Act
SPONSOR: Matsunaga
DATE INTRODUCED: May 6, 1985
SENATE COMMITTEE: Judiciary
OFFICIAL TITLE: A bill to direct the Attorney General to study the problems of indigent, elderly immigrants who wish to return to their home countries but cannot afford to pay the transportation costs to do so.
BILL DIGEST: Immigrant Repatriation Study Act - Directs the Attorney General to study the problem of indigent, elderly immigrants who wish to return to their home countries but cannot afford the transportation costs to do so.

Requires a report to the Congress within 12 months.

Bill S.1181

BRIEF TITLE: Home and Community-Based Services for the Elderly Act of 1985
SPONSOR: Hatch
DATE INTRODUCED: May 21, 1985
SENATE COMMITTEE: Labor and Human Resources
OFFICIAL TITLE: A bill to establish a program for the provision of home and community-based services to elderly individuals.
CO-SPONSORS: 14 Current Co-sponsors
BILL DIGEST: Home and Community Based Services for the Elderly Act of 1985 - Amends Title XIX (block grants) of the Public Health Service Act to authorize a block grant program for home and community based services for the elderly. Authorizes appropriations for FY 1986 through 1988.

Allots state funding based on a state's elderly population as compared with the elderly population of the United States. Makes Indian tribes and tribal organizations eligible grant recipients.

States that grants may be used to: (1) identify elderly individuals who are eligible for services; (2) plan and manage services to be provided; (3) educate the public and medical and social professionals concerning the availability of services; (4) encourage the participation of families and voluntary organizations; (5) train personnel; and (6) coordinate long-term care services.

Permits states to provide services for the elderly through grants to eligible organizations.

Prohibits the use of funds for: (1) inpatient services; (2) cash payments to intended recipients; (3) land purchase or construction; (4) purchases of major medical equipment; or (5) satisfying any requirement for the expenditure of non-federal funds.

Sets forth state application provisions.

Bibliography

The literature concerning elderly housing is extensive, and for this reason the scope of the bibliography has been selective. The citations, all published between 1980 and late 1985, pertain to the United States generally; very few focus on one particular city or state. Most of the publications concern housing options of the elderly (congregate housing, house sharing, retirement villages, etc.), but several areas closely associated with housing are represented—demographic characteristics of the elderly, financing of elderly housing, health and housing selection, housing and the delivery of services, federal housing policies and demonstration projects, effects of relocation on the elderly, etc. Literature about nursing homes and board and care facilities, however, is limited because the focus is primarily on housing which permits the elderly to live independently or semi-independently.

There are six parts to this bibliography: (I) books and monographs; (II) articles in books and journals; (III) congressional hearings and papers; (IV) conference and symposium papers; (V) dissertations and theses; and (VI) organizations. These parts vary in the extent of coverage; books, monographs, articles, and congressional hearings generally are more inclusive than are conference and symposium papers and dissertations and theses.

I. Books and Monographs

Action for Boston Community Development, Inc. *Planning and Developing a Shared Living Project: A Guide for Community Groups.* Boston, Massachusetts: Action for Boston Community Development, Inc., 1980.

Altman, Irwin, and Wohlwill, Joachin F. *Elderly People and the Environment.* Vol. 7 in *Human Behavior & Environment.* New York: Plenum Publishing, 1984.

American Bar Association. *Board and Care Report: An Analysis of State Laws and Programs Serving Elderly Persons and Disabled Adults.* Springfield, Virginia: National Technical Information Service, 1983.

Anton, Tom, and Dluhy, Milan. *Housing Policies and Programs for the Elderly*. Ann Arbor, Michigan: National Policy Center on Housing and Living Arrangements for older Americans, 1981.

Arnold, Gail. *Housing of the Rural Elderly*. Springfield, Virginia: National Technical Information Service, 1984.

Baxter, Raymond J., Applebaum, Robert, Calahan, James J., Christianson, Jon B., and Day, Stephen L. *Planning and Implementation of Channeling: Early Experiences of the National Long-Term Care Demonstration*. Springfield, Virginia: National Technical Information Service, 1983.

Beall, G. T., Thompson, M. M., Godwin, F., and Donahue, W. T. *Housing Older Persons in Rural America: A Handbook on Congregate Housing*. Springfield, Virginia: National Technical Information Service, 1981.

Browne, William P., and Olson, Laura Katz, eds. *Aging and Public Policy: The Politics of Growing Old in America*. Westport, Connecticut: Greenwood Press, 1983.

Burke, Paul. *Equality in Subsidized Housing*. Washington, D.C.: U.S. Department of Housing and Urban Development, Division of Housing and Demographic Analysis, 1981.

Carlin, Vivian F., and Mansberg, Ruth. *If I Life to Be 100—Congregate Housing for Later Life*. West Nyack, New York: Parker Publishing Company, 1983.

Carstens, Diane Y. *Site Planning and Design for the Elderly: Issues, Guidelines, and Alternatives*. New York: Van Nostrand Reinhold Company, 1985.

Chellis, Robert D., Seagle, James F. and Seagle, Barbara Mackey. *Congregate Housing for Older People: A Solution for the 1980s*. Lexington, Massachusetts: D.C. Heath, 1982.

Combs, J. Paul, Courbois, Jean-Pierre, Ellis, Larry, Narof, Joel, and Liro, Joseph. *Evaluation of the Section 8 Existing Housing Program in Rural Areas*. Springfield, Virginia: National Technical Information Service, 1982.

Cox, Harold. *Later Life: The Realities of Aging*. Englewood Cliffs, New Jersey: Prentice-Hall, 1984.

Diamond, R. C. *Energy and Housing for the Elderly: Preliminary Observations*. Berkeley, California: University of California, Lawrence-Berkeley Laboratory, 1983.

Directory of Federal Aid for the Aging: A Guide to Federal Assistance Programs Serving the Aged. Washington, D.C.: U.S. Government Printing Office, 1982.

Eckert, J. Kevin. *The Unseen Elderly: A Study of Marginally Subsistent Hotel Dwellers*. San Diego, California: Campanile Press, 1980.

Edelstein, J. and Timmons, R. *Use of Productive Resources: Pension Funds, Building Industry, Existing Housing.* Springfield, Virginia: National Technical Information Service, 1982.

Ferguson, Gary D., and Holin, Mary Joel. *Establishing a Home Maintenance Program for Elderly Homeowners: A Guidebook.* Springfield, Virginia: National Technical Information Service, 1983.

Ferguson, Gary D., Holin, Mary Joel, and Moss, William G. *Evaluation of the Seven City Home Maintenance Demonstration for the Elderly.* 2 vols. Springfield, Virginia: National Technical Information Service, 1982.

Gill, Deford. *Strategies for Meeting the Housing Needs of Older Americans: Public Policy Options Other Than Direct Service Delivery.* Washington, D.C.: National Senior Citizen Law Center, 1982.

Golant, Stephen. *A Place to Grow Old: The Meaning of Environment in Old Age.* New York: Columbia University Press, 1984.

Goode, C., Lawton, M. P., and Hoover, S. L. *Elderly Hotel and Rooming House Dwellers: The Population and Its Housing.* Philadelphia, Pennsylvania: Philadelphia Geriatric Center, 1980.

Gutowski, Michael, and Kimmich, Madeleine. *Shades of Gray: A Portrait of the Elderly in Five Metropolitan Areas.* Washington, D.C.: Urban Institute, 1981.

Hancock, Judith Ann, and Duensing, Edward. *Capital Gains Tax Exclusion for the Older Homeowner: A Bibliography.* Monticello, Illinois: Vance Bibliographies, June 1986.

_____. *Home Equity Conversions: Capital Liquidity for the Older Homeowner.* Monticello, Illinois: Vance Bibliographies, August 1986.

_____. *Housing the Elderly: Options and Policies.* Monticello, Illinois: Vance Bibliographies, April 1986.

Handler, Philip. *Housing Needs of the Elderly: A Quantitative Analysis.* Springfield, Virginia: National Technical Information Service, 1982.

Hare, Patrick H. *Accessory Apartments: Surplus Space in Single Family Homes.* American Planning Association, Planning Advisory Service Report No. 365. Chicago, Illinois: American Planning Association, 1981.

Hare, Patrick H., and Hollis, Linda E. *ECHO Housing: A Review of Zoning Issues and Other Considerations.* Washington, D.C.: American Association of Retired Persons, 1983.

Harkey, P. W., and Traxler, G. H. *Share-A-Home: A Unique Community-Based Residential Alternative for the Dependent Elderly—Economics and Logistics of Unrelated Elderly Living as a "Family".* Springfield, Virginia: National Technical Information Service, 1983.

Heumann, Leonard F. *The Elderly as Consumers of Subsidized Housing.* Urbana, Illinois: University of Illinois, Urbana-Champaign, Housing Research and Development, 1983.

Heumann, Leonard F., and Boldy, D. *Housing for the Elderly: Planning and Policy Formulation in Western Europe and North America.* New York: St. Martin's Press, 1982.

Hodges, S. J., and Goldman, E. G. *Allowing Accessory Apartments: Key Issues for Local Officials.* Springfield, Virginia: National Technical Information Service, 1983.

Houston, L. E. *Congregate Housing Demonstration Project for the Elderly.* Springfield, Virginia: National Technical Information Service, 1984.

Howell, S. C. *Designing for Aging.* Cambridge, Massachusetts: MIT Press, 1980.

Hunt, Michael E., et al., eds. *Retirement Communities: An American Original.* New York: Haworth Press, 1984.

Irwin, R. *The $125,000 Decision.* New York: McGraw-Hill, 1982.

Kennedy, Stephen D., and Wallace, James E. *Evaluation of Success Rates in Housing Assistance Programs Using the Existing Stock: Implications for the Housing Payment Certificate Program from the Section 8 Existing Housing Program.* Springfield, Virginia: National Technical Information Service, 1983.

Koncelik, Joseph A. *Aging and the Product Environment.* New York: Van Nostrand Reinhold, 1982.

Lawton, M. Powell. *Environment and Aging.* Monterey, California: Brooks/Cole Publishing Co., 1980.

———. *Social and Medical Services in Housing for the Aged.* Rockville, Maryland: Department of Health and Human Services, Public Health Service, Alcohol, Drug Abuse, and Mental Health Administration, 1980.

Lawton, M. Powell, and Hoover, Sally L. *Community Housing Choices for Older Americans.* New York: Springer Publishing Co., 1981.

Lazarus, Steven S., Edgerton, Peter W., Balicki, Brian J., and Deshaies, Kenneth J. *Cost of Alternative Care Study (Final Report).* Springfield, Virginia: National Technical Information Service, 1980.

Lidoff, Lorraine, and Theilheimer, Lucy. *Matched Housing Program Development Model.* Washington, D.C.: National Council on the Aging, 1983.

Liebman, J. *Congregate Housing Resource Manual.* Springfield, Virginia: National Technical Information Service, 1982.

Lowry, Ira S. *Managing the Existing Housing Stock: Prospects and Problems.* Santa Monica, California: RAND Corporation, 1982.

Lutz, Brian, and Rzeczkowski, Susan. *Housing and Living Arrangements for Older Americans: A Review of Policy Relevant Research.* Ann Arbor,

Michigan: National Policy Center on Housing and Living Arrangements for Older Americans, 1981.

Lyttle, Dorrett E. *Research Prospectus: Alternatives to Long-Term Institutional Care.* Springfield, Virginia: National Technical Information Service, 1980.

Mayer, Neil S., and Lee, Olson. *The Effectiveness of Federal Home Repair and Improvement Programs in Meeting Elderly Homeowner Needs.* Washington, D.C: Urban Institute, 1980.

McCarthy, Kevin F. *The Elder Population's Changing Spatial Distribution: Patterns of Change Since 1960.* Santa Monica, California: RAND Corporation, 1983.

McCarthy, Kevin F., Abrahams, A. F., and Huban, C. A., Jr. *The Changing Geographic Distribution of the Elderly: Estimating Net Migration Rates with Social Security Data.* Santa Monica, California: RAND Corporation, 1982.

McConnell, S. R., and Usher, C. E. *Intergenerational House Sharing.* Los Angeles, California: University of California, Andrus Gerontology Center, 1980.

Mollica, R. *Congregate Housing for Older People: An Effective Alternative. An Assessment of Its Cost Effectiveness.* Springfield, Virginia: National Technical Information Service, 1984.

_____. *Congregate Housing for Older People: An Effective Alternative. Final Report.* Springfield, Virginia: National Technical Information Service, 1984.

Mor, Vincent, and Sherwood, Sylvia. *Report of Administrative Structure of Domiciliary Care Programs Serving the Elderly in Six States.* Springfield, Virginia: National Technical Information Service, 1981.

Myers, Phyllis. *Aging in Place: Strategies to Help the Elderly Stay in Revitalizing Neighborhoods.* Washington, D.C.: Conservation Foundation, 1982.

Nathanson, Iric. *Housing Needs of the Rural Elderly and Handicapped.* Washington, D.C.: U.S. Department of Housing and Urban Development, Office of Policy Development and Research, 1980.

National Center for Housing Management. *Toward an Improved Quality of Living for Older Americans.* Springfield, Virginia: National Technical Information Service, 1983.

National Policy Center on Housing and Living Arrangements for Older Americans. *Policy Measures for Increasing the Supply of Elderly Housing: Incentives for Private Industry.* Springfield, Virginia: National Technical Information Service, 1982.

National Retired Teachers Association. *Energy Equity and the Elderly: Report from a Mini-Conference of the 1981a White House Conference on Aging.*

Springfield, Virginia: National Technical Information Service, 1980.
National Shared Housing Resource Center, Inc. *National Directory of Shared Housing Programs for Older People.* Philadelphia, Pennsylvania: National Shared Housing Resource Center, Inc., 1983.
Newman, Sandra, and Reschovsky, James. *Federal Policy and the Mobility of Older Homeowners: The Effects of the One-Time Capital Gains Exclusion.* Ann Arbor, Michigan: University of Michigan, Institute for Social Research, 1985.
Parker, Rosetta E. *Housing for the Elderly: The Handbook for Managers.* Chicago, Illinois: Institute of Real Estate Management, 1984.
Pitkin, John, and Masnick, George. *Housing of Young Adults and the Elderly: An Analysis of 1960 to 1975 Changes.* Springfield, Virginia: National Technical Information Service, 1981.
Rabizadeh, Masoud. *Housing the Elderly.* Eugene, Oregon: University of Oregon Books, 1981.
Rabushka, Alvin. *Old Folks at Home.* New York: Free Press, 1980.
Raschko, Bettyann B. *Housing Interiors for the Disabled and Elderly.* New York: Van Nostrand Reinhold, 1982.
Rausch, K. J., and Hoover, S. L. *Mobile Home Elderly: Structural Characteristics of Their Dwellings.* Philadelphia, Pennsylvania: Philadelphia Geriatric Center, 1980.
Reiger, A. J., and Engel, D. *Granny Flats: An Assessment of Economic and Land Use Issues.* Washington, D.C.: U.S. Department of Housing and Urban Development, Division of Building Technology, 1983.
Riley, P., Provus, S., Kandoian, E., Seibel, R., and Duson, J. *Development Models and Public Education in Home Equity Conversion for a Rural State.* Springfield, Virginia: National Technical Information Service, 1984.
Rose, Edgar A. *Housing Needs and the Elderly.* New York: Gower Publishing Company, 1982.
Rubin, Eleanor S. *Options for Living Arrangements: Housing Alternatives for the Elderly.* New York: National Council of Jewish Women, 1980.
Sager, Alan. *Some Opportunities and Methods for Promoting More Adequate, Decent, and Equitable Long-Term Care for the Elderly.* Springfield, Virginia: National Technical Information Service, 1982.
Scholen, Ken, and Chen, Yung-Ping, eds. *Unlocking Home Equity for the Elderly.* Cambridge, Massachusetts: Ballinger Publishing Co., 1980.
Sherwood, Sylvaia, Mor, Vincent, and Gutkin, Claire E. *Domiciliary Care Clients and the Facilities in Which They Reside.* Springfield, Virginia: National Information Technical Service, 1981.
Shifman, Carole R. *Increasing Housing Opportunities for the Elderly.* American Planning Association, Planning Advisory Service Report 381. Chicago, Illinois: American Planning Association, 1983.

Solomon, Carmen D. *Board and Care Homes and the Keys Amendment.* Springfield, Virginia: National Technical information Service, 1982.
Spivack, Mayer. *Institutional Settings: An Environmental Design Approach.* New York: Human Sciences Press, Inc., 1984.
Stephens, Joyce. *Loners, Losers, and Lovers: Elderly Tenants in a Slum Hotel.* Seattle, Washington: University of Washington Press, 1980.
Streib, Gordon F. *Old Homes, New Families: Innovative Living Arrangements for Older Persons.* New York: Columbia University Press, 1984.
Streib, Gordon F., and Folts, William E. *Shared Living Arrangements for the Elderly: An Evaluation (Final Report).* Springfield, Virginia: National Technical Information Service, 1981.
Struyk, Raymond, and Soldo, Beth. *Improving the Elderly's Housing: A Key to Preserving the Nation's Housing Stock and Neighborhoods.* Cambridge, Massachusetts: Ballinger Publishing Co., 1980.
Sumichrast, Michael, Shafer, Ronald, and Sumichrast, Marika. *Planning Your Retirement Housing.* Washington, D.C.: American Association of Retired Persons, 1984.
Taylor, Paul S. *Long-Range Research Agenda for Elderly Housing and Related Services.* Springfield, Virginia: National Technical Information Service, 1981.
Taylor, Paul S., Sclar, Elliott D., and Soldo, Beth J. *Research on Housing and Related Services for the Elderly: An Annotated Bibliography.* Washington, D.C.: Gerontological Society of American, 1981.
Thompson, Marie M., and Donahue, Wilma T. *Planning and Implementing Management of Congregate Housing for Older Adults.* Washington, D.C.: International Center for Social Gerontology, 1980.
Turner, Lloyd, and Mangum, Eglute. *Housing Choices for Older Americans: Summary of Survey Findings and Recommendations for Practitioners.* Washington, D.C.: National Council on the Aging, 1982.
Turner, Lloyd, Schreter, Carol, Zetick, Bonnie, Weisbrod, Glen, and Pollakowski, Henry. *Housing Options for the Community Resident Elderly: Policy Report of the Housing Choices of Older Americans Study.* Springfield, Virginia: National Technical Information Service, 1982.
Turner, Lloyd, Walz, Thomas, Pressler, Martha, and McArdle, Thomas. *Review of Policies Affecting the Housing Decisions of Older Americans.* Springfield, Virginia: National Technical Information Service, 1981.
Turner, M. A. *Building Housing for the Low-Income Elderly: Cost Containment and Modest Design in the Section 202 Program.* Springfield, Virginia: National Technical Information Service, 1984.
United States Conference of Mayors. *Assessing Elderly Housing: A Planning Guide for Mayors and Local Officials.* Washington, D.C.: U.S. Conference of Mayors, 1985.

United States, Department of Health and Human Services. *Board and Care Homes: A Study of Federal and State Actions to Safeguard the Health and Safety of Board and Care Home Residents.* Springfield, Virginia: National Technical Information Service, 1982.

United States, Department of Housing and Urban Development. *Alternative Housing Arrangements: A Selected Information Guide.* Washington, D.C.: U.S. Department of Housing and Urban Development, Office of Policy Development and Research, 1985.

———. *Conversion of Rental Housing to Condominiums and Cooperatives: Impacts on Elderly and Lower Income Households.* Washington, D.C.: U.S. Department of Housing and Urban Development, Office of Policy Development and Research, 1981.

———. *Evaluation of Leasing Practices in the Section 8 Existing Program.* Washington, D.C.: U.S. Department of Housing and Urban Development, Office of Policy Development and Research, 1982.

———. *Housing Needs of the Rural Elderly and Handicapped.* Washington, D.C.: U.S. Department of Housing and Urban Development, Office of Policy Development and Research, 1980.

———. *Report to the Congress: Social Security Benefits and Assisted Housing Rent Charges.* Washington, D.C.: U.S. Department of Housing and Urban Development, Division of Policy Development, 1981.

———. *Summary of Innovative Concepts Resulting from the Rural Assistance Initiative.* Washington, D.C.: U.S. Department of Housing and Urban Development, Office of Policy Development and Research, 1982.

United States, Department of Housing and Urban Development, and Atlanta Consortium for Urban Research and Evaluation. *Section 202: Housing for the Elderly and Handicapped.* Washington, D.C.: U.S. Office of Housing and Urban Development, Office of Program Planning and Evaluation, 1980.

United States, General Accounting Office. *How to House More People at Lower Costs Under the Section 8 New Construction Program.* 1 vol. plus Supplement. Springfield, Virginia: National Technical Information Service, 1981.

Urban Institute and Conservation Foundation, Inc. *Elderly and Urban Housing.* Washington, D.C.: Urban Institute, 1983.

Urban Land Institute. *Housing for a Maturing Population.* Washington, D.C.: Urban Land Institute, 1983.

Urban Systems Research and Engineering, Inc. *Seven City Home Maintenance Demonstration for the Elderly.* 2 vols. Springfield, Virginia: National Technical Information Service, 1983.

Verbeten, Eileen, and Fink, Alene. *The Nursing Home: A Potential Resource for In-Home and Community-Based Services. A Manual on the*

Development of Adult Day Care, Respite Care, Community Meals, Congregate Housing, and Home Care Service. Springfield, Virginia: National Technical Information Service, 1982.

Wendt, James C. *Why Households Apply for Housing Allowances. Housing Assistance Supply Experiment.* Santa Monica, California: RAND Corporation, 1982.

Williamson, John B., et al. *Politics of Aging: Power and Policy.* Springfield, Illinois, Charles C. Thomas Publisher, 1982.

Winklevoss, Howard E., and Powell, Alwyn V. *Continuing Care Retirement Communities: An Empirical, Financial, and Legal Analysis.* Homewood, Illinois: Richard D. Irwin, Inc., 1984.

Zais, James P., Struyk, Raymond J., and Thibodeau, Thomas. *Housing Assistance for Older Americans: The Reagan Prescription.* Washington, D.C.: Urban Institute Press, 1983.

Zais, James P., and Thibodeau, Thomas G. *The Elderly and Urban Housing.* Washington, D.C.: Urban Institute Press, 1983.

Zeisel, John, Welch, Polly, and Epp, Gayle. *Midrise Elevator Housing for Older People: Behavioral Criteria for Design.* Springfield, Virginia: National Technical Information Service, 1981.

II. Articles in Books and Journals

Adams, E. "Havens for Retirees and Empty Nesters," *Professional Builder/ Apartment Business,* Vol. 48 (February 1983), 104-11.

Aging. "Special Issue on Housing," No. 342 (December 1983-January 1984).

Anderson, Elaine A., Chen, Alexander, and Hula, Richard C. "Housing Strategies for the Elderly: Beyond the Ecological Model," *Journal of Housing for the Elderly,* Vol. 2, No. 3 (Fall 1984), 47-60.

Baker, Michael. "Arizona Retirement Communities and the Changing Needs of an Aging Population," *Arizona Review,* Vol. 32 (Fall 1984), 14-22.

Bergum, Christian Olson. "Models of Man in the Design of Housing for the Elderly," *Journal of Housing for the Elderly,* Vol. 1, No. 2 (Fall 1983), 3-17.

Bernstein, J. "Who Leaves—Who Stays: Residency Policy in Housing for the Elderly," *The Gerontologist,* Vol. 22, No. 3 (June, 1982), 305-13.

Biggar, Jeanne C., Flynn, Cynthia B., Longino, Charles F., Jr., and Wiseman, Robert F. "Sunbelt Update: Older Americans Head South," *American Demographics,* Vol. 6, No. 12 (December 1984), 22-25+.

Binstock, Robert H. "The Elderly in America: Their Economic Resources, Income Status, and Costs," in *Aging and Public Policy: The Politics of Growing Old in America,* ed. by William P. Browne and Laura Katz Olson. Westport, Connecticut: Greenwood Press, 1983, pp. 19-33.

Blackie, Norman K. "Alternative Housing and Living Arrangements for Independent Living," *Journal of Housing for the Elderly,* Vol. 1, No. 1 (Spring/Summer 1983), 77–84.

Boles, Daralice D. "Congregate Manor," *Progressive Architecture,* Vol. 66, No. 8 (August 1985), 99–103.

Boles, William. "A Sociological, Psychological, and Physiological Profile of Three Groups of Older Adults as Related to Housing Needs and Norms," *Journal of Applied Gerontology* (December 1982), 44–60.

Borop, Jerry H. "Relocation: Attitudes, Information Network and Problems Encountered," *The Gerontologist,* Vol. 21, No. 5 (October 1981), 501–11.

Borop, J. H., Gallego, D. T., and Heffernan, P. G. "Relocation: Its Effect on Health, Functioning, and Mortality," *The Gerontologist,* Vol. 20, No. 4 (August 1980), 468–79.

Bourestom, N., and Pastalan, L. "The Effects of Relocation on the Elderly: A Reply to Borop, J. H., Gallego, D. T., and Heffernan, P. G.," *The Gerontologist,* Vol. 21, No. 1 (February 1981), 4–7.

Brecht, Susan B. "Lifecare Comes of Age," *Urban Land,* Vol. 43 (August 1984), 14–17.

Broder, J. N. "Non-profit Housing for the Elderly in Highly Urban Settings—Using a Federal-Housing Program to Meet Urban-Renewal Goals," *Urban Lawyer,* Vol. 13, No. 1 (1981), 107–20.

Brown, D. S. "Housing for the Elderly—Federal Subsidy Policy and Its Effect on Age-Group Isolation," *University of Detroit Journal of Urban Law,* Vol. 57, No. 1 (1980), 257–93.

Bryant, Ellen S., and El-Attar, Mohamed. "Migration and Redistribution of the Elderly: A Challenge to Community Services," *The Gerontologist,,* Vol. 24, No. 6 (December 1984), 634–40.

Burstein, J. "Housing Ownership by Low-Income Families: Elderly Could Pave the Way," *Journal of Housing,* Vol. 40 (July/August 1983), 104–107.

Carrol, Kathy, and Gray, V. Katherine. "Exploding Some Myths about Housing for the Elderly: What do Senior Citizens Look For in New Housing?" *Real Estate Review,* Vol. 15 (Summer 1985), 91–93.

Carp, Frances M., Carp, Abraham, and Millsap, Roger. "Equity and Satisfaction Among the Elderly," *International Journal of Aging and Human Development,* Vol. 15, No. 2 (1982), 151–66.

Chevan, Albert. "Age, Housing Choice, and Neighborhood Age Structure," *American Journal of Sociology,* Vol. 87, No. 5 (March 1982), 1133–49.

Clifford, William B., Heaton, Tim, and Fuguitt, Glenn V. "Residential Mobility and Living Arrangements Among the Elderly: Changing

Patterns in Metro and Nonmetro Areas," *International Journal of Aging and Human Development,* Vol. 14, No. 2 (1982/82), 139-58.

Cohen, D. L. "Continuing-care Communities for the Elderly; Potential Pitfalls and Proposed Legislation," *University of Pennsylvania Law Review,* Vol. 128, No. 4 (1980) 828-49, 883-936.

Crossman, Sharyn M. "Mortgage and Lending Instruments Designed for the Elderly," *Journal of Housing for the Elderly,* Vol. 2, No. 2 (Summer 1984), 27-40.

Daily, Linda. "Housing Options for the Elderly," *Editorial Research Report,* Vol. 2, No. 5 (August 6, 1982), 571-88.

deLaski-Smith, Deborah L. "Housing the Elderly: Intergenerational Family Settings," *Journal of Housing for the Elderly,* Vol. 2, No. 3 (Fall 1984), 61-70.

"Developing for the Over-50s Market," *Urban Land,* Vol. 43, No. 2 (February 1984), 2-7.

Devlin, A. S. "Housing for the Elderly—Cognitive Considerations," *Environment and Behavior,* Vol. 12, No. 4 (1980), 451-66.

Dobson, Douglas, "The Elderly as a Political Force," in *Aging and Public Policy: The Politics of Growing Old in America,* ed. by William P. Browne and Laura Katz Olson. Westport, Connecticut: Greenwood Press, 1983, pp. 123-44.

Dolbeare, Cusing. "Housing Needs of the Elderly and How to Meet Them," *Social Thought,* Vol. 10, No. 1 (Winter 1984), 16-29.

Eckert, J. Kevin. "Dislocation and Relocation of the Urban Elderly: Social Networks as Mediators of Relocation Stress," *Human Organization,* Vol. 42, No. 1 (1982), 39-45.

Eckert, J. Kevin, and Haug, M. R. "The Impact of Forced Residential Relocation on the Health of the Elderly Hotel Dweller," *Journal of Gerontology,* Vol. 39, No. 6 (November 1984), 753-55.

Elrod, L. H. "Housing Alternatives for the Elderly," *Journal of Family Law,* Vol. 18, No. 4 (1980), 723-61.

"Empty Nesters, First-Time Buyers: Two Growth Markets for Builder to Romance in 1982," *Professional Builder/Apartment Business,* Vol. 47 (January 1982), 168-93.

Fairholm, Gilbert W., and Fairholm, Barbara C. "Property Tax Relief: Helping the Elderly to Keep Their Homes," *Aging* (January/February 1982), 12-17.

Felton, Barbara J., Lehmann, Stanley, and Adler, Arlene. "Single-Room Occupancy Hotels: Their Viability as Housing Options for Older Citizens," in *Community Housing Choices for Older Americans,* ed. by

M. Powell Lawton and Sally L. Hoover. New York: Springer Publishing Company, 1981, pp. 267-85.

Fengler, Alfred P., and Danigelis, Nicholas. "Residence, the Elderly Widow, and Life Satisfaction," *Research on Aging,* Vol. 4 (1982), 113-35.

Fengler, Alfred A., Danigelis, Nicholas, and Little, Virginia C. "Later Life Satisfaction and Household Structure: Living with Others and Living Alone," *Aging and Society,* Vol. 3, Part 3 (November 1983), 357-77.

Ferraro, Kenneth F. "The Health Consequences of Relocation Among the Aged in the Community," *Journal of Gerontology,* Vol. 38, No. 1 (January 1983), 90-96.

_____. "Relocation Desires and Outcomes Among the Elderly: A Longitudinal Study," *Research on Aging,* Vol. 3 (1981), 166-81.

Fields, C. "Housing Programs and Outreach Strategies for the Elderly," *Urban League Review,* Vol. 6, No. 2 (1982), 50-55.

Fillenbaum, Gerda G., and Wallman, Laurence M. "Change in Household Composition of the Elderly: A Preliminary Investigation," *Journal of Gerontology,* Vol. 39, No. 3 (May 1984), 342-49.

Fitzpatrick, K. M., and Logan, J. R. "The Aging of the Suburbs, 1960-1980," *American Sociological Review,* Vol. 50, No. 2 (February 1985), 106-17.

Foley, Donald L. "The Sociology of Housing." *Annual Review of Sociology,* Vol. 6 (1980), 457-78.

Friedman, J., and Sjogren, J. "Assets of the Elderly as They Retire," *Social Security Bulletin,* Vol. 44 (March 1981), 3-19.

Generations. "Housing," Vol. 9, No. 3 (Spring 1985), entire issue.

Golant, Stephen M. "In Defense of Age-Segregation Housing," *Aging,* No. 348 (1985), 22-26.

_____. "Individual Differences Underlying the Dwelling Satisfaction of the Elderly," *Journal of Social Issues,* Vol. 38, No. 3 (1982), 121-33.

"Graying of America: Over 55 Housing Market [panel discussion]," *Professional Builder/Apartment Business,* Vol. 49 (August 1984), 134-51.

"Graying of America: Power and Problems. A Symposium." *Human Ecology Forum,* Vol. 12 (Summer 1981), 4-25.

Guttentag, J. "Home Equity Conversion: A New Factor in Retirement Planning," in *Saving for Retirement,* ed. by P. Cagan. Washington, D.C.: American Council on Life Insurance, 1982.

Harvey, Thomas J. "A National Housing Vision: We Need More than a Dream," *Social Thought,* Vol. 10, No. 1 (Winter 1984), 3-15.

Hendrick, Clyde, Wells, Karen S., and Faletti, Martin V. "Social and Emotional Effects of Geographical Relocation," *Journal of Personal and Social Psychology,* Vol. 42, No. 5 (May 1982), 951-62.

Henig, Jeffrey R. "Gentrification and Displacement of the Elderly: An Empirical Analysis," *The Gerontologist,* Vol. 21, No. 1 (February 1981), 67–75.

Herbert, A. W. "Enhancing Housing Opportunities for the Black Elderly," in *Aging in Minority Groups,* ed. by R. L. McNeely and J. L. Cohen. Beverly Hills, California: Sage Publications, 1983, pp. 123–36.

Heumann, Leonard F. "The Elderly as Consumers of Subsidized Housing: Anticipated Impact of the Rent Voucher Program on Private Real Estate Investments," *Illinois Business Review,* Vol. 41 (February 1984), 6–9.

_____. "Rent Subsidies and the Elderly," *Journal of Housing for the Elderly,* Vol. 2, No. 3 (Fall 1984), 71–87.

_____. "The Function of Different Sheltered Housing Categories for the Semi-Independent Elderly," *Social Policy and Administration,* Vol. 15, No. 2 (Summer 1981), 164–80.

Howe, Elizabeth. "Homesharing for the Elderly," *Journal of Planning Education and Research,* Vol. 4, No. 3 (April 1985), 185–93.

Huth, Mary Jo. "Strategies for Crime Reduction in Public Housing." *Journal of Sociology and Social Welfare,* Vol. 8, No. 3 (September 1981), 587–600.

Jacobs, B. "The Potential Antipoverty Impact of RAMs and Property Tax Deferral," in *Unlocking Home Equity for the Elderly,* ed. by K. Scholen and Y. Chen. Cambridge, Massachusetts: Ballinger Publishing Co., 1980.

Jeffords, Charles R. "The Situational Relationship Between Age and the Fear of Crime," *International Journal of Aging and Human Development,* Vol. 17, No. 2 (1983), 103–11.

Kearl, M. C. "Political Implications of the New Ageism," *International Journal of Aging and Human Development,* Vol. 15, No. 3 (1982), 167–83.

Kelen, J. and Griffiths, K. A. "Housing for the Aged. New Roles for Social Work," *International Journal of Aging and Human Development,* Vol. 16, No. 2 (1983), 125–33.

Kendig, Hal L. "Housing Tenure and Generational Equity," *Ageing and Society,* Vol. 4 (September 1984), 249–72.

La Greca, Anthony J., Streib, Gordon F., and Folts, Edward W. "Retirement Communities and Their Life Stages," *Journal of Gerontology,* Vol. 40, No. 2, (March 1985), 211–18.

Lane, Terry Saunders, and Feins, Judith D. "Are the Elderly Overhoused? Definitions of Space Utilization and Policy Implications," *The Gerontologist,* Vol. 25, No. 3 (June 1985), 243–50.

Lawton, M. Powell. "Alternative Housing," *Journal of Gerontological Social Work,* Vol. 3 (1981), 61–80.

_____. "An Ecological View of Living Arrangements," *The Gerontologist,* Vol. 21, No. 1 (February 1981), 59–66.

_____. "Housing the Elderly: Residential Quality and Residential Satisfaction," *Research on Aging,* Vol. 2 (1980), 309–28.

Lawton, M. Powell, Greenbaum, Maurice, and Liebowitz, Bernard. "The Lifespan of Housing Environments for the Aging," *The Gerontologist,* Vol. 20, No. 1 (February 1980), 56–64.

Lawton, M. Powell, and Hoffman, Christine. "Neighborhood Reactions to Elderly Housing," *Journal of Housing for the Elderly,* Vol. 2, No. 2 (Summer 1984), 41–54.

Lawton, M. Powell, Moss, Miriam, and Grimes, Miriam. "The Changing Service Needs of Older Tenants in Planned Housing," *The Gerontologist,* Vol. 25, No. 3 (June 1985), 258–64.

Lawton, M. Powell, Nahemow, L., and Yeh. T. "Neighborhood Environment and the Well-being of Older Tenants in Planned Housing," *Journal of Aging and Human Development,* Vol. 11 (1980), 211–27.

Lawton, M. Powell, and Yaffe, Silvia. "Victimization and Fear of Crime in Elderly Public Housing Tenants," *Journal of Gerontology,* Vol. 35, No. 5 (September 1980), 768–79.

Lee, G. R. "Residential Location and Fear of Crime Among the Elderly," *Rural Sociology,* Vol. 74 (Winter 1982), 655–69.

Lee, G. R., and Lassey, M. L. "Rural-Urban Differences Among the Elderly: Economic, Social and Subjective Factors," *Journal of Social Issues,* Vol. 36 (1980), 62–74.

Leeds, Morton. "Inflation and the Elderly: A Housing Perspective," *American Academy of Politics and Social Science Annual,* Vol. 456 (July 1981), 60–69.

Liang, J., Kahana, E., and Doherty, E. "Financial Well-Being Among the Aged: A Further Elaboration," *Journal of Gerontology,* Vol. 35, No. 3 (May 1980), 409–20.

Logan, John R. "The Graying of the Suburbs: Trends between 1960–1980," *Aging* (June/July 1984), 4–8.

Longino, Charles F., Jr. "Changing Aged Nonmetropolitan Migration Patterns, 1955 to 1960 and 1965 to 1970," *Journal of Gerontology,* Vol. 37, No. 2 (March 1982), 228–34.

Longino, Charles F., Jr., and Biggar, Jeanne C. "The Impact of Retirement Migration on the South," *The Gerontologist,* Vol. 21, No. 3 (June 1981), 283–90.

Longino, Charles F., Jr., Wiseman, Robert F., Biggar, Jeanne C., and Flynn, Cynthia B. "Aged Metropolitan-Nonmetropolitan Migration Streams Over Three Census Decades," *Journal of Gerontology,* Vol. 39, No. 6 (November 1984), 721–29.

Massey, Douglas S. "Residential Segregation and Spatial Distribution of a Non-Labor Force Population: The Needy Elderly and Disabled," *Economic Geography,* Vol. 56, No. 3 (1980), 190-200.

Mayer, Mary J. "Demographic Change and the Elderly Population," *Social Work with Groups,* Vol. 5, No. 2 (Summer 1982), 7-12.

Mayer, Neil S. "Grants, Loans, and Housing Repair for the Elderly," *Journal of the American Planning Association,* Vol. 47, No. 1 (January 1981), 25-34.

Mayer, Neil S., and Lee, Olson. "Federal Home Repair Programs and Elderly Homeowners' Needs," *The Gerontologist,* Vol. 21, No. 3 (June 1981), 312-22.

Metropolitan Life Insurance Co. "Projections of Population Growth at the Older Ages (1970-2050)," *Metropolitan Life Status Bulletin,* Vol. 65 (April/June 1984), 8-12.

Michigan Planner. "Elderly Planning." Vol. 4, No. 1 (Winter 1984), entire issue.

Millas, A. J. "Planning for the Elderly within the Context of a Neighborhood," *Ekistics,* Vol. 47 (June 1980), 264-73.

Miller, A. H., Gurin, Patricia, and Gurin, Gerald. "Age Consciousness and the Political Mobilization of the Older American," *The Gerontologist,* Vol. 20, No. 6 (December 1980), 691-700.

Mindel, Charles H., and Wright, Roosevelt, Jr. "Satisfaction in Multigenerational Households," *Journal of Gerontology,* Vol. 37, No. 4 (July 1982), 483-89.

Montgomery, James E., Stubbs, Alice C., and Day, Savannah S. "The Housing Environment of the Rural Elderly," *The Gerontologist,* Vol. 20, No. 4 (August 1980), 444-51.

Moos, Rudolf H., and Lemke, Sonne. "Assessing the Physical and Architectural Features of Sheltered Care Settings," *Journal of Gerontology,* Vol. 35, No. 4 (July 1980), 571-83.

Nachison, Jerold S., and Leeds, Morton H. "Housing Policy for Older Americans in the 1980s: An Overview," *Journal of Housing for the Elderly,* Vol. 1, No. 1 (Spring/Summer 1983), 3-13.

Nelson, G. "Social Class and Public Policy for the Elderly," *Social Service Review,* Vol. 56 (March 1982), 87-107.

――――. "Tax Expenditures for the Elderly," *The Gerontologist,* Vol. 23, No. 5 (October 1983), 471-78.

Neubig, T. "Reverse Annuity Mortgages: A Dissaving Mechanism for Older Homeowners," in *Five Thousand American Families—Patterns of Economic Progress,* Vol. III. Ann Arbor, Michigan: University of Michigan, Institute for Social Research, 1980, pp. 315-37.

Newman, Sandra J. "The Availability of Adequate Housing for Older People: Issue Areas for Advocates," *Journal of Housing for the Elderly*, Vol. 2, No. 3 (Fall 1984), 3–13.

Newman, Sandra J., and Struyk, Raymond. "An Alternative Targeting Strategy for Housing Assistance," *The Gerontologist*, Vol. 24, No. 6 (December 1984), 584–92.

Noelker, L. S., and Harel, Z. "Residential Choice and the Well-Being of Aged and Disabled Public-Housing Residents," *Journal of Gerontological Social Work*, Vol. 4, No. 2 (1981), 17–29.

Norton, Lee, and Wozny, Mark C. "Residential Location and Nutritional Adequacy Among Elderly Adults," *Journal of Gerontology*, Vol. 39, No. 5 (September 1984), 592–95.

Nowesnick, M. "Looming Challenge: Helping Older Americans Keep Their Homes," *Savings and Loan News*, Vol. 102 (May 1981), 84–88.

Ollie, A. "Randall Symposium on Housing Policy," *The Gerontologist*, Vol. 25, No. 1 (February 1985), 30–46.

Osgood, Nancy J. "Patterns of Aging in Retirement Communities: Typology of Residents," *Journal of Applied Gerontology*, (December 1983), 28–43.

Pampel, F. C., and Associates. "Retirement Migration Decision Making," *Research on Aging*, Vol. 6 (1984), 139–62.

Parr, J. "The Interaction of Persons and Living Environments," in *Aging in the 1980s*, ed. by L. W. Poon. Washington, D.C.: American Psychological Association, 1980, pp. 393–406.

Pastalan, Leon. "Manufactured Housing for the Elderly: A Viable Alternative," *Journal of Housing for the Elderly*, Vol. 2, No. 3 (Fall 1984), 89–91.

Peirce, Neal R., and Choharis, Peter C. "The Elderly as a Political Force—26 Million Strong and Well Organized," *National Journal* (September 11, 1982), 1559–62.

Pritchard, D. C. "Art of Matchmaking: A Case Study in Shared Housing," *The Gerontologist*, Vol. 22, No 2 (April 1983), 174–79.

Pynoos, Jon. "Setting the Elderly Housing Agenda," *Policy Studies Journal*, Vol. 13, No. 1 (September 1984), 173–84.

Raper, H. David. "Converting the Elderly Homeowner's Equity into Income," *Real Estate Review*, Vol. 12 (Sumemr 1982), 123–27.

Regnier, Victor, and Bonar, James. "Recycling Buildings for Elderly Housing," in *Community Housing Choices for Older Americans*, ed. by M. Powell Lawton and Sally L. Hoover. New York: Springer Publisher Company, 1981, pp. 286–98.

Regnier, Victor, and Byerts, Thomas O. "Applying Research to the Plan and Design of Housing for the Elderly," in Urban Land Institute, *Housing for a Maturing Population.* Washington, D.C.: Urban Land Institute, 1983, pp. 24-49.

Regnier, Victor, and Gelwicks, Louis E. "Preferred Supportive Services for Middle to Higher Income Retirement Housing," *The Gerontologist,* Vol. 21, No. 1 (February 1981), 54-58.

Rogers, Walter B. "Change in Demand for Housing Among the Elderly," *Tennessee Business and Economic Review,* Vol. 11 (September 1984), 10-15.

Rotstein, Arthur H. "Vacant Schools: Are We Flunking the Test?" *Historic Preservation,* Vol. 32, No. 6 (1980), 16-21 [adaptive reuse]

Rowles, Graham D. "Between Worlds: A Relocation Dilemma for the Appalachian Elderly," *International Journal of Aging and Human Development,* Vol. 17 (1983), 301-14.

———. "Growing Old 'Inside': Aging and Attachment to Place in an Appalachian Community," in *Transitions of Aging,* ed. by N. Datan and N. Lohmann. New York: Academic Press, 1980, pp. 153-70.

———. "The Surveillance Zone as Meaningful Space for the Aged," *The Gerontologist,* Vol. 21, No. 3 (June 1981), 304-11.

Samuelson, Don S. "Accommodating the Graying of America: A Competitive Viewpoint," *Urban Land,* Vol. 40, No. 1 (January 1981), 4-10.

Schreter, Carol. "Residents of Shared Housing," *Social Thought,* Vol. 10 (Winter 1984), 30-38.

Schwartz, David C. "Housing America's Elderly: A State-Level Policy Perspective," *Policy Studies Journal,* Vol. 13, No. 1 (September 1984), 157-71.

Schwartz, Robert D. "Shopping Patterns of Residents in Detroit Area Government-Assisted Senior Citizen Housing," *Michigan Academician,* Vol. 12, No. 3 (Winter 1983), 333-44.

Shannon, Charles P. "Local Government Policy on Aging: New Challenges for Old Problems," *Journal of Sociology and Social Welfare,* Vol. 8, No. 4 (December 1981), 796-817.

Sjogren, J., and Feins, J. "Home Equity Conversion Through Reverse Annuity Mortgages: An Income Supplement for the Elderly," *Federal Home Loan Bank Board Journal,* Vol. 16 (January 1983), 15-25.

Slavik, J. Ronald. "Senior Housing: Practical Innovations," *Journal of Property Management,* Vol. 46 (July/August 1981), 229-32.

Soldo, B. J. "America's Elderly in the 1980s." *Population Bulletin,* Vol. 35 (November 1980), 2-47.

Steinhuber, M. B. "Housing Trends of the Elderly—Emerging Policy and Implications," *International Journal of Public Administration,* Vol. 3, No. 3 (1981), 283-312.

Stockman, Leslie Ensor, and Fletcher, June. "Retirement Housing: A Maturing Market," *Builder,* Vol. 8, No. 6 (June 1985), 70–91.

Streib, G. "The Continuum of Living Arrangements," in *Aging and the Human Condition,* ed. by G. Lesnoff-Caravaglia. New York: Human Services Press, 1982.

Struyk, Raymond J. "Future Housing Assistance Policy for the Elderly," *The Gerontologist,* Vol. 25, No. 1 (February 1985), 41–46.

———. "Housing Adjustments of Relocating Elderly Households," *The Gerontologist,* Vol. 20, No. 1 (February 1980), 45–55.

Struyk, Raymond J., and Turner, M. "Changes in the Housing Situation of the Elderly: 1974–79," *Journal of Housing for the Elderly,* Vol. 2, No. 1 (Spring 1984), 3–20.

Taylor, Robert Joseph and Taylor, Willie H. "The Social and Economic Status of the Black Elderly," *Phylon,* Vol. 43, No. 4 (December 1982), 295–306.

Teski, Marea. "Environment, Crime, and the Elderly," in *The Elderly Victim of Crime,* ed. by David Lester. Springfield, Illinois: Charles C. Thomas Publisher, 1981, pp. 45–60.

Tissue, Thomas, and McCoy, John L. "Income and Living Arrangements Among Poor Aged Singles," *Social Security Bulletin,* Vol. 44 (April 1981), 3–13.

Turner, Margery Austin. "Building Housing for the Low-Income Elderly. Cost Containment in the Section 202 Program," *The Gerontologist,* Vol. 25, No. 3 (June 1985), 271–79.

Varady, David P. "Determinants of Elderly Residential Mobility: How Well Do the Elderly Adjust to Housing Problems?" *Journal of Planning Education and Research,* Vol. 4 (December 1984), 103–10.

———. "Housing Problems and Mobility Plans Among the Elderly," *American Planning Association Journal,* Vol. 46, No. 3 (July 1980), 301–14.

Varady, David P., and O'Toole, Colleen K. "Neighborhood Revitalization: How Do the Elderly Fare in Homesteading Neighborhoods?" *Journal of Architectural and Planning Research,* Vol. 1 (December 1984), 173–81.

Varady, David P., and Sutton, B. "Utilization of Housing Cost Assistance and Social Service Programs by the Community Resident Elderly," *American Planning Association Journal,* Vol. 47 (October 1981), 421–33.

Warner, Katherine P. "Demographics and Housing." in Urban Land Institute, *Housing for a Maturing Population.* Washington, D.C.: Urban Land Institute, 1983. pp. 2–23.

Weinrobe, Maurice D. "Consumer Safeguards for Financial Instruments Unlocking Home Equity for the Aged," *Journal of Housing for the Elderly,* Vol. 2, No. 2 (Summer 1984), 55–72.

Wilner, Mary Ann, and Witkin, Janet L. "Shared Living for Elders: A Viable Alternative," *Challenge,* Vol. 11 (September 1980), 5-11.
Wiseman, R. "Why Older People Move: Theoretical Issues," *Research on Aging,* Vol. 2 (1980), 141-54.
Woodward, Anne. "Housing the Elderly," *Society,* Vol. 19, No. 2 (January/ February 1982), 52-57.

III. Congressional Hearings and Papers

United States, House of Representatives, Committee on Banking, Finance, and Urban Affairs. *Resolution of Disapproval for Certain Procedures for Elderly Housing. Report together with minority views to accompany H.J. Res. 488.* Ninety-seventh Congress, second session, 1982. Washington, D.C.: Government Printing Office, 1982.

_____. *Section 8 Rent Adjustments, Elderly Housing and Other Assisted Housing Issues. Hearing before the Subcommittee on Housing and Community Development.* Ninety-eighth Congress, second session, February 22, 1984. Washington, D.C.: Government Printing Office, 1984.

_____. *Section 202 Housing for the Elderly. Hearing before the Subcommittee on Housing and Community Development.* Ninety-seventh Congress, second session, March 11, 1982. Washington, D.C.: Government Printing Office, 1982.

United States, House of Representatives, Select Committee on Aging. *Alternative Housing Options for the Elderly. Hearing before the Subcommittee on Housing and Consumer Interests.* Ninety-sixth Congress, second session, Denver, Colorado, October 6, 1980. Washington, D.C.: Government Printing Office, 1980.

_____. *Condominium Conversions. Hearing before the Subcommittee on Housing and Consumer Interests.* Ninety-sixth Congress, second session, May 15, 1980. Washington, D.C.: Government Printing Office, 1980.

_____. *Congregate Housing Services. Hearing before the Subcommittee on Housing and Consumer Interests.* Ninety-seventh Congress, first session, May 19, 1981. Washington, D.C.: Government Printing Office, 1981.

_____. *Elderly Housing: Innovative Alternatives. Hearing before the Subcommittee on Housing and Consumer Interests.* Ninety-Eighth Congress, first session, Erie, Pennsylvania, October 17, 1983. Washington, D.C.: Government Printing Office, 1983.

_____. *Elderly Housing: Innovative Alternatives. Hearing before the Subcommittee on Housing and Consumer Interests.* Ninety-eighth Congress, first session, Portland, Oregon, August 12, 1983. Washington,

D.C.: Government Printing Office, 1983.

———. *Home Equity Conversion. Hearing before the Subcommittee on Housing and Consumer Interests.* Ninety-eighth Congress, first session, Mattydale, New York, October 22, 1983. Washington, D.C.: Government Printing Office, 1984.

———. *Housing Needs of the Elderly. Hearing before the Subcommittee on Housing and Consumer Interests.* Ninety-sixth Congress, second session, North Hollywood, California, September 13, 1980. Washington, D.C.: Government Printing Office, 1980.

———. *Housing the Elderly: Present Problems and Future Considerations. Hearing before the Subcommittee on Housing and Consumer Interests.* Ninety-seventh Congress, first session, July 29, 1981. Washington, D.C.: Government Printing Office, 1981.

———. *Shared Housing. Hearing before the Subcommittee on Housing and Consumer Interests.* Ninety-seventh Congress, first session, November 17, 1981. Washington, D.C.: Government Printing Office, 1981.

United States, Senate, Special Committee on Aging. *Alternative Approaches to Housing Older Americans. Hearing.* Ninety-seventh Congress, second session. Hartford, Connecticut, February 1, 1982. Washington, D.C.: Government Printing Office, 1982.

———. *Impact of the Administration's Housing Proposals on Older Americans. Hearing.* Ninety-seventh Congress, second session. Washington, D.C., April 23, 1982. Washington, D.C.: Government Printing Office, 1982.

———. *Life-Care Communities: Promises and Problems. Hearing.* Ninety-eighth Congress, first session. Washington, D.C., May 25, 1983. Washington, D.C.: Government Printing Office, 1983.

———. *Low-Cost Housing for the Elderly: Surplus Lands and Private Sector Initiatives. Hearing.* Ninety-eighth Congress, second session. Sacramento, California, August 13, 1984. Washington, D.C.: Government Printing Office, 1984.

———. *Minority Elderly: Economics and Housing in the 80's. Hearing.* Ninety-sixth Congress, second session. Philadelphia, Pennsylvania, May 7, 1980. Washington, D.C.: Government Printing Office, 1980.

———. *Section 202 Housing for the Elderly and Handicapped: A National Survey.* Ninety-eighth Congress, second session. Washington, D.C.: Government Printing Office, 1984.

———. *Sheltering America's Aged: Options for Housing and Services. Hearing.* Ninety-eighth Congress, second session. Boston, Massachusetts, April 23, 1984. Washington, D.C.: Government Printing Office, 1984.

IV. Conference and Symposium Papers

Baldwin, Leo. "A Review of Home Equity Conversion." Paper at the Gerontological Society of America conference, November 1983.

Birenbaum, Arnold. "Aging and Housing: Toward a Theory of Negotiated Status Acquisition." Paper at the Society for the Study of Social Problems conference, 1980.

Gelwicks, Louis E. "Housing: The 'Where' in the Continuum of Care," in U.S. Department of Health and Human Services, Health Care Financing Administration, *Proceedings, Long-Term Care Financing and Delivery Systems: Exploring Some Alternatives.* Washington, D.C.: Government Printing Office, 1984.

Gerontological Society of America. Annual Meetings. Various places, 1980 to date. (There are generally several sessions pertaining to housing at these meetings.)

Hankin, Janet R., and Goodman Allen C. "Co-Existing Needs among a Sample of Elderly." Paper for Society for the Study of Social Problems conference, 1983.

Hare, Patrick H. "Accessory Apartments: A New Housing Option for the Elderly Homeowner." Paper at the Gerontological Society of American conference, November 1983.

Howell, Joseph T. "Congregate Housing: Social Benefits, Financial Obstacles," in U.S. Department of Health and Human Services, Health Care Financing Administration, *Proceedings, Long-Term Care Financing and Delivery Systems: Exploring Some Alternatives.* Washington, D.C.: Government Printing Office, 1984.

Huth, Mary J. "The Current Economic, Residential, and Familial Status of Elderly Americans." Paper at the American Sociological Association conference, 1983.

Huttman, Elizabeth D. "Policies for Social Housing Problems: A Comparative Perspective." Paper at the Society for the Study of Social Problems conference, 1983.

Jacobs, Bruce, and Weissert, William. "Home Equity Financing of Long-Term Care for the Elderly," in U.S. Department of Health and Human Services, Health Care Financing Administration, *Proceedings, Long-Term Care Financing and Delivery Systems: Exploring Some Alternatives.* Washington, D.C.: Government Printing Office, 1984.

Mauer, Richard C., Christenson, James A., and Warner, Paul D. "Perspectives of Community Services among Rural and Urban Elderly." Paper at the Rural Sociological Society conference, 1980.

Mortgage Bankers Association of America. "The Multifamily Housing Conference." Nashville, Tennessee, November 18-22, 1985. Five sessions focused on elderly housing: 1) Introduction and Overview of Retirement Housing; 2) New Developments in Life Care Communities; 3) Developing and Financing Congregate Care Facilities; 4) A Look at HUD's Retirement Service Center Program; and 5) New Opportunities in Nursing Homes, Hospitals, and Board and Care Homes.)

Pies, Harvey E. "Life Care Communities for the Aged—An Overview," In U.S. Department of Health and Human Services, Health Care Financing Administration, *Proceedings, Long-Term Care Financing and Delivery Systems: Exploring Some Alternatives.* Washington, D.C.: Government Printing Office, 1984.

Regnier, Victor. "Design Criteria for Outdoor Space Surrounding Housing for the Elderly." Paper at American Institute of Architects conference, "Research and Design 85: Architectural Applications of Design and Technology Research," Washington, D.C., 1985.

———. "Planning Congregate Housing for the Elderly: An Integrative Research and Participatory Planning Model." Paper at American Institute of Architects conference, "Research and Design 85: Architectural Applications of Design and Technology Research," Washington, D.C., 1985.

Schreter, Carol A. "A Profile of Non-Relative House-Sharers." Paper at the Gerontological Society of America conference, November 1983.

Stanford, Barbara. "The Role of the House-Mate Matching Service." Paper at the Gerontological Society of America conference, November 1983.

Turner, Howard, and Bokemeier, Janet L. "Satisfaction of the Rural Population with Their Living Conditions: An Elderly/Nonelderly Comparison." Paper for Rural Sociological Society conference, 1983.

Van Scoyoc, Gardner. "Life Care Communities: A Housing Option for the Elderly." In U.S. Department of Health and Human Services, Health Care Financing Administration, *Proceedings, Long-Term Care Financing and Delivery Systems: Exploring Some Alternatives.* Washington, D.C.: Government Printing Office, 1984.

White House Conference on Aging. *A National Policy on Aging.* Washington, D.C.: U.S. Administration on Aging, 1981.

———. *Recommendations, Post-Conference Survey of Delegates.* Washington, D.C.: U.S. Administration on Aging, 1981.

———. *Report of the Mini-conference on Housing for the Elderly.* Washington, D.C.: U.S. Administration on Aging, 1981.

———. *Technical Committee on Physical and Social Environment and the Quality of Life: Full Report.* Washington, D.C.: U.S. Administration on Aging, 1981.

Bibliography

Witkin, Janet L. "Agency-Sponsored Co-op House for Older People." Paper at the Gerontological Society of America conference, November 1983.

V. Dissertations and Theses

Ahrentzen, Sherry Boland. "Women and the Housing Process: A Look at Residential Fit, Adjustments, and Constraints of Lower-Income Female-Headed Households." Doctoral dissertation, University of California, Irvine, 1983.

Arline, Peter James. "Alternative Housing for the Elderly." Master's thesis, California State University, Dominguez Hills, 1982.

Astler, Char Rae Long. "Analysis of the Housing Status of the Elderly." Master's thesis, North Texas State University, 1982.

Bergum, Christian Olson. "Architecture as a Humanistic Endeavor: A Study of the Changing Concepts of Man in the Design of Housing for the Elderly." Doctoral dissertation, University of Pennsylvania, 1981.

Boschetti, Margaret A. "The Older Person's Emotional Attachment to the Physical Environment of the Residential Setting." Doctoral dissertation, University of Michigan, 1984.

Burkart, Julia. "From Quarters to Castle: Home Ownership among Black, Sugar Cane Plantation Families (Louisiana)." Doctoral dissertation, Texas Woman's University, 1983.

Burki, Mary Ann. "Housing the Low-Income, Urban Elderly: A Role for the Single Room Occupancy Hotel." Doctoral dissertation, Portland State University, 1982.

Burston, Nancy Ann. "Housing Relocation Services for the Elderly and Handicapped: A Case Study." Doctoral dissertation, Cornell University, 1982.

Carlin, Vivian F. "A Model of Successful Old Age: A Participant Observation Study of a Congregate Residence." Doctoral dissertation, Rutgers University, 1981.

Chun, Dong Hoon. "Consistency of Property Tax Assessment Practice: The Case of Philadelphia, Pennsylvania." Doctoral dissertation, University of Pennsylvania, 1983.

Dubose, Otelia. "An Analysis of the Impact of Economic and Socio-Demographic Variables on the Success of Households in the Housing Allowance Demand Experiment." Doctoral dissertation, Cornell University, 1983.

Fitzpatrick, Annelle Marie. "The Social Integration of the Elderly and the Disabled Living in Congregate Housing." Doctoral dissertation, St. John's University, 1982.

Frantz, Sheryl Ruth. "Elderly in the Tenderloin: Low-Income Residents in Single Room Occupancy Hotels." Doctoral dissertation, University of California, Berkeley, 1981.

Freeland, James Gordon. "The Evangelical Church and Housing for the Elderly." Doctoral dissertation, Dallas Theological Seminary, 1984.

Golightly, William Hall, II. "Social Support, Congregate Life Satisfaction and the Elderly." Doctoral dissertation, University of Utah, 1983.

Griffin, Teresa Beverly. "Life Satisfaction and Self Concept of an Elderly Population Living in Congregate and Non-Congregate Housing in Knox County, Tennessee." Doctoral dissertation, University of Tennessee, 1982.

Groth, Paul Erling. "Forbidden Housing: The Evolution and Exclusion of Hotels, Boarding Houses, Rooming Houses, and Lodging Houses in American Cities, 1880-1930." Doctoral dissertation, University of California, Berkeley, 1983.

Hayslett, Carolyn Sue. "Predicting Independent Living After Age Sixty." Doctoral dissertation, West Virginia University, 1981.

Herriott, Martha Jane. "The Use of Three On-Site Services by Elderly Residents of Low Income Public Housing." Doctoral dissertation, University of Washington, 1982.

Hinrichsen, Gregory Allen. "The Impact of Age-Concentrated, Publicly-Assisted Housing on Older Person's Social and Emotional Well-Being." Doctoral dissertation, New York University, 1982.

Johnston, Roger Harrison, Jr. "Client Satisfaction with A Housing Program." Doctoral dissertation, Claremont Graduate School, 1982.

Korthuis, Kathleen Elizabeth. "Functional Characteristics Associated with Feelings of Loneliness in Older Persons Who Live Alone." Doctoral dissertation, University of Toledo, 1982.

Laird, Julie Ann. "Measurement of Elderly Persons' Satisfaction with Limited Housing Space." Master's thesis, University of Nevada, Reno, 1981.

Lucky, Irene. "Seniors Helping Seniors: Training Low-Income Black Elderly to Cope with Cold Weather Energy- and Housing-Related Problems." Doctoral dissertation, City University of New York, 1982.

Madden, Richard K. "In Their Own Words: The Psychosocial Adjustment of a Group of Residents Living at a Subsidized Housing Complex for the Elderly." Doctoral dissertation, Boston University, 1984.

Metz, Eleanor Louise. "A Comparison of Elderly Residents' Life Satisfaction, Happiness, and Social Integration in Residential Facilities With and Without Long-Term Care Units." Doctoral dissertation, University of San Francisco 1983.

Nichols, Linda Olivia. "Community and the Elderly: An Urban Example." Doctoral dissertation, Washington University, 1982.

Normoyle, Janice. "Age Mix, Physical Design, and Fear of Crime Among Elderly Public Housing Residents." Doctoral dissertation, Loyola University of Chicago, 1984.

Nugent, Anne E. "Toward a Housing Policy Proposal for the Elderly Homeowner." Doctoral dissertation, University of Idaho, 1980.

Onyenwoke, Nelson Onyegbula. "Urban Development and Quality of Life of the Elderly." Doctoral dissertation, University of Wisconsin, 1982.

Reschovsky, James David. "Aging in Place: An Investigation of the Housing Consumption and Residential Mobility of the Elderly." Doctoral dissertation, University of Michigan, 1982.

Salago, John. "A Study of the Attitudes of Males Residing in an Apartment Complex for the Elderly." Doctoral dissertation, University of Pittsburgh, 1981.

Schreter, Carol A. "Room for Rent: Shared Housing with Non-Related Older Americans." Doctoral dissertation, Bryn Mawr College, 1983.

Smithers, Janice A. "Determined Survivors: Coping Strategies Among the Urban Elderly." Doctoral dissertation, University of California, Los Angeles, 1981.

Soras, Constantine George. "Consumption-Expenditure Patterns of the Elderly." Doctoral dissertation, Columbia University, 1981(?).

Stressman, Roger Marlin. "The United Methodist Church and the Aging: A Development Study." Doctoral dissertation, School of Theology, Claremont College, 1980.

Stuart, Neil E. "Anticipating Long-Term Care Needs: An Analysis of Predictors of Future Functional Status among an Elderly Population." Doctoral dissertation, Brandeis University, 1983.

Sweeney, Richard Hugh. "The Prior Living Arrangements of the Elderly and Adjustment to an Age-Segregated Housing Apartment." Master's thesis, California State University, Dominguez Hills, 1983.

Toledo, Sarah. "Housing Satisfaction, Supportive Services and Social Networks as Related to Life Satisfaction of the Elderly." Doctoral dissertation, Oklahoma State University, 1982.

Underhill, Patricia Ann. "Policy Implications of a Comparison Between the Predictors of a Life Satisfaction Model and a Problem Indicator Model for Service Delivery to Persons 63 Years of Age and Older in Independent Living Situations. Doctoral dissertation, University of Colorado at Boulder, 1981.

Washburn, Lawrence Arnold, Sr. "Peace Dale House: Church-Sponsored Elderly Housing." Doctoral dissertation, Hartford Seminary Foundation, 1980.

Wyckoff, Shelley Ann Rice. "The Effects of Housing and Race Upon Depression and Life Satisfaction of Elderly Females." Doctoral dissertation, George Peabody College for Teachers of Vanderbilt University, 1983.

VI. Organizations as Sources of Information

Administration on Aging, Office of Human Development Services, Department of Health and Human Services, 200 Independence Avenue, S.W., Washington, D.C. 20201

American Association of Homes for the Aging, 1050 17th Street, N.W., Suite 770, Washington, D.C. 20036

American Association of Retired Persons, 1909 K Street, N.W., Washington, D.C. 20049

American Institute of Architects, 1735 New York Avenue, Washington, D.C. 20006

American Longevity Association, 1000 West Carson Street, Torrance, California 90509

Center for Independent Living, 318 East 15th Street, New York, New York 10013

Federal Council on Aging, 330 Independence Avenue, S.W., Room 4243, Washington, D.C. 20201

Gerontological Society of America, 1835 K Street, N.W., Washington, D.C. 20006

Gray Panthers (National Office), 3635 Chestnut Street, Philadelphia, Pennsylvania 19104

International Center for Social Gerontology, 600 Maryland Avenue, S.W., Washington, D.C. 20024

Metropolitan Center for Independent Living, Inc., 1728 University Avenue, St. Paul, Minnesota 55104

National Association of Area Agencies on Aging, 600 Maryland Avenue, S.W., Washington, D.C. 20024

National Association of Housing and Redevelopment Officials, 2600 Virginia Avenue, N.W., Washington, D.C. 20037

National Council of Senior Citizens, 925 Fifteenth Street, N.W., Washington, D.C. 20005

National Council on the Aging, Inc., 600 Maryland Avenue, S.W., West Wing 100, Washington, D.C. 20024

National Institute on Aging, National Institutes of Health, 9000 Rockville Pike, Bethesda, Maryland 20205

National Shared Housing Resource Center, 6344 Greene Street, Philadelphia, Pennsylvania 19144

Social Security Administration, U.S. Department of Health and Human Services, 6401 Security Boulevard, Baltimore, Maryland 21235

United States Department of Agriculture, Farmers Home Administration (Multiple Housing Program and Single Family Housing Program), 14th Street and Independence Avenue, S.W., Washington, D.C. 20250

United States Department of Housing and Urban Development, 451 Seventh Street, S.W., Washington, D.C. 20410

United States House of Representatives, Select Committee on Aging, 717 House Office Building, Annex No. 1, 300 New Jersey Avenue, S.E., Washington, D.C. 20515

United States Senate, Special Committee on Aging, Dirksen Building G 33, Washington, D.C. 20510

Index

AAHA (American Association of Homes for the Aged), 211-12, 218, 220
AARP (American Association of Retired Persons), xx-xxii, 211, 212, 218, 220-21
Abrams, Philip, 239
accessory apartments, xxxii-xxxiii, 101, 104-10, 216, 234, 236
Ad Hoc Coalition for Elderly Housing, 212, 219, 220, 221
adaptive reuse, xxxiii, 113-15
Adult Action (Arizona), 53
adult day care centers, 232-33
affordability, housing, xii-xxvi, xxxix, 110-13, 216-17, 239.
age consciousness, xxxvi, 197-202, 204
age-segregated housing: advantages of, xxxi, 51-56; criticisms of, 50-51, 55; demand for, 49-50; isolation of elderly in, 50-51, 56; political aspects of, xxxi, 52-53; profiles of people choosing, 54; retirement communities as, xxxii, 236-37, 269; security in, xxxi, 52; and support services, xxxi, 53-54.
aging-in-place: and housing options, 231; and migration, xxix; and politics of aging, 216, 217; and property taxes, xxxviii; and support services, xxxviii. *See also* home equity conversions
aging process: and housing options, xx-xxii, xxxii, 228-29; and politics of aging, 189-90, 195; and social isolation/integration, 40-42; and surveillance zone, xxxii
Alabama, migration to, xxix, 32, 33, 36n1
Albrecht, R., 63
Alexandria, Virginia, 237
American Association of Homes for the Aged (AAHA), 211-12, 218, 220
American Association of Retired Persons (AARP), xx-xxii, 211, 212, 218, 220-21
American Homestead Mortgage Corporation (New Jersey), 123, 170
American Institute of Architects (AIA), 6, 10, 45, 218
Annual Housing Survey. *See* long-term care: financing of
appropriateness of housing, xx-xxii, xxix, 11-12, 42-44. *See* also surveillance zone
Appropriations Committees (U.S. Congress), 211, 219
Arizona, xxix-xxx, 31-36, 53, 237

315

Arkansas, 33, 36n1
assets as economic resources of the elderly, 21
Augsberg, Germany, 42
Auster, Rolf, xxxvi, 177-84
availability, housing, xviii-xxvi, xxxix, 111, 113-15, 239-40

Babylon, New York, 101, 108-9, 236
Back, Kurt, 192
Bader, J., 59
Baldwin, Leo, 231-32, 236, 237, 242
Banking Committee (U.S. House of Representatives), 211
Bethesda, Maryland, 11
Biggar, Jeanne, xxix-xxx, 31-36
Binstock, Robert H., xxiv, xxix, 15-29, 195-96
Blake, Peter, 12
B'nai B'rith, 212
board and care homes, xxxviii, 70-73, 237-38
Borzilleri, Thomas C., 26
Boston, Massachusetts, 8-9, 232, 234
Brody, E. M., 66, 67-69
Brooklyn, New York, 233
Browne, William P., 194-95
Brunswick, Ohio, 99, 100-101, 103-4
Buffalo, New York, 124
business-related housing interest groups, 211, 218. *See also* name of group
Butler, Robert, 228
Byerts, Thomas O., xxii

Cain, Leonard, 195
California, xxix-xxx, xxxiii, 31-36, 109-10, 111, 125, 139-40, 163, 172, 233, 242n23, 248
Campbell, Angus, 193, 194
capital gains exclusions: basic requirements for, 177-79; and property settlements, 179, 184n5, 184n6; purpose of, xxxvi; repealing forgiveness of (Struyk proposal), xli, 261, 262, 265; and replacement home purchase, 182-83; and repossessions, 180-81; and Section 121 (Internal Revenue Code), xxxvi, 179-80, 184, 184n2; and Section 1034 (Internal Revenue Code), xxxvi, 179-80; and wastage problem, 183-84; when to elect, 181-83
case management, 251
cash income adequacy, 22-24
Chicopee, Massachusetts, 113-14

circuit breaker (property tax reduction), 20
Clark, Robert L., 27, 28
clearinghouse, information, xliii, 218, 232, 242-42, 277, 283-84
Clearwater, Florida, 100-101, 104, 115
cluster zoning, xxxiii, 110-11
Cohen, C., 63
Colorado, 33, 36, 72-73, 111-12, 241, 242n23
communes/cooperatives, 57-58
Community Development Block Grants, 75, 269
community housing, 67-69, 75
condominiums, 9, 61-63
congregate housing: alternatives within, 67-69, 75; in Boston, Massachusetts, 8-9; and case management, 251; demand for, xxxii; and federal housing policies, xlii, 215, 239, 262; and frail elderly, 249; and HUD, 239, 262, 268; in Philadelphia, Pennsylvania, 9; *See also* shared housing
Congregate Housing Services Act (1978), 239
Congress, U.S. *See* federal government; name of committee
Congressional Budget Office: in-kind benefit study (1977) by, 25; study about needed in-home services of, 232
Connecticut, 33, 99, 101, 105, 232
conservatism of elderly, xxx, 192-95, 202, 203
construction program of Reagan [Ronald] administration, 252-53. *See also* Section 202
consumer safeguards for home equity conversions: and comparison of plans, 127, 137-38; and counseling, xxxiv, xxxv, 127, 128, 137-38, 142-43; disclosure as a, xxxv, 127, 137-38; and FHLBB, 21, 140-41, 147; need for, xxxv, 127, 135-36, 147; and reverse annuity mortgages, 138-44, 147, 148n8, 148n13; and risk-taking, 132, 138-39, 142-43, 148n14; and sale/leaseback plans, 144-46, 148n14
continuum of living, xx-xxii, xxxix, xl, xli, 248-49
cooperative apartments, 61-63
counseling for home equity conversions, xxxiv, xxxv, 127, 128, 137-38, 142-43
Cutler, Neal E., 194
Cutler, Stephen J., 193

Daily, Linda, xxxviii-xxxix, 227-44

Day-Lower model, 8-9
deferred payment loans, 125
demand, housing, xiv-xviii, 95
demographics: and demand for housing, xiv-xviii, 95; and housing options, 228; and politics of aging, 187-88; and pressures on federal government, 241. *See also* migration
density bonuses/requirements, xxxiii, 97, 99-101, 104, 109, 110-13
Denver, Colorado, 72-73, 241
Denver [Colorado] Research Institute, 72-73
design, housing: and health characteristics, 11-12; and social isolation/integration, 42-44. *See also* surveillance zone
disclosure as a consumer safeguard for home equity conversions, xxxv, 127, 137-38
displacement of the elderly: and condominium/cooperative apartments, 61-63, 74; reasons for, 73-74; and SROs, 65. *See also* gentrification.
District of Columbia, 233
Dobson, Douglas, xxvi, xxxvi, 187-208, 194, 202-3
domiciliary/personal care homes, 70-73, 75
Dowd, James J., 195, 196-97

earnings as economic resources of the elderly, 17-18
echo housing, xxxiii, 101, 104-10, 234
Eckert, J. Kevin, xxxi-xxxii, 57-80
economic resources of the elderly, 17-21. *See also* income status; social security
educational background of elderly, xxiv, xxxvi
Ehrlich, P. A., 63
elderly; conservatism of, xxx, 192-95, 202, 203; definition of, 96; diversity among, xx-xxi, xxvi, 98, 203-4; educational background of, xxiv, xxxvi; housing preferences of, xxxi-xxxii; legislation for repatriation of indigent, immigrant, 284; status of, 202-3, 205; "typical", xxiv, xxvi
Elrod, L. H., 62, 69
entitlement program (proposed by Struyk), xl-xli, 256, 259-61
Epstein, Laurily Keir, 194-95
Erickson, R. J., 63
Experimental Housing Allowance program, 258, 260-61

federal government: budget/demographic pressures on, 241; and costs for elderly programs, 16-17, 26-28, 188, 256, 272; initiatives in housing assistance of, 256-59; reformulation of policies of, 245-54. *See also* housing policies, federal; HUD; politics of aging; Reagan [Ronald] administration; name of dept/agency and legislation; name of congressional committee
Federal Home Loan Bank Board (FHLBB), 21, 140-41, 147
financing of housing for the elderly. *See* Struyk, Raymond J.; name of legislation, e.g. Section 8, Section 202, Section 236
Florida, xxix, xxvi, 11, 31-36, 104, 115, 232, 241-42, 242n23
Flynn, Cynthia B., 31-36
FMHA Section 504 (Home Repair Loan Program), 7
Foner, Anne, 193, 196, 198
food stamps, 20
Fort Collins, Colorado, 111-12
foster care homes, 71-73, 75
frail elderly, xiv-xv, xl, 248-50. *See also* continuum of living
Fry, C. L., 61, 62

Garnett, Robert, 161
General Accounting Office, U.S., studies by, 230, 237-38
gentrification, 73-74, 75
Georgia, xxix, 32, 33, 36n1, 242n23
Gergen, Kenneth, 192
Gillan, R. B., 59
Gillies, James, 66-67
Glenn, Norval, 192, 193, 194
Golant, Stephen M., xxxi, 49-56
Goode, C., 63, 64
granny flat. *See* echo housing
Green Bay, Wisconsin, 263
Greenwich, Connecticut, 101, 105
Griesel, Elma, 230
Grimes, Michael, 192
group living. *See* shared housing
Grumman Modular Buildings, 10
Guttentag, Jack M., 144-45, 161

Handler, Benjamin, xv, xix-xx
Hanover, Massachusetts, 111
Hare, Patrick, 236

Hawaii, 33
health characteristics: and housing design, 11-12; and housing options, 228, 229
Health and Human Services, U.S. Department of, xxxviii, 210, 215, 230, 238
Health Interview Survey. *See* long-term care: financing of
Hebrew Rehabilitation Center for the Aged, 72
Hefner, Ted, 194
Heilig, Peggy, 194
HELP Program (Home Equity Living Plan, Inc.), 124
Hoeflich, Michael, xxxiv-xxxv, 129-33
home care: clearinghouse for, xliii, 283-84; home equity conversions for financing of, 161-66; legislation about, 277, 278, 279-80, 283-85; medicaid/medicare for, 232; public support for, 151; and Social Security Act, xliii, 279-80; and Veterans Administration program, xliii, 278, 283-84
home equity conversions: and aging in place, xxxviii; availability of, 126-28; consumer safeguards for, xxxv, 127, 128, 132, 135-49; costs and risks of, 126-27, 130-31, 132; and counseling needs, xxxiv, xxxv, 127, 128, 137-38, 142-43; and deferred payment loans, 125; and disclosure, xxxv, 127, 137-38; and federal government, 216, 218, 248; for financing home care, 161-66; for financing long-term care, xxxv, 151-76; and housing options, 231-32; HUD proposal for, 269, 283; impact of, 155-56; and income taxes, xxxiv-xxxv, 130-31, 145, 218; legislation about, xliii, 283; and lender problems, xxxiv, 127, 142, 144, 147; obstructions to development of plans for, 172; purposes of, xxiv, xxxiii-xxxiv, 121-22, 123, 125, 129, 135, 145, 153-54. *See also* name of plan, e.g., reverse annuity mortgages
Home Equity Living Plan, Inc. (HELP), 124
Home Repair Loan Program (FMHA Section 504), 7
home/house sharing. *See* shared housing
homeownership: and federal housing policies, xlii, 259-61, 262-65; and financing of long-term care, 151-76; problems of xxiv-xxv, 7, 21. *See also* home equity conversions
Homesharing for Seniors, 234

homestead exemption (property tax relief), 20
Hoover, S. L., 60
hotels, 63-66
Housing Act (1937), xxviii, xxxix, 214, 238, 247
Housing Act (1949), xiv
Housing Act (1959), 212
Housing Allowance Supply Experiment, 263-64
housing policies, federal: current, 245-56; and financing of housing for the elderly, 252-54; for frail elderly, 248-50; future, 255-56, 259-65; history of, 247; and long-term care, xlii, 259, 265; and social welfare system, xlii, 259, 262, 265; Struyk's assumptions for, 255-56; and support services, 248-49, 250-51; trends/issues in, 248-54. *See also* federal government; politics of aging; Reagan [Ronald] administration; voucher plan; name of agency/legislation
Housing and Urban-Rural Recovery Act (1983), 219
HUD (U.S. Department of Housing and Urban Development): AAHA recommendations about operations and administrative policies of, 220-21; analysis of housing assistance for elderly by, 212; congregate housing study of, xx, 239, 262; elderly testifying at appropriations hearings of, 221; in-kind services demonstration of, 263-64; low-rent public housing program of, 238-39; major programs of, 267-71; role in housing for elderly of, 210, 215. *See also* name of legislation/program
Hudson, Robert B., 188, 202, 203

Idaho, 36
Illinois, xxx, 33, 36n2, 100-101, 131, 132
in-fill development, xxxiii, 6, 111
in-kind benefits, 25
in-kind income programs, 19-20
in-kind maintenance program (Struyk proposal), xlii, 263-65
incentive zoning, xxxiii, 8, 111-13
income: and federal housing assistance, 257-60; and housing options, 228; legislators' perceptions of elderly, 203, 208n63, 208n64; level and politics of aging, xxxvi; and Section 8, 257, 258-60; sources of, xxii-xxiv, xl, 17-21, 250; and Struyk's pro-

posed voucher plan, 259-61. *See also* social security
income distribution, 21-22
income status, 21-26
income taxes: and adult day care, 233; and capital gains exclusions, 177-84; and current federal legislation, xliii; and home equity conversions, xxxiv-xxxv, 130-31, 145, 218; implications of sale/leaseback plan for, 218; and mortgage interest deductions, 261, 265; and tax credit legislation, 278, 279-80, 282-83
Indiana, 33, 263
Individual Annuity Mortality (IAM) Table, 164
information clearinghouses, xliii, 28, 232, 241-42, 277, 283-84
Institute for the Future, 12
intrafamily transfers, 20
Inz, J., 59
isolation. *See* social isolation/integration; surveillance zone

Jacksonville, Florida, 241-42
Jacobs, Bruce, xxxv, 151-76
Jewish Federation, 212
Johnson, S. K., 61

Kansas, 100-101, 103, 242n23
Kansas City, Kansas, 100-101, 103
Karns, David A., 202-3
Katz Activities of Daily Living Scale, 157
Kaufman, Robert L., 193
Keyes amendment (Social Security Act, 1976), 71, 73
Kowall, C., 63, 65-66
Kuhn, Maggie, 57-58

Lancaster County, Pennsylvania, 236
Larmer, Kay, 233
Las Vegas, Nevada, 11
Lawton, M. Powell, 57, 58, 59, 64, 66, 70, 71, 72, 241
Lazer, William, xxii-xxiv
Leeds, Morton, xxxix-xl, 245-54
legislation, federal. *See* name or subject of legislation
legislators, perceptions of elderly income of, xxxvi, 202-3, 208n63, 208n64
Leisure World (Silver Springs, Maryland), 237

lender problems with home equity conversions, xxxiv, 127, 142, 144, 147
life-care concept, 247-48. *See also* continuum of living
living arrangements: and age-specific zoning, 97, 99; and fourteenth amendment, 115n6. *See also* options, housing; name of arrangement, e.g., shared housing
lobbying. *See* politics of aging; name of legislation
local government, xxxix, 241-42
long-term care: costs of, xxxv, 151-53; estimating need for, 157-61; and federal housing policies, xlii, 259, 265; home equity conversions for financing of, xxxv, 151-76; lobbying for, 222; and medicaid, 151-53, 173, 174; and renters, 174; research needed about financing, 172-73; and reverse annuity mortgages, 155-57, 161-66, 168-71, 172; and sale/leaseback plans, 172; and state government, xxxv, 152-53, 172; who pays for, 151-53, 174. *See also* home care; nursing home(s)
Longino, Charles F., Jr., 31-36
Loveland, Colorado, 11
Louisiana, 32, 33, 35, 36n2

McConnell, S. R., 59
MacDonald, Jack, 231
Manchester, England, 42
Maryland, 33, 98, 237, 242n23
Massachusetts, 33, 111, 113-15, 232, 234, 242n23
means-tested cash assistance, 19
medicaid, 19-20, 151-53, 173, 174, 222, 231, 232, 238
medicare, 19-20, 151, 222, 231, 232, 233
Meeker, David, 6, 7
Meharg, James K., Jr., 237
Meiners, Mark, 170, 175n6
Menefee, John, 27, 28
Metropolitan Jewish Geriatric Center (Brooklyn, New York), 233
Michigan, 33, 36, 197, 236-37
migration, xxix, 31-36
Minnesota, 242n23
Mississippi, xxix, 32, 36n1
Missouri, 36
mobile homes, 60-61, 269
modular homes, 10-11

Montclair, New Jersey, 101, 105-6
Moon, Marilyn, 20
Moore v City of East Cleveland (1977), 115n6
mortgage insurance: HUD programs for, 268-69; legislation about, 275-76. *See also* name of legislation
mortgage interest deductions, xli, 261, 265
multi-mission national organizations, 211, 218-21. *See also* name of organization
Mumford, Lewis, xxvii, xxx-xxxi, 4, 5, 39-47
Murrey, Mary Ittman, xxxi-xxxii, 57-80

Nachison, Jerold S., xxxix-xl, 245-54
Nassau County, New York, 59
National Association of Counties, 241
National Association of Home Builders, 10, 11, 211, 218
National Association of Realtors, 154, 211
National Bureau of Standards, 238
National Catholic Charities, 212
National Caucus on Black Aged, 212
National Center for Health Services Research, 233
National Center for Home Equity Conversion (Madison, Wisconsin), 155, 218
National Council on Aging (NCOA), 211, 221-22, 233
National Council of Senior Citizens, 212, 221, 246
National Leased Housing Association, 218
National Low-Income Housing Coalition, 212, 219, 220, 221
National Nursing Home Survey. *See* long-term care: financing of
National Shared Housing Resource Center (Philadelphia, Pennsylvania), 218
Nebraska, 242n23
Nevada, 11, 33
New Bedford, Massachusetts, 114-15
New Haven, Connecticut, 99
New Jersey, xxx, 33, 36n2, 101, 105-6, 109, 123, 125, 170, 242n23, 248
New Mexico, xxix, 32, 33, 35
New Rochelle, New York, 100
New York (state), 33, 36, 59, 100, 101, 108-9, 124, 128, 233, 236, 242n23
Newman, E. S., 72
Newman, Sandra, xiii-xiv
Nie, Norman H., 191-92, 202
non-profit sponsors/organizations, xli, 211-12, 218, 262. *See also* Section 202; name of sponsor/organization
North Carolina, xxix, 31-32, 33, 35, 36n2
North Dakota, 242n23
nursing home(s): federal mortgage for, 152, 247; federal studies of, 229, 230; as a housing options, 229-31; medicaid/medicare expenditures for care in, 231; and personal care dependency, 157-61; population of, xxxviii; regulation by federal government of, 229-31; reverse annuity mortgages to finance insurance for, 168-71. *See also* long-term care

Office of Management and Budget, U.S., 210
Ohio, xxx, 33, 36n2, 99, 100-101, 103-4
Oklahoma, 33, 36
Older Americans Act (1965), 233, 238, 242n23
Olin Corporation, 10
Omnibus Federal Housing Bill (1983), 218
On Lok Senior Health Services (San Francisco, California), 233
options, housing: and adult day care centers, 232-33; and aging in place, 231; and aging process, xx-xxii, xxxii, 228-29; and demographics, 228; and economic/social issues, 240-41; and elderly preferences, xxxi-xxxii; and federal government, 255-56; and future policy issues, 241-42; and health characteristics, 228, 229; and home equity conversions, 231-32; incentives for increasing, 8; and income, 228; and information clearinghouses, 232, 241-42; non-institutional, 231-38; and politics of aging, 218-19; and property tax relief, 231; remodeling for increased, 8; research needed about, xxxii; and social isolation/integration, xxx-xxxi, 5-6; and support services, xxx, 96-97, 232, 240-41; variety of, xxxi-xxxii; and zoning, xxx-xxxi, xxxii-xxxiii, 7-8, 95-117, 234-36. *See also* design, housing; shared housing; name of option, e.g., condominiums
Oregon, 33, 125, 236
Orshansky, Molly 26

Palo Alto, California, 111
Papp, Lazlo, 110-11

parking-space requirements and zoning, 97-98, 100-101, 104, 109
Pennsylvania, xxx, 9, 33, 36n2, 68, 99, 234, 236
Philadelphia, Pennsylvania, 9, 68, 234
Philadelphia [Pennsylvania] Geriatric Center, 68
Pierce, Samuel, 172
Pittsburgh, Pennsylvania, 99
Plano, Texas, 100-101, 102
politics of aging: and age consciousness, xxxvi, 197-202, 204; and age-segregated housing, xxxi, 52-53; and aging in place, 216, 217; and aging process, 189-90, 195; and attitudes, 192-95, 197-202; and behavior, 189-90, 197, 202; and business-related housing interest groups, 211, 218; and competition among political groups, 219-20; conclusions about, 203-5; and congregate housing, 215; and conservatism, 192-95, 202, 203; and current housing agenda, 212-15, 219-20; and definition of housing problem, 217-17, 222; and demographics, 187-88; and diversity among elderly, 203-4; and educational background, xxxvi; and elderly influence on housing policies, xxxvi-xxxvii; and housing options, 218-19; and income level, xxxvi; and involvement, xxxvi; and legislators' perceptions of elderly, xxxvi, 202-3; major groups influencing, 210-16, 217-21; and migration, xxx, 36; and multi-mission national organizations, 211, 218-21; and new directions in housing policy, 216-17, 220-20; non-profit sponsors and, 211-12, 218; and political involvement, 190-92, 202-3, 206n14; and political movements, 195-97, 204; and priority of housing issue, 209-10, 216-17, 221-22; and public housing, 214-15 and Section 202 program, 212-14; and state government, 202-3 and status of elderly, 202-3, 205; and subculture of the aging, 195. *See also* housing policies, federal; Reagan [Ronald] administration; name of congressional committee
Portland, Oregon, 236
Poverty. *See* economic resources of the elderly; income; income status
President's [Reagan] Commission on Housing (1981), xxxix, 216-17, 239

Princeton, New Jersey, 101, 109
private pension plans, 19
private sector, 170, 216-17, 239, 247-48
Project Share (Nassau County, New York), 59
property taxes, xxiv, xxxviii, xl, 20, 125, 231
public employee retirement systems, 18-19
public housing, xxv, xxvi, xxxvii, 214-15, 267-68, 273-75. *See also* federal government; name of legislation/program
Pynoos, Jon, xxvi, xxxvi-xxxvii, 209-23

Ragan, Pauline K., 195, 196-97
Rausch, K. J., 60
Reagan [Ronald] administration: construction program of, 252-53, 258, 261-62; cutbacks of, xxxviii-xxxix, xli, 257-59; emphasis of, xxxix, xli, 258, 261-62; initiatives versus objectives of, 258-59; reduction of housing programs by, 256-57, 158-59; Section 202 proposals of, xxxviii, xxxix; Section 8 proposals of, xxviii; social security program of, 17; voucher plan proposal of, xxxix, xlii, 217, 220-21, 239, 252, 258, 259-61. *See also* federal government; housing policies, federal
Regnier, Victor, xxii
rental assistance. *See* name of program, e.g. Section 8, Section 202, public housing
renters: and federal housing policies, xxv, 257-62; and financing of long-term care, 174. *See also* public housing; name of program, e.g., Section 8, Section 202
repair/maintenance, home: costs of, xl; funding for, 75; in-kind maintenance services proposal (Struyk), 263-65; legislation about, 275. *See also* home equity conversions: uses of
retirement communities, xxxii, 236-37, 269. *See also* age-segregated housing
reverse annuity mortgages: consumer safeguards for, 138-44, 147, 148n8, 148n13; definition of, 148n6; FHLBB regulations for, 21, 140-41; and housing options, 231; and long-term care, 155-57, 161-66, 168-71, 172; overview of, xxiv, xxxv, 122-23, 126, 155-57; as a source of income, 250; state programs for, 248; to finance home care, 161-66; to finance nursing home insurance, 168-71
reverse mortgages. *See* reverse annuity mortgages

Riley, Matilda White, 193
Robert Wood Johnson Foundation, 161
rooming houses, 63-66
Rose, Arnold, 195
Rosow, Irving, 54-55
Rowles, Graham D., xxxii, 81-94

safety/security, 52, 102
St. Angelo, Douglas, 194
sale/leaseback plan, xxiv, xxxiv-xxxv, 123-24, 126, 129-32, 144-46, 148n14, 172, 218
San Francisco, California, 233
Scanlon, W., 157
Schweiker, Richard S., 230
Seattle, Washington, 234
Section 8 (HUD rental assistance program): accomplishments of, xxvi, 212; HUD role in, 238-39; and income levels, 75, 238, 257, 258-59; lobbying for, 211; purposes of, xxv, 267; and Reagan administration, xxviii, 218, 220-21, 257, 258, 261; and Section 202, 213; and shared housing, 218; and Struyk voucher plan, 259
Section 121 (Internal Revenue Code), xxxvi, 179-80, 184, 184n2
Section 202 (HUD rental assistance program): accomplishments of, xix, xxvi, 212, 220, 247; cutbacks in, xli; hearings about, 216; House of Representatives resolution about, 273; HUD role in, 238-39; legislation about, 280; lobbying for, xxxvii, 212, 220, 222; mortgage program of, 215; and nonprofit sponsors, xli, 218, 238-39, 262; and politics of aging, 212-14; popularity of, xliii, 221, 239-40, 247; purpose of, xxv, 267; and Reagan administration, xxxviii, xxxix, xli. *See also* voucher plan
Section 221 (HUD mortgage insurance program for elderly housing), 268
Section 231 (HUD mortgage insurance program for elderly housing), 268
Section 232 (HUD mortgage insurance program for nursing homes/intermediate care facilities), 268
Section 236 (HUD housing assistance program), xxvi, 75
Section 242 (HUD mortgage insurance for hospitals), 268
Section 312 (Weatherization and Urban Development Act Grant programs), 75

Section 504 (FMHA Home Repair Loan program), 7
Section 1034 (Internal Revenue Code), xxxvi, 179-80
Select Committee on Aging, 210-11, 215-16, 233, 215-16, 233
shared housing: advantages/disadvantages of, 58-60, 234; barriers to, xxxii, xxxviii; federal emphasis on, 216, 218; and housing options, 58-60, 234-36; private sector experiments with, 248; as a source of income, 250. *See also* type of shared housing, e.g. congregate housing
Shared Housing Resource Center (Philadelphia, Pennsylvania), 59
Shepherd, Betty, 233
Sherman, S. R., 72
Shifman, Carole, xxxii-xxxiii, 95-117
Silver Spring, Maryland, 237
social isolation/integration: and age-segregated housing, xxxi, 50-51, 56; and aging process, 40-42; attitudes about, 39-40, 42-43, 47; and economic resources of elderly, 40; and housing design, 42-44; and housing options, xxx-xxxi, 5-6; and zoning, 45
social security: and economic resources of elderly, 18; legislation for home care benefits from, 279-80; and major source of income, xxii, xxiv, 17; and SSI, 19, 238
Social Security Act, xliii, 71, 233, 238, 279-80
Sokolovsky, J., 63
South Bend, Indiana, 263
South Carolina, xxix, xxx, 31, 32, 33, 36n1
Special Committee on Aging (U.S. Senate), 121-22, 210-11, 215-16, 229
split equity financing, xxxiv-xxxv, 124, 126, 132-33
SRO (Single Room Occupancy), 63-66
SSI (supplemental security income) payments, 19, 238
standards, housing, 246-47
Stanford Research Institute Conference (1967), 10
state government: board and home care regulation by, 238; budget pressures on, 241; financing of housing by, 253; and home care, xxxviii; and long term care, xxxv, 152-53, 172; and politics of aging, 202-3; and reverse annuity mortgages, 248; and support services, 232

Steck, Peter, 108
Stephens, J., 63
Streib, G. F., 58
Streig, R. B., 58
Stockman, David, 221
Stouffer, Samuel A., 193
Struyk, Raymond J., xl-xlii, 255-66
Subcommittee on Housing and Consumer Interests (House Select Committee on Aging, 210-11
Subcommittee on Human Services (House Select Committee on Aging), 233
Sun City, Arizona, 237
Sunbelt. *See* migration
supply, housing, xviii-xxxvi, xxxix, 111, 113-15, 239-40
support services: and age segregated housing, xxxi, 53-54; and aging in place, xxxviii; cost effectiveness of, xxxviii; and federal housing policies, xlii, 232, 248-49, 250-51; and frail elderly, 250-51; and housing options, xxx, 96-97, 232, 240-41; and HUD study of congregate housing, xx, 239, 262; and local government, xxxix, 241-42; and state government, 232; studies about need for, xxxviii; and zoning, 102. *See also* congregate housing; continuum of living
surveillance zone, xxxii, 81-94

tax exclusions. *See* Capital gains tax exclusion
taxes. *See* income taxes
Teski, M., 63
Texas, xxix, 31-36, 100-101, 102, 242n23
Thompson, Marie McGuire, 9, 12
Trapnell, Gordon, 170, 175n6
Trichilo, Vincent J., xxxiv, 121-28

U.S. Bureau of Labor Statistics (BLS), income level determinations of, 165
U.S. Conference on Mayors, 241
U.S. Department of Housing and Urban Development. *See* HUD; name of program, e.g., Home Repair Loan Program
U.S. House of Representatives. *See* federal government; Select Committee on Aging
U.S. Senate. *See* federal government; Special Committee on Aging
University of Illinois, study about homeownership by Program for Housing Research and Development of, 131, 132

University of Michigan: Center for Political Studies of, 197; Institute of Gerontology at, 236-37
Urban Development Action Grants, 269
Urban Institute, 9
Urban Systems Research and Engineering, Inc., 66
Usher, C. E., 59
Utah, 36

Verba, Sidney, 202
Veterans Administration, xliii, 278, 283-84
Vice President's [Bush] Task Force on Regulatory Relief, 230
Village of Belle Terre v. Boraas, 98
Virginia, 32, 33, 36n1, 237
Volunteers of America, 212, 234
voucher plan (Reagan administration proposal), xxxix, xlii, 217, 202-21, 239, 252, 258, 259-61
voucher plan (Struyk proposal), xli, 259-61, 262-65

Warner, Katherine, xxiv, xxv-xxvi, 96
Washington (state), xxx, 33, 36n2, 234, 242n23
Weatherization and Urban Development Action Grant programs, 75, 312
Weinrobe, Maurice D., xxxv, 135-49
Weissert, William, xxxv, 151-76
welfare system, xli, xlii, 254, 262, 265
Westport, Connecticut, 101
White House Conference on Aging (1971), xxii
White House Conference on Aging (1981), xiv, 28, 239, 240
Wisconsin, 33, 125, 172, 248, 263
Wiseman, Robert F., 31-36
Wolman, Harold, 209
Woodward, Anne, xxvii xxix, 3-13

Zimmerman, Jeffrey, 102-3
Zion, Illinois, 100-101, 101
zoning: and adaptive reuse, xxxiii, 113-15; and affordability of housing, 110-13; arguments against age-specific, xxxii, 97-98; arguments for age-specific, 96-97; and availability of housing, 111, 113-15; categories of age-specific, xxxii; cluster, xxxiii, 110-11; community/congregate housing and,

69; and density bonuses/requirements, xxxiii, 97, 99-101, 104, 109, 110-13; districts, 101-3; and housing options, xxx-xxxi, xxxii-xxxiii, 7-8, 95-117, 234-36; incentive, xxxiii, 8, 111-13; and in-fill development, xxxiii, 6, 111; innovative, 104, 110-15; legality of age-specific, xxxii, 98-100; and living arrangements, 97, 99; and parking-space requirements, 97-98, 100-101, 104, 109; and security/safety, 102; and social isolation/integration, 45; and support services, 102